The Art and Science of Making the New Man in Early-Twentieth-Century Russia

The Art and Science of Making the New Man in Early-Twentieth-Century Russia

Edited by

Nikolai Krementsov and Yvonne Howell

BLOOMSBURY ACADEMIC
LONDON • NEW YORK • OXFORD • NEW DELHI • SYDNEY

BLOOMSBURY ACADEMIC
Bloomsbury Publishing Plc
50 Bedford Square, London, WC1B 3DP, UK
1385 Broadway, New York, NY 10018, USA
29 Earlsfort Terrace, Dublin 2, Ireland

BLOOMSBURY, BLOOMSBURY ACADEMIC and the Diana logo are trademarks of Bloomsbury Publishing Plc

First published in Great Britain 2021
This paperback edition published 2023

A catalogue record for this book is available from the British Library.

Library of Congress Cataloging-in-Publication Data
Names: Howell, Yvonne, 1960- editor, writer of conclusion. | Krement?s?ov, N. L., editor, author.
Title: The art and science of making the new man in early 20th-century Russia / edited by Yvonne Howell and Nikolai Krementsov.
Description: London ; New York : Bloomsbury Academic, 2021. | Includes bibliographical references and index.
Identifiers: LCCN 2021026866 (print) | LCCN 2021026867 (ebook) | ISBN 9781350232839 (hardback) | ISBN 9781350232853 (pdf) | ISBN 9781350232860 (epub)
Subjects: LCSH: Russia–Intellectual life–20th century. | Soviet Union–Intellectual life. | Sociobiology–Russia–History–20th century. | Sociobiology–Soviet Union–History. | Human evolution—Social aspects–Russia–History–20th century. | Human evolution—Social aspects–Soviet Union–History. | Human evolution in literature. | Art and science.
Classification: LCC DK247 .A78 2021 (print) | LCC DK247 (ebook) | DDC 947.084–dc23
LC record available at https://lccn.loc.gov/2021026866
LC ebook record available at https://lccn.loc.gov/2021026867

ISBN: HB: 978-1-3502-3283-9
PB: 978-1-3502-3284-6
ePDF: 978-1-3502-3285-3
eBook: 978-1-3502-3286-0

Typeset by Deanta Global Publishing Services, Chennai, India

To find out more about our authors and books visit www.bloomsbury.com and sign up for our newsletters.

"The work attempted is not so much special and technical as a work of reconciliation, the suggestion of broad generalizations upon which divergent specialists may meet, a business for non-technical expression, and in which a man who knows a little of biology, a little of physical science, and a little in a practical way of social stratification, who has concerned himself with education and aspired to creative art, may claim in his very amateurishness a special qualification."

H. G. Wells, *Mankind in the Making* (1903)

Contents

Figures

Notes on Names, Transliterations, and Translations

This volume covers roughly half a century of Russian history, from the decades leading to the Great War to the beginning of the Second World War. During this period the very name of the country—to say nothing of its borders or its political, economic, administrative, and social organization—changed radically several times. To avoid an unnecessary confusion and cluttering of the text, the contributors often use its colloquial name, Russia, to refer to the Russian Empire (before 1917), the Russian Soviet Federated Socialist Republic (1917–22), the Union of Soviet Socialist Republics (1922–91), and the Russian Federation (after 1991), even though strictly speaking it is not historically accurate. Furthermore, the country's numerous cities, regions, and municipalities also repeatedly changed their names. To give but one example, St. Petersburg became Petrograd in 1914, Leningrad in 1924, and regained its original name in 1991. Throughout the text the authors use that name for a particular locale, which was in use at the time they describe, occasionally noting its current name and administrative subordination.

In rendering various Russian names and words in the Latin alphabet, the authors use the Library of Congress's transliteration system, except for the commonly adopted spellings of well-known names, such as, for example, "St. Petersburg," "Alexander," "Leon Trotsky," and "Maxim Gorky," instead of "Sankt-Peterburg," "Aleksandr," "Lev Trotskii," and "Maksim Gor'kii," respectively. Except for the names of the country's two major newspapers, *Pravda* and *Izvestiia*, and a popular-science magazine, *Priroda* (*Nature*), the titles of various periodicals are translated into English in the text, with their Russian names given in transliterated form in the references.

The contributors also had to make certain choices in translating various Russian terms and expressions into English. In contrast to some other studies that use such expressions as "new being," "new human," and "new person" to translate the Russian phrase *novyi chelovek* (singular), we decided to use "new man" as its proper translation and to use "new men" as the translation of the Russian *novye liudi* (plural). Both of these phrases, *novyi chelovek* and *novye liudi*, represent our actors' categories. The Russian word *chelovek* is gender-neutral. Although grammatically the noun is masculine, its root *chelo* (face) and many of its derivatives, such as *chelovechishche* and *chelovechestvo*, are also gender-neutral, both grammatically and semantically. As much as we appreciate our current gender sensitivities, during the period covered in the volume the expression "new man" and its analogues in major European languages, such as *l'homme nouveau*, *neue Mensch*, *uomo nuovo*, and *hombre nuevo*, were all used largely in a generic, non-gendered sense, as was the popular term "mankind." During the same time period all of these expressions were translated into Russian as *novyi chelovek*, not as *novyi muzhchina*; and vice versa, the Russian expression was translated into contemporary English as "new man," not "new human," "new person," or "new being." To use the expression "new person" or "new being" would imply that the Russian speakers of the time somehow had a very different conception of what the English speakers called "new man," which is certainly not true and dangerously misleading. When the Russian speakers wanted to emphasize a gender-specificity they used the expression *novaia zhenshchina* in the same way their foreign counterparts used the expressions "new woman," "*neue Frau*," "*nouvelle femme*," "*nuova donna*," and "*nueva mujer*." Thus, we reserve the use of such expressions as "new man" and "new men" to the translations of our actors' categories, while the expressions "new human," "new person," and "new being" serve as our authors' analytical classifications.

Abbreviations

AGDM	*Arkhiv gosudarstvennogo darvinovskogo muzeia* (Archive of the State Darwin Museum Moscow)
AKhRR	*Assotsiatsiia khudozhnikov revoliutsionnoi Rossii* (The Association of Artists of Revolutionary Russia)
APO	*Agitatsionno-propagandistskii otdel* (the Agitation and Propaganda department of VSKhV)
ARME	*Arkhiv Rossiiskogo etnograficheskogo muzeia* (Archive of the Russian Museum of Ethnography)
BSE	*Bol'shaia Sovetskaia Entsiklopediia* (*Great Soviet Encyclopedia*)
Cheka	*Vserossiiskaia chrezvychainaia komissiia po bor'be s kontrrevoliutsiei i sabotazhem* (The All-Russian Extraordinary Commission)
DOPR	*dom prinuditel'nykh rabot* (House of Preliminary Detention)
FED	*Felix Edmundovich Dzerzhinsky* (35 mm camera)
GMA	*Gosudarstvennyi muzei arkhitektury imeni A.V. Shchuseva* (A.V. Shchusev State Museum of Architecture)
GVK	*Glavnyi vystavochnyi komitet* (Chief Exhibition Committee of VSKhV)
METLA	*Moskovskaia edinaia teatral'naia leninskaia artel'* (Moscow Unified Leninist Theatre Team)
Narkompros	*Narodnyi Komissariat Prosveshcheniia RSFSR* (People's Commissariat of Enlightenment)
Narkomzdrav	*Narodnyi Komissariat Zdravookhraneniia RSFSR* (People's Commissariat of Health Protection)
Narkomzem (NKZ)	*Narodnyi Komissariat Zemledeliia* (People's Commissariat of Agriculture)
NEP	*Novaia Ekonomicheskaia Politika* (New Economic Policy)
NKVD	*Narodnyi Komissariat Vnutrennikh Del* (People's Commissariat of Internal Affairs)
OGPU	*Obiedinennoe Gosudarstvennoe Politicheskoe Upravlenie* (Joint State Political Administration)

Proletkul't	*Proletarskaia kul'tura* (Proletarian Culture)
RGAE	*Rossiiskii gosudarstvennyi arkhiv ekonomiki* (Russian State Archive of Economy)
RGALI	*Rossiiskii gosudarstvennyi arkhiv literatury i isskustva* (Russian State Archive for Literature and Art)
RGASPI	*Rossiiskii gosudarstvennyi arkhiv sotsial'no-politicheskoi istorii* (Russian State Archive of Social-Political History)
RSFSR	*Rossiiskaia Sovetskaia Federativnaia Sotsialisticheskaia Respublika* (Russian Soviet Federative Socialist Republic)
SF	science fiction
SME	*Gosudarstvennyi muzei etnografii* (State Museum of Ethnography)
SNK (Sovnarkom)	*Sovet Narodnykh Komissarov* (Council of the People's Commissars)
TsK VKP(b)	*Tsentral'nyi Komitet Vsesoiuznoi Kommunisticheskoi partii bol'shevikov* (Central Committee of the All-Union Communist Party of the Bolsheviks)
USSR	*Soiuz Sovetskikh Sotsialisticheskikh Respublik* (Union of Soviet Socialist Republics)
VSKhV	*Vserossiiskaia sel'skokhoziaistvennaia i kustarno-promyshlennaia vystavka* (All-Russian Agricultural and Handicraft Industrial Exhibition)
VTsIK	*Vserossiiskii tsentral'nyi ispolnitel'nyi komitet* (All-Russian Central Executive Committee)

Introduction

On Words and Meanings

Nikolai Krementsov

In the course of one brief century, the human outlook upon the order of the world has been profoundly changed.

H. G. Wells, *Mankind in the Making* (1903), p. 16

In April 1901, *Fortnightly Review*, an influential British magazine, carried the first of a series of essays that would appear in each of its subsequent issues till the end of the year under the general title "Anticipations: An Experiment in Prophecy."[1] The author of this ambitious "forecast of the way things will probably go in this new century" was H. G. Wells, the "discoverer of the future," in a somewhat exaggerated characterization by his biographer.[2] At the end of the year this "rough sketch of the coming time," as the celebrated author of *The Time Machine* defined it, came out in book format and became Wells's first nonfiction best seller. The collection of nine essays explored profound influences that rapidly developing science and technology were about to exert "upon human life and thought" in the course of the unfolding new century.[3] It concluded that "the great swollen, shapeless hypertrophied social mass of today must give birth at last to a naturally and informally organized educated class, *an unprecedented sort of people*."[4] In the follow-up series, first published in the same magazine and expressively titled "Mankind in the Making," Wells expanded his vision by focusing specifically on the effects of anticipated scientific, technological, and social developments "upon the evolution of man."[5]

Both *Anticipations* and its sequel exemplified a resurgence of interest in millennia-old ideas about creating a "new man." Both the author and his audience were particularly concerned with new ways of approaching this goal. As Wells emphasized in *Mankind in the Making*, "In the past man was made, generation after generation, by forces beyond his knowledge and control. Now a certain number of men are coming to a provisional understanding of some at least of these forces that go to the Making of Man."[6] For Wells, as for many others of his generation, the forces that went "to the making of man" were not those of God, but those of Nature; and there was only one reliable source of knowledge and understanding of these forces—science. His essays testified to Wells's conviction that science held the key to harnessing forces of Nature. Furthermore, according to Wells, science was about to provide requisite "tools" for actually making "an unprecedented sort of people" out of the available "swollen, shapeless hypertrophied social mass" of the present man, and, as Wells put it poetically, to "make real and living the sustaining dreams of the coming time."[7]

The idea that some "new man" would replace the currently existing one has circulated in various cultures since the dawn of human civilizations. But as Wells's essays indicate, it acquired a new meaning around the turn of the twentieth century. To many *fin de siècle* intellectuals, the coming of the new, twentieth century offered a suitable vantage point to survey the past and contemplate the future of humanity. In their views, rapid scientific and technological advances that penetrated the very fabric of everyday life in industrialized nations over the course of the previous century gave the beginning of the new one a certain symbolic quality, while a neat scale of 100 years provided a convenient measure of human history. Whether looking backward or forward, with dismay, fear, or hope, many of them tried to envision the future that lay ahead by using the past as their guide.[8]

Wells was certainly not alone in his anticipations of the "coming time" and the "coming man." Scores of *fin de siècle* writers, scientists, philosophers, educators, theologians, and artists in Britain, France, Germany, Italy, Russia, the United States, and elsewhere produced their own visions of a new type of human beings destined to replace the existing ones, describing both the forces involved and the tools necessary to accomplish such replacement. Many cultural productions of the time contemplated the future of humanity epitomized by the imminent appearance of the "new man." They ranged from US writer Edward Bellamy's novel *Looking Backward* (1888), French physiologist Charles Richet's essay *Dans cent ans* (1892), and Italian psychiatrist Paolo Mantegazza's novella *L'Anno 3000* (1897) to German science popularizer Wilhelm Bölsche's duology *Die Eroberung des Menschen* (1901) and *Die Abstammung des Menschen* (1904), Irish dramatist Bernard Shaw's play *Man and Superman* (1903), and French writer Gustave Guitton's novel *Ce que seront les Hommes de l'An 3000* (1907). As it was for Wells, for many of these visionaries, it was contemporary science and technology that supplied ideas, ideals, and techniques to make those dreams "real and living."

Although (re)appearing *c.* 1900 across Europe and the Americas, the visions of the "coming man" seemed to enjoy particular popularity in Russia. This special interest was clearly manifest in that *all* of the aforementioned texts, including Wells's essays, were immediately translated into the Russian language. Numerous Russian authors also tried to envision the "new man of tomorrow" in their own works. Their efforts ranged from writer Zinaida Gippius's collection of short stories about *New Men* (1896), theologian Sergei Chetverikov's treatise on *New Attempt at Renewing Mankind* (1901), and botanist Konstantin Merezhkovskii's novel *Earthly Paradise* (1903) to journalist Wilhelm Bitner's speculation on *Whence, Whither, and What Are We?* (1903) and zoologist Vladimir Shimkevich's discourse on *The Future of Mankind from a Naturalist's Viewpoint* (1906).

But what did the expression "new man" actually signify in these numerous cultural productions? Who used it, why, how, and for what purposes? Why and how did science and technology become an integral part of these dreams about the "coming man"? What were the similarities and differences between the concurrent notions of the "new man" in various cultures? Was there something special about the "new man" visions circulating in Russia?

It was with an explicit goal of answering these questions that on May 16–18, 2019, more than fifty participants from Britain, Canada, Germany, Japan, Switzerland, the United States, and all corners of Russia convened in St. Petersburg for a conference on "Making a New Man: Scientific and Artistic Experiments (Russia-USSR, *c.* 1900–39)." The conference was organized by Lyubov Bugaeva and Nikolai Krementsov and cosponsored by St. Petersburg State University and the University of Toronto. It brought together historians, anthropologists, sociologists, and philosophers of literature, cinema, science, theater, education, art, architecture, and medicine. Its immediate purpose was to foster a conversation among the scholars of these major cultural fields in order to identify common themes and materials, to develop shared languages of descriptions and explanations, and to discover general principles of, and approaches to, the understanding of the multiple ways in which various cultural productions of the "new man" intermingled and cross-pollinated each other.

This volume presents a selection of reports discussed at the conference. For the first time it brings together different historical sources, historiographical traditions, disciplinary preoccupations, and methodological approaches. It illuminates the "new man" visions circulating in different cultural domains (from literature and cinema to visual arts and sciences), media (written and spoken word, still and moving images), and practices (from public displays to pedagogical principles to doll making). Most importantly, the contributors analyze the "new man" as the actor's category, uncovering the multitude of meanings attached to the expression by the actual historical figures who used it. The volume provides the first interdisciplinary analysis of ideas, ideals, and practices underpinning the notions of "making the new man" in Russia during the first four decades of the twentieth century. It encompasses, examines, and contrasts three different periods in the country's history: Imperial, Bolshevik, and Stalinist. The contributors adopt an explicitly comparative framework by exploring the similarities and differences of the "new man" visions in Russia with analogous visions elsewhere.

The volume thus offers a rich history of the complex relationship among various cultural fields involved in articulating the dreams and constructing the realities of the "new man" in Russia. With contributions from scholars of different cultural domains, the book presents a groundbreaking multidisciplinary exploration of the major function of the "new man" ideas, ideals, and practices as an influential *cultural resource* open for exploitation to any participant in the cultural process. It investigates the actual contents of this resource, focusing on the role of the life sciences in its formation and on its manifestations in countless cultural products and media, from sculptures, dolls, and posters to movies, exhibits, and books. Through a comparative analysis of the "new man" visions prevalent in Russian and other cultures, the volume challenges the traditional assumptions that in Russia such visions had originated with the Bolshevik revolution and were nothing more than rhetorical, propagandist, or, at best, aesthetic constructs. In contrast to previous studies often centering on the apparent disconnect between such "utopian" constructs and the harsh realities of everyday life in the Soviet Union, the contributors to this volume investigate complicated historical trajectories of the "new man" visions, their often obscure origins, constituent components, particular trends and stages in their development, acclaimed and forgotten champions and detractors, and mutual interrelations. The volume's ultimate goal, then, is to showcase the multiplicity of meanings, ideas, ideals, and practices associated with the "new man" visions in twentieth-century cultures in Russia and elsewhere.

In what follows I address four major themes that emerge from the individual contributions to the volume. The first theme concerns the multiple meanings hidden under the universal label "new man" and the actual contents of the cultural resource this label comes to signify in Russia and elsewhere. The second involves particular types of thought and argumentation in the public discussions on "making the new man." The third relates to different stages in these discussions, each characterized by the prevalence of specific thought types and particular networks of individual and institutional actors involved. The fourth encompasses the general and the particular in the "new man" visions circulating in different settings. I conclude with a look at promising avenues for further research on the twentieth-century scientific and artistic experiments in "making the new man."

Labels and Meanings: *New* Man and New *Man*

Scholars of Russian culture have studiously examined the various notions of the "new man" appearing in cultural productions in the course of that country's history.[9] Most of them have focused on exploring the visions of the "coming man" circulating in Russian culture after the Bolsheviks took power.[10] Alas, many of these studies have failed to differentiate between the understanding and use of the phrase "new man" (*novyi chelovek*) by the historical actors under investigation and by the authors of such investigations themselves; in worst cases, simply substituting the latter for the former. To give but one pertinent example, the expression "new Soviet man" (*novyi sovetskii chelovek*), used widely and indiscriminately in numerous historical studies, has practically never appeared in the Russian-language sources from 1917 to 1940 upon which such studies are supposedly based.[11] Similarly, the phrase "new woman" (*novaia zhenshchina*) was evidently much more popular during the prerevolutionary, rather than the post-revolutionary, period.[12] Ironically, the number of historical works that appeared in the last thirty years on the "new woman" in Soviet culture apparently exceeds the number of Russian-language publications from 1917 to 1940, which had actually used the phrase in their titles and texts.

Furthermore, until quite recently the examinations of the "new man" in Russian cultural productions have lacked a systematic comparison with other cultures, a comparison that might have helped substantiate (or reject) popular claims about a particular "Soviet" character of the notions of the "new man" circulating in the aftermath of the Bolshevik revolution.[13] Even more important, all of these studies have largely glossed over the critical question of what the expression "new man" actually meant to those who used it.

Notions of a "new man" have a very long history in the European cultural tradition. Scholars of all stripes have examined the role of such notions in different settings and cultural domains, ranging from religion, architecture, and cinematography to philosophy, social practices, and pedagogical theories.[14] Yet, sometimes, reading these numerous works, one cannot escape the feeling that in using the phrase "new man" their authors follow Humpty Dumpty's dictum: "When *I* use a word, it means just what I choose it to mean – neither more nor less."[15] Such conceptual disarray strongly suggests that the expression "new man," in and of itself, has no singular, strictly defined meaning. What exactly is covered by this phrase depends on *who* used it, *when*, *where*, *how*, and *for what purpose*. A comparison of what this expression signified in the writings of, say, early Christian theologians and Bolshevik ideologues, illustrates a close dependence of the notion of "new man" on the historical contexts of its usage.[16]

Nevertheless, the two words that make up the phrase refer directly to the two key concepts that underpin *any* notion of the "new man." The first one is the concept of *time*. It is impossible to talk about something "new" without knowing what "old" or "prior" was. As Wells's characterization of his "coming man" indicates, the very phrase "*new* man" points to the primacy of time in its three main incarnations: past, present, and future. It rests on belief in the possibility and necessity of *temporal change*, for there could be no "new" man without the existence first of some "prior" one.

Shifts in the understanding of what time is, as well as in the means and principles of its measurement, inevitably led to changes in the notions of the "new," "coming," "future" man. In thinking about the "new man," various actors operated with vastly different notions of time: astronomical and biological, historical and mythical, psychological and geological, linear and cyclical, infinite and finite. Eschatological expectations of the "end of time"; hypotheses of the eventual "death" of the Sun and the Universe; concepts of geological and biological evolution; theories of economic competition or class struggle as the motive force of history, all these and many other conceptions, which include time as their central component and attempt to predict possible futures, did (and still do) govern our ideas about the "new man."

It was this foundational role of temporal change in the very expression "new man" that determined its wide appeal in societies undergoing rapid historical developments and perturbations that triggered high anxieties—both hopes and fears—about *the future* of such societies. Even a cursory glance at available literature attests to the popularity of ideas about the "coming man" in Western Europe in the fervor of the Reformation, in revolutionary France and the frontier communities of North America, in Imperial Russia undergoing its Great Reforms, in the nations at once enchanted and terrified by the social consequences of the industrialization, in the host of new states that emerged on the ruins of the Hapsburg, Ottoman, and Russian empires, and in contemporary post-industrial societies. This is exactly why various notions of the "new man" circulating in Russia in the aftermath of the Bolshevik revolution have attracted the close attention of numerous scholars. Alas, they have largely neglected to examine how changes in the understanding and manipulating of time—not only Bolshevik experiments with the calendar and time schedules, but also new ideas about time-space relations engendered by the relativity theory—affected the concurrent notions of the "new man."[17]

The second key concept embedded in the phrase "new *man*" is that of human nature—in plain words, an answer to the question "What is Man"? Already the first thinkers pondering this question (from Egyptian priests and Greek philosophers to the authors of the Gilgamesh epic and Old Testament) have noted a certain *duality* of human nature. In different historical periods such duality was expressed in the familiar appositions of body and soul, death and immortality, flesh and spirit, the physical and the psychical, the biological and the social, the natural and the cultural.

The notions of human nature in fact imply a whole series of questions: Who are we? Where did we come from? And where are we going?—questions about human origin, the human place in the Universe, the meaning of human life and death, and human destiny, which have puzzled humanity's best minds since times immemorial. Heinrich Heine brilliantly depicted their timelessness and poignancy in an 1827 poem, titled simply "Questions":

> By the sea, by the dreary, night-colored sea,
> A young man stands;
> His heart full of anguish, his head full of doubts,
> And with pale lips he questions the billows:
> "Oh *solve me the riddle of Life,*
> The torturing, deathless riddle
> Which has cracked so many heads,
> Heads in hieroglyphic bonnets,
> Heads in black birettas and turbans,
> Heads in weighty wigs and a thousand other
> Poor, perspiring heads of people—
> Tell me, *what is Man? And what's his meaning?*
> *Where does he come from? Where is he going?*
> *Who dwells up there among the golden stars?*"
> The billows are whispering their eternal whispers.
> The wind blows on, the clouds go sailing;
> The stars keep twinkling, indifferent and cold.
> And a fool waits for his answer.[18]

A great variety of answers to these existential questions offered by theologians, philosophers, writers, artists, and scientists have continuously shaped and reshaped the understanding of human nature and the human future.

The interplay of the changing conceptions of time and human nature produces one of the most important elements of any notion of the "new man," namely—a set of *ideals* describing what a "man of the future" should (and should not) be. These ideals embody dissatisfaction with the past (and/or the present) and anxiety about the future. Indeed, any discussion of the "new," "coming," "future" man includes as its key component an account of perceived imperfections in the "old," "outgoing," "present" man.[19] Only by overcoming such failings, vices, and limitations, the "new man"—a perfected, transformed, enhanced, uplifted version of the "prior man"—could come into being. Various historical actors proposed a number of instruments they deemed suitable to accomplishing this task. Depending on specific shortcomings identified in the "previous man" by particular actors, a large variety of very different ideals of the "new man," as well as very different tools for making such ideals a reality, coexisted in any given culture during particular time periods.

The phrase "new man," then, serves merely as a convenient label covering a complex amalgam of ideas, models, visions, hopes, images, beliefs, ideals, fears, symbols, practices, clichés, and fantasies, regarding human nature and its temporal changes, circulating in particular settings and among particular groups of actors. An explication of what exactly is hidden under this universal label requires a detailed analysis of the actual contents of such an amalgam—its constitutive elements, their origins, historical changes, and interrelations. It also necessitates an examination of individual and institutional actors involved with its articulation and propagation.

The materials collected in this volume demonstrate that in Russian culture the ideas, practices, and ideals hidden under the label "new man" varied widely and changed considerably. Individual chapters show that different species and subspecies, as it were, of the "new man," created with the help of different sets of tools and techniques, populated all kinds of cultural productions. Particular versions of the "new men" appeared in literary fiction and doll making, philosophical treatises and theological discourses, theatrical plays and scientific research, policy pronouncements and museum exhibits, cinema and sculptures.

Yet taken together, the contributions to the volume allow one to discern in the multitude of these variations several discrete types of arguments in the debates over "making the new man." Each of these types is characterized by a particular mix of ideas about human nature, its perceived past and present shortcomings, its anticipated desirable and undesirable future changes, and the instruments available to effect or arrest such changes. Each has emerged during a particular period in human history and was advanced by a specific group of individual and institutional actors who produced a distinct "network of meanings"[20] hidden under the general label "new man."

Actors and Arguments

The first and the oldest among these distinct types of argumentation was based on theological interpretations of the two key concepts underpinning the very notions of the "new man": time and human nature. In the theological (Judeo-Christian) worldview, time was short and finite. It began with God's Creation of *Orbis et Hominis* and would eventually end in the Last Judgment. Human nature was defined by its God-given "essence"—immaterial and immortal soul (and/or spirit), while its material, mortal, bodily manifestation was nearly completely neglected.[21] Accordingly, the theological discourses on the "new man" revolved almost exclusively around "spiritual" improvements, consisting of overcoming the vices and failings fostered by diabolic and bodily temptations. Such improvements could be achieved only through the communion with God and the knowledge of God's Word (in its concurrent interpretation by the church authorities).[22]

Until the mid-nineteenth century, the very phrases "new man" and "new men" appeared only rarely in Russian-language materials, and, for the most part, their use was confined to theological literature.[23] The situation changed radically in the early 1860s, when the notions of the "new man" spurred a wide public debate informed by another, *nurturist* type of thinking about human nature.

This type of argumentation had emerged during the Enlightenment era in the works of its great thinkers, such as John Locke, Voltaire, Benedict Spinoza, Jean-Jacques Rousseau, Thomas Hobbes, Étienne Bonnot de Condillac, and Johann Wolfgang Goethe, which altered dramatically the earlier interpretations of human nature. Driven by atheistic and/or agnostic worldviews, the Enlightenment intellectuals elaborated a new array of ideas and ideals based on belief in *reason* as the essential element of human nature and conception of human mind as *tabula rasa*. In their works, the theological ideas and ideals of man's "spiritual improvement" morphed into deeply held beliefs in the foremost role of upbringing, learning, and education in the formation of the "new man." By the beginning of the nineteenth century these beliefs had spread widely across Europe and beyond. Their deep cultural imprint could clearly be seen in the first novel that took "making the new man" as its central theme—Mary Shelly's *Frankenstein or the New Prometheus* (1818). In the novel, it is not the monstrosity of the Creature's body, but the circumstances of his "upbringing"—first and foremost, his rejection by his creator Victor Frankenstein—that define and mold his "nature" and turn a benevolent being into a murderous beast.

During the eighteenth century the Enlightenment ideas and ideals filtered steadily into Russian discourse.[24] In 1802, Emperor Alexander I even established a special Ministry of People's Enlightenment. But it was half a century later that these ideas and ideals entered public discussions on the "new man." As a Google Books Ngram reproduced in Figure 0.1 demonstrates, the 1860s saw a virtual explosion in the use of the expression "new men" in the Russian-language printed materials, indicating the advent of a broad-ranging public debate. There could be little doubt that the debate was ignited by the Great Reforms that fundamentally reshaped the country's economic, political, and cultural landscapes.

The 1861 Imperial decree on the abolition of serfdom virtually overnight uplifted tens of millions of "human cattle," sold and bought by the landowners, to the status of free human beings, equal in many respects to their former masters. The questions of how to accomplish this transformation not just on paper but in reality became a pressing concern for Imperial bureaucracy and the country's budding civil society. Two novels, published in short succession—Ivan Turgenev's *Fathers and Children* and Nikolai Chernyshevskii's *What Is to Be Done?* (pointedly subtitled "From the Stories About New Men" [*iz rasskazov o novykh liudiakh*])—both reflected and helped define public discussions on the "new men" that flared up in the 1860s. Both novels were informed by Enlightenment ideas about human nature.[25]

These ideas gave the mid-nineteenth-century Russian discussions on the "new men" a distinct *nurturist* bent, in the sense that "nurture," rather than God or Nature, would play the primary role in the arrival of the "new men." They transformed human reason, language, will, and creativity from the divine faculties of the God-given soul into an immediate result of appropriate upbringing, education, and learning. They also made human failings and vices into the failures of education and upbringing, not the consequences of diabolic and bodily temptations. Indeed, the main characteristics of

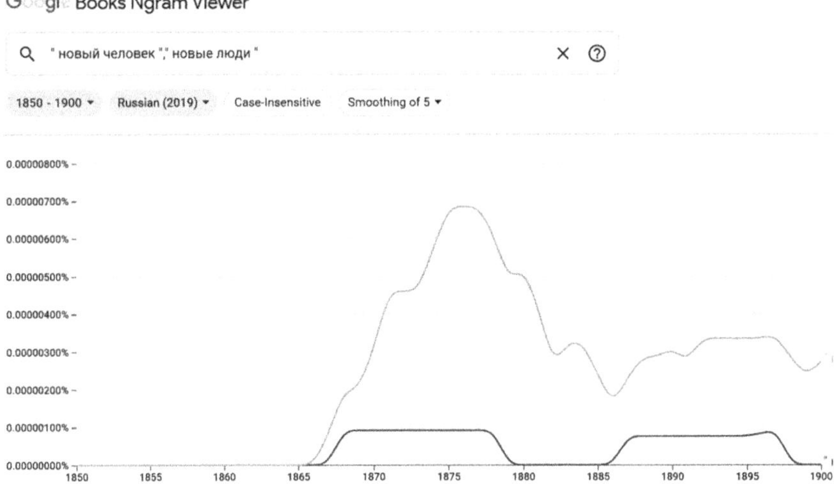

Figure 0.1 The frequencies of the expressions "new man" [*novyi chelovek*] (lower curve) and "new men" [*novye liudi*] (upper curve) in Russian-language books, from 1850 to 1900. Note that the frequency of the expression "new man" (singular) during this period barely raises above zero! A screenshot of Google Books Ngram Viewer that can be found here: <https://books.google.com/ngrams/graph?content=%22+%D0%BD%D0%BE%D0%B2%D1%8B%D0%B9+%D1%87%D0%B5%D0%BB%D0%BE%D0%B2%D0%B5%D0%BA+%22%2C%22+%D0%BD%D0%BE%D0%B2%D1%8B%D0%B5+%D0%BB%D1%8E%D0%B4%D0%B8+%22&year_start=1850&year_end=1900&corpus=36&smoothing=5#>; accessed on September 1, 2020. © Google Books Ngram Viewer.

the "prior men" frequently identified in the debate were ignorance, traditionalism/conservatism, servility, ineptitude, and superstition, all deriving from lack of knowledge and education. A variety of socially and politically active groups, from democrats, Slavophiles, and *narodniki* to socialists, monarchists, and anarchists, came to see education and upbringing as the main tools in shaping the future of the country and her people.[26] These ideas fueled the *narodniki* movement that was set on actually "making the new men" by bringing education, knowledge, and culture to the people (*narod*).[27] Numerous fictional and nonfictional writings elaborated on, critiqued, or ridiculed this particular array of ideas, ideals, and techniques, and reported on "What Has Been Done," as one of the authors titled his account.[28]

In the 1880s, the perceived failure of the *narodniki* movement in "making the new men" out of former serfs and their owners seemed to incite certain disillusionment with the efficacy of the nurturist ideas, ideals, and techniques. This disillusionment found expression in the resurgence of the theological and the rise of various "occult" (from spiritualist to theo- and anthroposophist) notions of human nature, all of which focused on its "spiritual" dimension, immateriality, and immortality.[29] This, in turn, sparked wide popular interest in various esoteric practices, from *magnétisme* and communication with "spirits" to yoga and telepathic or hypnotic suggestion, as suitable tools for molding human nature and, thus, "making the new men."

This *supernatural* argumentation gained particular currency after the defeat of the first Russian Revolution of 1905–6, which enhanced even further the disillusionment with the nurturist interpretations of human nature. The sheer number of various "occult" periodicals, along with their print runs, rose markedly.[30] A list of books issued by a publishing house, established in 1913 under the very name "New Man," provides a vivid illustration to this trend.[31] In this list, mystic Peter Ouspensky's *Search for a New Life: What Yoga Is* and diet enthusiast Aleksei Suvorin's *New Man* neighbored the translations of the latest edition of German physiologist Gustav Fechner's *Das Büchlein vom Leben nach dem Tode*, French hypnotist Fernand Girod's *Magnétisme expérimental*, and Canadian psychiatrist Richard M. Bucke's *Cosmic Consciousness*, along with writings by several other local and foreign "gurus."[32]

Yet during the very time when discourses on the "new men" were being saturated with the supernatural, another, *naturalistic* set of arguments was also gaining steam in the debate. As Krementsov's chapter in the present volume describes in detail, the advent of Charles Darwin's theory of temporal change (evolution) in plant and animal species, combined with the rapid development of new experimental medicine, psychology, and biology, radically altered the concurrent understanding of human origin and human nature. In the naturalistic worldview, the bodily side of human nature came to be seen as a highly adaptable chemical and physical "machine" molded by the millennia of biological evolution. At the same time, the "spiritual" dimension of human nature (mind, will, language, creativity, and so on) came to be regarded as a function of the body's nervous system, first and foremost, the brain.

In the decades around the turn of the twentieth century, new experimental bio-psycho-medical disciplines discovered multiple ways of manipulating in the laboratory such basic life processes as metabolism, growth, behavior, immunity, perception, ageing, and reproduction. These exciting discoveries engendered euphoric views of the experimental life sciences as powerful instruments of *control* over human nature and its future changes (evolution). According to these visions, the application of new bio-psycho-medical technologies—from hormone injections and blood transfusions to artificial insemination and sexual sterilization—could "correct" any human failings, be they physical, moral, mental, or social. Even more, they could make real any conceivable ideal of the "coming man," from immortality to telepathy to genius! Via a variety of fictional, semi-fictional, and nonfictional popular writings about contemporary science ("science fiction," "scientific fictional prose," and "entertaining science," as Matthias Schwartz defines them in his chapter), these euphoric views spread far and wide through every corner of Russian culture. They informed philosophical tracts, literary fiction, children education, motion pictures, and artistic works.

Circa 1900, yet another type of argumentation emerged in the debate—*Marxist*. Several members of the Russian Socialist Democratic Labor Party sought to "update" the Enlightenment-era nurturist ideas and ideals with Karl Marx and Friedrich Engels's political economy and philosophy. Led by Alexander Bogdanov—Lenin's rival for the party leadership—the group included eminent party members Anatolii Lunacharskii, Ivan Skvortsov-Stepanov, and Vladimir Bazarov, along with their influential sympathizers, such as writer Maxim Gorky. They reasoned that the limitations and shortcomings of the "prior men" were all the direct products of the capitalist economic system. But, according to Marxism, that system also produced the "new men"—proletarians conscious of their historical role as the "grave-diggers" of capitalism. The group, thus, saw its objective in raising the consciousness of the working class and advancing new "socialist" ideals. They defined these ideals as directly opposing what they saw as the "capitalist," "bourgeois" features of the "prior men." Ranging from individualism and competitiveness to mysticism and nationalism to mercantilism and piety, all of these "capitalist" features had to be overcome by the "new men" of the socialist tomorrow. In contrast to the proponents of the naturalistic approach, who in their discussions of the "coming men" focused largely on human biological, anthropological, and pathological types,[33] Marxists centered on social groups, classes, and hierarchies. Although Russian Marxists rejected the *political* ideas, ideals, and goals of the *narodniki* movement, they fully embraced their predecessors' *cultural* mission of bringing knowledge to the people. They emphasized the key role of upbringing, education, and learning in raising the consciousness of the "previously oppressed classes" and hence in "making the new men." This emphasis was apparent, for instance, in Bogdanov's project for a "proletarian encyclopedia" (investigated in Michael Coates's chapter) and in Gorky's pedagogical ideas (examined in Lyubov Bugaeva's contribution). But Russian Marxists were quite eclectic in their search for appropriate tools for "creating the new men." They borrowed freely from all the other types of arguments, advancing in one breath the ideas of "God-building," Darwinian evolution, the Nietzschean *Übermensch*, "physiological collectivism," and "socialist rituals."[34]

At the beginning of the Great War each of the five types of argumentation pertaining to "making the new men"—theological, nurturist, supernatural, naturalistic, and Marxist—had its proponents and opponents in Russia, and each was well represented in the cultural productions of the time. Yet, although their champions used the same expression—"new man"—the meanings they attached to this phrase differed substantially. As a result, the universal label "new man" came to cover multifaceted, partially overlapping, and shifting networks of meanings. These multiple meanings constituted a particular cultural resource rich in countless allusions, inferences, and connotations and readily available for exploitation to any interested party.

Phrases and Phases

The materials collected in the present volume indicate that during the first four decades of the twentieth century the discussions on the "new man" in Russia went through three distinct phases. A Google Books Ngram for the expression "new man" (*novyi chelovek*) in the Russian-language printed materials from 1890 to 1940 (see Figure 0.2) shows a precipitous increase in the frequency with which the phrase appeared in the Russian publications of the late 1910s to the early 1920s, and a no less steep decline in the late 1920s to the early 1930s. Despite all the limitations and imprecision of the Google Books research tools, the graph they produce is quite suggestive.[35] It points to a possible (cor)relation between the rise and fall in the usage of the phrase and the two catastrophic upheavals—customarily labeled the "Bolshevik revolution" and the "revolution from above," respectively—which completely overturned the country's political, economic, and cultural terrains during these very periods.[36]

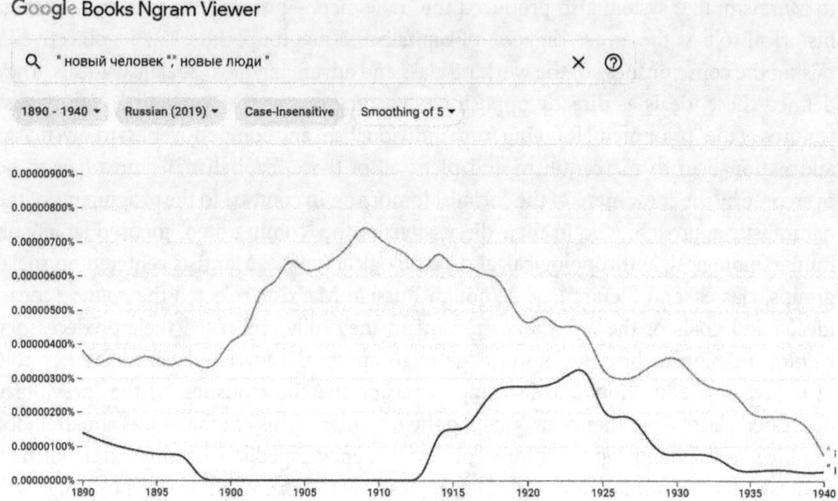

Figure 0.2 The frequencies of the expressions "new man" [*novyi chelovek*] (lower curve) and "new men" [*novye liudi*] (upper curve) in Russian-language books, from 1890 to 1940. A screenshot of Google Books Ngram Viewer that can be found here: <https://books.google.com/ngrams/graph?content=%22+%D0%BD%D0%BE%D0%B2%D1%8B%D0%B9+%D1%87%D0%B5%D0%BB%D0%BE%D0%B2%D0%B5%D0%BA+%22%2C%22+%D0%BD%D0%BE%D0%B2%D1%8B%D0%B5+%D0%BB%D1%8E%D0%B4%D0%B8+%22&year_start=1890&year_end=1940&corpus=36&smoothing=5&case_insensitive=true#>; accessed on September 1, 2020. © Google Books Ngram Viewer.

The first of these upheavals began amid the Great War with the fall of the Russian monarchy in February 1917 and the formation of a Provisional Government that was to ensure the country's transition from the autocratic empire to a democratic parliamentary republic. In late October, however, a coup d'état successfully carried out by the Bolsheviks, a radical faction of the Russian Socialist Democratic Labor Party led by Lenin, ignited a bloody civil war that ravaged the country for nearly four years. The Bolsheviks won the war. The new political system they implemented was stabilized by the adoption of the NEP (new economic policy) in late 1921 and by the establishment on the ruins of the former empire of the Union of Soviet Socialist Republics in December 1922.

The second upheaval began in the spring of 1928 with the infamous "Shakhty Trial" of several engineers accused of "wrecking" the coal mines entrusted to their management. The widely publicized show trial signaled a radical departure from the economic and cultural policies of the previous years. It inaugurated the abolishment of the NEP and the launch of the first Five-Year Plan with its neck-breaking industrialization, overt militarization, and the forced collectivization of the peasantry. By 1932, the upheaval subsided with the consolidation of Joseph Stalin's dictatorial rule over the party-state apparatus and of that apparatus's strict command and brutal control over all facets of life in the country.

The Google Books Ngram for the expression "new man" in Russian-language books seems to fully support a customary view that ideas about the "coming man" emerged and enjoyed particular popularity (presumably denoted by the frequency of the phrase's appearance in various texts) during the period between the two upheavals described earlier, and indeed were a characteristic cultural feature of that period. As is always the case with statistics, however, the curve hides a considerable bias deriving from specific criteria chosen for collecting and analyzing the data.

A curve generated from the same database for the expression "new *men*" (*novye liudi*) indicates that very similar ideas—expressed in a slightly different form—were increasingly popular during the preevolutionary period, from about the 1890s until the Bolshevik revolution of 1917 (see Figure 0.2).[37] Furthermore, the superposition of the searches for the expressions "new man" and "new men" shows that the popularity of ideas covered by the latter phrase was significantly greater than that of the former. It grew rapidly for nearly twenty years, from about 1895 to about 1914, when it began to drop. Around 1917, the popularity of ideas covered by the phrase "new man" began a proportionately somewhat smaller climb that lasted roughly a decade, while the frequency of the phrase "new men" remained fairly stable but still higher than that of the "new man." Toward the end of the 1920s, the popularity of both phrases went into a steady decline and reached the bottom at the end of the 1930s.

The Google Books Ngrams suggest that the two great upheavals—the Bolshevik revolution and the Stalinist revolution from above—did have some influence on the actual use and popularity of the ideas hidden under these general labels. The curves show that the period under study breaks into three distinct phases, which could be labeled Imperial (1890–1917), Bolshevik (1917–28), and Stalinist (1928–39). As materials collected in this volume demonstrate, each of these phases was distinguished by specific institutional settings, particular groups of actors involved, and the prevalence of certain types of argumentation in the debates over "making the new men."

During the Imperial phase, the theological, nurturist, supernatural, and naturalistic arguments coexisted in different institutional niches and were advanced by different large and vocal groups of actors, with only occasional "defectors" crossing the boundaries. The Marxist arguments during this phase remained virtually inaudible in the cacophony of multiple other voices. The arguments developed by clerics appeared predominantly in theological periodicals and treatises. Philosophers, psychologists, and educators advocated for the nurturist precepts in their own specialized publications.[38] Self-proclaimed spiritualists, theosophists, anthroposophists, and mystics defended the supernatural views in a variety of "occult" magazines and books. Physicians and scientists propagated the naturalistic interpretations in professional medical, psychiatric, and scientific, as well as popular science, publications. Marxists used party publications to spread their own views. Russian proponents of the five trends of thought were well informed about the works of their counterparts abroad. They translated practically all major publications on relevant subjects appearing in foreign languages.

The proponents of the five different types of argumentation did sporadically engage in boundary skirmishes, claiming their own exclusive cultural authority over particular ideas, ideals, and techniques.[39] Yet the five currents of thought coexisted rather peacefully, occasionally cross-pollinated, and coevolved in the rich cultural milieu of late Imperial Russia.[40] They generated multiple intersecting networks of meanings associated with the visions of the "new man." These networks formed an influential cultural resource easily accessible to anyone involved in the cultural process.

The cultural productions of the time reflect this haphazard mixture. Playwrights and satirists with equal venom made fun of the out-worldly claims of spiritualists and of the "hairbrained" schemes of scientists and physicians.[41] Fiction writers explored indiscriminately the supernatural, naturalist, and theological visions of the "coming man," along with the possible futures inspired by the nurturist and the Marxist ideas.[42] Dailies and weeklies regularly carried, often on the same page, advertisements for spiritualists' séances, hypnotists' public performances, theosophists' meetings, and scientific lectures. Literary and popular-science magazines printed under the same cover articles about "Spiritism and the Fourth Dimension" or "Thinking Horses" and reports on a lecture by eminent Moscow physician Fedor Sheremetevskii, exploring "The Physiological Foundations of Psychic Phenomena within the Limits of Scientific Cognition," or physicist Sir Oliver Lodge's address to the British Association for the Advancement of Science endorsing Spiritism.[43]

The Bolshevik revolution put an end to this equable mélange of very different approaches to "making the new men" and opened a new stage in the debate. The abolition of private property and the nationalization of economy accomplished by the Bolsheviks meant that all cultural spheres became dependent on party-state support and, hence, subjects to party-state control. One of the first top-level government agencies established immediately after the Bolsheviks had seized power was the People's Commissariat of Enlightenment (Narkompros). Headed by Lunacharskii, Narkompros oversaw virtually all educational institutions, from kindergartens to universities, and nearly all fields of culture, including literature, fine arts, theater, science, and cinema. Bolshevik agents and agencies, thus, came to define which ideas, ideals, and techniques would be culturally dominant by actively promoting what they perceived as "friends" and ruthlessly suppressing what they saw as "foes" of their regime.

The Bolsheviks' program of creating a new socialist society turned a "revolutionary dream" (in the apt expression of historian Richard Stites[44]) of "making the new men"—entertained by a few Marxist writers during the previous decades—into an urgent practical task. Since the Bolsheviks embraced the major tenets of the nurturist approach to human nature, they enthusiastically endorsed upbringing, education, and learning as the principal tools in "making the new men," as chapters by Michael Coates, Lyubov Bugaeva, and Olga Ilyukha show. Numerous government agencies mounted huge campaigns to combat illiteracy; to popularize all kinds of medical, technical, agricultural, economic, sociological, and scientific knowledge; and to promote the application of such knowledge to the everyday life of the populace. They mobilized all available types of cultural products: posters, songs, books, plays, paintings, illustrated weeklies, moving pictures, popular magazines, public lectures, sculptures, dances, buildings, music, public spaces, daily newspapers, monuments, exhibitions, museums, botanical and zoological gardens, radio programming, and even children's toys. Everything was deployed to enlighten, acculturate, and educate the "previously oppressed classes" of workers and peasants. Olga Elina's analysis of the 1923 All-

Russian Agricultural Exhibition illustrates the sheer magnitude, as well as range and extent, of the efforts the Bolsheviks put into making a "new peasant." At the same time, as Bugaeva's and Ilyukha's chapters demonstrate, the Bolsheviks considered children and adolescents the most suitable "raw material" for "making the new men" and employed all possible means, from literature to dolls to cinema, to inculcate them with new "socialist" ideas and ideals.

The Bolshevik revolution elevated Marxism, with its militant materialism and militant atheism, to the status of the country's official ideology. This resulted in the complete exclusion of all "idealistic"—first and foremost, theological and supernatural—arguments (including those advanced by some Marxists during the previous decades, such as "God-building") from public discussions on the "new man." By the end of the civil war in 1921, *all* theological and "occult" periodicals issued in large numbers during the Imperial era had disappeared. In 1922–3, about 200 eminent intellectuals accused of promoting "idealistic worldviews" were exiled from the country. Many supporters of theological and/or occult views emigrated. Those who stayed had to remain silent or hide and disguise their views. But even the masters of writing in between the lines could not always (or not for long) escape the merciless clutches of the Bolshevik censor, as Irina Golovacheva's chapter shows in the case of "Dog's Heart," a satirical novella written by Mikhail Bulgakov, a "mystical writer," as he defined himself.

At the very same time, the Bolsheviks' militant materialism and atheism, combined with the huge campaign to popularize all kinds of knowledge, greatly enhanced the cultural authority of the life sciences and their practitioners. The Bolsheviks hailed materials and techniques furnished by both evolutionary theory and new experimental bio-psycho-medical research as the ultimate proof of the Marxist atheistic and materialistic views of Nature in general and of human nature in particular. They gave a tremendous boost to the institutional development of new bio-psycho-medical disciplines and greatly enhanced the authority of the naturalistic arguments in the debate over "making the new men."

Indeed, the Marxist and the naturalistic modes of thinking were to a certain degree "hybridized," while the networks of meanings they produced became closely entwined. During the 1920s, Darwinism was incorporated into and became an integral part of the concurrent version of Russian Marxism.[45] Wide propaganda of the theories of biological evolution became a major focus of the state's considerable effort of bringing "science to the masses,"[46] as Pat Simpson's chapter on the Moscow Darwin Museum reveals. A number of leading Bolsheviks endorsed and promoted a variety of bio-psycho-medical ideas, ideals, and techniques as suitable pathways to "making new men." At the same time, a number of leading practitioners in bio-psycho-medical fields took up Marxist rhetoric and ideas in their own pronouncements on the subject.

Furthermore, scientists and physicians came to exercise considerable authority over the nurturist type of argumentation that underpinned much of Marxist thinking about "making the new man." They successfully "scientified," as it were, the principles of upbringing, education, and learning with the ideas, ideals, and instruments developed within such new scientific disciplines as criminology, reflexology, psychotechnology (*psikhotekhnika*), pedology (science of childhood), physiology of higher nervous activity, and scientific organization of labor (NOT). They even managed to appropriate certain ideas, ideals, and techniques previously advanced within the supernatural interpretations of human nature, such as hypnosis, immortality, and telepathy. They launched extensive research on these subjects, and firmly established their own intellectual and institutional authority over them.[47]

Moreover, the Bolshevik endorsement of the naturalistic approaches to human nature, coupled with the elimination of the theological and the spiritualist voices from the debate on "making the new man," created an atmosphere permissive of, and conducive to, certain kinds of bio-psycho-medical experimentation that would hardly be possible otherwise. For instance, the Soviet media widely publicized experiments with severed dog heads (by Sergei Briukhonenko),[48] with conditional reflexes in children (by Ivan Pavlov's students),[49] and with human-ape hybrids (by Il'ia Ivanov).[50] These scientific experiments generated much public excitement in Bolshevik Russia, manifest in their appearance in multiple cultural productions of the time.[51] Yet, although they did attract the close attention of the Western scientific community, and even inspired some of its members to advance certain visions of the "new man" based on these experiments, they were largely met with contempt and censure in the Western media. Nearly all chapters in the present volume demonstrate that numerous cultural productions of the time explored, reflected, and refracted through their particular media (written and spoken word, or still and moving images) this preeminence of the naturalistic, bio-psycho-medical approaches to human nature in the discussions over, cultural representations of, and actual efforts at "making the new men" in Bolshevik Russia.

The ascendancy of the naturalistic type of argumentation in shaping the "new men" visions and practices, however, did not last long. The "revolution from above" greatly increased the institutional power of party bureaucracy (in the first place, Stalin personally and his closest underlings), ideologues, and "professional" Marxists. It undermined the cultural authority of science and scientists and considerably diminished their role in predicting and shaping the future of the country and her populace, thus opening a new, Stalinist phase in the discussions on the "new men."

Already during the previous stage, some Marxists had begun to consider human nature not merely as a product of biological evolution, but as primarily the result of historical developments in social, first of all, labor and economic, relations. Taking their cue from Friedrich Engels's works, "The Role of Labor in the Origin of Man from Ape" and "The Dialectics of Nature" (first published in Russian in 1922 and 1925, respectively), some of them launched a noisy attack on the concurrent naturalistic, bio-psycho-medical interpretations of human nature. They accused their proponents of being "mechanistic," "reductionist," and "undialectical," and emphasized the role of labor, class, and society in defining what human beings actually are and will be.

During the "revolution from above" the debate over the interrelations of the biological and the social in human nature was (with Stalin's personal involvement) settled: the social "dialectically negated" the biological. All the bio-psycho-medical instruments of "making the new men," so popular during the three preceding decades, came to be seen—and summarily dismissed—as the "pernicious" *biologization* of human nature. The network of meanings produced within the naturalistic current of thought regarding the "new man" was severely truncated. Marxist ideologues replaced practitioners of bio-psycho-medical disciplines in the role of experts on human nature and humanity's future. Accordingly, social nurturist tools—upbringing, education, and learning—emerged as the primary instruments of modifying human nature and "making the new men." From that point on, the coming *Homo novus* was to be created not by managing reproduction or altering heredity and hormonal balance, but by manipulating upbringing and education. In the fall of 1930, Lev Vygotskii, one of the leaders of "Marxist" psychology and pedagogy, forcefully articulated this point in an article with a telling title, "Socialist Reconstruction of Man."[52] As a result, life scientists largely abandoned the futuristic visions of "making the new men," and confined themselves to the pursuit of their disciplinary, highly specialized research and clinical agendas.

Furthermore, party ideologues put forward a new set of "socialist" ideals, corresponding to the current priorities of industrialization, militarization, and collectivization. These ideals centered on such features as labor and military heroism, devotion to the party and its leaders, and loathing the internal "enemies of the people" and the external "enemies of socialism." In the mid-1930s, the party-state apparatus launched a huge propaganda campaign to demonstrate that the "new men of the socialist epoch," in the words of one of Stalin's lieutenants, had already come into being under the guidance of the party and its leader, Stalin.[53] Opened with the so-called Stakhanovite movement among industrial workers, the campaign quickly expanded to envelop the newly collectivized peasantry, hailing the "heroes and heroines of Stalin's fields."[54] As Schwartz's, Petriashin's, and Ilyukha's chapters show, during the 1930s, all elements of contemporary culture, including literature, museum exhibits, and doll making, were mobilized for the propaganda and inculcation of such "socialist" ideals of the "new man" and tasked with turning them into reality.

The General and the Particular

Materials collected in the present volume demonstrate the (co)existence of numerous species and subspecies of the "new men" in nearly all domains of Russian culture, as well as a plethora of instruments deemed suitable for actually "making the new men" out of the country's populace. How can we understand the multiplicity and pervasiveness of the "new men" visions in Russian cultural productions? Was there something that made the Russian visions of the "coming men" unique or special? Was there ever a truly Soviet version of the "new men," as some historical studies have postulated? And if there was, what made it "Soviet"?

Although *c.* 1900 multiple visions of the "new man" (re)appeared nearly everywhere, in particular cultures they met very different fates. These fates could be illustrated by the Google Books Ngrams for the expression "new man" and its analogues in the Russian-, French-, German-, Italian-, and Spanish-language printed materials for the period from 1890 to 1940.[55] Considerable differences among these Ngrams indicate that the actual use of this expression in particular cultures reflects variations in and adaptations to specific local conditions. At the same time, certain similarities in the curves' directions and fluctuations point to the possible influence of some common, "global" actors, factors, and contexts.

Materials collected in this volume allow one to examine which particular local and global contexts might have affected the debates on the "new man" in Russia. Several chapters have uncovered numerous similarities, as well as differences, between the notions of the "new man" circulating in Russia and elsewhere. Some of these similarities point to a certain commonality in the visions of humanity's future in different locales. In part, such commonality probably derived from the main purpose of these visions. Although produced by a variety of actors in a multitude of settings, all of these visions, in one way or another, sought to provide plausible answers to the same existential questions of human origin, human nature, and human destiny: Who are we? Where did we come from? And where are we going? Each of them presented certain ideals of the future and corresponding ideals of the human beings who were to enable and inhabit that future. Each addressed the issues of "raw materials" and special instruments necessary to make such ideals a reality. Each offered a time scale of change from the "old" to the "new" and plotted a route that ostensibly would take humanity from the past into the future. Some were overly optimistic, hailing the bright future being born in the nearest workshop, laboratory, school, labor commune, or factory and waiting just around the corner. Others were deeply pessimistic, prophesying the imminent catastrophic failure (or at best, the futility) inherent to any attempt to meddle with Nature in general and human nature in particular. But nearly all of them placed control over human nature and human destiny in the hands of humans themselves: the "making of mankind" was the job of mankind itself.

In part, such similarities and differences were undoubtedly a result of extensive filtering of some Western ideas, techniques, images, and ideals of the "coming men" into Russian cultural milieu. Russian actors were well aware of the multitude of the "new men" visions produced by their counterparts abroad. From the 1860s through the 1920s, they translated nearly all relevant works published in major European languages in all cultural fields: literature, medicine, education, philosophy, and science. Some of their own visions were obviously produced in response to, as a critique of, or as a further development of the visions developed elsewhere. Consider, for instance, Martians depicted in Alexander Bogdanov's 1908 novel *Red Star*. They are indistinguishable from Earthlings in their bodily appearance. Yet, thanks to mutual blood exchanges, they are much more advanced in their mental and physical capacities, immune to diseases, "physiologically collectivist," and long-living. There is little doubt that Bogdanov crafted his "future men" as a clear alternative to H. G. Wells's blood-sucking monsters killed off by the earthly bacteria in the *War of the Worlds*, as well as to Friedrich Nietzsche's utterly individualist *Übermensch*.

The flow of ideas, techniques, and ideals was never unidirectional, however. One example will suffice. In 1929, young British crystallographer John D. Bernal published a futuristic essay, provocatively titled *The World, the Flesh and the Devil* (alluding to the three sources of temptation and hence failings of the "prior men"). The essay advanced a particular vision of directed human evolution.[56] Asserting that "man himself must actively interfere in his own making and interfere in a highly unnatural manner," Bernal envisioned the human brain supported by intricate mechanical contraptions (what later would be called "brain-in-a-vat") as an inevitable next stage in human evolution. As he put it: "Normal man is an evolutionary dead end; mechanical man, apparently a break in organic evolution, is actually more in the true tradition of a further evolution." There is little doubt that Bernal's idea was inspired by Briukhonenko's experiments with severed dog heads kept alive by special machinery of his own design.[57]

Some similarities perhaps sprung from the common roots of the visions generated in Russia and elsewhere. Thus, the Enlightenment ideas and ideals of education, upbringing, and learning enjoyed wide popularity all over Europe and the Americas since at least the eighteenth century. This might well have contributed to the similarities between the pedagogical ideas and philosophies advanced in the United States and Russia during the first decades of the twentieth century, described in Bugaeva's chapter. Likewise, the notions of progress and positivist views of science as the only true way to understand and thus to "control" Nature (and humans as part of Nature) captivated many nineteenth- and twentieth-century intellectuals the world over. At the same time, beliefs in the "universality" of bio-psycho-medical knowledge and technologies might well have helped spread across national borders some contemporary notions of human nature and human destiny based on such knowledge and technologies. Certain anxieties about the future embodied in the perceived shortcomings of the "prior man"—particularly such "social ills" as crime, alcoholism, and prostitution—were widely shared across different cultures and might have also resulted in the similarities of the "new men" visions. Golovacheva's chapter uncovers remarkable parallels in the employment of the current ideas about the "criminal brain" in Bulgakov's 1926 novella "Dog's Heart" and James Whale's 1931 movie *Frankenstein*. Likewise, Krementsov's chapter reveals surprising similarities between Fedor Il'in's novel *Valley of New Life* (1928) and Aldous Huxley's *Brave New World* (1932) in the use of recent advances in bio-psycho-medical research as the foundations of their "new worlds" and the "new men" that populate them. Thus, contrary to the received wisdom asserting that the Bolsheviks were obsessed with constructing a unique "new Soviet man," the actual visions of the "new man" popular in 1920s Russia had very much in common with analogous visions circulating elsewhere.

A certain commonality of the "new man" visions in different settings, however, does not imply their uniformity. The contributions to the present volume also unveil numerous differences between the "new man" visions circulating in Russia and abroad. One could suggest that a major source of these considerable differences was the outright rejection of certain Western ideas, ideals, and techniques by some Russian actors. Since at least the nineteenth-century debate between the Slavophiles and the Westernizers, many eminent cultural figures in Russia have staunchly argued for the country's unique path to the future, profoundly different from other countries.[58] For various authors, this exceptionalism was rooted in the country's landscapes or religion, climates or economy, history or culture. But, most of them agreed that the key factor resided in the country's people who *by nature* (often referred to as the "mysterious Russian soul") differed from their neighbors to the West.

In the view of many proponents of the Russian exceptionalism, the most characteristic feature that distinguished the "Russian people" was their inherent, spiritual attachment to the communal way of living (*sobornost'*) embodied in the peasant commune (*obshchina*), which was seen as directly opposite to the individualism that imbued the lives of people elsewhere. The juxtaposition of "Western individualism" and "Russian collectivism" found expression in numerous cultural productions, from novels to scientific treatises. It was presented in the form of explicit oppositions between "I" and "We," individual and collective, private and public, competition and mutual aid, individuality and authority, autonomy and dependence, protest and orthodoxy, dissidence and conformity. These dichotomies certainly affected Russian discussions on the "coming man." This perhaps explains a much higher frequency of the phrase "new men" (plural) as compared to the phrase "new man" (singular) in the Russian corpus of printed materials collected by Google, as well as the differences in the curves' directions indicating the changes in the popularity of the two phrases over time (see Figure 0.2).

This also suggests that any form of exceptionalism (ethnic, national, racial, or cultural) would be reflected in the "new man" visions prevalent in particular settings. Indeed, a Google Books Ngram for the phrases "new man" and "new men" in the English-language materials differs substantially from that generated from the Russian-language sources.[59] In the English sources the singular "new man" appears more frequently than the plural "new men." The two curves closely parallel each other, suggesting that the plural perhaps represented merely a sum of the singular, and not a particular entity in itself. Furthermore, there is a marked difference between the Ngrams generated from the British and the American sources.[60] An Ngram generated for the two phrases "*neue Mensch*" and "*neuen Menschen*" in the German-language sources shows a similar parallelism, but the relation between the singular and the plural is reversed as compared to the English-language Ngram. It is basically the same as in the Russian-language Ngram, and it apparently reflects the rise and fall in the popularity of ideas about particular *Volksgeist*, a "national spirit," or "soul," of the German people.[61]

The Bolshevik revolution, with its emphasis on proletarian internationalism and its expectation of the forthcoming "world revolution," muted the arguments for the *Russian* exceptionalism, even though it reinforced the dichotomy between the individual and the collective. A major difference of the "new men" visions publicly advanced after the Bolshevik takeover from those propounded in other settings (including Imperial Russia) was that they were explicitly sanctioned by the party-state agents and agencies. They represented ideas, ideals, and practices overtly endorsed by the country's new rulers. Elsewhere in Europe and the Americas, it was the continuous interplay among a multitude of powerful interests, actors, and structures—ranging from public institutions, the church, and the market to private philanthropists, state agencies, and the media—that shaped such visions.[62] In Soviet Russia, it was the party-state apparatus that held all the power and thus molded such visions to fit its own agendas, policies, and interests.

During the first decade of the Bolshevik rule, however, this power was divided among numerous, not infrequently competing, government agents and agencies, each pursuing their own interests, policies, and agendas. From the very beginning of their regime, the Bolsheviks strove to control stringently the contents and distribution of all cultural products through several agencies set up specifically for this purpose (such as

Glavlit, *Repertkom*, and *Glavpolitprosvet*). As a result, the Bolshevik revolution did put a stop to the further development of the theological and supernatural approaches to the notions of the "new man," which had flourished during the Imperial period, and continued to flourish outside of Russia during the 1920s and beyond. Yet the division of power afforded a certain degree of variability in the "new men" visions produced and pursued under the auspices of different individual and institutional actors, such as Narkompros, Narkomzdrav, and even the secret police (OGPU), and their respective heads, Anatolii Lunacharskii, Nikolai Semashko, and Felix Dzerzhinsky. A partial restoration of private property under the NEP also allowed some private interests (such as commercial publishing, for instance) to exert certain influence on the availability and variability of such visions. The "revolution from above" concentrated the power in the hands of top-level party functionaries. It radically reduced the number of individual and institutional actors involved in both generating and propagating such visions and hence diminished considerably their variability and accessibility.

There were other sources of difference between the Soviet and the Western versions of the "new man." The exclusively state patronage of science engendered a particular configuration of bio-psycho-medical disciplines and research directions in Soviet Russia. Among available naturalistic interpretations of human nature, the Bolsheviks seemed to privilege the old Russian tradition of "nervism" (represented at the time by Ivan Pavlov's "physiology of higher nervous activity" and Vladimir Bekhterev's "reflexology") over both "humoralism" supported by many US and British physiologists and "psychologism" advanced by many German-speaking psychologists, psychiatrists, and psychoanalysts. The well-known case of the Soviet state first supporting, next suppressing, and then again promoting the development of (human) genetics provides another illuminating example. Naturally, such preferential treatments boosted the availability and popularity of ideas, ideals, and techniques generated by the privileged disciplines and research directions at the expense of those created by their competitors. At the same time, even though both Soviet and Western participants in the "new men" debates sometimes identified the same failings and shortcomings in the "prior men" (such as crime, degeneration, and prostitution), they often offered very different tools to overcome them. To give but one example, although eugenic ideas of "bettering human nature" found numerous proponents in Bolshevik Russia, nearly all of them rejected "negative" eugenic measures, such as coerced sexual sterilization, which were quite popular among US, German, and Scandinavian eugenicists. Furthermore, after the "revolution from above," all eugenic arguments vanished from the public discussions on the "new men" in Soviet Russia, being replaced with the nurturist precepts of education and upbringing.

Denouement: What Is to Be Done?

A short answer is "a lot." Of course, it is simply impossible to cover all the issues related to the "new men" visions circulating in Russian culture prior to the Second World War in a single volume, no matter how thick. Certain subjects and topics (for instance, gender relations embedded in the visions) have received very short shrift. Others, such as the role of technology, have barely been touched upon. Still others, such as the relative import of different cultural productions and different media—literature (word) and cinema (image), children's dolls and public displays—in articulating and propagating these visions, have not been addressed at all.

Although far from being comprehensive, this volume offers new approaches, sources, and frameworks to explore these and many other relevant subjects. Most important, it reveals the major constitutive elements of the "new men" visions: notions of time and human nature; ideals reflecting dissatisfactions with the past and anxieties about the future; and beliefs in the possibility and necessity of altering human nature as a way of both addressing such dissatisfactions and anxieties and making such ideals a reality. In one form or another, all of these elements are present in *any* vision of the "new man," regardless of its specific settings, creators, and media. By uncovering certain general types of argumentation and specific stages in the Russian discussions on "making the new men" during the first forty years of the twentieth century, contributions to the present volume also chart broad guidelines for examining such debates in other periods of Russian history, as well as in other settings. The aforementioned Google Books Ngrams for the expressions "new man" and "new men" in various languages beg for both a much more detailed analysis of individual "national" cases and a sustained comparative perspective in studying the "new men" visions in different cultures. For instance, a comparison of such visions produced by the large Russian diaspora abroad (especially after the Bolshevik revolution) with those of their compatriots living in Soviet Russia promises interesting results.

One of the most important finds articulated in several chapters is a key role of the life sciences and bio-psycho-medical technologies they produced in shaping the "new men" visions everywhere since the last decades of the nineteenth century. One could expect that every major development in the life sciences and associated technologies in the subsequent periods—from the rise of molecular biology to the emergence of new cognitive sciences—would also leave a deep imprint on both the concurrent discussions of the "new man" and their renderings in a variety of cultural productions. A systematic search for, and analysis of, such imprints should constitute an important part of the agenda for future research.

Practically all chapters demonstrate the defining role of the state—its agents and agencies, policies and interests—in the variability and availability of ideas and ideals of the "new men" circulating in Russian culture since the very beginning of the Bolshevik regime. We need to explore further the state's exact role in the fluctuating fortunes of various species and subspecies of the "new men." Were they merely an unintended by-product or an integral part of the state's shifting economic, political, and cultural policies and priorities? If, as Bugaeva's chapter seems to suggest, the latter was the case, we need to know much more about exactly who articulated, implemented, and enforced such specific policies, and how, why, and when did they do it. In any case, one could expect that all the major changes in the political leadership and corresponding policy shifts greatly affected the parameters of discussions on the "new men."

Even a cursory look at the next sixty years of Russian history supports this supposition. The Khrushchev "Thaw" rehabilitated, as it were, the bio-psycho-medical (first of all, genetic) approaches to human nature and reopened the discussions on the interrelations of the social and the biological in the future evolution of humanity. The so-called stagnation of the Brezhnev period effectively muted such discussions and eventually pushed them out of the public view, into specialized scientific/medical publications and into the underground—the tam- and the samizdat. The *glasnost'* of the Gorbachev era brought the discussions back into the public sphere. The dissolution of the Soviet Union saw the reinstatement of the theological and the occult as legitimate arguments in the public debate on the "new man," on the one hand, and, on the other, the extensive "borrowing" of contemporary Western post- and transhumanist ideas, ideals, and techniques. We obviously need to know much more about the particularities of each period, the role of various networks of individual and institutional actors involved, and the influence of Western developments on those in Russia and vice versa. Some recent works demonstrate that research along these lines could indeed be very illuminating.[63] By the same token, the focus on the state as a major player might prove useful in examining the "new men" debates in other settings.[64]

Given the explicit preoccupation with the future embedded in the very phrase "new man," one could safely postulate that major global events, which dramatically affected our views of possible futures (from the two world wars and the Cold War to the nuclear bombardment of Hiroshima and Nagasaki and the launching of *Sputnik*), shaped the waning and waxing popularity of certain ideas and ideals expressed in the concurrent discussions on the "new men." Similarly, since certain "local," "national" versions of the "new men" visions circulated between different settings, often cross-pollinated, hybridized, and intermingled, we need to know much more about the specifics of this interchange—its venues, interlocutors, and historical changes. Given how influential it was during the time period covered in the present volume, one could expect that this continuous interchange also left its mark on the subsequent visions, as Yvonne Howell's chapter shows for the post-Soviet period. A close examination of these issues could provide important insights into both the particularities and the interconnectedness of the "new men" visions in Russia and elsewhere. It could also shed new light on the general evolution of our understanding of human nature and human destiny, along with local and global factors that shaped it.

Part I

Nurturing the New Man

Across societies and continents, the turn of the twentieth century was marked by acute interest in the prospects of creating a "new kind of person" for what seemed to be, for better or for worse, the advent of a new kind of world. In Russia, ideas about how to create the men, women, and children of the future acquired momentum well before the Bolshevik revolution, and continued to evolve under the new Soviet regime. As the chapters in this section show, creating "new men" in the postrevolutionary era invoked fundamental questions about the nature of cognition, development, and the social order. How would the production and dissemination of knowledge have to change, in order to change the way "new people" think? How could American experiments in "progressive education" be adapted in reeducation schemes favored by the Soviet secret police? If a child's imagination is shaped by its toys, what would the new toys look like? Nurturing the "new man" was a task that occupied a wide range of innovative thinkers in the 1920s, but became more and more constrained by strict ideological considerations in the 1930s.

1

Encyclopedic Worldbuilding

Alexander Bogdanov and the Cognitive Creation of the New Man

Michael Coates

The new man, like the new world of communism he would inhabit, was not merely something to be imagined—he was something to be built. But what if these processes—imagination and construction—were fundamentally the same? What if imagining the new world could bring both it and the new men who would inhabit it into existence? Science-fiction writers have long seen the potential for their works to help bring about the utopias—or avert the dystopias—they describe. But there is another genre of writing that, perhaps more surreptitiously, has also fulfilled this function. That is the encyclopedia.

Encyclopedias have long been seen as tools for the transformation of human knowledge. One could trace the history of the idea back to the likes of Francis Bacon and Gottfried Wilhelm Leibniz (if not to ancient times), through Diderot and d'Alembert, and into the nineteenth century. Even if one limits oneself to those who sought to use an encyclopedia to build socialism, the list is extensive: Henri de Saint-Simon, Nikolai Chernyshevskii, Friedrich Engels, Georgii Plekhanov, Jean Jaurès, H. G. Wells, Otto Neurath, and many others planned to incorporate the writing of encyclopedic works into their political and philosophical programs.[1]

Encyclopedias are a particularly powerful tool because they, characteristically, claim to describe the entire world as it is. Yet the greatest encyclopedias have rarely been oriented toward the present. Rather, they look toward the future. Diderot himself understood this: an encyclopedia must not only "know the spirit of its nation" but also get ahead of it, working "only for the following generations." For Diderot this was, in part, a practical matter: encyclopedias frequently take many years to write, and any encyclopedia that is not forward-looking may be outdated before it has even been completed.[2] But it also suggests an imaginative role for the encyclopedia. Predicting the future means imagining the future, and writing for the next generation requires the imagining of both a future reader and a future world—the world that would be depicted on its pages.

In the years leading up to the Russian Revolution, there was no greater advocate for the necessity of a socialist encyclopedia than Alexander Bogdanov, the psychiatrist, philosopher, systems theorist, and Bolshevik revolutionary. There were also few who wrote as prolifically about the new man as Bogdanov did, and essentially none who worked toward his creation in so many ways, from philosophizing to teaching to writing fiction to conducting biological experiments. But out of all of Bogdanov's efforts, the encyclopedia stood as the most central to the new man's emergence. This is because the new man was, above all, new in his cognition—he would think in ways that were different from those of the previous generations, and all of his knowledge would be structured differently. He would hold a worldview that, while unified, was also adapted to the diverse components of modern society and conducive toward making scientific and technological progress in all areas. The creation of the new man meant the creation and propagation of this new form of cognition. The encyclopedia was to be the primary means by which both tasks would be accomplished.

Bogdanov made two efforts to produce a workers' encyclopedia: one in conjunction with a school held on the island of Capri in 1909, and the other as a part of the postrevolutionary Proletarian Culture (Proletkul't) movement. Neither was ultimately written, though their intellectual legacies persisted, in certain ways, into the Soviet era. The history of these projects has been examined in an article by Daniela Steila, who has reconstructed many of the discussions surrounding the Capri project in particular.[3] I am largely in agreement with her reconstruction of the events on Capri. The novelty of my approach to this topic comes from its integration of Bogdanov's ideas about encyclopedias with his cognitive theories. In particular, this chapter seeks to explain exactly why it was that Bogdanov thought that an encyclopedia was essential for achieving a cognitive, and consequently a cultural, revolution, and how his cognitive theories of the new man affected his conception of the encyclopedia. Encyclopedias had long been a structuring metaphor in his theories: I argue that, several years before Bogdanov had ever indicated a desire to produce an actual, written encyclopedia, he had already come to view being "encyclopedic" as an essential quality for any proletarian worldview or system of thought. I also emphasize the dissimilarities between the Capri encyclopedia and the later Proletkul't project. These were, I argue, fundamentally different projects, particularly in that the first was intended to be written by intellectuals for the proletariat (with some assistance from workers), whereas the second was to be written by the proletariat for itself (with some assistance from intellectuals). The difference is indicative of a major shift in Bogdanov's thought on the role of intellectuals in revolution and knowledge or cultural production that might be characterized as a general loss of confidence in their ability to lead such movements.

In Bogdanov's theory, the creation of the new man's proletarian form of cognition was in effect the construction of a new mental world. In English the term "worldbuilding" is one that is frequently used in relation to science-fiction and fantasy literature to describe the process by which imagined alternative worlds are created, with their own laws of nature, history, culture, and so on.[4] In using the word "worldbuilding" here I want to invoke not only that usage, but also (and more directly) the Russian version of this term, *mirostroitel'stvo*, which was employed by Bogdanov in his work *The Philosophy of Living Experience* to describe the process by which the members of a particular class or other group develop their own method for organizing their experience to form a single, coherent world-picture (*kartina mira*). In Bogdanov's case, the term, which he claims to have derived from the writings of the worker-philosopher Nikifor Vilonov, is in part an allusion to the god-building or *bogostroitel'stvo* advocated by Anatolii Luncharskii, Maxim Gorky, and others, which in basic terms sought to adapt elements of religion—particularly rituals and myths—to help imbue socialism with emotion, make it more understandable, and foster belief in it.[5] Bogdanov's worldbuilding, I would argue, also takes a key element from religion—the importance of a central, all-encompassing text that embodies a particular worldview and can answer more or less any essential question one might put to it. Bogdanov writes in *Tektology* that the Bible is the encyclopedia of the Judeo-Christian worldview; he also argues that the bourgeoisie had developed and crystallized its own worldview in the process of producing the *Encyclopédie*. Bogdanov accordingly believed that the creation of a new proletarian mental world, and thus a new man, could be realized only through a proletarian encyclopedia.[6]

Bogdanov's conception of the new man of socialist society included, especially in his later years, mixed biological and psychological components. This is perhaps best reflected in his famous blood transfusion experiments, which aimed at achieving "physiological collectivism."[7] While Bogdanov, in his early career, was not especially concerned with the creation of a man who would be new from a physiological perspective, he had recognized the significance of physiology to his goals, advancing a biologically rooted theory of cognition.[8] This theory, in turn, served as the basis for his theories of culture and cultural revolution, which were essential to his conception of the new man. I will argue that Bogdanov's ideas for an encyclopedia grew, to a significant degree, from these early theories of his, and that the idea of the need for an encyclopedia likewise had a reciprocal influence on the development of his thought by serving as a kind of metaphor that structured key components of his thinking on what proletarian forms of cognition were to be. Accordingly, I will begin with an exposition of some of Bogdanov's early theories, showing how they helped lead him to the idea of the necessity of the encyclopedia.

Bogdanov's Early Ideas on Cognition and the Making of the New Man

In order to explain the origins of Bogdanov's belief in the necessity of producing a socialist encyclopedia, I want to highlight a few aspects of Bogdanov's early philosophical works, which introduced ideas that remained core to his philosophy for the remainder of his life. Chief among these were the *Fundamental Elements of the Historical View on Nature* of 1898 and 1901's *Cognition from a Historical Point of View*. As Nikolai Krementsov has shown, these works (which grew out of Bogdanov's medical studies in Khar'kov) can be understood as an attempt to synthesize several different philosophical tendencies, placing at the center of these viewpoints a Darwin-derived evolutionary perspective (the title "historical view"), which he considered to be characteristic of the new way of thinking.[9] These works represent the beginnings of Bogdanov's social-constructionist epistemology, which rooted all knowledge claims in social interaction and viewed them as having a class character. He argues that every era has its own *istina* (truth), which is defined by the mental content of cognition (*poznanie*) existing in that era. *Poznanie* is developed through human activity—humans, in the course of their labor, develop mental content which is adapted to the tasks that they perform and the world that they live in—this mental content includes everything that we would think of as constituting knowledge, but also things like how cause-and-effect works in our minds and other laws of thought. The measure of the value of any particular version of *istina* is thus how well it enables humans to navigate and act in the world in which they live. Key to this process is the function of language and words themselves, which Bogdanov discusses extensively in the *Fundamental Elements*. Beginning to denote mental concepts with words both stabilizes them (making them less variable) and enables them to be socialized, spreading beyond the individual in which they arose to the society at large. However, the gap between the malleability of mental concepts and the relative permanence of words still poses a number of problems for Bogdanov: "people never, in essence, speak in exactly one and the same language. Two representatives of one nation, one tribe, estate [*soslovie*], class, even two members of the same family never attach entirely the same meaning to the same words. It is possible, finally, to say that about a single individual taken in different periods of their life." In daily life this does not present much of a problem, since, generally speaking, the differences in understanding are not so great that people are left talking past one another. But in the realm of science Bogdanov finds that the concepts associated with words vary sharply among individuals. What Bogdanov proposes as a solution is to redefine more specialized concepts in terms of more basic or general ones as a means for bridging understanding.[10]

The precise mechanism through which the mental adaptation that constitutes cognition takes place is what Bogdanov terms "psychological reactions," which are essentially energy-saving mental processes based on the plasticity of the brain, an idea that had been introduced only in 1890 by William James.[11] Bogdanov classifies the reactions into three categories based on how conservative they are: there are those that are highly plastic and are specific to individuals, having been developed in the course of their life; there are those that are highly conservative, being shared across the entire human species; and there is an intermediate level that Bogdanov associates with culture, and therefore with particular classes or other groups. Adaptations of the first, highly plastic category that arise in an individual can become socialized and shared across the cultural group if they prove to be useful to anyone other than the individual in which they developed; this is done through the process of communication.[12] They thus become a part of the intermediate, or cultural, level. One consequence of this theory is that any attempt to have a cultural revolution or otherwise transform culture will necessarily be an attempt to alter this intermediate level of psychological reaction. As I will argue, the production of the encyclopedia was to be the key venue for performing this task (just as blood exchanges were his method for altering the fundamental, biological level).

Bogdanov's theory of the reflexes or reactions and their implications represented the major intellectual development of *Cognition from a Historical Point of View*. In the few years following its publication Bogdanov became increasingly involved in revolutionary politics. In 1902 he became the leader of a radical discussion circle in Vologda that included his future collaborator Anatolii Lunacharskii, who would become Commissar of Enlightenment in the Bolshevik government. The group became particularly involved in debates over the philosophy of Nikolai Berdiaev, a onetime Marxist philosopher who had recently turned toward religion. Bogdanov and Lunacharskii criticized Berdiaev for his idealism. Ultimately this led Bogdanov and Lunacharskii to reach out to Vladimir Lenin, then working in foreign exile as the editor of the major socialist newspaper *Iskra*, asking for some of their work to be published. Lenin was already aware of Bogdanov at this time due to the latter's books, which Lenin viewed favorably. Ultimately *Iskra* did not publish the works sent to them, due both to disagreements with Lenin over the editing of the article manuscripts and to problems in communication with him. Bogdanov subsequently became involved in the establishment of a new journal in Moscow, *Pravda*. In 1904, at the conclusion of his sentence to exile, Bogdanov moved to Geneva with Lunacharskii and some other associates. In Geneva he met Lenin for the first time.[13]

The origins of Bogdanov's first encyclopedia project can be traced to his writings from this era. As far as the available documents reveal, Bogdanov had begun to use the concept of the encyclopedia metaphorically, as a kind of ideal of what knowledge or philosophy should be, even before he ever had the idea to write an actual, printed encyclopedia. In a 1904 essay titled "The Gathering of Man," Bogdanov presented an evolutionary view of humanity from primitive civilizations to modern society, focusing on the effects that the division of labor has had on human thought. In primitive societies, labor, and thus human experience, generally, was almost entirely undifferentiated—the vast majority of people did more or less the same things in their daily life, and so their mental content closely resembled one another's. That mental content was also more universal, in the sense that one individual's experience was a large subset of the sum total of human experience. In the modern world, however, experience and labor have become highly differentiated—and thus narrower and more specialized. The experience of any one person, their knowledge and mental content, is only a tiny fraction of that of the whole, and, while highly specialized, encompasses a range of human activity that is narrower than in primitive times. One effect of such specialization is that there has been a significant narrowing of perspectives across all of humanity; Bogdanov singles out intellectuals, and philosophers in particular, for blame. In Bogdanov's view the intellectuals have abandoned their duty to try to see the whole, to try to synthesize and generalize the various domains of human experience. In the words of Bogdanov, "the philosopher . . . stopped being an encyclopedist." They are no longer interested in the full scope of human activity, but instead get caught up trying to answer questions like "who am I?" that Bogdanov sees as meaningless.[14]

That essay, and the others published alongside it, constitute major attempts by Bogdanov to outline how to integrate his theories of cognition and of the constantly changing nature of the world with his political philosophy. Bogdanov follows Marx in offering what is essentially a version of historical materialism. Both, of course, rely heavily on the conception of the progression of the division of labor in making their arguments. But Bogdanov's approach differs in a number of ways. Notably absent from these essays is any direct conception of the problems raised by private property. In Marx the stages of history are marked by changes in the mode of production, with the crucial role being played by the nature of the ownership of property in a particular system, which serves as the basis for the social relations of production in that system. The social relations contained within the mode of production of a particular society then, to a large degree, determine the consciousness of individuals and groups within the particular system. The consciousness can ultimately give rise to class conflict, which serves as one of the major motive forces in history, along with the need to satisfy a growing list of human wants.[15] For Bogdanov the latter seems to take much greater precedence, but in his work it takes on a more biological and Darwinist tone. Humans are constantly developing new cognitive adaptations to help them better and more efficiently (from the perspective of energy and time) engage in activity meant to satisfy wants and respond to environmental pressures. These adaptations tend on the whole to be highly plastic and vary from individual to individual, especially in the higher stages of the development of society. For Bogdanov, the division of labor is in essence about cognitive specialization in relation to human activity, and thus in a certain sense not so much about the labor itself (though labor is still the driving force). The overriding concern is about producing forms of generalized cognition that would enable one to possess the adaptations of "a hunter, a fisherman, a herdsman or a critic" (as Marx would say) and not, in the immediate sense, of devising a way to organize human labor in a way which would make it possible to "hunt in the morning, fish in the afternoon, rear cattle in the evening, [and] criticize after dinner."[16] In fact, one can see here the roots of the idea (which would become especially prominent in Bogdanov's later work) that before one can have a communist society, or even a communist revolution, one needs to have a proletarian culture and a proletarian mode of cognition. A cooperative organization of production can never be achieved until the cognitive principles that would enable it have been developed. For Bogdanov, the increased use of machine technology in production was beginning to lead workers to develop the mental adaptations that would make them the most effective organizers of all of human experience and activity. Until then, one is stuck with the "authoritarian" organizers of human activity, such as capitalists and despots.[17]

Bogdanov's political philosophy thus becomes intimately linked with his theories of cognition-as-adaptation and about the plasticity of psychological reactions. But, as noted, the other key feature of *New World* (*Novyi mir*, which includes "The Gathering of Man") is that the essays mark the beginning of Bogdanov's thought on the subject of encyclopedism. Philosophy, which is supposed to be the "theory of cognition," had lost its way by becoming caught up in false "accursed questions," which were merely reflections of the fracturing of experience, especially in bourgeois society. Accordingly, the philosophers themselves became too specialized, failing to schematize all of human experience into a single, harmonic whole and thus failing in the aims of philosophy. In this way "the philosopher has stopped being an encyclopedist." At this point in the development of his thought, Bogdanov had not yet arrived at the conclusion that an actual encyclopedia was the solution to his philosophical problems, as least as far as can be discerned from the record available to me. That would come only a few years later, as will be discussed below. But it is important to note that the metaphor of the encyclopedia had already become a part of the way that Bogdanov thought.

Bogdanov's early thinking on encyclopedias stands in an interesting relationship to nineteenth-century trends on the encyclopedia as a metaphor for knowledge. Chad Wellmon has argued that in the late eighteenth and early nineteenth centuries, especially in Germany, the metaphor of the encyclopedia as a sort of ideal knowledge institution began to break down in the face of information overload.[18] In fact, Ann Blair and Richard Yeo have argued that the modern idea of the encyclopedia itself emerged in response to information overload, having developed from the practice of keeping a commonplace book. The encyclopedia was widely thought of as being a "book of books," one single book that could summarize and replace many others, allowing its reader to acquire information more efficiently.[19] Bogdanov shared a concern with information overload, in the sense that Bogdanov recognized that access to the totality of human experience was no longer possible.[20] Insofar as Bogdanov considered the world to consist of the experiences of all humans, informed by their individual cognitive structures, it thus had become impossible to know the world, except in fragments. Bogdanov, like Wellmon's German scholars, sought to find a way to relate the individual to the totality of human knowledge, or human experience, believing, again like the Germans, that this was essential for further progress (whether in the realm of science or in society in general). At the end of the day, this involved trying to find a way to relate the individual to the collective. But whereas for the Germans this meant the advent of the disciplines and in effect the acceptance of one's place as a member in a community of scholars governed by a particular ethic, all working toward the pursuit of further knowledge, for Bogdanov this was unacceptable. The only way to achieve real harmonization (a term that the Germans also used) was to find a way to actually reunite the experiences of all individuals into a single whole, making all experience and all of knowledge comprehensible to anyone.

In 1904 Bogdanov published the first volume of his *Empiriomonism* (*Empiriomonizm*), a work in which he further developed and synthesized his theories on cognition and its social implications, expanding upon and integrating his earlier work on cognition and Marxist sociology and economics to a high degree. Two more volumes would follow, with the work being completed in 1906. This work thus represented an expansion upon the ideas developed in his contemporaneous *New World*. Upon its publication, this work became a major source of controversy within the Bolshevik faction. The relationship between Lenin and Bogdanov had already been a rocky one, with the two having emerged as the most prominent factional leaders within the Bolshevik group. Bogdanov's theories, and especially *Empiriomonism*, had won him a large following within the Bolshevik faction. Disputes over whether epistemological works of the type Bogdanov and his followers were producing could be published in Party publications, combined with differences in revolutionary strategy over the failed Revolution of 1905 (Lenin wanted the Bolsheviks to stand candidates for the elections to the new Duma; Bogdanov rejected or at least was accused of rejecting participation in such politics), widened the gap between the two, eventually leading to open conflict. In

1908 Lenin published his *Materialism and Empirio-criticism* (*Materializm i Empirio-krititsizm*), attacking Bogdanov and his associates for deviating from what Lenin considered to be orthodox Marxist theory. In particular, Lenin attacked Bogdanov's characterization of his philosophy of perception and cognition as monist, rejecting the idea that the cognitive processes Bogdanov described could produce objective knowledge of the world, and instead claimed that Bogdanov was (like Ernst Mach and Richard Avenarius, who had influenced him) actually advancing a disguised Kantian idealist philosophy.[21] Lenin was ultimately victorious over Bogdanov, with the latter being voted off the Party's Central Committee the following year.[22]

During his struggles with Lenin, Bogdanov continued to attract new supporters. One figure drawn to Bogdanov's philosophy in this period was the writer Maxim Gorky, who had become involved in Party politics. Gorky's house on the island of Capri would serve as an important meeting point for Bolshevik leaders in the following years, and especially for the circle that included Bogdanov and Anatolii Lunacharskii.[23] Bogdanov and Lunacharskii became collaborators, and it was in conjunction with Gorky that Bogdanov's thinking on encyclopedias as a tool began to develop further.

The Capri Encyclopedia

Bogdanov's earliest thought on the idea of putting an actual encyclopedia to revolutionary use in Russia seems to have emerged from discussions held on Capri. This was the plan for an "encyclopedia for the study of Russia" (*entsiklopediia dlia izucheniia Rossii*), which had been discussed by Gorky in a letter from March of 1908 (to Bogdanov) and was further detailed by Gorky in a letter to the publisher K.P. Piatnitskii in April 1908.[24] Gorky attributed the genesis of the project to the collective effort of a group that included Bogdanov, Anatolii Lunacharskii, Vladimir Bazarov (an old friend of Bogdanov's from his time in Tula), Nikolai Rozhkov (a historian), Ivan Skvortsov-Stepanov (another old friend of Bogdanov's), and himself. Gorky evidently did not intend to write for the encyclopedia himself, but he seems to have taken on kind of organizing role, corresponding with publishers about the project and recruiting other writers.[25]

The project was to produce what was essentially a history encyclopedia, which would show the development of Russian history and the key institutions of Russia from a Marxist perspective. As described in the letter to Piatnitskii, it was to include seven sections on history: one on the "history of Russia—political," one on the "history of the economic development" of Russia, one on the "history of foreign relations—that is the history of international politics," one on the "history of the development of political thought," one on the "history of the development of legal ideas," one on the "history of the church," and one on the "history of literature" (*slovesnost'*). To this Bogdanov was to add a section on the "organization of experience and the types of class psychology." Altogether the work was to comprise twelve to fifteen volumes of about 300–400 pages each.[26]

By May the project had evolved somewhat: the new plan was to include the same sections on the organization of experience and the histories of literature (now *literatura*), foreign affairs, the church, domestic politics (this is presumably the same section on political history), "philosophical thought, that is ideology" (again, this would seem to be the earlier section on "political thought"), and one on "industry and trade" (an evolution of the earlier section on "economic development"). But now there was also to be a separate "history of the nationalities (*narodnost'*) that are part of Rus'." Another addition was a new volume, forming part of the introduction (along with Bogdanov's work) on the "history of people's creativity" (*istoriia narodnogo tvorchestva*), which would be "built on contrasting the strength of the collective psyche with the impotence of the individual in the spheres of myth, poetry, etc."[27] The individual sections would, it seems, have aimed to integrate the key components of each topic into a single narrative, rather than treating them separately. Grigorii Aleksinskii (who had been approached by Gorky, Bogdanov, and Lunacharskii about the project) notes, for example, that he and Bogdanov believed it necessary to write the section on the "nationalities" as "one general book with the characteristics of the development of the major nationalities and the relations between them," rather than a separate history of each nationality.[28]

The new encyclopedia was to be simultaneously "strictly scientific and entirely popular," and thus intended for distribution outside of the Party's intellectual elite.[29] The small size and (necessarily) generalizing character of the volumes would make them well suited for substantial print runs and distribution to the workers, to whom it could demonstrate their place in Russian history from the perspective of historical materialism, inculcating a world-historical consciousness.

Even if he did not originally propose the encyclopedia, Bogdanov seems to have been the most enthusiastic about the project, and played a key role attempting to recruit potential writers outside of the initial circle. This included his friend, the historian Mikhail Pokrovskii. In his letter to Pokrovskii Bogdanov evidently described the project as an "encyclopedia for workers" (*entsiklopediia dlia rabochikh*), a formulation that would become important later.[30] Pokrovskii expressed "ardent sympathy" for the idea in his February 1909 reply to Bogdanov, but noted that he was at the time preoccupied with the writing of his own "Course in Russian History for Self-Education" (*Kurs russkoi istorii dlia samoobrazovaniia*) for the Granat Brothers encyclopedia publishing house.[31] Gorky may have seen in this the opportunity to get their new encyclopedia sponsored or published by Granat,[32] and attempted to bring Pokrovskii and his work into the fold.[33]

By this point the plan of the work had been developed further, and the writers for most sections had been identified. Bogdanov would write his work on the organization of experience, Lunacharskii would handle the history of the people's creativity, Pokrovskii was proposed to write the history of Russia and history of Russian foreign affairs, Bogdanov and Skvortsov-Stepanov would collaborate on a "course in political economy in connection with the history of culture," and Skvortsov-Stepanov would write the history of industry and trade. An author for the section on the "church and sectarianism" had not yet been identified (though Aleksinskii was still interested in it), and a new section on the "contemporary situation" would be written by the authors collectively. But the striking addition to this list was the new section on the "history of the peasantry and the agrarian question," which was to be written by none other than "the old man" Lenin.[34] Gorky had, in spite of his closeness with Bogdanov, remained friends with Lenin, and had apparently convinced him to join the project at a meeting held on Capri in April 1908.[35]

By March 1909, when this plan was outlined, the relationship between Lenin and Bogdanov had decayed significantly, and Bogdanov was shortly to be removed from the Bolshevik leadership by Lenin and his supporters. Gorky's desire to include Lenin in the project suggests another purpose for the encyclopedia: that it was intended to help bridge the emerging split in the Bolshevik faction.[36] Gorky had frequently stressed that the entire encyclopedia needed to be a collective work, written from a single, coherent point of view. Writing the encyclopedia would have required all of the authors to come to a consensus about all of the topics that it would cover, helping to heal the divisions between the authors. The decreasing coherence of the plan of the work, as the project developed, was thus of great concern to Gorky. In his March 1909 letter responding to Bogdanov's letter about Pokrovskii, Gorky had noted that "everything is starting to unravel and become uncoordinated, because the interest is not going in the direction needed to unify all the intentions and interests, the whole work."[37] Likewise, in his letter to Pokrovskii, Gorky stressed the necessity that, if they were to agree to combine the two projects, "all work will be internally connected with a unified worldview and present itself as if it were a collective work."[38] Aleksinskii's letter of March 1909 suggests that Gorky had aimed to begin work on the encyclopedia shortly, possibly to try to halt this split before it worsened.[39]

The proletariat was still the intended audience of the work. At the same time, however, it is true that even though the encyclopedia was to be written for the workers, and not primarily as a contribution to the debates within the Russian Social Democratic Labor Party, it was still a work by the intellectuals for the proletariat, and not by the proletariat for itself. It would convey to the proletarian reader the thoughts and knowledge that these intellectuals had developed based on years of study, providing a digested version of the world in a manner similar to the "book of books" that encyclopedias are often understood to be. There were some ways in which the perspectives of the workers were to be integrated into the encyclopedia. Chief among these is the interrelation between the Capri Party School, which also took place in 1909, and the encyclopedia project.

Like the encyclopedia, the party school is an idea that evidently emerged from discussions among the Capri group. In March 1909 letter (in fact one of the same letters in which he discusses the encyclopedia), Bogdanov proposed to Gorky to bring twenty to twenty-five workers from Russia to Capri for instruction. The course of study would include both common lectures on general topics and individual lessons on the "issues of party practice."[40] The idea took off, and the school ran from August to December of that year.[41]

The course of study consisted of four broad areas: "party organization and affairs," focusing on practical issues like propaganda; "party theory," which consisted mainly of lectures on the history of the workers' movement and of Russia; the "philosophy of proletarian struggle," which focused on culture and historical materialism; and "the current moment" or "critique of the present situation." Of these, Bogdanov would lecture on economic theory as part of the course on "party theory" and on the "history of social worldviews" as part of the philosophy course (*istoriia obshchestvennykh mirovozzrenii*). Students would study the development these worldviews from a historical-materialist perspective, similar to the methodologies that Bogdanov employed in his works. Other lecturers would include Lunacharskii, Pokrovskii, and Gorky himself.[42]

Although this was not publicized, Bogdanov's letters reveal the role that he intended the party school to play in the creation of the encyclopedia. For Bogdanov, the school would be not only a place where the revolutionary intelligentsia might instruct the workers, but also a place where the intelligentsia could learn from the workers, to help bring their own thought into line with the workers' proletarian cognition, thereby making it possible for an *intelligent* such as himself to write an encyclopedia from the proletarian perspective, for the benefit of the proletariat. This would occur through both discussions and written work produced by the students. To this end, Bogdanov was sharply critical of those, such as Leon Trotsky, who did not appreciate this side of the school: "he looks at the school as just a propaganda circle . . . the *creative* side of the affair doesn't exist for him—that, which for us is developed in the connection between the school and the encyclopedia."[43] Lenin had decried the school as factional, claiming that the "philosophy of proletarian struggle" did not exist (being found nowhere in Marx, Engels, or elsewhere in European philosophy) and would have to be invented before it could be taught.[44] But for Bogdanov, the development of such a philosophy, in dialogue with the worker-students, was in fact a central goal of the school and the encyclopedia.

Bogdanov's experiences at the party school (and at a similar school the next year in Bologna) led him to write two key works in 1911. The first, the *Philosophy of Living Experience* (*Filosofiia zhivogo opyta*), is a development and summary of his philosophy of empiriomonism, which is considered to have been based on the lectures he gave at the two schools in his course on materialism. The second, *The Cultural Tasks of Our Time* (*Kul'turnye zadachi nashego vremeni*), represents a development of his thinking on the subject of encyclopedias.

Writing retrospectively, Bogdanov characterized his work on the party schools and what would become known as the Proletarian University as having been inspired by his experience of leading discussion circles (*kruzhki*) in Tula and Vologda when he was in internal exile. What he was most struck by was the curiosity of the workers—their thirst for knowledge from across many domains, as well as their intuitive sense of what they needed or wanted to know and what was unnecessary for them. Bogdanov reminisces about being asked difficult questions by the workers in his *kruzhki*, which pushed him and other participants of an intellectual background to expand their own knowledge and horizons in an attempt to be as helpful to the workers as possible.[45]

The Capri encyclopedia was never written, but Bogdanov had completed some work toward his section, which he further developed and published under the title *The Science of Social Consciousness* in 1914. Uniquely among Bogdanov's book-length works, this book is structured as a series of questions and answers; a kind of imagined questioning of Bogdanov by a worker or other person curious about the world. It is difficult to say whether Bogdanov had envisioned the encyclopedia itself to take this form, had it been written, but in any event I would argue that this reflects both the experience of the party school and a more general characteristic of encyclopedic works, which I alluded to at the beginning, as being the kind of work you could go to with a question to which you want an authoritative answer.[46]

Why was the encyclopedia never completed? Ultimately, I would highlight two primary factors. The first is that Gorky had not seen much success in securing a publishing advance to fund the research for the project.[47] The second, and more important of the two, was that the proposed participants were unable to come to the kind of unified viewpoint that the project demanded. Gorky complained to Bogdanov about how every participant wanted to go their own way and address their own parochial concerns; the intellectuals, in some sense, had fallen into the trap that Bogdanov had highlighted in "The Gathering of Man."

The failure of the Capri encyclopedia project, combined with expulsion of Bogdanov from the Party leadership and the formation of the Vpered group (a group focused on achieving a cultural revolution that included Bogdanov, Gorky, Lunacharskii, Pokrovskii, and others), I would argue, did much to shake Bogdanov's confidence in the intellectuals as a leading force in revolution. In the aftermath of the 1909 meeting of the editors of the Bolshevik newspaper *The Proletarian*, at which Bogdanov was removed from the Bolshevik Center, Bogdanov and his allies issued a statement calling, among other things, for a "broadening and deepening of socialist propaganda," which would entail developing a "propagandistic literature, illegal and legal, of a much more complete and encyclopedic content" that was also "popular in form".[48] In the years leading up to the revolution, Bogdanov continued, in his writings, to call for the production of a workers' encyclopedia, but never again was the encyclopedia to be primarily the work of the intellectuals. Now, it would be written by the proletariat itself, with intellectuals serving merely as a resource in that process.

Proletkul't and the *Workers' Encyclopedia*

Bogdanov's post-expulsion views on the new encyclopedia are expressed most clearly in his 1911 work *The Cultural Tasks of Our Time*. In discussing the encyclopedia, he begins with a comparison to Diderot: the bourgeoisie of the eighteenth century had emerged as a class, and was developing its own forms of organization, its own cognition. "An advanced group of bourgeois ideologues created then the famous *Encyclopedia*. It was the bible of a new worldview, as comprehensive as its content allowed it to be, inevitably in a large measure fractional according to the very nature of bourgeois experience and thought." The *Encyclopédie* became a sensation; one who read it "could confidently say that he knows his place in nature and in society, knows from where and to where he is going, what is necessary for humanity and every rational, active person." The *Encyclopédie* represented the "crystallized truth [*istina*] of its time." In the modern day, however, encyclopedias are written not by the ideologues of the bourgeoisie, but rather by the intelligentsia, which according Bogdanov lies between the bourgeoisie and proletariat. These are a poor imitation of *Encyclopédie*, in the sense that they do not possess "the strong spirit of struggle" found in the *Encyclopédie* and among the bourgeoisie of the eighteenth century as it did battle for its own truth. The contemporary petit-bourgeois intelligentsia does not experience this struggle; moreover, it is (as noted) not even really bourgeois. But if the intelligentsia cannot write an encyclopedia on the level of the *Encyclopédie* for the bourgeoisie, so too can it not write one for the proletariat that would truly capture its truth. The encyclopedias produced by the intelligentsia are

> relatively huge by volume, uncoordinated in content, and in most cases are not popular enough in form. In them there is not a unified point of view: such is the individualism of the *intelligent*, that he certainly must show originality of thought, necessarily have in view fundamental disagreements with his colleagues; there is no aspiration to come to agreement and, uniting their expertise, to come to a common position. They not only lack collectivism in their internal content, but also in their very method of work. They are much more a collection of individual works than a collective work.[49]

Here the old encyclopedias produced by the intelligentsia function as a metaphor for the intelligentsia itself. This is not to say that Bogdanov rejects entirely the role of the intelligentsia in creating a proletarian encyclopedia, or the value of these old encyclopedias for the present. On the contrary (continuing the allegory of encyclopedia as *intelligent*), Bogdanov notes that "in their rich scientific material and in their many successful generalizations of a private character they can, however, play a useful preparatory role in the preparation of the New Encyclopedia, especially in the part devoted to science and technology."[50] The best thing that Bogdanov and the rest of the intelligentsia could do, in other words, was to provide the working class with their accumulated knowledge and cognitive generalizations, so that the working class could use them as the starting ground for their own project of worldbuilding. Ultimately the working class itself would decide what was useful for productive life and what needed to be reformed or thrown out entirely. They would produce their own ways of understanding, and construct their own truth.

One concern expressed by Bogdanov is the difficulty of making new scientific theories comprehensible to the workers. To help alleviate this problem, Bogdanov developed the idea of "universal substitution," a process that allows ideas to be understood and reformulated in terms of other ideas by means of generalization. Bogdanov saw universal substitution as being necessary for the progress of science, but its results are not always easily comprehensible, especially at the highest levels of generality. The encyclopedia could, as in the sense noted above, teach its readers to see the world in terms of the overarching theories, learning how to relate their sense-perceptions to the grander scheme of things and harmonizing cognition across society. It would show how all of the particulars related to the generals, creating new forms of thought suitable toward approaching grander, more overarching general laws of organization. This would be a difficult project, but one which Bogdanov thought possible: "the new encyclopedia must replace this fragmentation … with comprehensive and complete explanations of these connections . . . What is demanded is an enormous and difficult collective work on the most varied fields of knowledge."[51]

The indispensability of the encyclopedia for this task is further demonstrated by the conclusion of Bogdanov's novel *Engineer Menni*, the 1913 prequel to his 1908 *Red Star*. At the very end of that book, a school of students, including both workers and young scholars, forms around the character Netti. It is this group that creates the *Workers' Encyclopedia*, the "pillar and banner of the ideological unity of the proletariat". As Bogdanov describes it, it was only in the process of writing the encyclopedia that Netti began to develop the principles of the new, universal organizational science—the organizational science, in other words, is a product of the encyclopedia, or at least the process of writing it, and not the other way around.[52] Bogdanov had not mentioned the encyclopedia at all in *Red Star*, as that book (having been written before the events on Capri) predated his coming to the conclusion that the encyclopedia was a necessary part of the revolutionary program. In concluding *Engineer Menni* in this way, Bogdanov retroactively writes the encyclopedia into the history of his Martian utopia: the world of *Red Star* becomes a depiction of the post-encyclopedia world.

The passage from *Engineer Menni* may also help explain why it was that Bogdanov was active in so many spheres of intellectual activity: Bogdanov, in his own person, embodied the kind of encyclopedic knowledge that the Proletarian University would, through its research and educational programs, develop. He aimed to be, as he put it in *Empiriomonism*, "the encyclopedic genius of his time." Now Bogdanov did not think that the worker had to emulate him: he did not consider it essential for every worker to be an encyclopedist or a polymath. But it was important for him that any worker has access to the knowledge that he wishes to have or needs to have in order to be able to live and work, and the encyclopedia, with its synthesis of all knowledge and experience according to the principles of organizational science, would provide it.

The October Revolution gave Bogdanov the opportunity to attempt, for the second time, to realize his dreams of a proletarian encyclopedia. Once again, the encyclopedia was to be linked with a school: in this case, the "Proletarian University" that he and others attempted to establish in Moscow as a part of the Proletarian Culture (Proletkul't) movement. The Proletarian University was not merely to be a center for education, but in fact a center of knowledge production—the production of the *Workers' Encyclopedia*.

The new university and encyclopedia were among the major topics of discussion at the First All-Russian Conference of Proletarian Cultural-Educational Organizations, held on September 15–20, 1918. Bogdanov himself addressed the new university and encyclopedia most directly in his speech "Science and the Proletariat" (*Nauka i proletariat*) delivered on the third day of the conference. In this speech Bogdanov took particular aim at those (such as Pokrovskii, with whom his relationship had deteriorated in the preceding years) who wished to educate the workers with fundamental, "pure" scientific knowledge as it existed at the time, that they may subsequently enter the country's public universities. Such approaches, per Bogdanov, failed to recognize the class character of scientific knowledge (by assuming that there could be anything like a "pure science") and ultimately would do harm to the proletarians attending the university by indoctrinating them with bourgeois knowledge. Bogdanov argued for the disposal of the idea of the "teacher" entirely: "In the proletarian university there is a different principle. Here there are no 'teachers', here there is comradehood, cooperation, living collaborative work, illuminated by the spirit of free critical thought . . . the fundamental task of the proletarian university is to give the workers the possibility to seize the means of scientific research. This can be achieved only through work, and best of all - collaborative, comradely work." The encyclopedia was to be the most direct and important product of these efforts as well as the means for their realization. Again invoking his frequent interpretation of the Bible as an encyclopedia, Bogdanov argued that each great class in history had written its own encyclopedia, and that not only the content of the encyclopedia, but also its structure, reflected the cognition of that class: the priestly class that created the Bible had a "historical-moral" viewpoint, which used revelations to provide guidance for many aspects of life, and the bourgeoisie had used the model of the dictionary for its encyclopedia, in which "pieces of knowledge are connected only by individual words"—one that is characterized by the division of knowledge, not by its unification. But the new encyclopedia was to be "an integrated picture of the methods and achievements both of labor and of cognition. In this sense it will be the best tool of the victorious class struggle and of creative construction."[53] The encyclopedia was to be not only a published work, but a "system of knowledge" in and of itself.[54]

This dual structure, of the university and the encyclopedia, directly reflects Bogdanov's ideas about how mental concepts arise and are communicated, but on a socialized level. As I described earlier, Bogdanov held that mental adaptations would arise in individuals in the course of their work and life, which could then become socialized through communication, and adopted by others, should the adaptations prove to be useful to them. The problem with this is that it relies on *stikhiinost'*—on spontaneity. One has to hope that someone will come up with an innovation, that it will be able to be communicated adequately, and so on. While Bogdanov had a bit more confidence in the ability of spontaneity to produce positive results than Lenin did, he still viewed it as something to be conquered by means of organization. What the Proletarian University represents is a site of socialized, organized knowledge production, in which a collective of worker-intellectuals, acting as a kind of single, collective brain, would collaborate to systematically examine and critique all of human knowledge, strip out any bourgeois metaphysics they may find, develop the basis for a new unified proletarian synthesis of knowledge, and in general make new discoveries, all in the process of writing the encyclopedia. The final, printed encyclopedia would then serve as the means for communicating this new synthesis to the workers at large, fixing the ideas in language and allowing these new cognitive adaptations to be socialized. More than a "book of books," it would be an authoritative, systematic presentation of the new proletarian worldview, reflecting new ideas, experiences, and forms of thought that could be found nowhere else.

Bogdanov's second encyclopedia project attracted interest from a number of other figures involved in the Proletkul't movement, most notably from Pavel Lebedev-Polianskii, who was at the time Proletkul't's head of publishing (subsequently serving as head of Glavlit, the Soviet Union's chief censorship organ). Lebedev-Polianskii had spoken in favor of the idea at the conference even before Bogdanov's speech on the topic, and in much the same terms as Bogdanov.[55] In speeches to Proletkul't organizations, he continued to support the idea even after the short-lived Moscow Proletarian University, also inspired by Bogdanov's ideas, had ceased to exist.[56]

Ultimately, this second iteration of the *Workers' Encyclopedia* also failed, in part due to the arrest of Bogdanov for his alleged connections to the opposition "Workers' Truth" (*rabochaia pravda*) movement and due to the loss of independence of the Proletkul't movement. In spite of the support that the project had attracted within Proletkul't, no major work appears to have been done toward it, and, unlike in the case of Bogdanov himself, many in the Proletkul't movement seem to have viewed the university and the encyclopedia being separable from one another, in the sense that there were efforts to launch proletarian universities as educational institutions with no plans for them to produce their own encyclopedias.[57] The Tula regional Proletkul't organization did include work on a "proletarian scientific encyclopedia" and a separate "proletarian encyclopedia of art" in the plans for its General-Theoretical Department, but no such work was ultimately produced.[58] The protocols and reports of Proletkul't organizations in Moscow and various other regions show no indication that Bogdanov's vision was discussed there, though the Moscow Proletkul't did produce an unrelated encyclopedia dedicated to the organization of workers' clubs in 1926.[59] It should also be noted that by the time of Proletkul't's fall, proposals for several new encyclopedia projects had begun to circulate within the Commissariat of Enlightenment and the Socialist (later Communist) Academy, from which the *Great Soviet Encyclopedia* (*Bol'shaia Sovetskaia Entsiklopediia—BSE*) ultimately emerged. Although Bogdanov remained active in the Academy even after his arrest, he had no documented role in any of these projects, and he does not appear to have made a third attempt to produce a workers' encyclopedia before his 1928 death, which came as the result of one of his blood transfusion experiments.

Conclusion: From Bogdanov's Projects to the *Great Soviet Encyclopedia*

As we have seen, Bogdanov viewed the proletarian encyclopedia as the key tool for the construction of the new proletarian system of cognition, which would define every aspect of the thought and communication of the new man. Through the writing of the encyclopedia, the proletariat would rework all existing knowledge in accordance with its emerging worldview, and through its publication that knowledge would become socialized. Although neither of Bogdanov's encyclopedia projects were ultimately realized, the Soviet Union did, eventually, produce a universal encyclopedia, which was intended to have been written from the perspective of the proletariat, and which shared some similar foundational principles. This was the *Great Soviet Encyclopedia* (*BSE*), the First Edition of which received its initial approval in 1924. A number of Bogdanov's collaborators played key roles in the development of the First Edition. First and foremost among them was Pokrovskii, who was a member of the project's editorial board and was, along with Valerian Kuibyshev, one of the two designated political overseers of the project. Skvortsov-Stepanov and Lunacharskii (also collaborators from the Capri encyclopedia) were likewise members of the editorial board, though they played a more limited role in the project than Pokrovskii. Also participating was one of

Bogdanov's collaborators from the Proletkul't encyclopedia, Lebedev-Polianskii, who was the First Edition's lead editor for literature, art, and linguistics from 1931 onward and was one of only three people (the others being Otto Shmidt, the First Edition's editor-in-chief, and Fedor Rotshtein) to serve as members of the editorial board throughout the 1930s and up to the final volume in 1947/8.[60]

Nearly all of Bogdanov's closest collaborators in his previous endeavors were thus involved with the *BSE*. Gorky, the major exception, was again living in Italy at the time of the launch of the First Edition; involving him would thus have been difficult. While these editors, in the documentation which I have located, did not explicitly frame their interest in working on the *BSE* in terms of their earlier experiences with the Capri or Proletkul't encyclopedias, the *BSE* can doubtlessly be said to represent a continuation (albeit in modified form) of those earlier interests.

Bogdanov himself took no direct role in the *BSE*, and I have located no references to it in his surviving writings. This is true in spite of the fact that Bogdanov remained actively involved in the work of the Communist Academy, which, while not formally controlling the work of the *BSE*'s editors, had an ownership stake in its publisher and would sometimes hold discussions of its draft articles or of problems that its editors were facing. Bogdanov was certainly aware of the new project from an early stage: the protocols of the Academy indicate that he attended a major presentation on the *BSE* given by Shmidt on June 2, 1925, along with Pokrovskii (who presided over the meeting) and Lebedev-Polianskii. Bogdanov is not, however, recorded as having asked questions or otherwise spoken at the meeting.[61] But even if Bogdanov had been asked to participate, it seems unlikely that he would have been interested. The First Edition of the *BSE* was a work by the intelligentsia for the whole Soviet population, including not only the proletariat but the intelligentsia itself. Such a work, as we have seen, was antithetical to Bogdanov's post-Capri views on the nature of the intelligentsia and its relationship to the working class, and could never actually result in the formation of a new, proletarian form of cognition and, correspondingly, a new, proletarian form of science.

Still, the First Edition of the *BSE*, organizationally, can be said to have much in common with the Capri encyclopedia. Its lead editors did view it as a constructive project even if, publicly, they did not typically frame it as such.[62] It was an effort to systematically rework all existing knowledge in accordance with a new, class-based viewpoint. And it did have some organizational links with new, nominally proletarian educational and research institutions, although structurally these were much more conventional than the Proletarian University that Bogdanov envisioned.[63]

Let me now return to the concept of worldbuilding. Fiction is of course a powerful venue for achieving this task. But for Bogdanov, and for many other thinkers, encyclopedias are also a key tool for fulfilling this function. We tend to think of encyclopedias as being works that reflect the knowledge and culture of their times, and they of course do. But the world that encyclopedias reflect does not have to be the real one: it can be an imagined one or, as is particularly relevant here, a world that one hopes to bring into existence. And the power of encyclopedias in this respect comes both from their totalizing nature—they characteristically claim to encompass everything and make it all available—and the fact that, with the exception of some literary creations, they claim that the world that they reflect is real even when it is imagined. Bogdanov believed that every era needed to build its own mental world—and, in the process of doing so, produce its own new men. To do this required one to take the workers' childlike curiosity—Bogdanov characterized children as the "spontaneous creators of new little worlds"—and organize it into a conjoined research and informational program. The writing of the Encyclopedia was, for him, the only way in which this could happen.[64]

2

"The Road to Life"

Educating the New Man

Lyubov Bugaeva

The self is not something ready-made, but something in continuous formation through choice of action.

John Dewey (1916)

They just talk and write about a new man, while we in practice try helping him to grow up.

M. Gorky (1928–9)

The 1920s in Soviet Russia was a time of daring pedagogical experiments designed to transform the *besprizorniki*, juvenile delinquents, and street children, into the "new men" of the communist future. Surprisingly, major sites of these experiments were "children's labor-education communes" created by the Joint State Political Administration (OGPU), the secret police of the young Soviet Republic. Even more surprising, the actual practices of "making new men" in these secret-police installations were to a large degree based not on the prevalent ideology but on prerevolutionary Russian experimental pedagogy, the American ideas of progressive education, and John Dewey's philosophy of education.

The experiments resonated widely through various domains of Soviet culture. Writers and educators tried to capture their essence and to convey the enthusiasm of a "new-world-in-the-making" that permeated the life of these communes in numerous literary works. Nikolai Ekk's *The Road to Life* (*Putevka v Zhizn'*) (1931), a full-length feature film commissioned by the OGPU, presented the experiments in the reeducation of the *besprizorniki* on the silver screen.

This chapter explores the OGPU's children's labor-education commune by examining the intricate interactions of life, literature, and cinema, as well as the pedagogical principles, both Russian and American, which underpinned the Soviet experiments in "creating the new man." It argues that the children's labor-education commune, created, ironically, by one of the most feared and rigid institutions of control of the Soviet state, was an "island of freedom" that for a short period embodied the most audacious aspirations and ideas of American progressive education and prerevolutionary Russian pedagogy. The labor-education communes did not create a "new man," but they certainly tried.

The Soviet School as a Pilgrimage Destination

The "new-world-in-the-making" caused genuine interest around the world, and foreign guests—teachers, scientists, philosophers, writers, physicians, and others—rushed to the Soviet Union. As Michael David-Fox noted, the "pilgrimage to Russia" was "one of the most notorious events in the political and intellectual history of the twentieth century," one that marked a period of intensive cultural and intellectual interactions between Soviet Russia and the Western world.[1] Soviet newspapers regularly reported about foreign guests coming to the USSR. Thus, the July 1928 newspapers informed their readers about an "American excursion to the USSR," the arrival in Leningrad of "a group of 31 American educators headed by the Vice-President of the American Academy of Sciences Jean Dew."[2] The "Jean Dew" mentioned in the news was the American pragmatist philosopher and education reformer John Dewey (1859–1952), who laid out his theory of education in a number of publications, for example, "My Pedagogical Creed" (1897); *The School and Society* (1900); *The Child and the Curriculum* (1902); *Democracy and Education* (1916); and *Schools of Tomorrow* (1915).[3] One year before his visit to the Soviet Union, Dewey joined the board of directors of the newly created American Society for Cultural Relations with Russia. In 1928, Anatolii Lunacharskii (1875–1933), People's Commissar of Enlightenment, invited Dewey to visit the Soviet Union to have a close look at Soviet schools.[4] For Dewey, who had traveled before to Mexico, China, and Turkey, it was one more meeting with the "revolutionary world." *Time* magazine half-mockingly reported on Dewey's trip to Russia:

> Number Six on the Boulevard Sretensky in Moscow is the People's Commissariat for Education. There excited Russians are awaiting this week the coming of a great U. S. citizen who is chiefly famed on other Continents—John Dewey. [. . .] "The two contributions of America to world culture are Professor Dewey and Negro jazz." [. . .] Now he could leave behind his duties as a professor of philosophy at Columbia University. Ahead lay Europe, then broad, fertile Russian plains, and Moscow, and Number Six Boulevard Sretensky.[5]

The infamous Bureau of Investigation, later renamed the Federal Bureau of Investigation, hurried to label as communist supporters the delegation, the Society for Cultural Relations with Russia that sent the delegation, and assuredly Dewey himself because of his interest in the Soviet experiment.[6] Meanwhile, Soviet Russia had been eagerly awaiting the American philosopher whose name and works were widely known. *The School and Society*, one of Dewey's major works on education, appeared in Russian already in 1907 and was reprinted in 1922, 1923, 1924, and 1925, with a new chapter and an introduction by Stanislav Shatskii (1878–1934), an important Russian and Soviet educator and educational administrator. Other works published in Russian were "My Pedagogical Creed" (1913–14); *How We Think* (1915, 1919, 1922); *Schools of Tomorrow*, written with Evelyn Dewey[7] (1918, 1922); *Democracy and Education: An Introduction to the Philosophy of Education*, with an introduction by Stanislav Shatskii (1921); and *The Child and the Curriculum* (1922, 1923).

The itinerary for the American delegation proposed by the People's Commissariat of Enlightenment (Narkompros), the agency responsible for public education and culture, included visits to Leningrad and Moscow, with several side trips. It was designed to demonstrate to the American professors and educational administrators "the art of education in the USSR."[8] Anatolii Lunacharskii also had in mind the application of Dewey's ideas in Soviet schools. He was looking for authoritative conceptions and for allies to rely on for his mission of building new schools for the new society. Education was to be the education of the "new man," since the "old man," "which was raised in a chaotic and a-cultural capitalist society, was not acceptable." In order to organize the educational process accordingly, school was to be reformed. As Lunacharskii put it, "it is in the arena of the school that we will change the old world."[9] For him, creation "of the new man" required both self-training and self-education, and, therefore, the theory of education required "anthropology," that is, "human studies."[10] The Commissar was then a passionate advocate of the complex method, a concept of the educational process that replaced traditional subjects in a school program with complex themes, for example, "The USSR and the world." The goal was to develop a child's understanding of the natural and social environment and to encourage group work in the process of study. Lunacharskii believed that instruction, for example on how to cook, could simultaneously provide insights into chemistry, physics, botany, and zoology, as well as into hygiene and physiology. He found parallels between the Soviet complex method and the American project method[11] and was eager to pursue turning them into an effective Soviet educational model. Shatskii, whose thought was greatly influenced by the works of John Dewey, promoted in Russia the project method as early as 1905. The Russian publication of *The Project Method* by William Kilpatrick, Dewey's pupil and colleague, opened the door for applying American ideas in Soviet schools.[12]

Dewey was interested in the Soviet school system and in Soviet life in general; he wanted to understand Soviet society. During his visit, Dewey "slept soundly, stayed out at parties, gave dinners, visited night clubs, attended every event, and never experienced a day of dysentery [. . .] He managed to see as much art as possible, the icons, the folk art, and modern paintings in Moscow. But he also went on every obligatory excursion and found those nearly as interesting."[13] Soviet Russia really shook Dewey, who saw in Soviet people the energy and a kind of almost religious feeling, reminiscent of the enthusiasm and religious rise of the first American settlers. In the first chapter of the essay "Impressions of Soviet Russia" (1929), written in the wake of the trip, Dewey shared his understanding of the Russian Revolution. For him it was in the first place a transformation of human consciousness, not a social change; "the more basic fact of a revolution—one which may be hinted at, but not described, by calling it psychic and moral rather than merely political and economic, a revolution in the attitude of people toward the needs and possibilities of life."[14] He had an insight that "the Revolution was a great success, while Communism was a frost."[15]

Dewey discussed nurturing the aesthetic taste of Soviet people in the metaphors of agricultural engineering, as if the new consciousness, like a plant, required cultivation: "Perhaps the most significant thing in Russia, after all, is not the effort at economic transformation, but the will to use an economic change as the means of developing a popular cultivation, especially an esthetic one, such as the world has never known."[16] The American philosopher wanted to see how the new consciousness could be "cultivated" through the application of the methods of progressive education. He got the opportunity when he visited the experimental stations of Narkompros in the Moscow and Kaluga regions, and the children's labor colony near Leningrad. Dewey was enthusiastic about what he saw:

> Education affords, once more, the material for a striking illustration of the role of experiment in the future evolution of Soviet Russia. In a region something less than a hundred miles from Moscow [. . .] there is an educational colony under the direction of Schatzsky. This colony is the center of some fourteen schools scattered through a series of villages, which, taken together, constitute an extensive (and intensive) educational experiment station for working out materials and methods for the Russian rural system. There is not in my knowledge anything comparable to it elsewhere in the world.[17]

The American philosopher was particularly impressed by the labor-education commune Krasnye Zori (Red Dawns) near Leningrad, which was located in the former palace of Grand Duke Mikhail Romanov.[18] The director of the commune was a biologist and a former pilot Ignatii Ionin (1893–1939). Dewey wrote about the wayward children whom he met there:

> I have never seen anywhere in the world such a large proportion of intelligent, happy, and intelligently occupied children. They were not lined up for inspection. We walked about the grounds and found them engaged in their various summer occupations, gardening, bee-keeping, repairing buildings, growing flowers in a conservatory (built by a group of particularly tough boys who began by destroying everything in sight), and making simple tools and agricultural implements, etc. Not what they were doing, but their manner and attitude is, however, what stays with me—I cannot convey it; I lack the necessary literary skill.[19]

The Labor-Education Commune and the Joint State Political Administration

The labor-education commune that fascinated Dewey was a project born in the OGPU and implemented by the Chekists. Felix Dzerzhinsky (1877–1926), nicknamed "Iron Felix," the head of the secret police and of the Commission for the Improvement of

Children's Lives at the All-Russian Central Executive Committee of the RSFSR, saw *besprizorniki* as the most important and urgent problem that the secret police should deal with. He once noted that the "care for children is the best means of exterminating the counterrevolution."[20] Genrikh Iagoda (1891–1938), the head of the OGPU until 1931, followed Dzerzhinsky's priorities and actively supported the idea of *perekovka*—literally re-forging—reeducating former criminals and turning them into new Soviet people. Maxim Gorky (1868–1936), a Russian and Soviet writer and a political activist, who was a longtime friend of Iagoda since their first meeting in Nizhny Novgorod before the Revolution, once noted that the difficult task of educating young generations was the responsibility of the so-called terrible Chekists, whom "the bourgeoisie of all countries usually portrayed as being devoid of any human likeness." Only the art of the future would be able to illuminate their "amazing cultural work."[21] The Chekist idea of "re-forging" perfectly met the mood of the time. "Re-forging" meant a reeducation of the criminal, not necessarily a juvenile, through creative work and in the course of solving large-scale problems.[22]

In his efforts to introduce "re-forging" Iagoda followed the decisions of the government of the RSFSR that in March 1926 adopted the Regulations on the Struggle against Homelessness, and in September approved the three-year plan that included the liquidation of child homelessness. However, Cheka and Narkompros started the fight against homelessness even earlier. Labor-education communes became the main weapon in this fight. Several communes were opened under the auspice of the OGPU, that is, Krasnye Zori near Leningrad, the Gorky colony near Poltava, the Dzerzhinsky colony near Kharkov, and the Bolshevo commune near Moscow.[23] The first inhabitants of the communes were teenagers, usually from thirteen to seventeen years old, each with a criminal past and a prison term.[24]

In 1936, Ida Auerbach, the wife of Iagoda, advocated for the countrywide creation of labor camps for adult criminals for their "re-forging," claiming that "the general situation of 'being', the general scheme of the production process in the prison camps already has in itself a number of objective possibilities for solving the seemingly insoluble, as the square of a circle, the task of redesigning the consciousness of the declassed and the class-hostile elements, re-forging them into the workers of the socialist society."[25] According to Auerbach, those elements are reconstructed "in a forge of conscious productive labor connected with all forms and methods of cultural and educational influence."[26] The practice of Stalin camps in the 1930s was, of course, fundamentally different from that of the children's commune labor schools; however, the rhetoric of stories about them, especially that of transforming mentality, came from the narratives of the 1920s. The "liquidators of homelessness,"[27] Matvei Pogrebinskii, Ignatii Ionin, and Anton Makarenko, colorfully narrated their experience of reforming juvenile delinquents.[28] Gorky, in his essay "Across the Union of Soviets" (1928–9), branded the work of the "liquidators of homelessness" as "the insanity of realists."

Education in communes was based on several principles. The commune was a community of co-thinkers and a "school of action," where the residents decided all important questions collectively. The basic principles of the commune structure from the very first days were voluntariness and independence. The voluntariness differentiated a commune from a penal colony. The prospective members of the commune decided on this principle at the very first meeting, "the arrival and departure of a commune is voluntary, no fences, no guards. The doors are always open."[29] Being in a commune voluntarily implied the responsibility and duties of communards. The Chekists who supervised the communes explained that everything was given as a credit. Therefore, the well-being of the commune would depend on work. The answer to the question "who to work for?" was "for your community, work for yourself." Members were responsible for each other and for discipline; accordingly, they exercised control functions and took disciplinary action: "No one has the right to punish them. The supreme body is the general assembly. All issues will be resolved by this assembly."[30] The recent juvenile delinquents made the selection of prospective communards from prisons, camps, and detention points: "Further on, the new members of the commune will be received by the communards themselves. They themselves will go to the prison, and they themselves will select the guys."[31] Among other rules was compulsory work. Communes were self-sufficient economic units: they practiced agriculture, beekeeping, and various crafts. For example, the Kharkov labor colony, named after Dzerzhinsky, became the site of the production of cameras called FED (for Felix Edmundovich Dzerzhinsky).

The set of rules and principles of commune life was impressive, especially taking into account the time period. Juvenile delinquents enjoyed a high level of independence. The Cheka, which was considered one of the most rigid controlling organizations of the Soviet state, supported their self-rule, autonomy, and initiative:

> Do you want a good life? You will have a good life! Today you have workshops but they're pathetic: tomorrow you'll have powerful factories. Today your only meagre nag escaped from you. Tomorrow you'll have garages with your own cars. Today you walk to the station, to the cooperative store, right? Tomorrow you'll drive trucks with goods to your own store. You'll have schools, hospitals, stores, everything. But you should make it happen. You should do that with your own hands.[32]

When visiting the Dzerzhinsky OGPU Labor Commune in the Ugresha Monastery, Gorky was deeply impressed with the variety of labor activities of the communards who were making shoes, manufacturing beds, cooking and baking bread, doing carpentry and stone works. Most important, among all those activities there was a place for art and science, and the environment in the colony was set up to support and develop creative imagination:

> About fifty boys are working in a "sculptural" studio, their instructor is a young artist invited from the DOPR [House of Preliminary Detention], where he was serving his sentence apparently for embezzlement. [. . .] Some sixteen-year-old, a face amazingly similar to Fyodor Chaliapin in his young years, arranged a so-called "bio-garden" from a huge cage of wire [. . .]. In the cage there are magpie's chicks, blind little owls, a hedgehog and a large toad, which he calls Banker. The guy is a dreamer, a romantic [. . .].[33]

By the time of Dewey's visit Krasnye Zori was a multi-sector self-sustaining farm, where the communards worked in horticulture, animal husbandry, poultry farming, beekeeping, and seed production. They even took part in film production.[34] The motto of the commune was "Let's make our educational facility a model polytechnic school laboratory."[35] Ionin was proud of the "industrial science" that he had created. Every year students moved to the next class with a different type of agricultural activity. For example, poultry farming was taught in the fourth grade, and seed and beekeeping in the seventh. Ionin was convinced that the labor community is an effective way of educating "new people," and the commune was the "forge" in which they were created.[36] Gorky voiced a similar idea: "I'm not against the epic of old fairy tales, but I'm for the new ones that could transform a drudge and indifferent master into a free creator of a new culture."[37]

Gorky linked this transformation with purification and with the hygiene of the body. Yet in Gorky's *Mother* (1906), purification was seen as preceding an inner radical transformation:

> Man ought to be renovated—that's what I think! When a man grows scabby, take him to the bath, give him a thorough cleaning, put clean clothes on him—and he will get well. Isn't it so? And if the heart grows scabby, take its skin off, even if it bleeds, wash it, and dress it up all afresh. Isn't it so? How else can you clean the inner man? There now![38]

Not surprisingly, a clean body became the first step toward the reeducation of street urchins:

> They appeared in incredible rags, with faces covered with dirt and soot; gloomy, angry, they seemed sick, tortured, trampled by the ruthless life of the city. It was even more strange to see them an hour or two later, when, washed, dressed in clean clothes, strong, as if cast in bronze, they walked freely in the workshops of the dispensary, curious and suspicious, while observing other children, already quite skilled carpenters, fitters, blacksmiths, shoemakers. Almost all the guys seem healthy on the outside, well-built, and muscular.[39]

The reeducation of young criminals into responsible builders of a bright future was an experiment, like physical, chemical, or natural science experiments. Consequently, juvenile criminals were the material for those experiments, though the first pools of prospective communards were "not especially good," as Pogrebinskii observed. Gorky used similar language, though in his view the "biomaterial" was of good quality, "All healthy, smart, well-built guys; very rarely flicker degenerate, stupid or painful faces. [. . .] you don't immediately believe what you see, but you see healthy children."[40] For him it was Darwin's theory in action, "natural selection of the toughest" over those who were "weak, poisoned by cocaine and alcohol, destroyed by a premature sex life, and already dead."[41] It seemed coherent that street urchins "with bad heredity and susceptible to the temptations of the street" died, while only strong ones who were able "to fight for life" were left.[42] No wonder that communards, who ran the selection process themselves, took recruitment of new members very seriously, weighing the "quality" of the material and bringing in the "best, healthiest and smartest."[43] A healthy body guaranteed the "healthy spirit" and productivity that were required for successful *perekovka*: "Yet seventeen, Val'ka already had a prison sentence; a former gangster, she escaped the death penalty being a minor. Today she is a woodworker and earns 108 rubles because she is fit and healthy."[44] Once Iagoda made a Freudian slip while describing a "happy socialist country" that did not have "the hungry, poor, and freaks."[45]

The results of the pedagogical experiment impressed the experimenters themselves. Pogrebinskii, for instance, enthused:

> Enemies are angry, while allies look at the factory that produces new Soviet people with admiration and love. It is unbelievable, and the facts are irrefutable. Recent scoundrels of society, those who have got their education in a harsh school of life, start a new life. This is the implementation of Dzerzhinsky's idea, this is the OGPU contributing its experience to the construction of socialism. Thanks to the enormous energy of the OGPU leaders, the commune lives and expands, not as an experiment, but as a fact proved by life itself.[46]

The newspaper *Leningradskaia Pravda* (Leningrad's Truth) reported that in the course of the fifteen years of its existence, the labor commune Krasnye Zori had trained hundreds of qualified builders of socialism. Among the former pupils of Krasnye Zori were "six scientists, fourteen engineers, six doctors, six party workers, seven commanders of the Red Army, and 27 teachers."[47] The "liquidators of homelessness" made the pedagogical experiment-in-progress possible. Gorky recognized them as "neither dreamers nor romantics" but as "a new type of teachers," who had an "active love for children."[48]

From Life to Screen: *The Road to Life*

In the early 1930s, in his effort to contribute to the reeducation of juvenile criminals, Gorky wrote a movie script, titled *Criminals*, which was based primarily on his impressions of the labor communes. Striving for accuracy and credibility, the writer even discussed it with communards. However, the script never made it to the screen, because another film, *The Road to Life*, had already filled the niche.

The Road to Life (1931, Mezhrabpomfilm, directed by Nikolai Ekk, script by Alexander Stolper, Nikolai Ekk, and Regina Yanushkevich) is one of the first Soviet blockbusters and one of the first Soviet feature sound films, often referred to as "the first." The film explores the struggle against homelessness in the 1920s that resulted in the creation of an experimental labor commune headed by the Chekist Sergeev (Nikolai Batalov). The main characters are former petty criminals in the gang of Zhigan (Mikhail Zharov) and then the first communards, Mustapha, nicknamed "Fert" (Dandy) (Ivan Kyrlia), and Kol'ka, nicknamed "Whistle" (Mikhail Dzhagofarov). The gang leader throughout the film makes serious efforts to repossess his former assistants. He tries to humiliate them by suggesting that they are "bought" by the police, and to seduce them with drinks and "girls." At the end of the film, when all attempts to get Mustapha and Kol'ka back fail, Zhigan sabotages the newly built railroad that connects the commune with the outer world and kills Mustapha.

At the time of filming *The Road to Life* Nikolai Ekk (1902–1976) was a young director, whose creative activity began in the Meyerhold Theater and in the theater abbreviated as METLA (a broom), The Moscow Unified Leninist Theatre Team. Ekk was the author of scripts and plays that were mostly about youngsters (including some coauthored with Regina Yanushkevich, his wife, and Alexander Stolper, a Russian and Soviet film director and screenwriter).[49] He was a "man of both unrestrained and logical imagination; he could flash like gunpowder, and he did not hesitate to undertake the most audacious enterprises,"[50] and was constantly in a search for new forms and new themes. The symbol of the theater where he worked, a broom, was rather transparent: the goal of the theater, as well as of Ekk, was to clear the space for experiments using Meyerhold's biomechanics as a new method of creating a theater performance.[51] *The Road to Life* also was an experiment in a number of ways.

The OGPU commissioned Ekk, Stolper and Yanushkevich to write a script for a *kul'turfilm* (cultural film, from German *Kulturfilm*), a propaganda or educational film about homeless children.[52] The authors decided to "immerse themselves" in the material; they "visited prisons and other places not so remote, came to several children's communes, talked to the Chekists, criminal investigation officers, and met with street children on Moscow streets." They quickly discovered the limitations of the Kulturfilm format and convinced the Chekists that "the film would be deeply human and would stir up millions of people."[53] As a result, the Kulturfilm became a full-length feature film. A dedication to Felix Dzerzhinsky, recited by the theater actor Vasilii Kachalov in the film's finale, reminds the viewer of its original assignment:

> To you, the enthusiasts of the homelessness front, and to you,
> the first chairman of the Children's Commission of the All-Russian Central
> Executive Committee and the best friend of children,
> to you, Felix Dzerzhinsky, we dedicate this film.

The film reflects the experiences of several communes and shows the role of the OGPU in creating them. It opens with an introductory section, which gives background information, sets the stage for the story, and provides the main theme: street children and offenders, described as "skeletons in dirty tatters, looking angry, looking wild." Their fate seems predestined, "Today he is homeless, tomorrow he is the enemy of labor, a bandit!," but they get a chance to start anew in a Soviet labor-education commune:

> What will save them? Charity? Teaching? It's all funny to them and to us!
> We know more: man is created by the environment.
> The Republic of the Soviets will give them a ticket to life,
> Because it understands the power of free, universal labor.

The reeducation of urchins is presented as "remodeling," or "remelting":

> We build metallurgical giants in uninhabited taiga.
> We have found the live lever to the fate of humanity.
> We will teach the homeless to break through to the new world.
> We'll melt them into the workers at the construction sites of the world.[54]

The Cheka oversees the "remelting" of the former offenders into "the workers at the construction sites of the world." The leading Chekist Nikolai Sergeev (Nikolai Batalov)[55] sets the basic principles of commune life, which are freedom, voluntariness, trust, and independence. In the commune, there is no guard, no authoritarian leader, no permanent control of the former criminals, and no apparent control of the OGPU. Though Sergeev occasionally reports to the OGPU on the progress, he does not receive any orders. In general, there is no interference or pressure from the authorities.[56] Sergeev meets children, the future communards, at the railway station when they arrive voluntarily and without guards. The journey to the "new life" is their first decision and the first lesson of trust. Sergeev entrusts Mustapha, a skillful pickpocket in his previous life, with the money to buy food for the trip. It is risky, and Sergeev himself doubts the success of his little pedagogical experiment: "Will he escape?" Mustapha, though, does not run away but comes back with purchases, thus justifying the unexpected trust of the Chekist Sergeev.[57] Pogrebinskii, describing a similar episode in his story of the commune, imagines the thoughts and feelings of the juvenile criminals at that time: "But here starts an extraordinary thing: they, the prisoners, receive the money for their train tickets and no guards escort them, just the head of the commune. Like free people, really? Maybe to escape? No, better to wait, it is unclear what is going on. Besides, it's flattering—they trust!"[58]

Communards also had a high degree of autonomy. They organized their work activities, determined the punishment for the guilty, and made strategic decisions for the future of the commune. Not the Chekists but the communards themselves conducted the operation to neutralize the gang leader Zhigan, who tried to seduce the communards with a good life, alcohol, and "girls." Besides, Mustapha and Kol'ka arrived armed to detain Zhigan, and even used their guns, though pointed in the air.

Another important element of reeducating *besprizorniki* was compulsory handicraft-type production. A "new man" was to be a master of his craft. By organizing labor activities in the communes, the educators sought to employ the skills from the criminal past of their pupils. Thus, Mustapha, who could, right in the street, masterfully carve decent size pieces from the fur coats of fashionably dressed ladies, used his criminal skills in a communal shoe shop. Mustapha's reorientation and the application of his "talents" to production were not a product of the film director's fantasy. Rather it was an illustration within the pedagogical scheme of the assumption that "biologically unambiguous mechanisms of social behavior can be turned by intense and skillful work on re-forging in the opposite direction; the social meaning of biological mechanisms, like the current of the Volga River, can be turned [. . .]."[59]

The film supports the idea that the reeducation of juvenile criminals begins with the hygiene of the body. In one of the episodes, an off-screen voice asks: "Fathers and mothers, what if somebody pushes your neat child into the mud and beats him badly?" The answer is apparent; your child will be dirty. Thus, a bathhouse becomes an obvious metaphor of purification and almost an obligatory element of the narrative about the new man.[60] The bath corresponds to the liminal phase in the rite of passage, which former criminals undergo. Along with mud, water washes away the previous identity—there is a transition to a new state. In *The Road to Life*, the bathing ritual naturally takes place immediately after the arrival of the *besprizorniki* in the commune, that is, before entering a new life. The nudity of the boys in the bathhouse alludes to the initial human nudity. It marks the first stage of the pedagogical experiment. The footage of the youngsters merrily soaking in the steam room of the bathhouse alternates with the footage in which OGPU workers rejoice at Sergeev's wired message: "No one escaped. Experiment successful." The text of the message emphasizes the experimental nature of what is happening. Besides, the *besprizorniki* in the film, like those described by Pogrebinskii and Gorky, is the good quality "material" that could be used for creating a new man. Screen communards are never sick, and the film's hallmark is Mustapha's white-toothed smile along with the laughter of the Chekist Sergeev revealing his healthy strong teeth (see Figures 2.1 and 2.2).[61]

When *The Road to Life* was released in the United States in 1931, Harry Alan Potamkin, a film critic of the "left," announced the new turn in Soviet cinema:

> Today the Soviet kino is [. . .] arriving at the terminal contact, which is, after all, the human experience. [. . .] Instead of the actor, there is the character, the human personality. Instead of the oratory of the "grand" films of Eisenstein and Pudovkin, there is intimacy of contact. [. . .] we get a *Road to Life* and a *Golden Mountains* in which collectivism is experienced through its florescence, the human personality.[62]

Figure 2.1 Ivan Kyrlia as *besprizornik* Mustapha, a screenshot from Nikolai Ekk's *The Road to Life* (1931) © Mezhrabpomfilm, 1931.

Figure 2.2 Nikolai Batalov as Chekist Sergeev, a screenshot from Nikolai Ekk's *The Road to Life* (1931) © Mezhrabpomfilm, 1931.

Potamkin claimed that as a result of "the ideological re-armament," "the picture becomes luminous with a new reality, that of the advance of Soviet culture."[63] Defending the film from criticism for its technical shortcomings, the critic argued, "The movie is not just technology; it is technology informed by philosophy—the latter is the more important."[64] In his view, the substance of *The Road to Life* greatly exceeded certain imperfections of its form.

Indeed, *The Road to Life* was more than relevant to American viewers during the Great Depression. American teenagers whose parents lost their jobs were leaving their homes and riding the rails in search of income that was not easy to find. *The Road to Life* influenced several American films made in the 1930s that told the stories of homeless children in the times of Great Depression, for example, *Wild Boys of the Road* (1934, directed by William A. Wellman, Warner Brothers) and *Boys Town* (1938, directed by Norman Taurog, MGM). In the latter a priest, Father Flanagan, created a "boys' town," a commune for troubled teenagers, where he reeducates them. Like Soviet communards, American boys in their "town" exercised self-governance and determined the rights and responsibilities of the community members. They were also judges, and they decided on punishment in case of guilt.

In the Soviet Union, the official reception of *The Road to Life* was cold. The General Directorate for the Theater Repertoire (Glavrepetkom) and the Children's Commission of the Central Executive Committee banned the film, and only Stalin's reaction, "I do not understand what should be banned here?"[65] saved it. But in the movie theaters the film was a success, running for months in the same movie theater. However, critics, especially from the left, found in it "the most alarming symptoms of lagging behind the practice of socialist construction."[66] According to A. Mikhailov, the critic for the "left" magazine *Proletarian Cinema*, the theme of homeless people was presented too romantically, thus creating the impression of a "robinsonade." The social roots of homelessness associated with the capitalist system, for example, unemployment and wars, were not shown; the anti-bourgeois nature and the specific features of the struggle against homelessness were not disclosed; "the growth of children, their remake" was "not felt as a process."[67] According to the newspaper *Izvestiia*, the film was "our defeat on the ideological front" and revealed the need for "some measures to eliminate the homelessness of this art."[68] Striving for the political control over film production and demanding the "communist reflection on the plot," the critic considered a mistake the film's "lyrical appeal to the hearts of the audience." He also saw as a mistake the very attempt of reeducating *besprizorniki* that was based on trust.[69] The review reflected the change of political climate. The 1930s brought fears of initiative and of independence. No wonder that for the critic "the film showing the struggle of the Soviet power and the Soviet public with homelessness" missed "nine tenths of the Soviet power and of the Soviet public."[70]

Authorities were worried by the popularity of the negative character Zhigan (Mikhail Zharov) and his thief's songs. Also puzzling was the freedom that the communards had and the fact that the OGPU backed them. The reaction to the film, both on the right and on the left, came together with the realization that the educational experiment shown in the film was not strictly controlled. It was an initiative project with unpredictable consequences and with an open end. Whatever critics perceived as amateurism and a "robinsonade" was in fact the result of the introduction of the principles of voluntariness, autonomy, initiative, and responsibility. The principles that underlined the "re-forging" of juvenile criminals transgressed the boundaries of the purely "Soviet" experiment tied to a certain time. Those principles and their practical application connected the OGPU educational project with advanced pedagogical experiments in the United States and Europe, and in the first place, with Dewey's philosophy and pedagogy.

Dewey's Philosophy and Soviet Experimental Education

The OGPU project of labor-education communes found its roots in the prerevolutionary Russian experience of progressive education, in particular the ideas of Stanislav Shatskii and Alexander Zelenko. Before the Bolshevik revolution, Shatskii and Zelenko worked on a number of projects, such as the Settlement, an educational institution, modeled on Hull House, a settlement in Chicago that was cofounded in 1889 by Jane Addams and Ellen Gates Starr; the Day Shelter for Children in Moscow; and the Invigorating Life, a summer children's colony. Shatskii and Zelenko in turn, before and after the revolution of 1917, were inspired and guided by the American experience of progressive education and by the ideas of John Dewey. Zelenko, who was for many years in correspondence with Dewey, visited the United States several times. In 1903–4, he lived in Hull House, where Dewey was a trustee and a frequent guest. Although Shatskii met Dewey in person for the first time in 1928 in Moscow, he had known of the latter's works for a long time and was the author of prefaces to several Russian editions of Dewey's books. The two spent several days together at the experimental station of Narkompros[71] in the Kaluga region. For Dewey, meeting Shatskii was a meeting with the new; the practical application of the ideas of American pedagogy in Soviet education engaged the philosopher's imagination. For Shatskii, on the contrary, he was meeting the author of a theory he was very well familiar with.[72]

Several key concepts of Dewey's pragmatism resonated with the Soviet educational model, in the first place the concept of experience based on the organism-environment interaction and problem-solving in the process of inquiry. In 1896, Dewey wrote a short, but important, article, "The Reflex Arc Concept in Psychology," where he argued against the conception of the reflex arc, common in psychology at the end of the nineteenth century. The reflex arc conception treated sensory stimulus, central connections, and motor responses as separate entities (sensation-idea-movement), while for Dewey such separation was an erroneous evocation of the mind/body distinction. Assuming the continuity of body and consciousness, he argued for the wholeness of experience as "the result of interaction between a live creature and some aspect of the world in which he lives."[73] As he put it, "in actual experience, there is never any such isolated singular object or event; *an* object or event is always a special part, phase, or aspect, of an environing experienced world—a situation" (italics in the original).[74] So, experience in the first place was "the manifestation of interactions of organism and environment";[75] interactions were necessary conditions for defining "the self" that was "a factor *within* experience and not something outside of it to which experiences were attached as the self's private property" (italics in the original).[76] Experience rested at the heart of how people think and imagine the world; new experience, which was the result of interaction with the environment, opened new possibilities and new perspectives.

Such understanding of experience is the core of the John Dewey's philosophy of education. If the body and consciousness are inseparable, and experience is the result of the interaction between the body and the environment, then the learning process requires problematic situations that are solved through the interaction of the student with the environment:

> When a pupil learns by doing he is reliving both mentally and physically some experience which has proved important to the human race; he goes through the same mental processes as those who originally did these things. Because he has done them he knows the value of the result, that is, the fact. A statement, even of facts, does not reveal the value of the fact, or the sense of its truth—of the fact that it is a fact.[77]

Education necessarily means discovery; it is the ongoing growth and richness of experience in the sequence of "discoveries," "reconstruction or reorganization of experience which adds to the meaning of experience, and which increases ability to direct the course of subsequent experience."[78] For Dewey, education is experimental, in the sense that is situational, based on experience and is an ongoing process of decision-making and problem-solving. Besides, the inclusion of the student into a wide social context is a critical condition for the educational process. Dewey states that the student is a social being, and the school is "simply that form of community life in which all those agencies are concentrated that will be most effective in bringing the child to share in the inherited resources of the race, and to use his own powers for social ends."[79] "The democratic man," which is the final goal of education, is created through active interaction with the community in the process of "growth," that is, realizing his potential in the process of learning. This personal growth depends not so much on the political system in the society as on the way of thinking and interaction among its members. Openness, communication, and dissemination of ideas are far more important than democratic institutions.

In Soviet Russia, Dewey found to his excitement the practical application of the philosophy of pragmatism in his instrumental and experimental version. The complex method, supported by Lunacharskii, implied a contextual approach. Considering the context was akin to looking at the organism in its interaction with the environment, which was one of the key points in Dewey's instrumentalism. The laboratory-brigade method applied in Soviet schools was a variant of the Dalton plan, a secondary-education technique based on individual learning, created by Helen Parkhurst, an American educator, author, and lecturer, under the influence of Dewey. The plan presumed active and independent students, free choice of school subjects, and the individual speed of progress. It gave freedom to the student's manifestation of individuality. In Russia, the Dalton plan replaced the classroom system shortly after the publication in 1923 of *Dalton Laboratory Plan* by Evelyn Dewey, with a foreword by Nadezhda Krupskaia.[80] On the first pages, Evelyn Dewey declared, "The children are the experimenters. The instructors are observers, who stand ready to serve the community as their special talents are needed."[81]

In Soviet commune schools, Dewey liked the experiment per se. Besides, Soviet teachers, like Dewey himself, understood the importance of the educational environment. For Dewey, the ideal learning environment was life itself. The learning process was to provide access to experience and knowledge that would help a student enter the social space. After his visits to the commune Krasnye Zori and to the Shatskii's experimental station, Dewey concluded that the Soviet education system succeeded in that

> The idea of a school in which pupils, and therefore, studies and methods, are connected with social life, instead of being isolated, is one familiar in educational theory. In some form, it is the idea that underlies all attempts at thorough-going educational reform. What is characteristic of Soviet education is not, therefore, the idea of a dovetailing of school activities into out-of-school social activities, but the fact that for the first time in history there is an educational system officially organized on the basis of this principle.[82]

Moreover, the construction of life in labor communes was in line with Dewey's philosophical principles, as the learning environment there was created within and by the commune, and there were no distracting or detracting influences, of benighted and stogy parents, for example. Hence, the educational process in a commune school was easier to model. Dewey, who devoted a considerable part of his writings to developing liberal ideas and for whom democracy was the "idea of community life itself,"[83] saw a great democratic potential in the labor commune.

From his trip to the labor communes Dewey brought back an excursion diary and a drawing by a fourteen-year-old boy given to him in memory of the school that "opened eyes."[84] He also brought to the United States the belief that, as a result of the "grand psychological experiment" in Soviet Russia, a new form of human association was born, experimental, creative, alive:

> But I cannot but suppose that the Russian people will, in the end, through a series of adaptations to actual conditions as they develop, build something new in the form of human association. That these will be communistic in the sense of the leaders of the revolution, I doubt; that they will be marked by a high degree of voluntary cooperation and by a high degree of social control of the accumulation and use of capital, seems to be probable.[85]

Inspired by the application of his ideas of active interaction with the environment, learning through problematic situations, connecting school and life, community-building based on common interests, and so on, Dewey stated that "however rigid and dogmatic the Marxian symbols may be, actual practices are affected by an experimental factor that is flexible, vital, creative"; the desire and readiness to experiment "marks the Russian school leaders to an extent unknown in other countries."[86] According to the philosopher, "the simplest and most helpful way to look at what is now going on in Russia is to view it as an enormous psychological experiment in transforming the motives that inspire human conduct."[87] Upon his return to the United States, the welcome-back reception at the Astor Hotel in New York became "a tribute to the vision, the courage, the freedom and spiritual integrity of a great American educator whose influence [. . .] has reached overseas to help make school a rich and joyous experience for little children in the back streets of ancient cities and the remote villages of Russia's once illiterate hinterland."[88]

However, the story that connected the United States and Soviet Russia, Dewey's philosophy of education and the Soviet pedagogical experiment, the reality of labor communes and a film about them, did not end there. After *The Road to Life* premiered at Mussolini's first Venice Film Festival (1932), where spectators recognized Ekk as the best director, the film made its way to the United States, where it ran in movie theaters for almost a year. Amkino (American Cinema), a special agency established in New York in 1926, was responsible for its distribution. Amkino was prominent in spreading Soviet cinema in the United States; during thirteen years of its existence it delivered to American viewers more than 160 Soviet films. For several months in a row, *The Road to Life* was on screen in the very heart of New York City, in Times Square at the Cameo movie theater, which could accommodate 600 spectators. At that time, the movie theater was directed by Matti Radin, who was actively promoting Soviet cinematic art. A year later, Eisenstein, speaking in the Cameo before the screening of *Golden Mountains*, a film by S. Yutkevich, praised the movie theater "for the good work that the Cameo is doing in bringing Communism to Times Square."[89] The poster for *The Road to Life* announced that "all New York is startled by the first Soviet talking picture."

In the Russian version, the film starts with an introduction performed by the actor Vasilii Kachalov. In the world distribution the introduction has different "voices," and their choice is telling.[90] In the American version, John Dewey introduces the film with the following remarks:

> Ten years ago, every traveler in Russia came back with stories of hordes of wild children who roamed the countryside and infested the streets. They were the orphans of soldiers killed in the war, of fathers and mothers who perished in the famine after the war. You will see a picture of the old road to life, a road of vagabondage, violence, thieving. You will see their new road to their new life, a road constructed by a brave band of Russian teachers. After methods of repression had failed, they gathered these children together in collective homes, they taught them cooperation, useful work, healthful recreation. Against great odds they succeeded. There are today no wild children in Russia. You will see a picture of great artistic beauty, of dramatic action and power. You will also see a record of a great historic episode. These boys are not professional actors. They were once wild children, they once lived in an actual collective. You will also see an educational lesson of the power of freedom, sympathy, work and play to redeem the juvenile delinquent; a lesson from which we too may learn.[91]

In Dewey's "Impressions of Soviet Russia", in Nikolai Ekk's movie *The Road to Life*, in the works by Maxim Gorky, and in literary narratives of the "liquidators of homelessness," Soviet Russia of the late 1920s and early 1930s is presented as an experiment-in-process, unfolding in time and space, "a new world and a new man in the making."

Conclusion

In the Soviet Russia of 1928, Dewey caught the pathos of "re-forging" a criminal into a new man. The spirit of Bolshevik educational experimentation resonated with Dewey's vision of the "school of tomorrow." He praised the transformational power of the revolution that unlocked the creative potential of man: "I can hardly do better than record the impression, as overwhelming as it was unexpected, that the outstanding fact in Russia is a revolution, involving a release of human powers on such an unprecedented scale that is of incalculable significance not only for that country, but for the world."[92] Yet educating a "new man" did not necessarily mean educating a democratic citizen. Despite his admiration for the pedagogical experiments in Soviet Russia, Dewey believed that, in order to build communism without dictatorship, "the most essential thinking" about how to achieve this goal "still remains to be done."[93] It is also important to note that one of the reasons Dewey was enthusiastic about what he found in Soviet educational experiments was that they put into practice his conception of the transactional nature of experience. This approach to experience, which is to say the mutually constructive interaction of an individual with his environment, was in turn central to Dewey's idea of democracy as a way of life. Unfortunately, contemporary commentators on Dewey's reactions to the educational experiments of the 1920s do not appreciate this point.

Dewey thought that in the end "all education is experimental, whether we call it that or not. [. . .] practically everything we do, every course we lay out, every class we meet, is in its effects an experiment for good or for bad."[94] However, the labor communes stand out compared to other attempts to educate children as democratic citizens. The commune was shaped by a number of ideas: prerevolutionary Russian, early Soviet, and Dewey's ideas of the organism-environment interaction, inquiry, and education as experience. It was a complex phenomenon based on its own rules. It produced workers as well as engineers, scientists, and artists. It never became single-personality-centered; the general idea of experimental and practice-based education was greater than the personal or institutional ambitions of its Chekist organizers. It turned out to be more successful in generating a productive atmosphere than many schools not based on commune living. The labor commune was an example of progressive education in the USSR, but it was also more than that. It was a new form of life created in Soviet Russia as a result of international pedagogical experiential thinking.

The period of pedagogical experiments in the Soviet Republic was short. On September 5, 1931, the Central Committee of the All-Union Communist Party of Bolsheviks adopted a resolution "On Primary and Secondary Schools," which called for "a struggle against frivolous methodological fantasies and implementation of methods not previously tested in practice." The resolution singled out and stigmatized the project method that made impossible any future reference to the American ideas of progressive education: "All attempts to make the so-called 'project method', which springs from anti-Leninist theory of a dying school, the basis for schoolwork actually led to the destruction of the school."[95] Moreover, Dewey's influence, even his very name, came to be ignored in subsequent histories and commentaries during the Soviet period.[96]

The 1920s were a golden time for pedagogical experimentation, a period of the most fruitful activity of the OGPU labor communes. In the 1930s, the communes no longer fit into the new Soviet administrative and command system. They were either reorganized into factory schools or closed. In 1936, Makarenko admitted that "ten years of experience of Chekists, brilliant experience of world importance" were totally forgotten.[97] In 1937, when the NKVD began its "purging" operation, the head of the colony Krasnye Zori Ignatii Ionin was arrested, and soon after the colony was disbanded. In 1937, Pogrebinskii shot himself. As Michael David-Fox notes,

> With Pogrebinskii's suicide following the arrest of Iagoda, Bolshevo's fate was sealed. In a mere three days in 1937, more than 400 people were arrested in the commune, many of whom were shot. In the course of 1937–38, all the secret-police labor communes for children were liquidated as educational institutions; the Bolshevo Commune was turned into a "Plant for the Production of Sporting Goods Inventory."[98]

The book of Pogrebinskii was removed from the libraries, Ivan Kyrlia (Mustapha) was arrested on charges of Mari nationalism, and all direct references to the Bolshevo commune were removed from the film. *The Road to Life*, balancing between the avant-garde language of the 1920s and the aesthetics of the 1930s, between the pedagogical experiments of the 1920s and the pedagogy of the 1930s, did not fit the reality of the 1930s. A unique Soviet experiment in educating the "new man" was over.

3

The New Man in the Nursery

Making Soviet Dolls and Regulating Children's Play in the 1920s and 1930s

Olga Ilyukha

From the very beginning of their regime, the Bolsheviks turned the dream of "making a new man," the builder of a future communist society, into an urgent practical task.[1] They found a suitable "raw material" in "wax-like" children[2] and made childhood a special interest sphere for their newborn state: one of the first top-level government agencies established immediately after the Bolsheviks took power was the People's Commissariat of Enlightenment (Narkompros). The new agency took charge of creating a new system of children education and upbringing, from nurseries to universities, from children literature and theater to museums and social organizations. Speaking to the Seventh Congress of the Union of Enlightenment Workers in 1929, the head of Narkompros Anatolii Lunacharskii explained the reasons for such close attention to childhood:

> If we want to bring up the new man, i.e. cultivate new reflexes, new aptitudes, we must keep in mind that <. . .> at the pre-school age an individual can be molded and bent, at the Komsomol age – only broken, while after that, it's [just like] "a humpback only the grave could cure."[3]

Unlike adults, children "born by October" and not familiar with the pre-Soviet past did not need to be "re-forged."[4] Yet, proper molding of their worldviews required close attention to what books they read, to what imagery they were exposed, and what games they played. This was clearly articulated in the very title of a book, *To New Children—New Games*, published in 1925. Written by Evgenii Radin, the head of the department for the protection of children's and adolescents' health at the People's Commissariat of Health Protection (Narkomzdrav) and one of the founders of Soviet pedology, together with his wife, Mariia Radina-Kornil'eva, a lecturer at the Central Institute for Physical Culture, the book was continuously expanded and reprinted five times in as many years.[5] As the authors put it: "a child of the proletarian dictatorship period is a child of the October [revolution]—a new child, and new children also need new games."[6]

The Bolsheviks closely scrutinized children's play. They paid special attention to a particular object children were supposed to play with—the doll. In their views, dolls and playing practices inherited from the pre-revolution era transmitted to the children the "antiquated form of family," the attributes of "former" life, and obsolete forms of upbringing. Considering that the ultimate task of the Bolshevik revolution was to eliminate the bourgeoisie as a class, Bolshevik pedagogy could not allow non-proletarian-looking dolls in children's games, for dolls were supposed to act as an important means of socialization and self-identification.

Scholars have approached the history of Soviet dolls from various perspectives. They have explored in more or less detail philosophical, anthropological, culture-, literature-, art- and education-related aspects of this history. Yet much remains to be done. Yurii Lotman, an eminent Soviet semiotician and cultural theorist, explained the inexhaustibility of discourses around the history of dolls:

> From the first toy to a theatrical stage, a man creates for himself a "second world," and playing there he doubles his life, mastering it emotionally, esthetically, [and] cognitively. In this cultural orientation, the stable elements of the game—a doll, a mask, a character—play an enormous socio-psychological role. Whence derive the exceptionally important and wide opportunities the doll carries in the system of culture.[7]

Children's play and its transformation during Soviet times have attracted some attention of childhood historians. They have viewed the game as an element of children's daily life, which adults strove to put under strict control and subordinate to Bolshevist ideology.[8] Their detailed analyses of the games of Soviet children have revealed an underlying matrix derived from traditional folk games, which Soviet educators infused with time-relevant contents.[9] Childhood scholars have explored the role of toys in the upbringing process, but have rarely made the toy, and especially the doll, an object of focused examinations. Using collections of the Toy Museum in St. Petersburg, some scholars have charted chronological stages in the general evolution of Soviet toys and their characteristic traits.[10] Others have investigated the doll as a character in Russian and, partly, Soviet literature, placing this character at the crossroads of playing and reading—key structural elements (practices) of children's daily life.[11]

In the context of childhood history, research on toys, including dolls, is hindered by the "historical invisibility" of children due to the scarcity of sources illuminating children's own views of and their reactions to the adult-given objects and rules of play.[12] Yet there are numerous other sources, ranging from party and government documents to specialized journal publications and memoirs, which make possible a systematic study of Soviet dolls in the context of the country's political, technological, and cultural history.

This chapter examines the history of mass-produced dolls during the first two decades of the Soviet regime. It focuses on how the "new man" image was represented through dolls, and how they were used for bringing up the "new child." The interwar period is of special interest in this respect, because it was during that very time that the pedagogical and aesthetic requirements for Soviet dolls were taking shape, and the realistic representation was gaining ground in their manufacturing. Whereas manufacturers in capitalist countries were primarily guided by fashion-shaped tastes and preferences of consumers, and children were agents of commercial interests, the vector of search for an ideal doll appearance in the USSR was largely defined by political ideology.[13] The creation of the Soviet doll and the attitudes toward it were influenced by the shifting Soviet policies, especially in the areas concerning gender, age, class, and ethnicity.

This chapter traces the continuities and discontinuities in the public narratives regarding the doll, which shaped and reflected the changing attitudes toward dolls by examining the roles of scientists, educators, artists, writers, and politicians in creating the image of an ideal doll. Through exploring the stages and turning points in the evolution of Soviet dolls, it investigates the special place that dolls occupied in the system of Soviet pedagogy and culture. The major questions this chapter seeks to answer are what features of the "new man" Soviet ideologists sought to embody in a doll and how officially approved practices of playing with a doll emerged and changed over time.

The Polyphony of the Doll Discourse, from "the Great Revolution" to "the Great Break"

Before the Bolshevik revolution doll making in Russia was governed by the market. Most children had to make do with homemade toys. Manufactured dolls were mostly imported from abroad: before the First World War the Russian toy market was saturated with German-made "dummy faced" dolls.[14] Wealthier families bought foreign-made dolls with bisque porcelain heads, sleeping-rolling eyes, and movable limbs. The most expensive dolls were French-made—true ladies, furnished with clothing and accessory kits, available at high-end shops. Only a few domestic doll-making factories operated in the Moscow Province and in the kingdom of Poland, which was part of the Russian Empire.

The First World War triggered a "change of power" in the world of dolls. Production volumes in Germany plummeted, and the leadership in doll mass production was taken over by the United States.[15] The United States became an influential arbiter of doll character types, promoting plump baby shapes—the kewpie doll—in production. In Russia, during the years of wars and revolutions, domestic doll manufacturing virtually ceased to exist, and imports of foreign toys stopped. The Soviet state inherited feeble backyard production, which during the NEP period (1921–9) developed into a network of cooperatives making cheap toys that most of the population could afford.[16]

Since the late nineteenth century, educators in Russia, as in many European countries, increasingly sought to control children's games, including playing with dolls. This control was not limited to using dolls as a means of educating girls in personal hygiene or sewing but was also meant to impose the rules and conditions to prevent "adverse games" through which child aggression and early sexuality could be expressed.[17] After the Bolsheviks took power the didactic side of child play attracted considerable attention and the management of children's games turned into a state affair, shaping both the distinct features of dolls and the practices of playing with them.

As early as 1918, less than a year after the Bolshevik takeover, Commissar of Enlightenment Anatolii Lunacharskii urged educators to encourage children's play, steering their games "in a favorable direction."[18] The same year, Narkompros opened in Moscow a toy museum (headed by art critic and collector Nikolai Bartram) and established a number of commissions for the control of game and toy manufacture. Numerous publications by specialists in children's play theory and practice articulated the state policies in this area.

A new discipline of pedology—science of the child—provided scientific underpinnings for these policies.[19] Pedology had emerged as a multifaceted research area and a professional movement early in the twentieth century in many countries undergoing rapid modernization, which realized that the success or failure of their future development was in the hands of children. Russia was a pioneer among them. The "science of the child" studied its objects through the prism of various disciplines, combining anthropological, sociological, psychological, psychoanalytical, genetic, physiological, pedagogical, pediatric, and criminological perspectives on childhood.

Narkompros actively promoted this kind of research, and early in the Soviet era the country advanced the furthest in the institutionalization of pedology. During the 1920s, a large network of pedological organizations emerged in Soviet Russia, assimilating the institutions established before the revolution. Studies of *infans ludens* were pursued at research institutes in the capitals and numerous pedological offices and units in the provinces.[20]

Pedologists enjoyed much intellectual freedom and employed a variety of methods, including Freudian psychoanalysis and psychological tests; achievements of Vladimir Bekhterev's psychoneurology and Ivan Pavlov's reflexology; educational psychology and anthropometric indicators of development; so-called defectology (special education) and sociological surveys permitting children to have their own say, alongside the latest psychophysiological approaches to studying "juvenile delinquents."[21] At the same time, they increasingly incorporated the Marxist-Leninist "class approach" into their theoretical constructs and research practices. Influential Bolsheviks, including the Commissar Anatolii Lunacharskii, his deputy Nadezhda Krupskaia, and member of the Politburo Nikolai Bukharin, took an active interest in these studies. Pedologists were expected to produce practical recipes for quickly creating the "new socialist man" on a mass scale.

Games children played and toys they played with quickly became subjects of pedological research. Some of the first recommendations on using dolls (human figures) in nursery schools were developed by a special Commission on Child Toys set up at the Central Pedological Institute established in Moscow in 1921 and headed by psychologist Nikolai Rybnikov. After a careful study of Russian and foreign pedagogical literature, the Commission suggested making a collection of colorful, voluminous wooden toys for children of different ages. The collection provided very schematic portrayals of a human body for younger preschoolers and more sophisticated versions representing urban and rural types of human figures for children in their last years before school. It also included a set of trees and shrubs, as well as toy vehicles. The institute's specialists especially insisted that in designing the doll's appearance excessive details, such as accurate coloring, for instance, should be avoided, arguing that such details would "confine the child's imagination."[22]

Researchers encouraged parents and childcare workers to observe closely children playing with dolls, and designed a special questionnaire to record their observations. Pedologists were interested not only in doll-playing activities (e.g., dressing, bathing, walking, feeding, putting to sleep, paying visits, attending funerals and weddings) but also in the methods of disciplining dolls, their names, "family connections," and even contents of dolls' "dreams." This questionnaire shows that they were trying to unlock the world of children's play and the psychology of the playing child: to understand how his/her morals were forming, how religious feelings were reflected, and parenting qualities were developing.[23] Konstantin Kornilov, a leading psychologist at the Central Pedological Institute (and future director of the Institute of Experimental Psychology), wrote in 1924 that "to resolve the question of a child's play means to resolve the central question of a child's life."[24] Admitting that studies on child's play in general had a long history, he asserted that the issue of dolls for children remained "insufficiently covered and poorly analyzed."

In the 1920s, pedologists who worked with the "utterly mutable child material" were fascinated with the reflexological approach developed by physiologist Ivan Pavlov and psychiatrist Vladimir Bekhterev. Emphasizing the role of social factors in determining human nature, adherents of reflexology assumed that children's behavior can, and should, be formed at the level of reflexes; that is, ideologically commended personal and social behavioral practices could be turned into the child organism's physiological demands.[25] They recognized the significance of the playing domain for developing new reflexes. For instance, physical games were supposed to contribute to the development of "attack" and "defense" reflexes. In their experimental research, they treated toys, including dolls, as particular stimuli triggering specific responses. The reflexologists focused on the study of collective games, where complex forms of social interactions between children were exposed, organizers and leaders emerged, children learned to help each other, exchanged toys, let each other use them in turn. Special attention in these studies was given to the ability of children, as future "builders of communism," to act as a team, adapt to changing environment, and overcome obstacles and barriers.[26] Bekhterev's followers emphasized the ability of a children's collective to "modify the organism's responses" and to correct "social reflexes" as needed.[27] Pavlov and his students sought to prove experimentally the "transformation" of conditional, acquired reflexes into unconditional, "hereditary" ones, as a possible instrument of modifying behavior and, thus, "making the new man."[28]

These approaches were taken up by education practitioners who were developing new games. Multiple repetitions of the same actions within games carrying "revolutionary" content, while steering children's imagination in a proper direction, were also supposed to induce and fix the desired reflexes. "The formation of conditional reflexes is channeled by these games towards class war phenomena surrounding children both inside the USSR and globally," stated the authors of a teacher's manual.[29]

Pedologists coupled the social practices of children's behavior with their "natural instincts." Thus they interpreted playing with dolls as a manifestation of girls' innate "maternal instinct" that was worth cultivating. Pedologist-physician Alexander Antonov, for instance, suggested that "parents should be advised to give their children baby dolls, rather than dressed-up damsels."[30] This recommendation did concur with the general idea that innate instincts could be regulated, which was popular in terms of bringing up the "new man." But the encouragement of "maternal instincts" contradicted the political narrative of making a worker and social activist woman in the 1920s Soviet project aimed at gender equality. It also ran contrary to the widespread predictions that family as an institution would soon disappear and that the upbringing process would be communalized. Proceeding from these assumptions, some educators dismissed dolls that looked like children, endorsing instead "adult-type" dolls representing Red Army soldiers, workers, peasants, or various professionals, whose roles a child was to "try on" while playing. Boys and girls were supposed to be equal in playing with dolls.

The pedological studies of children's playing practices were expected to clarify what traits an ideal doll should best satisfy children's demands. Kornilov, for instance, described such an ideal doll as an artistic-psychological being conceived through co-creation by an experimenter psychologist and by a specialized artist. Kornilov's ideas emerged out of an extensive study based on questionnaires filled out by fifteen- to sixteen-year-old Moscow schoolgirls regarding their experiences of playing with dolls. Kornilov did not proceed from state interests in child upbringing. Rather, he tried to "picture a doll [that] girls would fall for." He utilized the girls' utterances to create a composite portrait of such a doll:

> large, blonde—"with long wavy hair that can be combed,"—"with fine complexion,"—"with large blue sleeping-rolling eyes, with long eyelashes,"—"with a small nose, chubby cheeks, small, scarlet, half-open lips, fine pearly teeth,"—with movable head and limbs "with well-sculpted fingers and toes," talking, "clad in light-colored dress."[31]

There is little doubt that these traits were named by girls who had seen foreign-made pre-revolution dolls (or, perhaps, their pictures in children's magazines and books). Kornilov stressed that the ideal doll image he had extracted from the questionnaires was little more than a rough draft. It had to be elaborated experimentally to make it suitable for working with an artist on creating the model doll.

The overall "doll motif" broadcasted in the 1920s press contained distinct notes of criticism of not only "bourgeois" (hair in locks, dressed up, cold-eyed face) but also folk dolls. While supporting artisan crafts in general, as their products were in demand abroad and earned hard currency, Soviet propagandists were eager to update the range of products, urging craftsmen to mold images of workers, Red Army men, and "Young Pioneers"[32] out of clay and wood.[33] They severely criticized the traditional handcrafted heavily stylized human models: the "slavishly bowing" *van'ka-vstan'ka* (roly-poly boy) and *matryoshka* (nesting doll) with a "humble look in her eyes" associated with the mother of a large family.[34] Both toys failed to meet the realistic requirements of dolls' appearance and to reify the modern ideals of a builder of socialism. *Matryoshkas* and roly-poly toys, however, continued to be manufactured, as both were goods for export. Inside the USSR, parents also continued buying them for their offspring, inciting critical reactions from propagandists well into the 1930s. Thus, the newspaper *Pioneer's Truth* asserted in April 1932: "Our nearest task is to make a revolution in toy manufacturing. There is no place for old pre-revolutionary *matryoshkas* and *van'ka-vstan'kas* among our kids."[35]

The most heatedly debated issue was the doll's place in new revolutionary imaginaries. The new man—a revolutionary, a committed fighter in the quickwater of change was juxtaposed to a petty bourgeois in the stale quiet of domesticity. The doll in its traditional form was harshly criticized. This critique resonated closely with the concurrent debates about fairy tales. Some critics attempted to discredit fairy tales as a pedagogical tool and dislodge them from children's readings under the rationale that they drove children away from the real world.[36] For instance, dolls representing the Red Riding Hood and dwarfs were considered pedagogically impermissible. In this situation, the founder and director of the Research Institute for Games and Holidays Vladimir Marts, together with the puppet theater director Natalia Sats, spoke out to defend dolls representing fairy-tale characters.[37]

The aspiration to project the structure of human society onto "doll society" sometimes took rather radical forms. The Soviet regime in its early years experimented with creating toys depicting its enemies. Such dolls were made deliberately ugly, to be detested by children. Evgenii Shvarts, a renowned author of books and plays for children, recalled his impressions of the situation in his diary. He wrote that the opponents of anthropomorphism and fairy tales, who believed that fantasizing makes it difficult for a child to know the real world, captured key positions in Soviet pedagogy. These educators, he noted,

> ... removed [traditional] dolls because they [ostensibly] stimulated the hypertrophy of the maternal element, and replaced them with goal-oriented dolls, e.g. fat and homely clerics designed to elicit antireligious sentiment in children. These elderly theoreticians were self-assured. They cared not that girls in nursery schools were cradling ugly priests and putting them to sleep and washing them in toy bathtubs, driven by the blind and ineradicable maternal instinct. Because it is not for being good-looking that a child is loved.[38]

The doll-playing domain thus emerged as a place for children's resistance against the adult culture and for their own interpretation of cultural messages.

The new state priorities resulted in a change in the composition of the country's "doll population" (see Figure 3.1). A story related by the director of the Toy Museum Nikolai Bartram about a toy exhibition in the late 1920s portrays the structure of the new "doll society": "Red Army soldiers walked in the front rows; after them there appeared pioneers and a militsiia officer ... Then followed a worker with a club hammer, *Mossel'prom* tradesmen, figures of peasant men and women, junior schoolchildren, and an occasional 'Soviet damsel' with a briefcase."[39] Trusting the dummies of adults into the hands of young puppeteers rushed them to grow up, emphasizing children's responsibility for the fate of the country.

Figure 3.1 Doll types of the early Soviet era. Unknown artist. From the journal for young children *Murzilka*, 1924, 7: cover. © Out of copyright.

Red Army men dolls, whose backyard production had started already during the civil war of 1918–22, became "a fixture" in childcare institutions in the 1920s. As time has passed since the October Revolution and the civil war, the doll representing a Red Army man did not vanish but became an element of "defense toys," occupying a prominent position among the versatile troops ready to defend the virtual Soviet doll country. As peace was returning to daily life, a new iconic figure emerged in adult-organized child's play—the *militsiia* (Soviet police) officer. This figure was juxtaposed to the policeman of the Imperial era and emblematized the new order with its declaration of care for "the ordinary man."

The revival of traditional family values in the late 1920s to the early 1930s changed the attitude toward dolls decisively. As the ideal woman was now supposed to combine the social functions of a worker and a wife,[40] so too baby dolls again became legitimate toys for girls. Tellingly, a book about handmade toys published in 1927 paired a cardboard Red Army soldier for boys with a swaddling doll for girls.[41] The ideological assault on baby dolls was halted.

The Doll in the Context of Accelerated Industrialization and "Victorious Socialism"

During the NEP period, it was largely up to the producer what dolls to make. The market was full of poor-quality backyard products and homemade dolls were widespread. With the beginning of the Great Break, as the NEP was being curtailed, resolute actions were taking place on the "toy front" as well. For instance, in early 1928 a Narkompros order shut down the Zhuravlev & Kocheshkov toy factory (a prerevolutionary survivor). Following the order, the porcelain heads of "damsel" dolls that the factory was manufacturing were publicly destroyed.[42] This emblematic event, resembling archaic practices of destroying the images of enemies to harm them,[43] took place shortly after the First Pedological Congress (December 27, 1927 to January 3, 1928), a harbinger of the Great Break in Soviet pedagogy and the human sciences more generally.

At the congress, leading Bolsheviks, including member of the Politburo Nikolai Bukharin, head of Narkomzdrav Nikolai Semashko, head of Narkompros Anatolii Lunacharskii, and his deputy Nadezhda Krupskaia, addressed the challenges of "making a new man" corresponding to the new priorities of industrialization, militarization, and the collectivization of the peasantry introduced by the Great Break. The congress signaled a turn in the development of Soviet pedology toward the consolidation and strengthening of its status as the official state science of childhood. As the formal leader of Soviet pedology and the congress's chairman Aron Zalkind declared, Soviet pedologists had overcome a "lengthy and profound ideological crisis."[44] Some congress participants, however, voiced fears that children were still influenced not only by the "revolutionary socialist creative environment" but also by the "fading, yet still quite strong, small bourgeois element."[45] They called for eliminating all "toxic" manifestations of this "element." The principal task was to transform the toy from an "object of commercial exploitation" into an instrument for the communist upbringing of "children's masses." The Fourth All-Russian Congress on Preschool Education held a few months later in December 1928 articulated similar tasks. The centralization of education processes was anchored in its resolution concerning the programming of nursery school activities, which introduced "elements of political upbringing" into preschool institutions.[46]

During the Great Break, the USSR educational system was turning back from the revolutionary pedagogical experiments of the 1920s to the traditional schooling model based on the teacher's authority and discipline. In light of the goals formulated by their professional congress in 1928, Soviet pedologists saw their new mission as the study of the "rate of development of a child organism," with vocational education and "labor evolution" moving to the top of their research agendas. Studies of games closely associated with the themes of labor, along with the production of related technical toys, construction sets, and building blocks, were prioritized. Research on doll playing became part of the politically important tasks of "cultural handling of women's masses," inculcating appropriate social references in girls, and studying the "gender typology" of children in various social and ethnic environments.[47] At the same time, the production of dolls representing various ethnic types was pushed forward to accord with evolving ethnic policies.[48]

After the introduction of five-year planning in 1928, toy design and production fell under strict state control and toy manufacturing grew rapidly. In 1928–9, small-scale and backyard facilities produced toys worth only 7–8 million rubles in toto. A decade later, in 1938, the output volumes grew fiftyfold and reached an estimated 350 million rubles.[49] Toy-making cooperatives mushroomed, producing most of the output (see Figure 3.2). Seeking to improve the situation in "toy affairs," in the second half of the 1930s the state resorted to the use of disabled manpower in cooperatives; prisoners and wives of repressed military personnel were also involved in toy manufacturing.

The heightened importance of toys was clearly reflected not only in the climbing production figures, but also in setting up new institutions and articulating new policies. In 1930, Narkompros and the All-Russian Cooperative-Industrial Council (an agency in charge of promoting the creation of cooperatives in industry) established a joint Interdepartmental Scientific and Artistic Council on Toys and Playing Materials. The purpose of the new agency was to bridge the gap between the theory of toys and the practice of their mass manufacturing, and to "rework [both of] them fundamentally." On July 14, 1931, Narkompross issued a special resolution "On the Soviet toy." It

Новинка артели инвалидов «Коммуна» (Москва).

«Пупс». Мягкая кукла с мастичной головкой, с открывающимися и закрывающимися глазами; размер 50 см; платье из легкой бумажной ткани. Модель тов. Матяткиной, головка работы тов. Власовой. Цена 17 р. 60 к. В 1939 году будет выпущено 10—15 тыс. экземпляров.

«Люсик». Мягкая кукла с мастичной головкой; размер 35—38 см; одежда из фланели или трикотажа. Модель тов. Матяткиной, головка работы тов. Власовой. Цена 17 р. 60 к. В 1939 году будет выпущено 10—15 тыс. экземпляров.

Figure 3.2 Models of baby dolls made by the "Communa" artel of disabled people as samples for mass production. Artists Matiatkina and Vlasova. From the journal *The Toy (Igrushka)*, 1939, 1: 8. © Out of copyright.

emphasized that "too little has been done for replacing the old bourgeois toy with the new one," and "the attempts to deliver a modern character type in dolls sometimes end up in a biting caricature of the modernity."[50] The Narkompros new policies demanded that the upbringing process be built upon the "burning, bright material of modernity," and the programs of childcare institutions should be "profoundly soaked with modernity."[51]

The same year, the Interdepartmental Scientific and Artistic Council on Toys was transformed into the Toy and Playing Materials Resource Center under Narkompros. This Center was expected to "create the truly Soviet, healthy, polytechnic toy."[52] Its tasks included the development of new designs, control over their manufacturing, coordination of the activities of departmental stakeholders, and organization of pedagogically oriented trade in toys. A year later, in 1932 Narkompros also founded a new Toy Research and Development Institute on the basis of the Toy Museum that had by then been moved from Moscow to Zagorsk.

The activities of these new institutions and the general directions of the early 1930s policies in toy design and production are well exemplified by the writings of Evgeniia Flerina, an active member of the Interdepartmental Scientific and Artistic Council on Toys and Playing Materials and later of the Narkompros Resource Center. A graduate of the Imperial Stroganov Central College for Industrial Arts and a specialist in child drawings and toy theory, she authored numerous "policy articles," clearly defining the requirements the Soviet doll should fulfill.[53] Thus, in 1931, Flerina lamented that "a modern character type is hardly ever to be seen among dolls. Even if a single Young-Pioneer girl does appear among a thousand of 'damsels', she still has a frisette, white curled hair, painted lips, etc." Flerina stressed that the production of padded sofas, little dressers with mirrors and flowers, and miniature samovars for dolls' tea parties fosters old bourgeois habits, instead of endorsing the new collectivist living. She also pointed out the poor quality of dolls representing "ethnic types": "The grotesque design makes these dolls counter-revolutionary. These dolls scare, repulse, [and] prompt utterly perverse ideas about various nationalities and ethnicities." Flerina demanded that toys be realistic, and criticized their anthropomorphism: "Bunnies in pants and satin cloaks [and] cats in boots are worthless, unneeded, baneful toys," which could mislead the child, who perceives them as "straightforward reality." Flerina did not object to the use of toys depicting such "negative social types" as a capitalist or a cleric, but only if they were caricaturized, "inciting relevant emotions." She considered it premature, however, to give such toys to a preschooler, in whose hands a negative character could turn into a positive one ("my little priest"). Urging civil activists and manufacturers to pay close attention to the doll, Flerina expressed a general sentiment popular among the Soviet theoreticians of child play: "The doll often fulfills the function of a teacher." As a result of such criticisms, toys representing "anti-socialist character types" were to be destroyed and withdrawn from production.

A variety of commissions and councils on toys also criticized dolls deviating from the Soviet beauty standard. A 1931 publication by the Scientific and Artistic Council on Toys declared, for instance, that "the smartly dressed, white-handed damsel in tight curls, bows and lace, with rouged lips <. . .> should be regarded as an anti-social and anti-pedagogic toy."[54] Public inspectors went to toy-making enterprises to spot such baneful dolls. For example, an inspection by the Komsomol Central Committee in 1931 found the appearance of toy soldiers, sailors, peasants, and workers deplorable. Participants of the raid concluded that "Such toys cause aversion towards the main social groups in the Soviet Union. If doll toys are to be produced at all, they should be Komsomol and Young-Pioneer girls, but certainly not what is being produced now." [55]

As the Great Break gained momentum, the spears of criticism by the Communist Party also targeted pedology as both a professional movement and a scientific discipline, challenging its research methodology. The rationale behind pedologists' inquiries was the making of a creative and active individual. They focused on studying children's interests, fantasies, and wishes. This approach came into conflict with the new policies, and pedology came under attack as "pseudo-scientific" and "anti-Marxist." Studies of reflexes and reactions in playing children were declared to signify "bourgeois idealism," as were investigations of the manifestation of instincts in games. Pedologists were accused of approaching children's behavior without due regard to the class environment and of being disconnected from children's life realities. Such leading proponents of pedology as psychologists Konstantin Kornilov and Anatolii Smirnov, along with many other 1920s researchers of *infans ludens*, were accused of "overbiologizing" the childhood. Their critics proclaimed that "we know that a child's play is thoroughly social," and a child must be regarded "as an individual, class-specific child."[56]

Thus Smirnov's influential study of *Child and Adolescent Psychology* (first published in 1926 and reprinted four times in as many years) was virtually ostracized. The critique of his book demonstrated in what directions children's playing practices were expected to be developing. One of the critics, for instance, was enraged by Smirnov's statement that "while living in one's utterly special world—the world of play, a child cannot be too intimate with or sensitive to our actual reality." The critic inquired indignantly: "how can such slander against kids be allowed, especially in our Soviet country <. . .>, where children at perhaps 2 or 3 years of age begin to comprehend public life in their own way and get involved?"[57] He contrasted Smirnov's views with the party-approved ideal image of the "new child": "Don't we see the facts of children taking a heroic part in the civil war, don't we know how children help adults build socialism, is it rare that a village child convinces the old father or grandfather to join the collective farm, or the mother to get rid of icons."[58] Similar accusations were leveled at Kornilov. The psychologist's interest in how natural instincts are expressed in children's games and behavior was deemed to be harmful for Soviet educational science.[59] His conviction that "the nature of doll playing is primarily intimate"[60] ran contrary to the aims of raising the "new collectivist man" articulated in the new pedagogical principles and policies, which called for active interference in and close supervision of the playing process in preschool institutions and schools.

Another tangible change in the attitude toward doll playing occurred in 1934, when Narkompros introduced new programs for nursery schools with clear-cut instructions on the matter. The Narkompros instructions made dolls an obligatory element in child's play at all preschool institutions throughout the country. They defined the composition of doll characters to be played by children of different ages. The instructions recommended that three-year-olds be given large dolls dressed as children, while four-years-olds receive the same dolls but with the addition of some special character types, such as Young Pioneers, Red Army soldiers, and militsiia officers. The range of such doll character types was to be expanded annually as children grew older.[61] A year later, in 1935, the Toy Research and Development Institute jointly with the Narkompros Committee on Toys began to publish a specialized journal, *The Soviet Toy* (renamed *The Toy* in 1937). The journal became a clearinghouse and a regulator of standards in toy production and consumption.

The critical campaign against pedology in the press and specialized publications reached its climax in the summer of 1936. On July 4, the country's highest political authority, the Central Committee of the Communist Party (TsK VKP(b)), issued a special resolution "On Pedological Perversions in the System of Narkomproses," which sealed the fate of pedology in the Soviet Union.[62] The resolution banned pedological research and theorizing that had provided the foundation for much of Soviet pedagogy during the previous years.

There is every reason to call 1937 the year of the toy, for it saw an unprecedented attention lavished on the subject by the Soviet authorities. That year, the RSFSR Sovnarkom (Council of People's Commissars—the republic's highest government office) instituted a special commission on children's toy manufacturing and a permanent inspectorate for toy quality control. At the same time, government agencies in various industrial sectors involved with toy production created "artistic councils" that were charged with overseeing toy designs. In their turn, state trade agencies began to build a network of specialized toy shops, and introduced regulation of toy pricing (in 1937, prices were reduced by a whole of 11 percent).[63] Production plans were urgently revised, projecting a more than 50 percent increase in output volumes.[64] Old production facilities were modernized and new ones founded. Thirty-two toy-making enterprises were either built anew or expanded substantially in 1937. Echoing Stalin's well-known declaration that "life has become better and merrier,"[65] in addition to dolls per se, the industry started manufacturing various doll accessories, such as household items and clothes. As philologist Marina Kostiukhina has observed, "Smartly dressed dolls with a stock of dresses and household items were meant to symbolize [the growing] Soviet prosperity."[66]

The rapid modernization of the Soviet toy industry entailed much more than a tremendous increase in the sheer numbers of produced dolls. The transition from handmade to machine-made toys also signaled a departure from creating dolls with more or less individualized looks and the move toward cranking out identical artificial bodies according to a specific design approved by the powers that be. This transition could be seen as a particular manifestation of the general trait of all disciplinary industrial societies, which seek to control corporeality.[67] These global phenomena of sociopolitical control over corporeality were projected onto the doll and clearly reflected in the design of its appearance in accord with the regime's goals and its current body ideals.[68] The doll was expected to portray a physically fit, sanguine child, and artists were instructed accordingly. In December 1936, the journal *The Soviet Toy* proudly reported:

> Finally, we have obtained quite a cultured, "qualified" doll. Artist M.P. Kiseleva has delivered baby-doll models. They are large, smartly dressed, highly artistic dolls, a

> boy and a girl, that could compete with the best foreign specimens. The artist has rendered a realistic image of a healthy, jovial child: the body, head, and clothes are fashioned thoroughly and expressively.[69]

The journal, however, identified in the doll a flaw "alien to Soviet people," an "excessively mannered facial expression," which the artist had to correct. With the doll's flesh matching the physicality of the Soviet person, its face also had to render Soviet spirituality.

Foreign achievements in doll making were a major reference point for Soviet doll ideologues and producers. The Western toy domain was both an unattainable ideal and a target of harsh criticism. In 1939, the newspaper *The Soviet Art* carried a note by a certain educator, L. Vorontsova, who drew explicit comparisons between Soviet and "Western" dolls. She lamented that "we still do not have cheerful toys equal in popularity to Disney's characters," and called on doll manufacturers to look for inspiration at "remarkable characters in the literature of all the peoples [of the USSR], which children love and which could be reproduced in making dolls." Vorontsova berated artists and toy craftsmen, stating that "The doll common in our country is just a slightly modified foreign doll model from the second half of the 19th century." But the major source of her dissatisfaction with the appearance of such dolls was "An ordinary, blank, mask-like face."[70]

The task of creating dolls portraying children of different ethnic groups and races took quite a while to fulfill. In 1931, the Narkompros Council on Toys approved for manufacturing the doll set "Children's International" created by craftsman Stulev. The set included four dolls: a Japanese girl, a Chinese boy, an African boy, and a Karelian girl.[71] The mission of these dolls was to evoke sympathy for children of all ethnicities in the USSR and oppressed children abroad. Such dolls were often marked ideologically: a common attribute of their outfits was a red tie, the emblem of the Young Pioneers. However, early experiments in this sphere were bitterly criticized:

> Truly harmful is the "international doll." Blacks, Chinese, Gypsies made of rags, pottery, and papier-mâché are caricatures. All these dolls are nothing more than vicious mockery of other ethnicities and races. The manufacturing of these toys in their present form is a straightforward sabotage on the front line of the communist internationalist upbringing of children.[72]

Yet, toward the end of the decade, the situations in the toy section of this "battlefield" improved: the models "Kyrgyz boy" and "Nenets on a reindeer" were recognized as successful (see Figure 3.3). A telling fact is that these specimens portrayed traits of the peoples of the USSR and, as was especially emphasized, their faces were smiling and merry.

Mass production of dolls designed by professional artists faced major difficulties, however. Leaving the factory, they often looked rather different from the original, due to low qualification of personnel, technical issues, and shortage of necessary raw materials, such as fabric for sawing the doll body, which would then be stuffed with sawdust. The high proportion of defective products in the output was an issue,

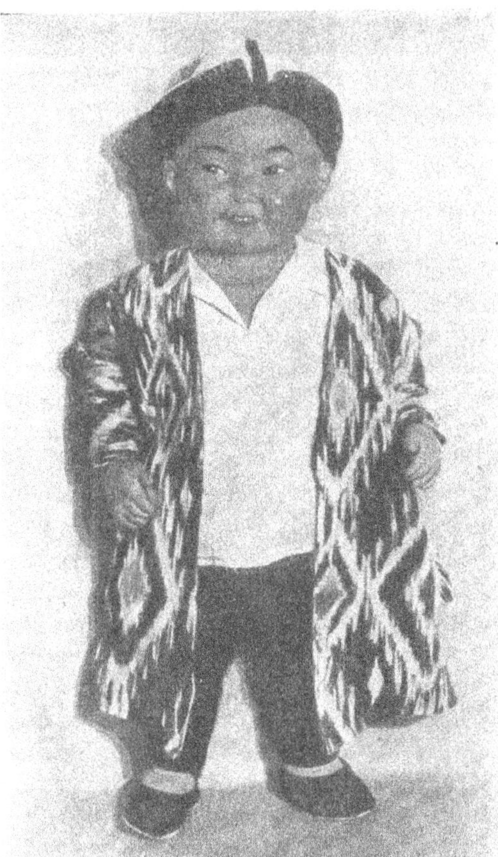

Кукла-«киргиз», работы худ. М. Киселевой

Figure 3.3 A doll, "Kirgiz," artist M. Kiseleva. From the journal *The Toy (Igrushka)*, 1938, 2: 23. © Out of copyright.

and many dolls with defects reached shop shelves. Such defective toys were labeled "counter-revolutionary." "Authorized organizations have started to deal with toys. Out of the 10 thousand product range, they culled 67.8 per cent as ideologically harmful, bluntly counter-revolutionary toys," reported the *Pioneer's Truth* in April 1932.[73] A whole column in the newspaper was headlined "Stop producing kewpie dolls. Launch broad-scale production of polytechnic toys." An argument against the kewpie doll was, not least, its poor quality. Close-up photographs of defective kewpie dolls were accompanied with matching captions: "An ugly creature with a swollen belly and a squint. Such is the baby as depicted by the doll factory," and "Another creep also representing a child." The critics demanded "urgent surgical intervention" in the production process.[74] Such accounts reflected the Soviet attitude toward human body: a cult of healthy and athletic physicality, and the unwillingness to accept deviations from the accepted standards.[75] People with disabilities were, in fact, outcasts in Soviet society, and the word "handicapped" applied to a doll served as an indicator of its defectiveness. A comment by a drama critic highlights the marginal status of a disabled individual in theatrical doll images: "What we see on the stage is some hoppers, amputees with prostheses instead of heroes."[76]

The year 1937, remembered for mass repressions, was also harsh on toys failing to satisfy government standards and requirements. Thus, the withdrawal of "ugly doll creatures" from production and sale turned into another mass campaign. The authorities were especially irritated by failures in the production of military toys, including "defense dolls." As the country was getting increasingly militarized, the production of this category of toys became a priority. Toy troops were required to be "sturdy and movable," but soldier figures cut out of plywood or stuffed with cotton wool were rather clumsy, unsteady on their feet, and did not live up to the desired ideal.

The appearance of "defense dolls" was evaluated at the highest level. For instance, at the beginning of 1938 Marshal Semen Budenyi, Hero of the Soviet Union Valerii Chkalov, and Deputy Head of the Political department at the Frunze Military Academy Major M. Moskovtsev visited a defense toy exhibition in Moscow. Moskovtsev, for one, was quite critical of tin Red Army soldier sets and character dolls depicting military personnel, such as a border guard, a pilot, and an infantryman. He noticed "faulty representations of the uniform, awfully bad figures, [and] dull, sometimes even stupid faces (of dolls)," emphasizing that "the lack of proper bearing, fitness, [and] gallant posture so typical of our brave young soldiers is absolutely unacceptable in a toy."[77] Special attention was given to the face of the toy soldier. It had to be expressive, energetic, yet stern. The invention of a mechanism for making dolls with opening and closing eyes unexpectedly affected the defense toy: such dolls did not correspond to the ideal of a vigilant, sleepless warrior safeguarding the "nation's peace and calm" day and night. Alongside the military doll, representing the vanguard of the toy counterpart of Soviet society, the dolls representing the "creators of the new world" were also in high demand: for instance, some dolls were modeled after polar pilots and explorers, who became celebrities in the decade before the Second World War.

Overall, during the 1920s and 1930s Soviet industry produced a limited range of doll types, which was variegated by means of different clothes and accessories. For instance, performing rather poorly in manufacturing dolls with adult bodies and faces, the industry had to fulfill "defense doll" production plans with plump kewpie dolls dressed in Red Army uniforms. By dressing the same doll differently, the manufacturer could supply it to retail chains as either a "kewpie baby doll" or a "Red Army man." That is, one and the same doll body (and face) was supposed to acquire a new meaning for the child when covered up in (and set off by) new clothes (see Figure 3.4 a–c).[78]

Another problem, which Soviet pedagogy has since long solved for the "ordinary" doll, became a stumbling block when it came to the "defense doll": dressing and undressing the doll. Such manipulations with kewpie dolls were considered normal and even encouraged, for they thought to promote hygienic habits and skills. Finding didactic grounds for such practices with the dolls representing the military or the militsiia was rather problematic. A compromise, however, was found: the overclothes of such dolls were made removable, while underwear was affixed to (or painted on) the doll body to prevent children playing with a naked "official." Evgeniia Flerina

Figure 3.4 The same doll model with different clothing patterns: (a) worker; (b) kindergarten children; (c) Red Army soldier and commander. A doll could acquire a new "social status" simply by changing clothes. Artist I. Kholodov. From L. N. Kurlova and F. S. Litvin, *Igraem s kukloi* (Playing with a doll) (Sverdlovsk, 1936). © Out of copyright.

suggested applying this technique to all dolls of "adult, Soviet character types." She also demanded that such figures "be well-poised," flexible, with artfully and thoroughly made faces portraying the best, expressive traits of the character.[79]

New objectives required not only appropriate changes in the doll appearance but also considerable modifications in doll-playing practices. Doll playing was increasingly regulated, both directly and indirectly, to serve current political and ideological agendas. Nursery school teachers acted as game organizers and facilitators, guided the playing process, gave hints, and corrected the course of the game. There was hardly any free doll playing in nursery schools—dolls were handed out to children for a certain predefined period of time and then stacked away. The teacher's control was aimed at avoiding a risk of game transformation into a representation of inappropriate behaviors: boozing, squabble, or fighting.[80] But it has broader aims as well.

Drilling children in contemporary political issues became a required element of pedagogical practices. Children were obliged to play with dolls following preset narratives such as "Red Army on tactical exercise," "Ski rally Sverdlovsk–Moscow and Northwards," and "Collective farm." In the ski rally game, for instance, children were seeing off a doll delegated to go to a congress in Sverdlovsk, with the doll-making appropriate speeches along the rally route. Teachers claimed that such games helped children comprehend social realities, while in fact they merely reproduced the fictional world of slogans and front-page news stories. Thus, at the conclusion of the "collective farm" game, kindergartener Petia, who played the role of the "collective farm director," addressed the dolls in the following manner: "You're tired, collective farmers, we've had lots of work today, now eat to the full. We did a good job, so let's now go to the theater."[81]

Personal characteristics of six- and seven-year-old children written by the staff of the Sverdlovsk Regional Nursery School described them as "politically competent and aware of the country's public life." Formulating their findings from the study of doll playing, the teachers from Sverdlovsk emphasized its role in committing children to the Soviet way of life:

> Dolls help anchor the love for everything that's ours: our factories, plants, Red Army soldiers, pioneers, workers, collective farmers . . . children emotionally consolidate, clarify their likes and dislikes. There is so much anger in how the 7-year-old Vova says to the laggard Donat—the destroyer of his laborious edifice: "Hey, vermin, we build and you destroy." And there is so much willingness and power in children's exclamations from the dais: "We don't want war but are ready to fight!" and "Long live our leader, the great Stalin!"[82]

The educators were well aware of how important the strong emotions incited by dolls were for achieving the desired result in bringing up a "socially active person." The use of Soviet hackneyed phrases by children playing with dolls, emulation of approved behavioral templates, and political labeling were welcomed by the teachers and disseminated through the press as "benchmarking."

Soviet educators "creatively" subdued children's personal desires and propensities to their pedagogical goals. For instance, a problem arose in playing out games with an adversary: no child wanted to perform as the enemy, whether an infiltrator, a spy, or an enemy soldier. Adults offered their own solution: they suggested that the infiltrator hiding in the scrub could be represented by a flap-eared monkey or a teddy bear "that children disliked."[83] The description of a game for junior schoolchildren, modeled after the Red Army invasion of Poland in 1939, offered a similar recipe.

The Toy journal urged teachers around the country to emulate the knowhow of the Moscow City Pioneer Center, where children supervised by a tutor created a game, titled "Red Army meets the children of Western Belorussia and Western Ukraine." In this game, the roles of "negative characters" also went to the dolls. One doll, dressed in a top hat and a cape collar, portrayed a fat landowner. Another, wearing a bonnet, represented the landlord's peasant-offending evil wife. A table was brought outside, surrounded by trees—it represented the landowner's house. A mock-up church was built next to the house. Dolls representing Polish officers were seated at the windows, armed with two cannons. The tutor enthusiastically described the way children played the game:

> Raia was unanimously chosen to be the commander. Children took shotguns, grenades (made of pieces of construction materials). "Units, fall in!"—commanded Raia—"Comrade soldiers! We're going to liberate our brothers, Belorussians and Ukrainians, those who live in Poland. Gentry and landowners made them toil, taking everything produced for themselves and not giving anything to the workers. They starved, they didn't have collective farms, not even their own schools. Come on, soldiers, for the Motherland, for Stalin!"[84]

Children's feelings were sacrificed to ideological causes: children had to betray their dear, beloved dolls, which following the will of "pedagogues" were transformed into diabolized landowners, bourgeoisie, clerics, and enemy officers and were "doomed to share the same fate: be exposed, defeated, annihilated."[85]

Conclusions

The doll—a small object of children's games and affection—got caught in the twists and turns of early Soviet history. It came to embody the Bolsheviks' visions of the "new man" and became an instrument for instilling in the new generations the bodily image, behavioral traits, and social attributes of the "builder of socialism." In contrast to the interwar Western discourses that saw the doll's major function in steering girls toward proper motherhood and the latest understanding of hygiene and childcare,[86] Soviet attitudes toward dolls clearly reflected the regime's general policies of secularization, industrialization, militarization, and collectivization, as well as its shifting priorities in such particular areas as gender, age, class, and ethnicity.

The story of the Soviet doll during the interwar period falls into two distinct phases. In the 1920s different vectors coexisted in the use of dolls in the child's play, ranging from dolls as a means to make boys and girls equal in their games to the replacement of baby dolls with adult characters to traditional "mother-daughter" game practices. The doll became a subject of extensive research by the new "science of the child"—pedology—that made a careful study of children's own voices, wishes, and views and aimed at making the "new child" into a creative and active person. During the Great Break, "serving socialism in practice" became the motto of all pedagogical studies and procedures,[87] and the attitudes toward dolls changed accordingly. In the 1930s, the state invested heavily in doll manufacture and increasingly strove to control the children's playing domain, by endorsing clear-cut standards of doll appearances and game narratives. Dolls were supposed to represent the best qualities of the "new man" and the "new child": physical health was rendered via bodily shapes and proportions, while moral health via facial expressions. Such features as frisette, rouged lips, or use of lace in the doll's dress were berated as indicators of "bourgeoisness," turpitude, and excessive care for one's looks. Artless smile, direct look, facial expression without guile or flirtation, and a determined and courageous expression in the military dolls became the characteristic features in the appearance of a Soviet doll.

The materialization of these traits in the doll model of the new man, however, often encountered insurmountable technical barriers in the manufacturing process. Nonetheless, the doll—a proxy of an ideal Soviet person—became a symbolic guide for a playing child to emulate and to identify with, an unambiguous cultural message from adults to children. The changing composition of the "country's doll population"—now dominated by workers, soldiers, pilots, and militsiia men—reflected the changing human ideal in Bolshevik ideology and the new symbolisms of Soviet life, with the sanctity of state authority projected onto the bodies of dolls representing the military and militsiia officers.

The doll no longer remained an object in children's freestyle play, but was committed to didactic causes. The doll moved from the private sphere to state-controlled children's collective loci—nurseries, kindergartens, schools, orphanages, and children's summer camps. In these institutional settings the doll as a means of a dialog, a symbolic interaction, and a cultural exchange between the adult and the child simply disappeared. Dolls turned into mere props in the games narrated, manipulated, and controlled by adults. In the private domain, however, favorite dolls certainly lived far more diverse lives, beyond ideologized templates and imposed clichés.

Acknowledgments

This study was carried out under state order for the Karelian Scientific Center of the Russian Academy of Sciences.

Part II

Imagining the New Man

The rise of the modern life sciences, whereby the investigation of biological, pathological, and psychological phenomena was subjected to rigorous experimentation, resulted in unprecedented new understandings of how human life is created, shaped, and changed through objectively verifiable processes. In the first decades of the twentieth century, this scientific revolution coincided in many parts of the world with rapid social change and the collapse of old empires, leading to euphoric—or anxious—visions of the future. In the Americas, in Europe, and in Russia alike, imagining the "new man" who would populate this future now involved scientific (and often explicitly eugenic) presuppositions. As the chapters in this section show, although the scientific advances that undergirded fantasies of making a "new man" were everywhere the same, local and culturally specific visions of the "new man" took on very different features in different countries. Popular literary and film depictions of scientifically altered beings (monster, or marvel?) reinforce the contention that the *idea of creating a new man* was a broad and capacious cultural resource, from which a variety of memorable fictional images, as well as actual policy decisions, could be derived.

4

New Sciences, New Worlds, and "New Men"

Nikolai Krementsov

The year was 1927. The Soviet Union was gearing up to celebrate the tenth anniversary of the Bolshevik revolution and the Union's own fifth birthday. The entire country was trying to grasp the enormity of change that had occurred over the course of the past decade and to anticipate the changes yet to come. Politicians, journalists, engineers, theater directors, physicians, artists, educators, scientists, writers, filmmakers, and state officials—all were preparing laudatory accounts of past accomplishments and optimistic prognoses of future achievements. In the midst of this jubilant atmosphere, Andrei Platonov, a twenty-eight-year-old engineer and aspiring litterateur, wrote an essay, evocatively titled "The Man That Will Be."[1]

Platonov explicated the purpose of his essay as follows: "our theme is to explain a future type of man that must replace the currently existing type." Considering humanity's past, he observed that "laboring on remaking the world, man has been forgetting to remake himself. Therefore, the great natural sciences have brought humanity not benefit and salvation, but death. The example is the war of 1914." According to Platonov, the Bolshevik revolution has changed this situation: "the creation of the new man has begun in Soviet Russia." "The new man already exists, . . . already acts," the author asserted. For the writer, the arrival of the "new man" was a major promise of the Bolshevik revolution, a promise whose realization Platonov would continue to examine in his subsequent writings, including now-famous novels, *Chevengur* and *The Foundation Pit*, written in the late 1920s.

Platonov's essay captured a notable feature of postrevolutionary Russian culture: its main subject, the "new man," was an important component—a major meme, if you will—of Bolshevik culture, migrating with ease from one cultural domain to another. The "new man" figured prominently in numerous cultural productions, ranging from movies, scientific treatises, and novels to paintings, philosophical tracts, and theatrical plays. It was hailed in speeches of government leaders, embodied in monuments and buildings, and sung of in symphonies and hymns. But contrary to Platonov's belief shared by many of his compatriots that Soviet Russia was the birthplace of the "new man," the very idea that a "new man" would somehow replace the currently existing one has long predated the Bolshevik revolution and has never been a feature of exclusively Russian culture. Rather, variations on the theme of the "new man" have reverberated far and wide in many cultures since the beginning of human recorded history.

So, what exactly did the expression "new man" mean in Platonov's writings? According to his essay, the very arrival of this "fantastic creature of the future" was the main "*internal-biological* consequence of the October [1917] Revolution," and the new man "necessarily is better equipped *biologically*." Furthermore, the essay's first draft bore the title "The Breeding Pen of the New Man," with the words *breeding pen* (*pitomnik*) apparently signifying both where and how this "future type of man" would appear.[2] Platonov's word choices indicate that biology played a key role in his ideas about the "new man." But why would a railroad engineer with a passion for electrical technologies define his "new man" as a biological being? Was this "biological trend" something specific to Platonov's thinking and confined to the visions of humanity's future in Bolshevik Russia? When, why, and how did biology—the study of life—enter the millennia-old notions of what Platonov characterized as a "fantastic creature of the future"? In what follows, I look for answers to the questions raised by Platonov's essay through a particular lens provided by comparison of Aldous Huxley's 1932 classic *Brave New World* with a little-known novel, *Valley of New Life*, published by Russian physician Fedor Il'in four years prior.

The Biology of the New Man

Who are we? Where did we come from? Where are we going? What is the meaning of life and death? Since time immemorial humanity's best minds have puzzled over these existential questions of human origin, human nature, human place in the Universe, and human destiny. For millennia, priests and poets, philosophers and physicians, astrologists and artists found answers to these questions in theological conceptions of Creation. According to a theological worldview, humans are the pinnacle of God's creation, the center of the Universe, and the stewards of Nature. Their own nature is defined by the unity and duality of material body and immaterial soul, while their destiny is to suffer their earthly lives in the name of God and to spend the eternity of afterlife either in Hell or in Heaven, according to the Last Judgment.

Many intellectuals have doubted and questioned these answers. But it was only during the nineteenth century, when the systematic pursuit of knowledge about Nature—*science*—became professionalized, that the theological view of the world was openly and thoroughly challenged.[3] During that century, science fully acquired distinct features of a particular social institution, with its own system of organizations, practices, languages, patronage, careers, communications, ethos, and personnel. The word "scientist" first appeared in the English-language only in the 1830s. It was during this time that the differentiation of sciences and formation of separate scientific disciplines, according to the subjects, objects, and methods of study, began in earnest, and the study of life acquired its modern name, biology.[4] And it was during this time that science began to contest openly the cultural authority of theology over the existential questions.

The first blow to the theological outlook was delivered by geology that during the first third of the nineteenth century completely rewrote the "history of Earth." Numerous studies, summarized and elaborated by Charles Lyell in *Principles of*

Geology (1830–3), increased the age of Earth by several orders of magnitude—from less than ten thousand years that had ostensibly passed from the days of Creation described in the sacred books to untold millions written into the recently uncovered and deciphered geological record.[5] Furthermore, Lyell argued that vast past changes of Earth's crust, which had occurred over those millions of years, were results of the same "causes" that he and his contemporaries could observe and study.[6] This conclusion opened a possibility of not only elucidating the past history and the present state of our planet, but also envisioning its (geological) future.

The second, far heavier blow was delivered by biology that drew much inspiration from the facts and theories of the new geology. In 1859 Charles Darwin published his book *On the Origin of Species*. His revolutionary work described actual mechanisms, "laws," which govern the process of *temporal change* (evolution) in plant and animal species in Nature: the laws of variability and heredity, of struggle for life and natural selection. In Darwin's view, these laws determine the differential survival and propagation of some ("fit"), and, at the same time, the differential mortality and fertility of other ("unfit"), members of a species. It is the differential fertility and mortality that assure the species' continuous adaptation to changing environmental conditions and that over the course of time lead to its preservation, its modification, its divergence into different species, or its extinction. Along with many of his contemporaries Darwin believed that the "laws of evolution," like other laws of Nature discovered by scientists—from the laws of celestial mechanics to the laws of thermodynamics—are inevitable and inexorable. These laws, therefore, could not only explain the past and the present, but also help predict the future: "improvement" and emergence of new species or "degeneration" and extinction of existing ones.

Only a single sentence in Darwin's entire volume mentioned humans, promising that his theory could throw "light . . . on the origin of man and his history."[7] Nevertheless, even before Darwin himself would attend to the task in his monumental, two-volume treatise on *The Descent of Man* (1871), many other scientists inspired by his work did shed light on these issues.[8] According to Darwin's theory, zealously developed, promoted, and popularized by his "bulldog," T. H. Huxley, man was not the favorite creation of God, the center of the Universe, and the steward of Nature. He was merely one particular species of the animal kingdom, *Homo sapiens*. This species did not appear out of God's hand, but evolved (in accord with the laws discovered by Darwin) over hundreds of thousands, if not millions, of years from some other ancestral species, common to man and apes.[9] As witnessed by Huxley's famous dispute with the Oxford bishop Samuel Wilberforce at the June 30, 1860 meeting of the British Association for the Advancement of Science, for him, as for many others, the explicit anti-theological dimension of Darwin's theory's implications for the issues of "the origin of man and his history" constituted its major strength and cultural importance.

Furthermore, some scientists almost immediately attempted to use Darwin's "laws of evolution" not only to fulfill his promise of illuminating "the origin of man and his history." They also tried to envision a possible future of man and even to intervene into such future. It followed from Darwin's theory that the "evolutionary destiny" of *Homo sapiens* is no different from that of any other animal species: the human species will inevitably continue to evolve. This evolutionary process could lead to three possible outcomes. The species could remain the same and preserve its present form through time. It could "improve" further and generate (or diverge into) new "modified" species of *Homo*. Alternatively, it could "degenerate" and eventually go extinct, as happened to countless species that had inhabited Earth in past eons.

Already in the 1860s, scientists in France, Britain, Russia, Germany, and elsewhere began exploring possibilities of applying Darwin's "laws" to overcome the "evolutionary destinies" and to shape the future of man.[10] These scientists elaborated various schemes aimed at preventing the "degeneration," and promoting the "improvement," of mankind. Their schemes were all based on Darwin's principles of heredity, variability, struggle for life, natural and artificial selection, and differential fertility of "fit" and "unfit" individuals. At that time, such projects did not go beyond proposals of introducing a "hygienic" or "rational" marriage by articulating the rules and methods of regulating unions between spouses from different social (ethnic, class, racial, confessional, familial, occupational, etc.) groups.[11]

Darwin's theory and its possible applications to the human species profoundly influenced the ideas about the "nature" of man and his possible futures, the "new man," which circulated in European cultures in the last decades of the nineteenth century.[12] It will suffice to mention the embodiment of the "laws of evolution" in the writings of one "failed biologist," who had learned these laws under the tutelage of their leading champion T. H. Huxley. This former biology teacher was none other than a founding father of a new literary genre, soon-to-be-named science fiction (SF), H. G. Wells.[13] His popular articles, such as "The Man of Million Year" (1893) and "Extinction of Man" (1894), as well as his SF novels, *The Time Machine* (1895), *War of the Worlds* (1897), and *The First Men in the Moon* (1901), were little more than literary projections of the possible outcomes of Darwin's theory's main principles of struggle for life and natural selection. They offered their readers artistic depictions of the possible future consequences of Darwin's "laws" for *Homo sapiens*, such as adaptation, divergence, improvement, degeneration, and extinction. Wells also attempted to examine the forces that could affect the future of the human species in nonfiction format. He published two series of essays: one in 1901 "Anticipations: An Experiment in Prophecy," and another in 1903 "Mankind in the Making."[14]

Wells was not alone in turning to Darwin's works in search of answers to the existential questions and attempts to envision possible human futures. The theory of evolution inspired many others the world over. In Russia, for example, Wilhelm Bitner, the publisher and editor of *Herald of Knowledge* (*Vestnik znaniia*), the country's most influential popular-science magazine, produced in 1903 a multivolume overview of the "greatest scientific and cultural acquisitions of the nineteenth century." The entire third part of this overview was titled "Whence, Whither, and What Are We?" and devoted to the implications of Darwin's theory to the past and the future of mankind.[15] The same year, Konstantin Merezhkovskii, a well-known botanist, published simultaneously in Russian and German a futuristic novel, titled *Earthly Paradise*, which, as Ricardo Nicolosi has recently demonstrated, was part and parcel of the extensive debate on degeneration spurred by Darwin's theory.[16] Three years later, Vladimir Shimkevich, an eminent zoology professor at St. Petersburg University, published a popular brochure, expressively titled *The Future of Mankind from a Naturalist's Viewpoint*, that was repeatedly updated and reissued up to its author's death in 1923.[17]

The Experimental Sciences of the New Man

Science, however, does not stand still. By the time H. G. Wells published his first SF novels, the scientific knowledge that underpinned them had become obsolescent. Another revolution had engulfed the studies of life. Its theoretical and methodological foundations were articulated in a number of seminal publications, including physiologist Claude Bernard's *Introduction à l'étude de la médecine expérimentale* (1865), psychologist Wilhelm Wundt's *Grundzüge der physiologischen Psychologie* (1874), chemist Louis Pasteur's *La théorie des germes et ses applications a la médecine et a la chirurgie* (1878), and physicist Hermann von Helmholtz's *Das Denken in der Medizin* (1878). This revolution prompted the formation of three new, closely entwined fields: experimental medicine, experimental psychology, and experimental biology, which together provided the foundation for what today we call the life sciences. The very names of these fields allude to the essence of the new revolution: the introduction of experimentalist spirit and experimental methods, largely borrowed from physics and chemistry, into the study of life. Armed with the new research techniques, numerous scientists around the world enthusiastically attacked the mysteries of human nature in both its material (bodily) and its immaterial (psychic) aspects. They launched systematic studies of basic life processes and their pathological alterations, including metabolism, reproduction, nervous and endocrine regulation, cell division, behavior, variability, sensory perception, aging, immunity, growth, and heredity. This new research dramatically changed the understanding of life and death, health and disease, the normal and the pathological, the psychical and the physical, and, as a result, of human nature and human destiny. Building on the works of René Descartes, Julien Offray de La Mettrie, and their numerous followers, these new studies developed the view of the bodily side of human nature as a chemical and physical "machine." At the same time, they promoted the understanding of the "spiritual" dimension of human nature (reason, will, language, creativity, mind, etc.) as function of the body's nervous system, first and foremost, the brain.

Circa 1900 this experimentalist revolution stimulated the rapid differentiation of new research directions and new disciplines within the life sciences, such as biophysics and immunology, biochemistry and developmental mechanics, endocrinology and reflexology, genetics and psychophysics, biogeochemistry and psycho-neurology, gerontology and hematology, biomechanics and psychotechnology, and many others. To pursue their new agendas, practitioners of these disciplines built new research institutions, including the Stazione Zoologica in Naples (1872), Institut für experimentelle Psychologie in Leipzig (1880), the Institut Pasteur in Paris (1888), the British Institute of Preventive Medicine in London (1891), the Rockefeller Institute for Medical Research in New York City (1901), and many others. New knowledge they produced quickly found applications in various branches of medicine, generating new diagnostic techniques, therapeutic treatments, surgical operations, and preventive measures. It underpinned exciting successes in tissue and organ transplantation; X-ray- and sero-diagnostics; sexual sterilization; blood transfusions; artificial insemination; cell and tissue cultivation; and hormone-, vitamin-, radium-, chemo-, and sero-therapies. It helped decipher certain basic mechanisms of sensory perception, behavior, heredity, cognition, and embryonic development. Most importantly, it changed the very image of the life sciences and scientists, engendering euphoric visions of science as an instrument of *control over life* and scientists as *engineers of life*.[18] Mikhail Zavadovskii, a leading Russian experimental biologist, put it succinctly:

> The time is near when successes in the study of living nature will create conditions for the flourishing of biotechnology (*biotekhnii*), alongside the technology of dead matter; the biologist's tasks in the field of creating new life forms, which at the moment seem akin to Wells's fantasy [*The Island of Dr. Moreau*], will become as mundane as those of a construction engineer.[19]

Captivated by such "visionary biology," as science historian Mark B. Adams has aptly named it, numerous scientists around the world came to believe that experimental research could provide them with new technologies to control the spread of diseases, expand individual lifespan, manipulate human reproduction, and create new life forms.[20] Indeed, to many scientists, it seemed that the new knowledge and the new technologies would enable them not merely to improve the present well-being of humanity dramatically but also to control its further development and evolution—plainly speaking, "making the new man."

As did their colleagues elsewhere, Russian scientists actively participated in the experimental revolution that engulfed the life sciences. In the decades *c.* 1900, they built institutions for the pursuit of their new research, including the Imperial Institute of Experimental Medicine (1890) that became a major base for Ivan Pavlov's studies, Vladimir Bekhterev's Institute of Psycho-neurology (1907), Georgii Chelpanov's Institute of Psychology (1912), and Nikolai Kol'tsov's Institute of Experimental Biology (1916). They also readily embraced the visions of control over life and death, human mind and body, and, ultimately, human nature and human destiny.

In 1903, the soon-to-be Nobel Prize winner Il'ia Mechnikov published a lengthy treatise, *Essays on Human Nature*, which became an international bestseller. Originally issued in French, and very soon appearing in Russian, English, and German versions, the book powerfully expressed its author's belief that "bettering human nature requires first of all deep knowledge."[21] According to Mechnikov, only science was capable of delivering the required knowledge and, hence, tools for such betterment: "To change human nature . . . [one] needs first of all to be aware of an ideal to which to strive, and then to use all the means science could provide to the realization of this ideal."[22]

Mechnikov's beliefs were echoed by Pavlov, who openly admitted in his Nobel lecture of 1904:

> Essentially, only one thing in life really interests us: our psychical nature. Its mechanism, however, was and still is shrouded in profound mystery. All of man's resources—art, religion, literature, philosophy, and the historical sciences—all

> have united in the attempt to shed light on this mystery. But man also has at his disposal one more mighty resource: natural science with its strictly objective methods. This science, as we all know, is achieving gigantic successes every day.[23]

According to Mechnikov, Pavlov, Bekhterev, Kol'tsov, and many other scientists, among all the various elements of culture—"art, religion, literature, philosophy, and the historical sciences"—only the experimental life sciences with their "gigantic successes" were capable of discovering "true" human nature and of finding means to "better" it.

During the first decades of the twentieth century, this belief in science facilitated rapid spread across the globe of the eugenics movement set on arresting the "degeneration" and assisting the "improvement" of the human species.[24] Successes in experimental studies of life led to the rethinking of the ways to intervene in humanity's evolutionary destiny. In the last third of the previous century these goals had been pursued through advocating for "hygienic" or "rational" marriages. The development of new tools for manipulating human reproduction—from sexual sterilization by surgery and irradiation to the use of sex hormones, sex-gland transplants, and artificial insemination—enhanced the appeal of ideas about "controlled" human evolution. It aided considerably the formation of a special discipline, eugenics, as Darwin's cousin Francis Galton had christened it, which became an important component of "visionary biology." The very subject of this new discipline became "the self-direction of human evolution."[25] During the first three decades of the twentieth century, eugenics was institutionalized in more than forty countries all over the world, including Russia. With Kol'tsov as a major "prophet" of the new discipline and his Institute of Experimental Biology as its major base, Russian psychiatrists, jurists, hygienists, gynecologists, sociologists, pediatricians, anthropologists, and especially practitioners of new experimental medicine, biology, and psychology, from geneticists to endocrinologists, enthusiastically organized eugenics laboratories, institutes, societies, journals, and conferences. They elaborated and passionately debated new instruments for "bettering human nature," as one Russian proponent of eugenics titled his 1927 textbook on the subject.[26]

New Worlds for New Men

"Visionary biology" exerted an enormous influence on the ideas about human nature and humanity's future, which permeated European cultures during the first third of the twentieth century.[27] Arguably, the most famous example of this influence is *Brave New World*, a futuristic novel published in 1932 by another "failed biologist," Aldous Huxley—a grandson of the very same T. H. Huxley who had taught biology to H. G. Wells and a younger brother of Julian Huxley, a leading British experimental biologist of the time.[28] There is no need to recount the novel's contents or legacies here.[29] But it is worthwhile pointing out certain circumstances of its creation and, especially, some of its scientific underpinnings.[30]

In 1929, Julian Huxley, together with H. G. Wells and his son, zoologist G. P. Wells, published a monumental, three-volume treatise addressed to the general public and titled simply *The Science of Life*.[31] According to Julian Huxley, he and Wells Jr. wrote the bulk of the treatise, for Wells Sr. "had forgotten much of his biology and what he remembered was by now old-fashioned."[32] The volumes thus offered their readers in a very accessible form a virtual encyclopedia of nearly all the latest and coming advances in the study of life. Many of these advances of new experimental research in biology, medicine, and psychology described in the volumes—ranging from Pavlovian conditioning and Freudian psychoanalysis to the chemical manipulation of embryonic development and the hormonal regulation of fertility—became the very foundations of the future New World and the humans who inhabit it envisioned by Aldous Huxley.

Aldous undoubtedly incorporated into his novel many facts and conceptions engendered by new research in the experimental life sciences that his older brother had described in *The Science of Life*. As Julian Huxley recounted in his memoirs, during the winter of 1927–8, Aldous witnessed his work on the treatise directly and participated regularly in the discussions of its contents.[33] But the book's general idea that this new knowledge could provide suitable instruments to control human life and to affect dramatically humanity's future came not from his brother but from Aldous's longtime friend (since his school years at Eton), J. B. S. Haldane, a rising star of British experimental biology.

In November 1923, a special book series established by a London publisher under the evocative title "To-day and to-morrow" was inaugurated by Haldane's lengthy essay on *Daedalus, or Science and the Future* that forcefully articulated this very idea.[34] The "science" in the essay's title was not physics or chemistry, but the new experimental science of life. As Haldane emphatically put it: "The centre of scientific interest lies in biology"; and further: "The biologist is the most romantic figure on earth at the present day." It was not Daedalus's invention of flight or the engineering feat of creating the Labyrinth, but his role in producing the Minotaur, the first "interspecies hybrid," "part man and part bull"—his "only recorded success in experimental genetics," in Haldane's words—that justified his prominent place in the book's title.

The essay proved very popular and highly influential: in just three years it went through seven printings.[35] It sparked heated polemics among and elicited responses from a number of famous British intellectuals, including Bertrand Russell's rebuff pointedly titled *Icarus, or the Future of Science* and published in the same series in 1924.[36] Haldane continued to advocate for this idea in many subsequent essays and books. Indeed, as Mark B. Adams has convincingly argued, it became an essential part of his lifelong credo. He further elaborated it in a sequel to *Daedalus*, titled "The Last Judgement," which was published in 1927 nearly simultaneously in Britain and the United States.[37] The US version carried a subtitle, "A Scientist Turns to Prophecy," that unobtrusively invited its readership to appreciate the essay's differences from the much older "Experiment in Prophecy" published by H. G. Wells at the turn of the twentieth century.

Aldous Huxley attentively followed the polemics spurred by Haldane's futuristic visions. Indeed, one of the principal foundations of his Brave New World, "ectogenesis"—growing human embryos in artificial wombs—came straight from Haldane's *Daedalus*. But his cautionary tale of "the world controllers" and the possible abuses of the power furnished by new biological knowledge derived directly from Russell's *Icarus*, as well as from his older brother's experiment in literary fiction, a "biological phantasy" published in 1926 under the title "Tissue Culture King."[38] In the foreword written for the Vanguard Library edition some twenty years after the novel's first publication, the author himself explained its "biological" focus:

> The theme of Brave New World is not the advancement of science as such; it is the advancement of science as it affects human individuals. The triumphs of physics, chemistry and engineering are tacitly taken for granted. The only scientific advances to be specifically described are those involving the application to human beings of the results of future research in biology, physiology and psychology. It is only by means of the sciences of life that the quality of life can be radically changed.[39]

Brave New World then was a pointed literary commentary on the projects, promises, and prophesies of scientists preoccupied with the search for the means to control human nature in the hope of shaping humanity's future and "making the new man."

The profound impact of the new experimental life sciences on the visions of the "coming man" was by no means confined to the 1920s British cultural scene. It was manifest in a variety of cultural productions in France and Germany, Italy and the United States, and elsewhere. As witnessed by Platonov's writings, Russia was no exception. Indeed, scores of writers, philosophers, theater and cinema directors, state officials, scientists, and artists in Bolshevik Russia grounded their own visions of the "new world" and the "new man" in the knowledge supplied by the new bio-psycho-medical disciplines. A 1928 novel, titled *Valley of New Life*, provides a close parallel and a precursor (both literally and figuratively) to *Brave New World*.[40]

Published under the enigmatic pseudonym Theo Elie, this novel came from the pen of Fedor Il'in, a physician who had been engaged in experimental studies of new exciting biomedical subjects, ranging from the effects of radium on malignant tumors to the possibilities of using artificial insemination to fight infertility.[41] It depicts the first stages, as it were, in the creation of what could become a "brave new world," whose basic contours Aldous Huxley would have no trouble recognizing. Set in an isolated valley in the Himalayas and narrated by one of the valley's inhabitants, French electrical engineer Rene Ger'e, the novel portrays a new civilization being created by a clan of American billionaires, the Queensleys. With the help of leading scientists and engineers, whom they "import" by co-option or coercion to the valley from around the world, the Queensleys populate this new Atlantis with a race of super-advanced human beings. According to their plans, this new race—armed with superior science and technology, including the use of atomic energy, synthetic foods, and mind control—is destined to conquer and remake the "old" world.

The "valley of new life" exemplifies humanity's triumph over Nature through science and technology. The valley's inhabitants enjoy technologies still unheard of in the "old" world. They use atomic energy, ride superfast "magnetic" trains, transmit electricity wirelessly, and fly on "electrical wings." But, much as in *Brave New World*, it is incredible advances in various bio-psycho-medical technologies that make the valley a true place of the future. The narrator apologizes tongue in cheek for "possible inaccuracies" in his descriptions of these technologies because he "lacks fundamental biological training." But he asserts that he "cannot avoid biology because it occupies such a prominent place in everything I had lived through." Indeed, the most astonishing feature of the valley—a new race of human beings, which comprises its "native" population—is created by the application of new biotechnologies developed by scientists and engineers the Queensleys brought to the valley from all over the world, including Russia. In fact, the creator of the new race is a "Russian zoologist, renowned for his work in artificial insemination and animal hybridization," named Petrovskii.[42] As in the "brave new world," the ultimate goal of all the efforts by the inhabitants of the "valley of new life" is to make humanity happy. But, in the words of Petrovskii, "the only way to reach happiness on earth is to re-make humanity."

Much like Huxley's novel, *Valley of New Life* also offered its readers a wide-ranging anthology of contemporary advances in the life sciences that could enable such remaking of humanity, along with the hopes and fears, expectations and anxieties, promises and concerns spurred by these advances. As the narrator explains, "there was nothing fantastic, in the exact sense of the word," in all the bio-psycho-medical technologies employed in the valley: "There were only the advances of science, the beginnings of which had been known in Europe."[43] Like the inhabitants of the "brave new world," the race of super-humans populating the "valley of new life" is created by means of in vitro fertilization and ectogenesis—gestation of human embryos in "incubatoriums." Like the residents of the "brave new world," various manipulations on the embryos divided them into different "casts" destined to perform specific tasks. In both novels, the accelerated development, upbringing, and education of these new humans are based on the use of hormones and chemical preparations, "mind control" and conditioning. In both "new worlds," the thoughts, emotions, and general mental states of their inhabitants are carefully manipulated: in Huxley's by hypnopedia, Community Sings, and Solidarity Services; in Il'in's by "séances of joy" and "telepathic suggestions."

In both novels, the new biology brings about a new sociology. The family is no longer the main unit of social organization among the natives of both "new worlds." They have no parents, siblings, spouses, and children, indeed, no relatives at all. They do not experience feelings, sentiments, and emotions associated with such biological and social roles. They have no family names. Il'in's creatures carry only numbers (echoing Eugenii Zamiatin's famous novel *We*) and occasionally nicknames, while Huxley's possess the names referring to the cultural heroes and founding fathers of their "brave new world," from Ford and Freud to Marx and Lenin to Darwin and Helmholtz. In Huxley's world, the very words "mother" and "father" are obscenities; in Il'in's, they are used only in figurative ways: one of the "natives" declares that "our mother is Nature, and our father is Science."

Furthermore, in full accord with the grim predictions of Russell's *Icarus*, in both novels it is the powers that be—the ten world controllers in Huxley's and the Queensleys in Il'in's—that use various instruments furnished by science to control their populations. Even more, the same powers seek to control science itself. As the Resident Controller for Western Europe Mustapha Mond puts it in *Brave New World*: "Science is dangerous; we have to keep it most carefully chained and muzzled. . . .

It has given us the stablest equilibrium in history. . . . But we can't allow science to undo its own good work."[44] As if in support of this declaration, in *Valley of New Life*, it is the very same scientists who had provided the Queensleys with "mind control" technologies who also invented a special device that shields their own minds from being "read" and "controlled," which becomes a critical means of the novel's narrator's escape from the valley.

What could explain such remarkable parallels, as well as certain notable differences, in the writings of the British and the Russian authors? What could they tell us about the intersections of the life sciences and culture over the notions of the "new man" in their respective homelands?

The New Man as a Cultural Resource: Professional, Popular, and Fictional Science

Huxley's and Il'in's novels epitomized the end results of the transformation of specialized, often quite arcane, new scientific knowledge about human origins and human nature (both body and soul) into an element of a particular *cultural resource* identified by the general label "new man," which became a constitutive component of both British and Russian contemporary cultures.[45] This transformation included three interconnected processes: the production of new knowledge; its translation into a language accessible to the general public; and its uses by a variety of interested parties, including philosophers, educators, theologians, politicians, literati, artists, and scientists.

The professionalization and differentiation of knowledge production, which unfolded in the course of the nineteenth century, rested on developing research practices and instruments, building organizational structures, securing patronage, recruiting and training personnel, and establishing social legitimacy. It also involved creating a specialized vocabulary in each particular area of scientific studies. The major purpose of this vocabulary was to build internal consensus over specific research subjects, objectives, and practices shared by a group of scientists. It also served to erect intellectual, methodological, and institutional boundaries with other, often competing groups and cultural domains, such as religion, philosophy, and literature. Created within all scientific disciplines, such highly specialized vocabularies were often completely incomprehensible to the uninitiated. Yet the necessities of maintaining the social infrastructures of their vocation (particularly patronage, legitimacy, and recruitment) also required scientists to make their esoteric pursuits understandable to a broader public, especially to prospective patrons and students, critics and supporters.

These conflicting demands of internal coherence and external legitimacy led to the eventual divergence of scientific writings into two subgenres: professional and popular.[46] Each subgenre developed its own styles, norms, conventions, and venues. Most important, the popular-science writings translated (both literally and figuratively) the decidedly technical vocabularies of professional scientists into a language accessible to any literate person. But they did more than that. To explicate and explain scientists' professional jargons, popular-science works infused particular pieces of knowledge with highly metaphorical connotations, subtexts, inferences, and allusions by referring their readers to the popular images, icons, and clichés of world cultures. As we saw on the previous pages, these popular images ranged from the Greek myths of Daedalus and Icarus to the "monsters" of Wells's Dr. Moreau. As a result, scientific knowledge was transformed into a cultural resource readily accessible not just to scientists working in particular disciplines and their colleagues, but to any other social group. Each of these groups sought to exploit this resource to their own ends that quite often were at odds with the stated goals of scientists who had produced the knowledge in question.[47]

Around the turn of the twentieth century, the rapid and massive infusion of popular-scientific knowledge into contemporary cultures prompted the arrival of a new literary genre, called variously scientific romance, scientific fantasy, scientific fiction, scientifiction, and finally, science fiction.[48] As its very names clearly attest, this genre became a preferred vehicle for exploiting the new resource by scores of cultural figures. The use of words "science" and "scientific" as modifiers of such nouns as "romance," "fiction," and "fantasy" signaled unambiguously the cultural recognition of the rapidly growing role of science in the life of humanity and its great potential in shaping humanity's future. Not surprisingly, concurrent advances in the life sciences that claimed to answer the existential questions of human nature and human destiny became favorite subjects of numerous SF stories.

Wells, Huxley, Il'in, and many others used their SF writings to address the implications of the new sciences of human body and soul for the human future, embodied in the notions of the "new men." They created a variety of "subspecies"—particular ideals—of the "new men" that scientists' discoveries promised to make real in the nearest future.[49] They sought to identify the basic units, from which the "new men" would be created: individual, family, labor collective, clan, nation, race, or humanity as a whole. They discussed possible directions of the future development: spiritual, anatomical, physiological, moral, intellectual, technical, and social. Some writers focused on bodily forms and functions, depicting beautiful, healthy, and even immortal bodies of the "coming men," or special modifications that would adapt them to the extreme environmental conditions of life in oceanic depths, on other planets, and in space, and even bodiless human brains supported by complex machinery as the next step in human evolution. Others explored psychical developments, ranging from mind-reading villains and all-around geniuses to "communal" and "disembodied" minds. Still others examined social roles, relations, and structures that would characterize the "new men" of the future. They pondered possible outcomes of such developments: divergence, degeneration, and extinction of humankind, or, to the contrary, improvements and further progress, leading to the emergence of "men like gods" (H. G. Wells), "physiological collectives" (A. Bogdanov), "super-organisms" akin to ant hills or beehives (K. Merezhkovskii), "group minds" (O. Stapledon), "robots" (K. Čapek), and "amphibious men" (A. Beliaev). They debated the motive forces of such developments: the will of God or the desires of Man, the laws of Nature or the laws of History, scientific technologies or esoteric practices, the agendas of state institutions or the ambitions of individual scientists, physicians, and engineers. They estimated their speed: a slow millions-year-long evolution, as in Wells's *The Time Machine* and Olaf

Stapledon's *Last and First Man*, or a rapid revolution, taking just a few centuries, as in Bogdanov's *Red Star* and *Engineer Menni*. They considered various instruments for "making the new man"—from organ transplants and blood transfusions to telepathic suggestion and interspecies hybridization to ectogenesis and artificial insemination.[50] Some of these SF visions were optimistic, hailing the bright new future ahead and the "men like gods" who would inhabit it. Others were pessimistic, prophesying inevitable catastrophes triggered by scientists' meddling with Nature in general, and human nature in particular. Taken together these SF writings articulated the hopes and fears, expectations and anxieties, promises and concerns inspired by the recent advances of the life sciences in the imaginations of members of the educated public and expressed in the visions of the "coming men."[51]

Given the multiplicity of the subspecies of the "new men" created by a variety of actors, the very phrase "new man" acquired numerous different and often contradictory meanings. Indeed, the phrase itself is nothing more than a convenient label. It obscures what exactly is hidden under this universal label. It covers an amalgam of a dizzying array of ideas, conceptions, images, symbols, ideals, fears, expectations, practices, beliefs, clichés, and fantasies regarding human nature and its possible (desirable or undesirable) future changes, circulating in a particular setting. Only a detailed analysis of the actual contents of this amalgam—its constitutive elements, their origins, historical changes, and interrelations—coupled with an examination of the particular networks of actors involved in its articulation and propagation, could reveal what the phrase "new man" actually means in the cultural productions of particular historical figures, be they writers, scientists, theologians, cinematographers, artists, or politicians.

Traditionally, scholars of culture focus predominantly on images and texts, manifestos and symbols, styles and techniques, characters and plots, contexts and discourses. They often pay very little, if any, attention to scientific and technological ideas, objects, agents, and practices that figure in the cultural products they examine.[52] However, a study of metaphorical and nonmetaphorical uses of science and technology in any cultural field allows one to discern not only the interrelations between science and other cultural domains as relatively independent social institutions. It also uncovers ideas, anxieties, expectations, biases, promises, fears, ideals, concerns, and hopes, spurred by advancing science and technology in the minds of individuals and social groups comprising a particular society.

In this respect, an examination of "undergirding" scientific/technological elements in various cultural products opens interesting possibilities, especially for illuminating the particular features of the "new man" visions in specific settings. Such particularity could be determined only by careful comparison of visions prevalent in different settings.[53] Indeed, comparison is the absolutely crucial, but alas often neglected, foundation for any pronouncements on temporal and/or spatial particularities of ideas about the "new man."

In light of a comparative approach, analyses of scientific/technological elements in various visions of the "new man" could be particularly instructive, because, in the popular belief actively promoted by scientists themselves, the most characteristic feature of science is its *universality*. In plain language, such universality means that scientific knowledge—be it the laws of mechanics, thermodynamics, or evolution—is true no matter where such knowledge was produced, say, in Britain or in Russia. As Platonov put it in his essay:

> Science has never been national. The way of human thinking is the same in all countries. Nature made the [human] brain the same everywhere. Any scientific discovery happens only once and only in one country. It is absurd to discover, say, radio twice. After the first discovery, the second makes no sense. Radio cannot be Russian, German, or Italian, it is simply radio.[54]

Such universality implies that the results of scientific studies conducted in one locale could—indeed must—be verified in another setting. It is in this sense that science and scientific knowledge are customarily considered to be inter- or transnational.[55] Therefore, according to this viewpoint, experimental studies of life, along with knowledge, technologies, and visions they generate, must also be universal and transnational. It is then quite likely that this universality might explain certain similarities among various local versions of the "new man" based on scientific knowledge, technologies, and visions, whether such "subspecies" are found in Britain, Russia, Germany, Italy, or elsewhere. For instance, it is possible that some of the parallels between Aldous Huxley's and Fedor Il'in's novels derived not only from the common bio-psycho-medical knowledge they incorporated but also from both authors' familiarity with the visions expressed in Haldane's *Daedalus* and Russell's *Icarus*; both essays were translated into Russian and published under the same cover in 1926.[56]

The New Man in Bolshevik Culture

Historians of science, however, have long questioned claims regarding the universal and transnational character of science considered merely as an organized system of knowledge. They have argued that not only the organization and operations of science as a social institution but also the production of scientific knowledge is always intrinsically *local*.[57] Science is deeply enmeshed in the social fabric of a specific time, place, society, state, language, and culture. This "social dimension" is necessarily reflected in the contents of cultural resources formed on the basis of scientific knowledge, and it might explain certain differences in the "new man" visions popular in separate settings or among different groups of people.

Russia presents a particularly illuminating case in this regard, for the Bolshevik social revolution coincided with the peak of the experimentalist revolution in the life sciences. Prior to 1917, the social and cognitive arrangements of the life sciences in Russia had differed little from those elsewhere. But after the Bolshevik revolution, they underwent considerable transformations.[58] The most important one was "nationalization"—the establishment of *exclusively* state patronage for all scientific research and researchers. Science, in a sense, became a "property" of the state. The nationalization stimulated the rapid development of mutually beneficial, "symbiotic" relations between the Russian scientific community and the newborn Bolshevik state. It enabled the unprecedented quantitative growth of scientific institutions and personnel. It made "doing science" a mass occupation and increased the prestige of science and scientists in Soviet society considerably. In just two decades the country was transformed from a quiet province into a bustling center of world science.

The nationalization affected, however, not only the size and social relations of science. It also considerably modified its cognitive structures and epistemic boundaries.[59] The absence of alternative funding sources made science and scientists hostages to the party-state apparatus's shifting priorities in all spheres of life: economy, politics, ideology, and culture. Under such conditions, those directions of scientific research, which were perceived by the apparatchiki as corresponding to their priorities, received nearly unlimited funding and developed rapidly; those, which were not, lost state support and withered away, or were outright banned.

In this respect, during the first decade of the Bolshevik rule, the life sciences appeared very fortunate. The Bolsheviks considered them a principal foundation for the rapid modernization of three vitally important areas: medicine/public health, agriculture, and education. Furthermore, they also deemed them critical for fulfilling the many promises the Bolsheviks made to their social base, the previously oppressed classes of the proletariat and the peasantry, in improving the miserable conditions of life and labor they had endured under capitalism.[60] Moreover, the recent advances in the life sciences (both evolutionary theory and experimental results) became the Bolsheviks' favorite weapon in the fight against their sworn ideological enemy—religion and its notions of God-created *Orbis et Hominis*.

More important, however, new "visionary biology" resonated deeply with the "revolutionary dreams" (in historian Richard Stites's astute characterization) of creating a "new world" and a "new society," which thoroughly imbued Russian culture in the aftermath of the Bolshevik takeover.[61] A key element of these "revolutionary dreams" was the "new man." From its very birth, the Bolsheviks' foundational doctrine, Marxism, had been saturated with ideas about a "new man"—the "gravedigger" of capitalism and the builder of a future communist society; and the construction of such communist future was the proclaimed ultimate goal of the Bolshevik revolution.[62]

It comes as no surprise, then, that some Russian Marxists greeted with much enthusiasm the intense studies and development of various bio-psycho-medical technologies for "making the new man" pursued by "visionary biologists" before and particularly after the Bolsheviks seized power. Aside from the well-known case of Alexander Bogdanov, who had been deeply engaged in both philosophical analysis and practical applications of one such technology—blood transfusions,[63] it will suffice to recall the oft-cited 1923 statement by Leon Trotsky. The second-in-command in the Bolshevik leadership at the time spoke eloquently about the creation "under our own fingers," with the help of "the most complicated methods of artificial selection and psychophysical training," of a "higher socio-biological type, an overman (*sverkhchelovek*), if you will."[64] A year later, another prominent Bolshevik, Nikolai Semashko, the head of the Commissariat of Health Protection (Narkomzdrav) and arguably the most important patron of Soviet bio-psycho-medical research and researchers, emphasized the role of "biological analysis" in addressing any social problem. A "Marxist-naturalist," as he characterized himself, lamented on the pages of a leading literary magazine that "In our country, little attention has so far been paid to biology (perhaps because our leading Marxists were sociologists, economists, and politicians, not biologists)." But, he insisted, "it is biological elucidation that is often necessary to solve even seemingly pure social and economic problems."[65] Trotsky, Semashko, and many other top-level Bolsheviks became influential and eager patrons of the new experimental life sciences.

This resonance between the "visionary biology" of Russian scientists and the "revolutionary dreams" of their patrons in the party-state apparatus prompted the tremendous expansion of research in, and rapid institutionalization of, new bio-psycho-medical disciplines during the first postrevolutionary decade. The Bolsheviks generously funded the revival of the old, and the establishment of numerous new, research institutions in biophysics and biochemistry, genetics and endocrinology, hematology and developmental mechanics, eugenics and psychotechnology.[66] They supported the creation of research establishments for the experimental studies of physical and mental labor, maternity and infancy, childhood and adolescence, endemic and occupational diseases, as well as many other subjects they deemed relevant to their "revolutionary dreams."

The country's new rulers also put considerable efforts into the widest popularization of the life sciences and their latest discoveries. Hundreds of articles, posters, plays, pamphlets, films, and books produced during the 1920s by scientists, writers, doctors, state and party officials, theater and cinema directors, journalists, artists, and philosophers successfully translated arcane specialized knowledge generated by the experimental life sciences into the language accessible to any literate person.[67] It was this huge mass of popular-science productions that became the main source of scientific knowledge for all participants in cultural processes, from writers like Platonov to moviemakers like Vsevolod Pudovkin. It was these productions that enabled the rapid and extensive infusion of the life sciences' newest advances into the cultural resource hidden under the label "new man."

This, in turn, led to very considerable changes in the contents of this resource. The Bolsheviks' active support of the life sciences "scientified," as it were, the beliefs in the leading role of upbringing, learning, and education in "making the new man," which had been a key component of this resource since the Enlightenment. Such "scientification" could be readily seen in the rapidly growing during the 1920s popularity and institutional structures of two new disciplines. One of them was pedology (*pedologiia*) that advanced bio-psycho-medical studies of childhood.[68] Another was psychotechnology (*psikhotekhnika*) that focused on experimental studies of particular physical and mental abilities, and developing methods of specialized training, for different professions, occupations, and vocations in all spheres of life, from opera singing to operating steam engines.[69] Both of them embraced the popular interpretations of upbringing, education, and learning as little more than the formation of new reflexes actively promoted by Bekhterev, Pavlov, and their numerous students. At the same time their practitioners persistently attempted to apply such interpretations to pedagogical practices. For instance, one of Pavlov's collaborators produced a monumental volume titled *The Doctrine of Conditional Reflexes as a Foundation of Pedagogy*, while a popular book, written by one of Bekhterev's followers and titled *Reflexology and Pedagogy*, was issued six times in as many years.[70] Of course, similar processes unfolded in the West, as witnessed by the oft-cited boast by the founder of behaviorism John Watson:

> Give me a dozen healthy infants, well-formed, and my own specified world to bring them up in and I'll guarantee to take any one at random and train him to become any type of specialist I might select—doctor, lawyer, artist, merchant-chief and, yes, even beggar-man and thief, regardless of his talents, penchants, tendencies, abilities, vocations, and race of his ancestors.[71]

But during the 1920s such radical approaches arguably did not attain as much popularity in the West as in Bolshevik Russia, even though "Pavlovian conditioning" figures prominently in *Brave New World*.

The Bolsheviks' strict control over the contents and distribution of all printed materials (as well as all other cultural products) also completely excised from the notions of the "new man" nearly all "idealistic" (theological, mystical, theosophist, spiritualistic, occult, and anthroposophist) interpretations of human nature and humanity's future, which had been very much in vogue prior to 1917.[72] At the same time, such control effectively muzzled any critique of the Bolsheviks' own "materialistic" interpretations of these issues, as happened, for instance, to Mikhail Bulgakov's novella "Dog's Heart," whose publication was explicitly forbidden by the direct order of Lev Kamenev, a leader of the Bolsheviks.[73]

Even this very short description suggests that cultural resources in particular societies are much more local and specific than the scientific knowledge that often undergirds such resources. A comparative analysis of the scientific contents of the "new man" visions, then, allows one to discern the differences in the very position of the life sciences within the culture of a society, in the societal attitudes toward bio-psycho-medical research and researchers, in the evaluation of their results, and in their acceptance or rejection by the society.

For example, the disappearance of the family as a result of new bio-psycho-medical technologies leads to very different outcomes in Il'in's and in Huxley's novels. In *Brave New World*, founded as it is on Sigmund Freud's theories of mind and human development, sex becomes the major instrument of upbringing, socialization, and social interactions among its inhabitants (recall its main motto, "every one belongs to every one else"). In contrast, in *Valley of New Life*, sex is completely absent, men and women live in separate settlements, and its "native" population lost "all sexual features and passions so detrimentally affecting the modern man all over the world."[74] Even more, the entire "production" of women is limited to just 5,000 per year, for "they appeared unsuitable for the Valley of New Life, because they are physically weaker than men and distinguished by a less stable character."[75] Such drastically different societal consequences of applying basically the same technologies that separated sex and reproduction undoubtedly reflect not merely the personal tastes of the novels' authors. They also point to significant differences between their respective homelands as regards both particular directions of scientific research on, and societal attitudes to, the "sexual revolution" that unfolded *c.* 1900.[76] Many of Platonov's 1920s essays, including "The Breeding Pen of the New Man" and especially the essay evocatively titled "Antisexus," treat the questions of sex in a manner very similar to Il'in's.

The image of "mad" or "evil" scientist that became extraordinarily popular in Western cultures in the first third of the twentieth century offers another revealing example. The popularity of this image was manifest in the cinematographic revival of Mary Shelly's 1818 classic, *Frankenstein*, and the popular identification of Victor Frankenstein, not as Prometheus of the novel's subtitle, but as the "monster" he created.[77] In the cultural productions of Soviet authors, this image appeared predominantly in "capitalist" settings, as exemplified by Queensley Jr. in the *Valley of New Life* or the lead protagonists of two very popular SF novels by Alexander Beliaev, the American Kern in *The Head of Professor Dowell* (1926) and the German Shtirner in *Ruler of the World* (1926). It appeared in "socialist" settings only as a "spy" and/or an "enemy" set on destroying the Soviet Union and its people. Furthermore, the image of "evil" or "mad" scientist was nearly always directly juxtaposed to the image of "true Soviet" scientist. Under the pens of Soviet writers, scientists working in the land of victorious proletarian revolution could be "naïve," "politically illiterate," "impractical," "childish," and "eccentric" (such as, for instance, Dugov and Kachinskii from the same *Ruler of the World*), but never "mad" or "evil." Even in openly critical and satirical portrayals, for example, in Bulgakov's famous novellas "Fateful Eggs" and "Dog's Heart," it is not the scientists, but the world surrounding them that "goes mad" with the Bolshevik revolution. The protagonists themselves, Professors Persikov and Preobrazhenskii, retain the full ability to diagnose (albeit not to cure) this madness. Moreover, attempts by some contemporary Western observers to characterize certain Soviet research (for instance, Sergei Briukhonenko's experiments with severed dog heads) as "inhumane," and scientists themselves as "servants of Satan" and "creatures of Hell," were immediately rebuffed by the Soviet press.[78]

From the Engineers of Life to the Engineers of Human Souls

This necessarily brief overview indicates that the expression "new man" is but a simple label affixed to a complex amalgam of very different and often contradictory ideas and ideals of the future and human nature, circulating among certain groups of people in particular settings. This amalgam forms an influential cultural resource open for exploitation to any participants in the cultural process, including writers, scientists, politicians, philosophers, artists, theologians, and educators, who use this resource to their own ends.

Since the last few decades of the nineteenth century, in many countries around the globe, this resource became saturated with scientific knowledge generated by the systematic studies of life. Circa 1900 rapid advances of experimental research produced a variety of bio-psycho-medical technologies, which transferred control over humanity's future from the "blind" laws of Nature into the capable hands of "engineers of life"—scientists engaged in this kind of research and creating such technologies. During the first third of the twentieth century the place that the life sciences came to occupy in the contents of this cultural resource rapidly expanded, thanks to the translation of scientists' esoteric findings into the language accessible to any literate person accomplished by the massive popularization of scientific discoveries. This cultural expansion was manifest in the rapid growth of a large subset of a new literary genre, SF, that provided pointed commentary on the projects, promises, and prophesies of scientists preoccupied with the search for the means to control human nature in the hope of shaping humanity's future and "making the new man."

In Russia, the Bolshevik revolution that coincided with the peak of the experimentalist revolution gave these worldwide processes particular forms. In the first postrevolutionary decade, the popularity of proposals to employ bio-psycho-medical technologies for "bettering human nature" and "making the new man," rose dramatically, thanks to a deep resonance between the "visionary biology" of Russian scientists and the "revolutionary dreams" of their Bolshevik patrons. As Platonov's "The Man That Will Be," Il'in's *Valley of New Life*, and many other cultural productions of the time make clear, these proposals became a major component of the cultural resource hidden under the label "new man." They displaced all "idealistic," especially, theological and supernatural, elements from the contents of this resource. They also "scientified" the beliefs in the important role of upbringing, learning, and education in "making the new man," which had been a key component of this resource since the Enlightenment.

The ascendancy of bio-psycho-medical technologies and scientists creating such technologies in defining the contours of the "new man" visions and actual efforts of bringing such visions to life did not last long in Soviet Russia. Just half a year after the countrywide celebrations of the tenth anniversary of the Bolshevik revolution, a new "revolution from above" radically reshaped the economic, political, and cultural landscapes of the Soviet Union. This new revolution led to the consolidation of Joseph Stalin's personal rule over the party-state apparatus, and of that apparatus's tight and brutal control over the country's population.[79] It extinguished the "revolutionary dreams" of the preceding decade, replacing them with a rigid, though constantly shifting, "party line" and five-year plans. It sharply diminished the cultural authority of both bio-psycho-medical technologies and scientists, creating such technologies, in envisioning and shaping the future of humanity and in the notions of the "new man." Despite Platonov's determined efforts, he was unable to publish his essays "The Man That Will Be" and "Antisexus," or his novels, which articulated and examined some of those "revolutionary dreams." Neither did the second volume of Il'in's *Valley of New Life* see the light of day.[80] The dissolution of the Russian Eugenics Society in 1930 and the subsequent disappearance of eugenics from the discussions on the "new man" became a telling sign of the new times.[81]

In the course of the 1930s, all attempts at bio-psycho-medical "controls" of the future came to be seen—and summarily dismissed—as the "pernicious" "bourgeois" *biologization* of human nature, as demonstrated by a special party edict that banished pedology in 1936 and by the curtailment of research on human genetics around the same time.[82] They were rapidly replaced by the Marxist interpretations of man as a product of *exclusively social*, first and foremost, labor and economic, relations, as witnessed by an unsigned article that appeared in 1929 in the journal *Revolution and Culture* under the title "The Thoughts of Marx and Lenin on the Social Division of

Labor and the 'New Man.'"[83] Soviet Marxists did not deny the role of such biological factors as variability, heredity, and natural selection (which formed a foundation of Darwin's theory) in the *past* evolution of the human species. But, for them, that role had ended with the emergence of "labor" and "class society," at which point social, economic, and cultural factors took over the determination of a further development of humanity. As one young Marxist philosopher put it, in the human evolution there occurred a "transition from the leading role of natural selection to the leading role of labor."[84]

In the 1930s, party ideologues and functionaries, not scientists, spearheaded efforts to envision and define the future of the country, its populations, and humanity as a whole. They shunned the new technologies offered by the experimental life sciences. Instead, they resorted to propaganda, inculcation, and terror. In this situation, the Enlightenment era's beliefs in upbringing, learning, and education as the main tools of "making the new men" reclaimed the primary place in the contents of cultural resources covered by this label.[85] From now on, the future *Homo novus* was to be created not by managing reproduction or altering heredity, but by manipulating upbringing and education. It was no longer the scientist, but the writer who was given the role of the *engineer* responsible for "making the new man." The only subject of such "engineering" became not the human body, but "human souls."[86] By the end of the 1930s, in the familiar duality of human nature, the social had "dialectically negated" the biological.[87]

5

Entertaining Sciences, Unlikely Horrors

The Changing Image of Man in Soviet Popular-Scientific Literary Genres

Matthias Schwartz

Science, art, and literature are hothouse plants demanding warmth and respect and service. It is the paradox of science that it alters the whole world and is produced by the genius of men who need protection and help more than any other class of worker.
H. G. Wells (1921)[1]

It was on August 1, 1934 that a memorable meeting took place in the famous Hotel Astoria, a neoclassical Art Nouveau building on St. Isaac Square in Leningrad. The English writer H. G. Wells had come for a two-day visit from Moscow, where he had conducted his legendary interview with Joseph Stalin a few days before.[2] During his first day in Leningrad, he had already visited some prominent sightseeing places, accompanied by a delegation including the Noble Prize–winning physiologist Ivan Pavlov and the most prominent writer of the time, Aleksei N. Tolstoi, author of the allegedly first "Soviet" science-fiction novel *Aėlita* (1922–3).[3]

The following evening, here in the hotel, he was to meet a small circle of three of his greatest admirers, all professionally engaged in the popularization of science, as well as two representatives of publishing houses and one translator. The first devotee was Nikolai Alekseevich Rynin, a key activist, organizer, and pioneer in early aeronautics and space rocket developments, but also author of the first encyclopedia on space travel worldwide, the comprehensive nine volumes of *Interplanetary Communications*, published between 1928 and 1932.[4] The second was the most well-known science popularizer of the early Soviet Union, Iakov Isidorovich Perel'man, author of hundreds of books and articles mainly on physics, astronomy, and space flight.[5] The third was Alexander Romanovich Beliaev, then the country's most successful and important writer of the emerging genre of science fiction, the "Soviet Jules Verne," as he was later called.[6]

Three decades later, Grigorii Mishkevich, one of the publishers' representatives, wrote a memoir of this meeting, according to which the two science popularizers and the two writers talked about one thing in particular: the function of literature in times of political conflicts and war.[7] In Wells's words: "The task of any writer, especially those working in the science fiction genre, is to foresee the social and psychological shifts generated by the progress of civilization. The task of literature is to improve humanity."[8] Even if this transcript of a memory is anything but reliable,[9] it does point precisely toward the topic that Wells had been working on for the last decades: to participate in creating a better mankind through his popular-scientific and literary works. Moreover, as I will argue in this chapter, this meeting of the three Soviet writers and the English author is highly symbolic. As the careers of the four persons show, the challenge of constructing a "new man" with the help of science and literature was approached very differently in Western Europe and the Soviet Union.

For H. G. Wells, this meeting was symbolic also because it was already his third visit to Russia.[10] The last time he had been in the city, in September 1920, the town had been devastated by the First World War, the revolution, and the civil war. This shocked him deeply: Only ruins remained of the former glory, of the flourishing metropole, of the Russian tsarist Empire, the restaurants and shops were closed, the people were starving.[11] What appalled Wells most, however, was the condition of the scientists he met in the House of Sciences, who not only suffered from physical hunger but were also completely cut off intellectually from all new scientific developments and publications: "Seeing all these distinguished men living a sort of refugee life amidst the impoverished ruins of the fallen imperialist system has made me realize how helplessly dependent the man of exceptional gifts is upon a securely organized civilization."[12]

This insight into the total collapse of a civilization that was deficient, but somehow still functioning, strengthened his view that the Bolsheviks had taken the wrong path in Russia. And when Wells, through his longtime friend and fellow-writer Maxim Gorky's mediation, was given the opportunity to meet Vladimir Lenin in the Moscow Kremlin, the Bolshevik leader appeared to him as an unrealistic "dreamer" who, while being an intelligent and critical interlocutor, did not seem to foresee the disastrous consequences of the alleged "inevitable class war" and "downfall of capitalist order."[13] Instead of risking destruction and dictatorship, the "wonderful spirit" of science must be protected at all costs, and therefore Wells insisted in his talk to Lenin on his belief "that through a vast sustained educational campaign the existing capitalist system can be *civilized* into a collectivist world system."[14]

In the decade that followed, Wells dedicated himself more than ever to this project of civilizing the capitalist system with the help and for the benefit of the sciences. But no matter how hard he tried to convince his own society through a political *Open Conspiracy* or an educational *Science of Life*,[15] he remained powerless: Scientific-technical inventions continued to be used in the service of profit and war. Instead of a better civilization came the world economic crisis and the rise of the fascists and Nazis. This disillusionment is expressed in Wells's fictional works.

In the Soviet Union, the development seems to have been quite different. Here, after Wells's departure and the end of the civil war, the "hothouse plants" of science seemed to have finally been given the "warmth and respect and service" they deserved. Ivan Pavlov, who, according to Wells, raised "potatoes and carrots" for survival in 1920,[16] was given his own laboratory financed by the Bolsheviks, and new research institutes and scientific institutions sprang up all around. Everywhere the optimistic notions of the artistic and political avant-gardes, the "laboratories of dreams," and the utopian visions of man's transformation with the help of revolutionary experimental practices and groundbreaking inventions spread.[17] There were very different biopolitical visions of what the new mankind should look like: Some dreamed of a eugenic perfection of body and mind, some saw a machine-human ideal in a mechanical conditioning of all movements, while others envisioned a bio-cosmic transgression of the human body itself.[18] To all these scientific dreamers, the political revolution seemed to make possible a "scientific revolution" that promised to remedy all the societal ills of the past by conditioning, breeding or training a Soviet new man.[19]

However, in his study on *Revolutionary Experiments* (2014), Nikolai Krementsov has pointed out that at this time in Soviet history, there is a strange discrepancy. While new research institutions of a collectively run "Big Science" are being established on a massive scale, literary fictions abound in which isolated "mad scientists" continue to tinker individually with their own inventions.[20] Krementsov's numerous literary examples show that within the literary discourse of this period, scientific inventions are rarely associated with positive developments and instead are mostly linked with fatal social consequences. But what does this discrepancy between the goals of research institutions, on the one hand, and the topics of popular fiction, on the other, mean if we ask about the role of sciences in constituting a new image of man? In this chapter, I explore this question by analyzing the development of three popular-scientific genres and discussing how—in the words attributed to H. G. Wells—the "task of literature" to "improve humanity" was realized in different ways in the Soviet Union depending on the changing political circumstances of the 1920s and 1930s.

In order to develop this argument further, I return, in the next section, to H. G. Wells for some more general considerations about the relationship between scientific progress, political formations, and the changing image of man in works of art (first section : Whither Mankind?). In the following sections, I will examine this connection on the basis of the development of Soviet popular-scientific literature of the 1920s and 1930s in more detail. In the second section (Unlikely Horrors), I discuss how the emerging genre of so-called scientific fantasy served authors like Alexander Beliaev to imagine the ambivalent consequences of a scientific reshaping of man. Against these ambiguous literary fantasies the newly founded genre of "scientific-fictional literature" propagated, in the 1930s, a heroic image of scientists as masters of nature (section three: "Bad Anticipations"). However, despite all political turmoil, the older concept of an enlightened man of science survived in so-called entertaining science publications and institutions and gained even more popularity in times of Stalinist terror and show trials (section four: "House of Wonders"). In the concluding part (section five: "Changing Images of Man"), I will contextualize these changing popular-scientific literary images of men in a broader perspective, followed by a short postscript.

Whither Mankind? H. G. Wells's Anticipations of Scientific Progress and Human Future

A year and a half after H. G. Wells's return from the Soviet Union, in the spring of 1936, one of the most influential SF films ever was released in the cinemas: William Cameron Menzies's *Things to Come*, based on a novel (1933) and screenplay (1935) by H. G. Wells.[21] The film, a box-office hit at the time, dealt with all the hopes and anxieties that had been associated with modern societies, technical progress, and the future development of mankind in the preceding decades.

Originally, Wells had wanted to give the film *Things to Come* (1936) the title *Whither Mankind?*, indicating that he attributed a fundamental sociopolitical significance to the work that addresses humanity as a whole.[22] In fact, the work is, above all, a cinematic revision and a rethinking of Wells's own speculation over the past decades about the future of man. Beginning with his renowned best-selling 1901 book *Anticipations of the Reaction of Mechanical and Scientific Progress upon Human Life and Thought*,[23] which at the time made Wells famous as a public intellectual, his thoughts culminated in the numerous editions of his 1928 "Blue Prints for a World Revolution," *The Open Conspiracy*.[24] In contrast to Wells's dystopian novels of the time, the *Anticipations* were carried entirely by the technological optimism of the industrial age. However, they were also heavily criticized because of their last chapter in which Wells presented a eugenic vision of future mankind based on the selection of the best and strongest.[25]

The film is set in such a distant future: 100 years later, in the year 2035. A technocratic mankind has ultimately triumphed, but not by eugenic selection rather through scientific-technical superiority. Toward the end of the story, however, the herald and visionary of this new humanity, the engineer "Cabal," is confronted by the skeptical humanist "Passworthy." Criticizing the incessant striving for progress on earth, he instead calls for a little respite and happiness in the here and now, even for fragile human beings. Cabal counters by shouting:

> Rest enough for the individual man. Too much of it and too soon, and we call it death. But for MAN no rest and no ending. He must go on—conquest beyond conquest. This little planet and its winds and ways, and all the laws of mind and matter that restrain him. Then the planets about him, and at last out across immensity to the stars. And when he has conquered all the deeps of space and all the mysteries of time—still he will be beginning.[26]

When Passworthy insists on some indulgence for the "little creatures" of men who are "so fragile—so weak," Cabal declares: "If we are no more than animals—we must snatch at our little scraps of happiness and live and suffer and pass, mattering no more—than all the other animals do—or have done." And pointing to the stars, he confronts his opponent with the alternative: "It is that—or this? All the universe—or nothingness . . . Which shall it be, Passworthy?"[27]

This dialogue addresses our question about the changing image of man for two reasons. On the one hand, it narrows down the question "Whither Mankind?" to the question "What kind of mankind?" And second, it links this issue closely to the political order in which such a humanity exists. Clearly, Wells's sympathy lies with the image of a fragile, yet happy humanity.[28] However, in view of the political context—the rise of the National Socialists in Germany and the violent industrialization of the Soviet Union under Stalin's "iron fist"—this conception of mankind seems doomed to irrelevance.[29]

Moreover, in the film, not only are scientific and technical inventions not associated with peace and happiness, but, on the contrary, with political repression, war, and exploitation. This fear of progress was generally characteristic of popular culture in modern times, but after the First World War, it intensified.[30] In *Things to Come*, this fear is closely linked to the image of man in capital letters: For it is only the sciences that give MAN the tools and weapons to exercise his dictatorial power over the weak and his opponents.[31] This skepticism toward modern forms of government is also clearly demonstrated at the end of the film, when a huge crowd gathers around the moon cannon—not to cheer its launch, but to protest against it. The "new men" are literally put to flight.[32]

It is precisely this general skepticism toward any political and scientific revolutions that the Bolsheviks were confronted with in the young Soviet Union. This must be considered when investigating why there were so few utopian and forward-looking fictional works in the 1920s. As mass literature, the popular-scientific genres responded to the taste and demand of the general public in different cultural ways. The emerging genre of Soviet science fiction tried to incorporate skepticism into its narratives and showed—as Beliaev's work demonstrates—that progress does not inevitably entail the rise of bloody dictators, but always poses new challenges for a humanistic view of man. Perel'man, as the inventor and guiding rector of the nonfiction genre of "entertaining science," on the other hand, tried to dispel widespread fears by enchanting ordinary people with the wonders of technology. In contrast to these two opposing modes of science writing, a third genre of "scientific-fictional literature" emerged in the beginning of the 1930s. It sought to simply ignore and ban the existing fears instead propagating a man of science who, like Wells's Cabal, subjects the earthly and cosmic nature to his will—"conquest beyond conquest."[33]

Unlikely Horrors: Alexander Beliaev and the Precarious Limits of Men in "Scientific Fantasy"

When the Bolsheviks finally won the civil war and founded the Soviet Union in December 1922, they had no clear concept of how to artistically convey the promises of scientific progress to the broad masses, and neither Leon Trotsky nor Anatolii Lunacharskii or Nikolai Bukharin—as the most influential politicians in the field of culture at the time—had a coherent idea of what such art might look like. Relying on the transforming power of science and technology, they all trusted that the enthusiasm of the scientific avant-garde and the promotion of scientific knowledge would gradually spread among larger parts of the population.[34]

Survey results of the time show, however, that the increasingly literate masses of workers and peasants rather preferred to read all kinds of adventure literature in the broadest sense, featuring fictional stories about dangerous scientific inventions, frightening discoveries, and dystopian civilizations. All kinds of "scientific romances" and "extraordinary adventures" that came from the West, which were still being translated on a massive scale well into the 1930s, enjoyed much greater popularity than the works of local writers. H. G. Wells is probably the most prominent example in this regard, as he was one of the best-selling living foreign authors ever in those years in the Soviet Union. After the revolution, several editions of his collected works were published along with hundreds of individual book releases. *Time Machine* (1895) alone was published twelve times as a book from 1918 to 1935, and *War of the Worlds* (1898) ten times in the same period. By the mid-1930s, Wells's total circulation in the Soviet Union was already more than two million copies, which far exceeded his sales figures in England.[35] And although *Things to Come* was not able to make it into cinemas of the Soviet Union after 1934, still Wells's screenplay was printed in 1937 as a popular booklet with a circulation of 20,000 copies.[36]

In order to meet this widespread demand and at the same time to redirect it somewhat, a huge number of popular-science journals was founded in the 1920s, such as *Worldwide Pathfinder* (*Vsemirnyi sledopyt*, 1925–32), *Knowledge Is Power* (*Znanie—sila*, 1926–) or *The World of Adventures* (*Mir prikliuchenii*, 1922–30), who all published all sorts of Western adventure stories but also aimed at establishing similar Soviet light fiction stories (see Figure 5.1).[37] It is exactly in this context that Alexander Beliaev was able to kick-start his literary career, becoming the most widely read author of Soviet science fiction with his stories that all dealt with transformations between man, animal, and machine, facilitated by science. In one of the most famous stories from the cycle, *Inventions of Professor Wagner* (1926–36), for instance, it is an elephant with a

Figure 5.1 Front pages of the Soviet illustrated popular-scientific journals of the 1920s, left to right: *World of Adventure* (No. 2, 1928), Around the World (No. 1, 1927), and *Worldwide Pathfinder* (No. 6, 1927). © Out of copyright.

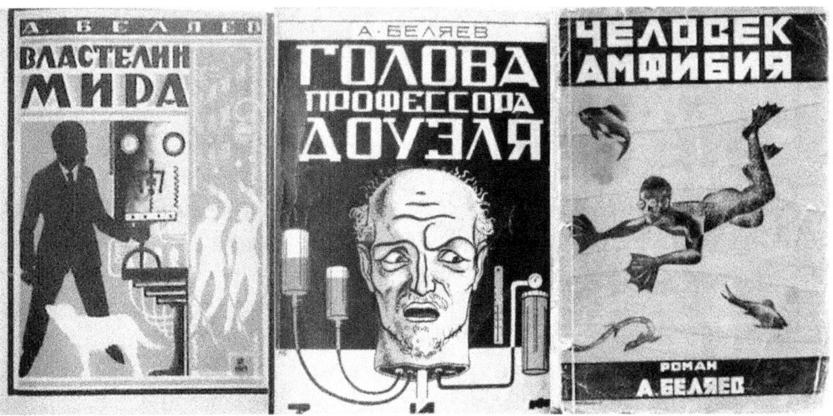

Figure 5.2 Book covers of Alexander Beliaev's novels, left to right: *Ruler of the World* (Moscow, 1929), *Head of Professor Dowell* (Moscow, 1926), and *Amphibian Man* (Moscow, 1928). © Out of copyright.

human brain that shocks the world, whereas in the *Amphibian Man* (1928) a human is partly transformed into a sea creature. World conquest enabled by new machines is treated in novels like *The Ruler of the World* (1926) and *The Air Seller* (1929) (see Figure 5.2). In the latter, however, the Soviet government succeeds in the end, taking over the invention for the sake of the people.[38]

It was only with the announcement of the first five-year plan at the end of 1927, when a massive collectivization of agriculture and industrialization of the country was imposed by force, that these entertaining stories of miraculous human transformations, wonder weapons, and megalomaniac dictators suddenly came into the focus of criticism.[39] Now every kind of light adventure literature was rejected as unrealistic and counter-revolutionary contraband from the capitalist West that fueled fear among the readers instead of actively promoting the construction sites of socialism.[40] In this context, the genre of science fiction was first conceptualized by critics as well as activists who sought to save their favorite literature by labeling it "*nauchnaia fantastika*" (scientific fantasy)—a compound noun that had previously been used only occasionally by publishers to advertise this sort of fiction.[41] By combining the creative quality of imagination—"fantasy"—with the objective accuracy of the natural sciences—the "scientific"—they defined this literature as ideally suited to propagating the building of socialism.[42]

One of the first people to provide a more elaborate conceptual formulation of the term "scientific fantasy" was the young science-fiction author Abram Ruvimovich Palei (1893–1995), whose first novel *Gulfstream* had been published in 1927.[43] According to Palei, "scientific fantasy" was first and foremost to correspond to scientific standards, that is, to popularize actual scientific facts. Second, it was to introduce readers' imaginations to new research questions—to inspire. Third, it was to satisfy high literary standards by consisting of well-written and excitingly presented subject matter. It was to promote the image of self-confident, competent scientists instead of telling frightening adventure stories about science gone wrong.[44]

Tellingly, the enforcement of this definition met with considerable resistance among the readers and supporters of those scientific wonder stories. For example, when the largest journal for scientific-fictional literature, *Worldwide Pathfinder*, announced in the same year a nationwide competition for the best scientific-fantastic story and received hundreds of submissions from all over the Soviet Union, the disillusioned editors of the journal had to admit, in the end, that not a single one of the submitted works had met their criteria.[45] According to the editors, none of the authors had cared about the scientific integrity of their fiction and instead only offered "unlikely horrors."[46] What emerged in the following years as a compromise between these different interests in science popularization was a "scientific fantasy" that incorporated the "unlikely horrors" as something that Soviet new men were able to master.[47]

A vivid example of this compromise is Alexander Beliaev's novel *The Star KETs* (1935), which appeared in the same year as Wells's film script to *Things to Come*. The title—a compound of the initials of Konstantin Eduardovich Tsiolkovsky's first name, patronymic, and surname—suggests that this novel popularizes Tsiolkovsky's ideas about space flight and the human colonization of the universe.[48] And indeed, many of Tsiolkovsky's scientific ideas are described in detail in the novel, but these are combined with the "unlikely horrors" of fantasy.[49] Hence, the first flight to the moon ends with the shocking discovery that the back of the moon, eternally turned away from earth, does not actually exist. Instead, it turns out it was once destroyed by a meteorite and the moon exists only as a single hemisphere.

At the same time, this scientific endeavor also challenges the limits of man. After the protagonist returns from the far side of the moon, he joins research at the space station "system KETs" and comes into closer contact with the researchers working under the conditions of zero gravity and cosmic rays. He finds out that daily exposure to these conditions has damaging effects. People are becoming demoralized. Some turn into "eccentric fellows" (*chudaki*), others into "primitive, insane humans"[50] that are full of jealousy, vanity and mistrust, and are even ready to kill someone for their own sake. Some lose their minds, confuse everything and forget elementary things. Others despair over their scientific work, when, with the help of biological mutation, they manage to raise more fertile animals in their laboratories: "'Somehow, in the last time I got lost completely, I directly dumped down . . . You know', he told me in a frightened silenced tone, 'it won't take long and I'll go mad, when in front of your eyes these nightmarish monsters are born.'"[51]

One of the most frightening monsters born in the cosmic laboratories is a dog called Gipsy that has the body of a monkey, the mouth of a dog, and the face of a human. This intelligent "nightmarish monster" becomes the only friend of the narrator in a world of demoralized and mad scientists. "Thus, step by step, we offered our thoughts one to another. The only uncomfortable thing was that Gipsy nevertheless remained a 'stranger', whom only I was able to understand. For that he esteemed and loved me even more."[52]

If one reads this novel against the background of the time, the function of "scientific fantasy" becomes clearer. After the First Soviet Writers' Congress in 1934 especially, the focus was increasingly set on the positive hero who, thanks to the glorious successes of Soviet scientists and inventors, exceeded his human limits: on the great industrial projects, in aviation, in the Arctic or in agriculture.[53] This new heroic subject was tightly integrated into the collective and was led by the Party. "Scientific Fantasy" negotiates the uncertainties and doubts about this canonical norm and, with the help of the "unlikely" scientific adventures, shows where the precarious limits of the new man lie.[54] In Beliaev's case, it is the officially propagated scientific heritage of Tsiolkovsky, who died in 1935, that is being tested on the "Star KETs."

Whereas in the 1920s the emerging genre of Soviet "scientific fantasy" was dedicated to dystopian narratives of wonder weapons in the hand of "mad scientists" who initiate "wars of the worlds," in the 1930s, in contrast, this kind of disputed fiction addressed the precarious limits and fragility of the Soviet new man. It incorporates the fantastic "unlikely horror" into scientific fiction but encodes it, in the Soviet sense, as man's struggle against untamed, dangerous nature. If we compare Beliaev's *The Star KETs* to Wells's *Things to Come*, the contrast could not be greater. While in *Things to Come* the storming of the universe is the ultima ratio against nothingness, here it is the universe itself that fundamentally confronts people with their fragility. Outer space is not the first refuge, but a testing ground for the limits of the human condition on earth, namely, Stalin's "socialism in one country."

As the few remarks on Beliaev's novel have already shown, these scientific fantasies were not overly concerned with implanting scientific progress into their narration of the socialist present. The big construction sites of socialism and five-year plans, if addressed at all, served, at most, as a framework for the plot. Even a new "socialist" understanding of science and its influence on the "new people" of the Stalin era is only hinted at. In order to compensate for this lack of ideological suitability, attempts were made from the end of the 1920s onward to establish an alternative semi-fictional literature that would put forward the official images of Soviet scientists as the masters of nature, the so-called scientific-fictional literature (*nauchno-khudozhestvennaia literatura*).

Bad Anticipations: M. Il'in, Alexander Ivich and the Propagation of the Soviet New Man in "Scientific-Fictional Literature"

While the "unlikely horrors" of "scientific fantasy" aimed to relieve the fears of progress, the "probable inventions" of "scientific-fictional literature" were intended to show a "realistic" picture of ordinary laboratories of everyday scientific life. Whereas "scientific fantasy" presented fictional scenarios to explore the precarious limits of man, "scientific-fictional literature" sought to anticipate the limitless power of man, which Soviet science brought to him. This idea was first raised by Maxim Gorky and the famous children's literary writer Samuil Marshak (1887–1967) in the aftermath of the first five-year plan on the eve of the Soviet Writers Congress in 1934. Beginning in the autumn of 1933, both started to use the term "scientific-fictional prose" (*nauchno-khudozhestvennaia proza*), which invoked the Russian term for "fiction" (*khudozhestvennaia literatura*), more frequently to promote a new genre of literature aimed at educating and inspiring young readers in particular, but not exclusively.[55] In doing so, the "fictional-scientific" works of literature were intended to bring about a whole new way of seeing the relationship between man and his social and natural environment. As Marshak put it during his opening speech at the first Writers Congress in 1934:

> Instead of presenting nature, men and morality as unchanging, they strive to show readers the changing connections between phenomena and to provide a description of the world that is so passionate and unequivocal that people feel the need to fight and to restructure life and nature.[56]

Scientific-fictional storytelling was not just a matter of propagating nature's dialectical transformability or humankind's meddling with life and nature but a categorical breach with an otherwise supposedly "objective and disinterested" understanding of science.[57]

The most important writer in this field in the 1930s was M. Il'in, the penname of Samuil Marshak's younger brother Mikhail (1895–1953). In 1930, Il'in had already channeled the zeitgeist successfully with his book *Story of the Five-Year Plan* (1931)—and Gorky praised him to the skies (see Figure 5.3).[58] The book was reprinted several times in the same year and immediately translated into the major languages of the world.[59] Taking a closer look at the book, its narrative perspective and tonality distinguish it clearly from typical popular-science books. Here is an omnisciently educated "scientific" narrator, who, as a participating observer and operative writer, is the only one who knows how to interpret the Soviet five-year plan correctly in terms of its social and

Figure 5.3 Book covers of the first editions of M. Il'in, *Story of the Five-Year Plan* (Moscow, 1931) and M. Il'in and E. Segal, *How Man Became a Giant* (Moscow, 1940). © Out of copyright.

historical contexts. All horror is dialectically externalized as a product of capitalist exploitation or as a human weakness to be overcome vis-à-vis the forces of nature. The "new man," as an idealized worker hero from the socialist construction sites, is inflated into a fairy-tale giant who overcomes all the natural obstacles with ease.[60]

The most vivid example of this new semi-fictional perspective was certainly M. Il'in's Opus Magnum (which he wrote together with his wife, Elena Segal) *How Man Became a Giant* (first volume, 1940; second volume, 1946; see Figure 5.3). It took the new Soviet man as its point of departure, reconsidered as the inevitable result of the entire history of mankind. The first volume uses simple language to describe the development of Homo sapiens from the first monkeys to antiquity and shows that man survived only in virtue of his fighting courage, his scientific spirit, and the gradual submission of nature.[61] Thus, the socialist new man appears here as an almost inevitable result of a long historical process—the pinnacle of evolution.

This "scientific-fictional" focus on the social conditionality of every human evolution was most clearly illustrated conceptually by the science historian, writer, and critic Alexander Ivich (Ignatii Ignat'evich Bernshtein, 1900–1978). First publishing his scientific-fictional book *The Adventures of Inventions* in 1930, two further editions followed suit in the next nine years.[62] Here, the social conditionality of science is addressed from a popularly understandable angle: New scientific inventions will be successful only if they correspond to the current state of knowledge and if there is also a socioeconomic demand for them.[63] According to this view, there had been many great inventions that had come too early for their time, because nobody understood or needed them, and, equivalently, there had been great discoveries that had come too late, because technology and society had already developed in a different direction.[64]

To illustrate this thesis, Ivich points to none other than the "great utopian" H. G. Wells. According to Ivich, Wells is a bad social prophet, because he thinks entirely in the well-trodden paths of his time and never moves beyond the current techno-scientific horizon. Citing the *Anticipations*, Ivich argues that Wells had only ever made "bad anticipations" (*plokhie predvideniia*): "Wells only combines known natural phenomena with inventions" and does not suspect that an innovation, "in order to be perfect, must take advantage of some completely new inventions. Inventor's thought can take a new path."[65] In contrast, this was exactly the task of "scientific-fictional literature," which sought to open up new perspectives on scientific research beyond the "well-trodden paths" of bad anticipations.[66]

The problem with this new form of scientific popularization, promoted by state institutions, major publishing houses, the members of the Writers' Association, prominent academics, writers, and critics, was that despite the huge circulation of its books, neither young readers nor the new technical intelligentsia or even scientific circles wanted to read these propagandistic works.[67] For instance, Il'in's *How Man Became a Giant* was harshly criticized at an internal meeting of the Writers' Association in 1939 because of its inadmissible simplification of connections, a gross distortion of scientific facts, and, above all, because it was excruciatingly boring to read.[68] It was seen as "bad anticipation" itself, not just because of its content but especially because of its style.

But even if this sort of semi-fictional literature had been written more excitingly, the people of the Soviet Union, caught, in the 1930s, in a time of purges, terror, arbitrary arrests and the Gulag, were tired of being ideologically strong men. And as the supply of "frightening horror" stories of "scientific fantasy" waned in the aftermath of censorship, especially in the 1930s, readers turned to another, less politically ideologies genre of science writing. It had existed long before the revolution and now experienced a comeback: the nonfictional form of the "entertaining sciences."

House of Wonders: Iakov Perel'man and the Making of Educated People in "Entertaining Sciences"

The notion of a new man as an educated, rational, always curious, and open-minded subject, solving all problems with the help of scientific knowledge, is an old project of the enlightenment.[69] But whereas in Imperial Russia this was mainly directed in opposition to the backward state politics and forms of government, in the Soviet Union it seemingly fitted perfectly into the scientific enthusiasm of the 1920s. In the second half of the 1930s, after some initial difficulties, it became the preferred political project to educate a new Stalinist technical intelligentsia.[70]

One of the activist supporters of this educational project in Russia was the aforementioned Iakov Isidorovich Perel'man (1882–1942), a graduate forester who had devoted himself since his early twenties to science popularization. A regular author and later chief secretary of the "illustrated journal for science, art and literature" *Nature and People* (*Priroda i liudi*, 1889–1918), he was made chief editor in 1913.[71] Perel'man was one of the early popularizers of Konstantin Tsiolkovsky's ideas and made them accessible to a larger audience. In 1915, he published the booklet *Interplanetary Travels*, which was subsequently published in ten further editions. He went on to found the first Soviet popular-science journal *In the Workshop of Nature* (*V masterskoi prirody*, 1919–29; see Figure 5.4) in 1919, and in the 1920s worked in the People's Commissariat for Education on the Soviet school reform. With the publication in 1913 of his book *Entertaining Physics*, he became a successful author (see Figure 5.4). After a second volume came out in 1916,[72] he published ten more similar books in the mid-1920s, such as *Entertaining Geometry* (1925), *Entertaining Mathematics* (1927), and *Entertaining Astronomy* (1929). Altogether, Perel'man published more than eighty popular-science books with a circulation of millions of copies.[73] His "entertaining sciences" were so successful that they soon found countless imitators in the 1920s and 1930s.[74]

This format for the popularization of science, presented primarily in large illustrated journals and daily newspapers, engagingly written brochures, and general educational nonfiction books, tried to reach its readers by making scientific research more vivid and, above all, more easily accessible through historical excursions, curious anecdotes, surprising comparisons, logical paradoxes, riddles, jokes, and humorous illustrations.[75] The "light and exciting" form of representation was supposed to "ignite our tired youth through the fire of wandering and wandering, through an outbreak of scientific research," as Alexander Fersman wrote in 1924.[76] The authors of these works gladly used fiction and mythological models and repeatedly crossed the border between the "fantasies of novelists" and the "sober spirits of engineers."[77] But no matter what topic they dealt with,

Figure 5.4 "Entertaining science" publications by Iakov Perel'man, left to right: book cover of *Enterteioning Physics. Book Two* (Moscow, 1932); front page of the journal *In Nature's Workshop* (1919, No. 5–6); book cover of *Miracle of Our Times* (Leningrad, 1925). © Out of copyright.

these works contained almost no politics at all, no social context that went beyond very general historical and geographical settings. There was no such thing as a Soviet hero either; here there was only the enlightened human, curious about and believing in science, fascinated by the wonders of technology, seen as the solution to all the world's evils.[78]

This absence of any political framing in the genre of entertaining science was repeatedly criticized sharply, especially by the proponents of "scientific-fictional literature" during the first five-year plan.[79] And yet, as "scientific fantasy" continued to be criticized for its alleged remoteness from everyday socialism and "scientific-fictional" literature was so unpopular with readers, the established genre of entertaining science gained more and more followers.

The "House of Entertaining Science" (*Dom zanimatel'nykh nauk*) manifested how Stalinist cultural politics promoted this genre exclusively while sidelining the ideologies "scientific-fictional literature" and certainly the scary "scientific fantasies."[80] This institution, opened in Leningrad in the autumn of 1935 on the initiative of Iakov Perel'man, was directly subordinate to the Section for Mass Political-Cultural Educational Work of the Lensovet, the Leningrad town council. It was housed in a prestigious location, the former Sheremetev Palace, a magnificent baroque building on the Fontanka River.[81] In the beginning, this House of Entertaining Science had only three rooms in the spacious building. But due to the enormous success among the public, it quickly grew and within a few years developed into a huge science museum, which soon occupied most of the building and counted hundreds of visitors every day. The "House of Wonders on Fontanka,"[82] as it was then known, had all the attractions, interactive installations, slides, dioramas, model-making, and astonishing special effects that were technically possible at the time. The "temple of enchantment" was built on the principle that all exhibits could be touched and tested by the visitors.[83]

Everyone was invited to try out all the equipment and experiments presented in the four sections of astronomy, geography, mathematics, and physics, expanded in 1940 to include a section on electricity.[84]

At the same time, the "miracle of Leningrad"[85] developed an extensive accompanying program with lecture series, competitions, Olympiads, and a large number of publications.[86] In addition to the "red corners" in pioneer houses, factories, and collective farms, "corners of the House of Entertaining Science" for locals to carry out experiments by themselves were set up in Leningrad and the surrounding area.[87] Because of its huge success, on the occasion of Perelman's fortieth professional anniversary, the house even dedicated its own exhibition to the "science propagandist"[88] and "outstanding science popularizer" in December 1939.[89] By the first half of 1941, more than half a million visitors had come through the museum's doors.[90]

But how far this museum of scientific wonders and instructive experiments really was from the ideal of a "socialist hero," often perceived as typical for the 1930s, became most apparent in the last section to be opened just before the German invasion of the Soviet Union. It was a hall dedicated exclusively to Jules Verne, whom Perel'man had praised repeatedly as a "master of scientific propaganda" and the "true founder of entertaining science."[91] In this room visitors could climb into the submarine Nautilus and admire the underwater worlds or follow the eighty-day journey of the English gentleman Phileas Fogg and his servant Jean Passepartout on an electronic world map.[92]

Here, man is no longer a practical fighter who becomes a giant in the struggle for existence, as in Ivich's and Ilin's understanding, but the adventurous professor of the nineteenth century who discovers exotic worlds and undertakes educational endeavors.[93] Instead of collective effort, this man tinkers, puzzles, marvels, and learns for his own sake (see Figure 5.5).[94] However, if one takes into account the political context of the

Figure 5.5 The foyer of the House of Entertaining Science in 1941, from *Tekhnika—molodezhi,* (1941) 4: 58. © Out of copyright.

1930s, this image of man indeed corresponded quite well to the educational policy of the Stalinist era. Hence, instead of the politicized "red universities" of the 1920s, now the emphasis was on the practical training of a new "technical intelligentsia," which was urgently needed on all fronts.[95] In a time when the "war of the worlds" was already on the doorstep, utopian (as well as dystopian) visions were reserved for the Bolshevik leadership and Stalin in particular. Such idealized image of man had no place in the realm of "entertaining sciences."

Changing Images of Man: Conclusion

The fictional, semi-fictional, and nonfictional popular-scientific literature barely mentions the term "new man," but all genres deal in different ways with the topic of how scientific and technological progress changes the (self-)image of humans. What is treated as "new" in all respects is the sociopolitical environment of socialism, which opens up hitherto unknown possibilities for the development of the sciences.

The scientific "genius of man," whom Wells had seen as still facing an existential threat in 1920, received more state support than ever before—if those concerned were willing to endorse the political conditions. It was these conditions that in the 1920s gave the numerous experimenters and inventors reason to hope for reshaping human civilization into a better "new mankind." However, popular literatures only rarely adopted this scientific optimism; rather, they addressed the educational and emotional needs of the newly literate and growing reading masses. Whereas works of "entertaining science" portrayed an enlightened image of man, occupied with solving the riddles of nature, the fictional adventure stories of the emerging genre of "scientific fantasy" depicted all the fears and nightmares associated with the potential transformation of and by man.

However, state support for the sciences in the Soviet Union also brought with it an increasing dependency, which was noticeable in the literary genres of scientific popularization, especially since the late 1920s. While censorship in the "first-rate literature," at least since the first congress of Soviet writers in 1934, prescribed a certain heroic image of man in accordance with the principles of Socialist Realism, such a canon could not—at first—be found in the genres of science popularization, children's literature, and science propaganda. In the corresponding genres, diverse images of man were created during the entire 1930s. Only the genre of "scientific-fictional literature" was politically initiated to project a socialist perspective of man as a giant onto the construction site of life. "Scientific fantasy," on the contrary, adapted to the new reality by portraying scientists of the future whose pioneering deeds suddenly confronted them with the precarious limits of human supremacy and subjectivity. The "entertaining sciences," on the other hand, designed written and physical spaces brimming with scientific curiosities for scientifically curious humans—a tempting self-image for the newly emerging technical intelligentsia of the 1930s. However, all three genres not only dealt with the challenges for the sciences under the conditions of a "socialism in one country" and developed different images of man. They also subtly indicated and partly incorporated the violence experienced in their own reality into their plots and intrigues. Soviet works of science popularization demonstrated that even if humans are powerless and fragile in times of "revolution from above" and "great terror," they may still keep their humanity (Beliaev), their spirit of adventure (Ivich), and their curiosity in intriguing phenomena (Perel'man). The "unlikely horrors" of Stalinist repression were integrated into the fictional, semi-fictional, and nonfictional writings more or less evidently as entertaining narrations of the challenges and dangers associated with scientific "adventures of inventions" (Alexander Ivich).[96]

Postscript

Only seven years had passed after Beliaev, Perel'man, and Rynin met with H. G. Wells in the Leningrad Hotel Astoria and discussed the future of an "improved" humanity, when, on June 22, 1941, the German Wehrmacht attacked the Soviet Union. It reached Leningrad in September and destroyed all exhibits in the House of Entertaining Science—and, with it, its propagated image of man. None of Wells's three passionate followers were to survive the war. Alexander Beliaev died of malnutrition under German occupation on January 6, 1942 in his home in Pushkin (the former Tsarskoe Selo) near Leningrad. Iakov Perel'man followed him two months later; he passed away on March 16, 1942, as a result of privations during the siege of Leningrad. Nikolay Rynin, who was seriously ill, was rescued from Leningrad by plane in the spring, but the help came too late, and he died of the consequences of hunger and lack of medical care in the evacuation on July 28, 1942.[97]

The changing image of man evoked by scientific inventions, linked with unlikely horrors, giant struggle, and thrilling entertainment, was finally buried in the Great Patriotic War. Now it was again the war heroes dying for their home and motherland who became the benchmark of all things to come. After 1945, the war then gripped the sciences themselves: in the late-Stalinist "science wars,"[98] the political authorities attempted to completely redefine the relationship between man, society, and science. But that is a different story.[99]

Acknowledgments

My thanks to Diana Aurisch and Anna Simon-Stickley for polishing my English.

6

The New Man as a Monster of Eugenic Imagination

The Criminal Brain in James Whale's *Frankenstein* and Bulgakov's "The Heart of a Dog"

Irina Golovacheva

Introduction

The purpose of this chapter is to answer the question of how the idea of "making a new man" by changing human nature, globally accentuated in the 1920 and 1930s, was reflected in two works produced at the time—in an American science-fiction horror film that was an immediate success and a fantastic Russian tale that was first published and got wide recognition only many decades later.

The first speculative text that directly dealt with "making a new man" was Mary Shelley's novel *Frankenstein* (1818). "The birth" of the monster whom the protagonist created out of different dead body parts marked the birth of a Frankenstein motif representing experimental science as a "monstrous" force that is out of human control. That motif was revived more than a century later in James Whale's *Frankenstein* (1931), a loose cinematic interpretation of the novel. In the first section, I discuss Whale's innovative treatment of Shelley's plot, since his film clearly signaled renewed interest in the old idea of "making a new man" in the context of contemporary science, especially of eugenic understandings of human nature. In the second section, I look through a similar lens at the representation of a "new man" in "The Heart of a Dog" (1925), a fantastic novella by Mikhail Bulgakov that reflected specific Russian scientific contexts.

I place the two works together because, besides employing the common theme of out-of-control monsters, they provide a similar "dysgenic" explanation of their behavior: the brains of these characters are abnormal. The comparison of the two plots allows me to show the two "subspecies" of "new man" and to highlight the similarities and the differences between American and Russian views on the rigid dichotomy of heredity and environment.

The Brain of Frankenstein's Monster

In 1931, James Whale released *Frankenstein*, a Universal Studios adaptation of Mary Shelley's original 1818 novel.[1] In the film, as compared to the novel, numerous characters, scenes, and narratives are missing: the whole frame story told by Captain Walton, the murder of Victor Frankenstein's bride, Elizabeth, and so on. The action in the movie takes place not in eighteenth-century Switzerland but in early 1930s Germany. Victor is renamed Henry and given a hunchbacked assistant, Fritz.

Shelley's humanoid monster is characterized as proportioned and his limbs as "beautiful." What disgusts his creator Victor Frankenstein are the creature's watery colorless eyes, complexion, and straight black lips. The Monster in the film adaptation is ugly. In the novel, the Creature is intelligent, eloquent, and literate, whereas Whale's monster is a mute degenerate incapable of adequate communication. However, both in the film and in Shelley's novel, the image of the Monster can be seen as a metaphor of threat.[2]

The film director who made the preparatory sketches and the Universal Studios chief makeup artist, Jack Pierce, rejected the idea of making their Monster resemble some extraterrestrial alien. Instead, they decided to make their Monster look subhuman.[3] The script written by Garret Fort and Francis Ford Faragoh specifies that the Monster "does not walk like a robot." Rather, it resembles "a lost animal."[4]

The author of the review in the *Hollywood Reporter* published after the movie release characterizes the protagonist, Henry Frankenstein, as "a young medical student. He is interested in what makes for life, what brings the fruit upon the trees, why one son of a mother is an honest and upright man, another a criminal, maybe a murderer."[5] Clearly, the reviewer unfailingly detected the heredity topic in the cinematic text. He was right—under the influence of the popular sociobiological rhetoric of the time, the makers of *Frankenstein* depicted the Monster in such a way that the viewer could explain his behavior by the "legacy" of the criminal acts and corrupted spirit of the donor whose brain was implanted. Apart from housing the spiritual part of human nature, the brain could be seen in the context of popular eugenic beliefs of the time as a standby for heredity. Such was the point of view of the "naturists." However, as shown further, the opposing "nurturist" approach, according to which social environment played a major role in human behavior, was not completely overlooked by the moviemakers.

In an early episode, Frankenstein, who seems to have as many dead bodies as needed for his work, sends his assistant Fritz to find an ideal brain for the operation. However, Fritz brings him the wrong preparation jar, neglecting the label: "Abnormal brain." It is worth noting that back in 1921, ten years before the release of the movie, the International Exhibition of Eugenics at the American Natural History Museum in New York City displayed the enlarged photographs of fifty preparations of supposedly abnormal brains that had belonged to criminals: the display propagated the achievements of forensic psychiatry in particular as well as the eugenic movement in general.[6] The Massachusetts Department of Mental Health that provided the exhibits issued a related poster that gained vast popularity in the United States (see Figure 6.1).

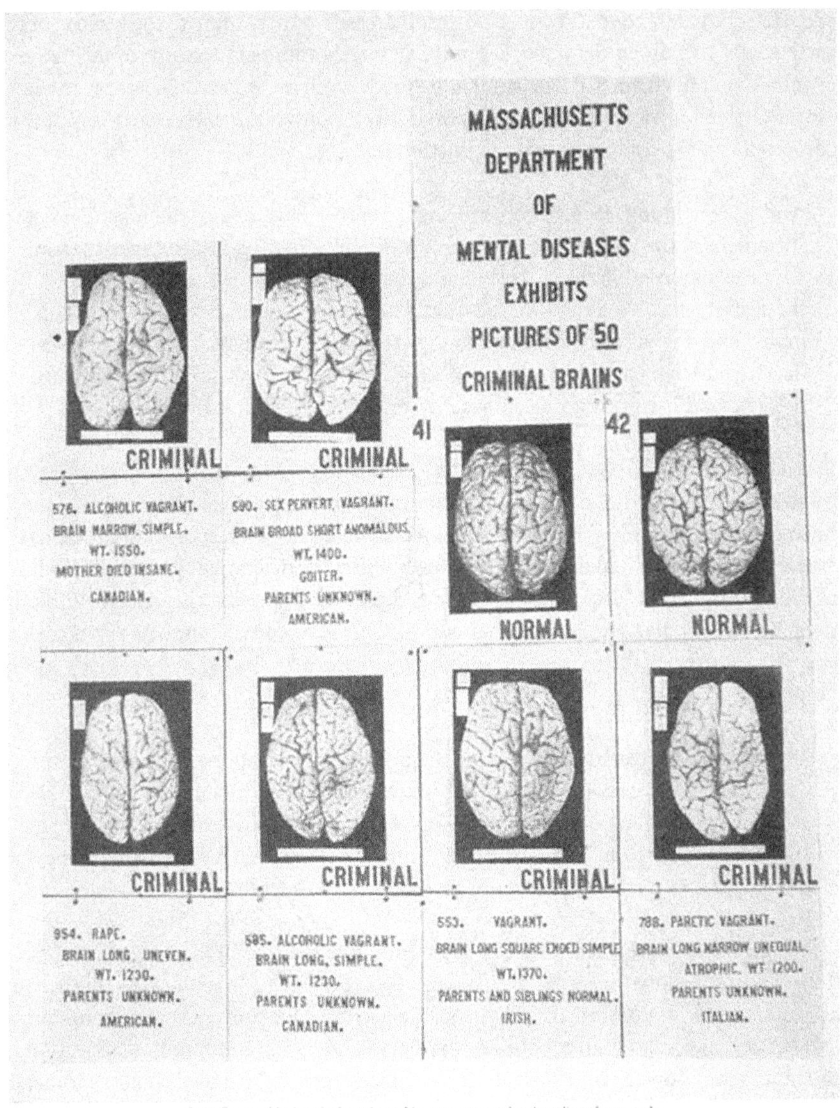

Figure 6.1 Poster "the brains of criminals," from Harry H. Laughlin, *The Second International Exhibition of Eugenics* (Baltimore, 1923). Courtesy of the Pennsylvania State University Libraries. © Out of copyright.

The episode in which Fritz steals the brain is preceded by the scene at Goldstadt Medical College, which was added to the scenario by Robert Flory and John Russel. In it, Dr. Waldman, while giving a lecture on pathological anatomy in the light of mainstream eugenics, the trend of that time, demonstrates a corpse and anatomical preparations to attentive students who are all dressed up according to the fashion of the early 1930s. Waldman definitely supports Cesare Lombroso's concept of the "inborn criminal" and his theory of atavism that defined criminals as hereditary savages whose deviant behavior was closely related to their inborn physical anomalies. This is how he comments on the content of two preparation jars:

> And in conclusion, ladies and gentlemen, here we have one of the most perfect specimens of the human brain ever to come to my attention at the university. And here the abnormal brain of the typical criminal. Observe, ladies and gentlemen, the scarcity of convolutions on the frontal lobe as compared to that of the normal brain, and the distinct degeneration of the middle frontal lobe. All of these degenerate characteristics check amazingly with the history of the dead man before us, whose life was one of brutality, of violence and murder.

Indeed, the frontal lobes are mostly responsible for cognitive skills. Because the frontal lobes of the donor's brain are abnormal, the subsequent deviant behavior of the recipient, the Monster, is easily explained since it fully corresponds to the deficient anatomy.[7] The moviemakers not only showed the atavistic craniology (skull structure) of the Monster. They also exhibited his "degenerative" brain, in this way providing the reference to popular phrenology that conceptualized a connection between the skull and the features of the cortex. Describing his work on Monster's image, Jack Pierce points out:

> If the monster looks like something I dreamt of after something I ate, don't blame me . . . blame science. I made him the way textbooks said he should look. I didn't depend on imagination. In 1931, before I did a bit of designing I spent three months of research in anatomy, surgery, medicine, criminal history, criminology, ancient and modern burial customs and electrodynamics.[8]

The books that Pierce chose to study apparently focused on phrenology and eugenics. The Monster's now-classic final makeup (see Figure 6.2) testifies to the artist's acquaintance with Lombroso's drawings. The Lombrosian concept of the criminal was still echoed in some popular books of the 1920s and 1930s and found its reflection in the cinematic monster of a special kind—the degenerate.[9] Probably, anthropometric data either of Francis Galton, the scientist who coined the word "eugenics," or those of Charles Davenport, the eminent eugenist, attracted Pierce's attention. However, most likely, he made use of Havelock Ellis's *The Criminal* (1890), its fourth edition appearing in 1910. Ellis paid much attention to cranial characteristics, that is, to the importance of the shape and size of the skull, the forehead, nose and ears:

> Considerably greater importance was formerly attributed to the shape and measurements of the head than we can now accord to them, although the subject still retains much interest <. . .>. The defect of low or flat-roofed skull is also found among criminals, and is characteristic of degeneration. <. . .> Receding foreheads,

Figure 6.2 Boris Karloff as the Monster in James Whale's *Frankenstein* (1931), a screenshot. © Universal Studios, 1931.

> very commonly observed among criminals, have always been regarded as evidence of low mental and moral organization, not without reason.[10]

Ellis specifically points out the "small-size brains" and the "scarcity" and poor condition of brain convolutions of criminals.[11]

The brain preparations that Dr. Waldman demonstrates in the Medical College episode of the film allude, among other things, to the aforementioned Massachusetts poster showing the pictures of criminal brains (see Figure 6.1). The Monster's skull and brain, as Jack Pierce thought, were not only crucial for making this horror-movie character sensational. They had to correlate with the contemporary views related to bio-criminology. Pierce recollects that, having decided to underline the Monster's atavistic characteristics, he gave him "a primitive, Neanderthal appearance, that would stress [the Monster's] low intellect" by "slop[ing] the brow of the eyes in a pronounced ape-like ridge of bone."[12] He also came up with a visual image of longer arms and legs so that the Monster would look atavistic, like "a gorilla."[13] At the final stage of the Monster's makeup design, Pierce made the creature's face pale, possibly guided by Ellis's words: "Most writers on criminals speak of the pallor of the skin."[14] As Boris Karloff, the talented actor who played the Monster, recollects: "We found the eyes were too bright, seemed too understanding, where *dumb bewilderment* was so essential. So I waxed my eyes to make them heavy, half-seeing."[15]

The plot of the movie and its sensational visuality, the joint effort of the director, the makeup artist, and the actor allowed them to create a convincing degeneration discourse. Waldman's lecture provides a logical and scientifically grounded explanation of the Monster's behavior in the light of contemporary theories of the "criminal brain."[16] However, it is amazing that, despite a supposedly deep knowledge of anatomy, Henry Frankenstein does not seem to notice that the brain that Fritz brought him has evident pathological characteristics. Curiously enough, the creator of the new man underestimates (perhaps, due to his overwhelming monomania) the influence of the brain anatomy on consciousness:

> WALDMAN: . . . Wake up and look facts in the face! Here we have a fiend whose brain. . .
> HENRY: The brain must be given time to develop. It's a perfectly good brain, doctor. You ought to know: it came from your own laboratory.
> WALDMAN: The brain that was stolen from my laboratory was a criminal brain!
> HENRY [*playing down his visible consternation*]: Oh well, after all, it's only a piece of dead tissue.

Thus, Frankenstein's failure to identify the abnormal brain is not an oversight in the plot, but key moment that helps to rationalize the Monster's behavior.

In the end of the episode, the Monster appears on the screen going backward, which, at first sight, should just tell the audience of the childish awkwardness of his first steps. However, this extravagant "backward" step is an excellent theatrical invention symbolizing the devolution or degeneration of *Homo sapiens*.[17] The rest of the storyline convinces the audience that the Monster's aggressive behavior is a result of the "inherited" brain anomaly. Therefore, the audience has to think that he commits crimes not solely because his environment (*nurture)* is most unwelcoming but, rather, because his heredity (*nature*) is bad.

The New Man Sharikov

Mikhail Bulgakov's novella "The Heart of a Dog," written six years before the release of Whale's *Frankenstein*, is a story of a prominent surgeon, Professor Preobrazhensky, whose research and practice are sponsored by the Bolshevik authorities despite his opposition to the new political regime. He adopts a stray dog, gives it the typical name Sharik ("little ball"), and takes good care of it. Soon, the professor operates on the dog by implanting the endocrine glands—the pituitary and testes—of a deceased human donor.[18] The dog quickly transforms into a man; however, the new man created by the operation bears all the "birth-marks" of the donor, who was a petty criminal. The dog-man Sharikov develops into a primitive *lumpen*, adapts with alarming ease to the political realities of his time, acquires a governmental job, and then progressively terrorizes Preobrazhensky and his assistant Bormenthal. The surgeons have to take action: they operate on Sharikov to transform him back into the dog Sharik.

While discussing Preobrazhensky's experiments, one should not overlook the medical allusions of his last name. "Preobrazhensky" invokes the similarly liturgical last names of several Bulgakov's acquaintances, who were icons of the medical profession of that time: his Kiev neighbors Professor Nikolai Pokrovskii (the writer's uncle), Ivan Voskresenskii, and Nikolai Bogoiavlenskii.[19] The latter was known to successfully operate on the pituitary gland.[20] Another allusion, no less transparent, would be to the eugenist Sergei Preobrazhensky, who published an article with a notable title "Surgical Prevention of Degeneration."[21] Besides, the alliterative choice of the first name and patronymic for Bulgakov's character—Philip Philipovich—was probably prompted by the last name of the famous eugenist Iuri Filipchenko (Philipchenko in another spelling). The latter headed the Eugenics Bureau in Petrograd and published a book with the characteristic title *Ways to Improve Human Kind (Eugenics)* (*Puti uluchsheniia chelovecheskogo roda [Evgenika]*, 1924) and a year later, an article "Intelligentsia and Talents" (*Intelligentsiia i talanty*, 1925) that claimed the special value of intelligentsia as the hereditary carrier of the best human qualities. Bulgakov's novella perfectly resonated with this statement.

The eugenic motif articulated in "The Heart of a Dog" was a specific response to a contemporary scientific debate. The writer was certainly aware of the issues of heredity, its role in shaping the body and psyche of men—such topics were widely discussed by anthropologists, physiologists, psychologists, sociologists, medical doctors, and pedagogues. He also knew of the disputes around the inheritance of acquired characteristics. A great variety of biological essays, including those on heredity, regularly appeared on the pages of *The Medical Gazette* (*Vrachebnaia gazeta*) that he used to read when he was a medical practitioner and continued to subscribe for in the 1920s when eugenics was firmly rooted in the minds of educated classes both in Russia and in the West.

As is clear from Bulgakov's text, the primary objective of Professor Preobrazhensky's experiment was rejuvenation.[22] For that purpose, the appendage of the human brain—the pituitary—was transplanted to the stray dog Sharik. In addition, dog's testicles were replaced by human testes. (The text does not comment on the role of the latter in the metamorphosis of the dog into a man, and back). Preobrazhensky does not doubt the major role of the pituitary in manufacturing the "unfit" creature, since he specializes in the quickly advancing field of endocrinology. The pituitary is the central organ of a human endocrine system controlling the activity of other endocrine glands. It is clearly specified in the novella that "the pituitary is a magic box which determines the individual human image."[23] In Bulgakov's text, it functions metonymically: "It's the brain itself in miniature."[24]

Let us discuss the results of Preobrazhensky's pioneering experiment in the light of the master narratives of the time—eugenic, endocrinological, anthropological and bio-criminal that frequently combined in the degeneration narrative.[25] Being a front-runner in medical experimentation, Bulgakov's professor clearly ranks himself among the adepts of eugenics. Explaining the goal of his work, Preobrazhensky declares that it is "the improvement of the human race."[26] Apparently, he treats the term "eugenics" very broadly, as an amalgam of ideas, values, and practices connected with the intervention into human reproduction and heredity and the implication of such intervention for the future. A broad spectrum of eugenic ideas addressed urgent social problems, while the goal of eugenic practices was to shape the future of a particular society and/or of humanity as a whole. Eugenic practitioners suggested appropriate measures to come up with tools to better human beings.[27] In fact, all medical science of the epoch reflected the eugenic trend.[28]

The previously unseen corporeality and eccentric behavior of Sharikov very soon transforms into the unpleasantly familiar image and modus vivendi of a declassed man. Bulgakov presents the readers with a medical and biological puzzle rather than with just another fantastic metamorphosis. We should tackle the same question as the one Philip Philipovich asks: "What is this creature?"[29] The unplanned and unprecedented effect of brain surgery that accidentally brought about a new human being makes the scientist professionally assess the case in order to find out why is it that his patient becomes an alcoholic and a *lumpen*, demonstrating violence and stealing propensities. Philip Philipovich, "the enemy of unsupported hypotheses," as he attests himself, thinks through the nature of the new man Sharikov, in no way employing the Darwinist evolutionary approach.[30] Preobrazhensky does not share Bormenthal's ecstatic reaction: "Oh, what a glorious confirmation of the theory of evolution! Oh, the sublime chain leading from a dog to Mendeleev, the great chemist!"[31] Contrary to Bormenthal, who thinks hard of the recipient's medical history, the professor analyzes that of the donor's. As it turns out, the pituitary implanted in Sharik came from Klim Chugunkin, a petty criminal and habitual alcoholic. From Preobrazhensky's point of view, the only convincing interpretation of the dog's mysterious transformation into a Chugunkin-like man is that character is not only endocrinological, but also "hereditary."

Reflecting on the physical and personal characteristics of Chugunkin and matching his medical history with Sharikov's anatomy and psyche, the two components of human nature, Philip Philipovich comes to the conclusion that the two individuals are almost identical. Sharikov "gives an impression of a short, ill-knit human male" and Klim is characterized as "short, poor physical shape" with "enlarged liver (alcohol)."[32] The new citizen is the "reincarnation" of Chugunkin, who, under the previous political regime, would have spent a lot of time behind bars, whereas, under the new one, was "saved by his social origin, the third time put on probation with a conditional sentence of 15 years hard labor."[33] In all probability, Sharikov fully "inherited" his behavior and criminal predisposition. Hence, the new man who settles in the apartment at Prechistenka is a chronic alcoholic and a thief.

Sharikov's case study is directly connected to the concepts of "burdened heredity" and "criminal brain." From the end of the nineteenth century and all the way to the end of the 1930s, both Chugunkin and Sharikov would have been considered by many medical and legal professionals as *hereditary criminals*. This point of view took its roots in the specific mixture of degeneration theory and criminal anthropology, the ideology that was typical for Russian pre-Revolution life sciences. Such were the views of Pavel Kovalevskii, who since 1883 had been the editor of *The Archives of Psychiatry, Neurology and Psychopathology*, the first Russian journal in the field, of psychiatrist Vladimir Chizh, of jurist Dmitry Drill, and of many others.[34] Psychiatric analyses of court cases by Kovalevskii contain passages on healthy/invalid brain.[35] The latter organ, in Kovalevskii's view, is prone to all kinds of behavioral deviations. In 1908, at the opening ceremony of the Russian Psychoneurological Institute, the outstanding neurologist Vladimir Bekhterev claimed that, in some cases, criminals clearly demonstrated certain hereditary deviations from the norm.[36]

Psychiatrists and anthropologists also studied the role of hereditary brain diseases in such "social evils" as alcoholism.[37] Bulgakov accentuates alcohol addiction as the manifestation of Sharikov's "burdened heredity" in the novella more than once. As Bormenthal registers quite early in his case-notes, "Today, after the dog's tail had fallen out, he quite clearly pronounced the word 'liquor.'"[38] One of the dinner scenes contains the following symptomatic description: "Sharikov tossed the glassful down his throat, blinked, lifted a piece of bread to his nose, sniffed it and then swallowed it as his eyes filled with tears. 'Phase' Philip Philipovich suddenly blurted out, as if preoccupied. <...> 'It's a phase,'<...>'There's nothing we can do about it. Klim.'"[39] Under the "phase," one surely needs to understand an inevitable phase in the unfolding development of the operated dog into its organ donor, Klim Chugunkin.

Mikhail Bulgakov was very well aware of forensic psychiatry, as his university curriculum, when he was a medical student in Kiev, included two special courses: "Forensic Medicine" and "Medical Aspects of a Human Being Tried in the Court of Law." The textbooks recommended for these courses—*Lectures on Psychiatry* and *The Textbook on Psychology for the Court of Law*—were authored by Vladimir Chizh.[40] Bulgakov's interest in psychiatry did not cease after his medical career was over: in "The Heart of a Dog," he vaguely alludes to the perspective of psychiatric approach to the strange patient, which did not materialize due to a different specialty of the two doctors. As Bormenthal puts it, "However, I am no psychiatrist."[41]

One of the distinctive features of the early post-Revolution criminology was its "biologization."[42] Criminologists tended to explain the failure of the Soviet power to eradicate crime even under the new "democratic" regime not by the criminals' lower social status but, rather, by their anthropological and psychological characteristics, thus addressing the general issue of "human nature." The Bolsheviks, when looking for the root causes of the colossal problems of the new country, and especially those of the unprecedented crime rate, leaned to the idea that one should blame "the heritage of the previous regime." Being the engineers of futuristic utopia, they believed that its builders should be the "people of the future," a "communist mankind" that would emerge "out of the communist mankind of the capitalist epoch."[43] And that dictated "a radical transformation of the coagulated *homo sapiens*."[44] The most famous of Soviet eugenists, Nikolai Koltsov, hoped that "people who are incapable of understanding contemporary knowledge and contemporary culture will slowly but surely give way to the bearers of a much more perfectly organized type of the brain."[45]

Psychiatrists, criminologists, anthropologists, and jurists—the professionals supported by Bolshevik patrons—tried to find means for social stabilization and decriminalization, for ways of "healthification" of the gene pool, that is, of health promotion of Russia's population that was weakened and catastrophically depleted due to wars, famine, and general devastation.

The devastation seems not to have touched the professor's luxury apartment at Prechistenka (a fashionable part of Moscow), which serves as a perfect choice for the setting of the novella. First of all, the House of Scientists opened on Prechistenka in 1922. It served as a venue for regular meetings of the Russian Eugenic Society. Second, a great change occurred in that same neighborhood in the early 1920s: the Prechistenka City Psychiatric Hospital was reformed as a special psychiatric ward for prisoners of the Moscow region, and subsequently renamed as the V. P. Serbsky Institute of Forensic Psychiatry. Among the goals of the Institute was the research of hereditary factors in crime, which coincided with the mainstream tendency of criminal psychiatry of the day. In the mid-1920s, specialized "criminology offices" opened all over the country. They were labs centered on studying crime and criminals from a general biological standpoint. Specialists carried out anthropological investigations, for example, the criminal's constitution was assessed, her/his hair, teeth, nails were inspected. A "criminal-anthropological profile" was subsequently compiled, alongside a "family list" with all kinds of data concerning the convict's occupation, her/his family status, and biographies of all family members. Scientists also screened alcohol dependence, intellectual potential, and moral views. The offices published reports on rationales for deep and wide anthropological and psychiatric examination of people whose criminal behavior, as the scientists believed, testified to their "biological insufficiency."[46]

Unlike many of their Western colleagues who openly supported the so-called negative eugenics, very few Soviet eugenists entertained the idea of purifying the germ plasm from degenerative heritage by sterilizing or segregating "criminal elements."[47] Thus, for instance, Boris Slovtsov propagated the idea of increasing childbirth of the "positive" (high-quality) part of the population, while sterilizing the "scumbags." He gave his voice in support of the Indiana-like eugenic sterilization statute.[48] Similarly, Mikhail Volotskoi, who saw in a criminal the deviation from the norm similar to the deviation found in a "defective person," also stood for sacrificing personal interests of a dysgenic individual for the interests of society.[49] These eugenists, provided the state gave them chance, would have adopted the radical approach. Their opponent, the anthropologist Victor Bunak denied the very existence of the "criminal gene," though asserting the role of heredity in the formation of the criminal.[50]

If one looks into the case study of Sharikov who is both grotesque and typical, she will unfailingly notice that with every passing day, his appearance and behavior reveal those of Klim Chugunkin. Sharikov's savagery is not the consequence of a life in the wilderness, unlike the savagery of Rudyard Kipling's Mowgli, who had spent many years in the jungle. Sharikov's body and primitively instinctive behavior are connected not to his animal (canine) nature; rather, they result from the "inherited"/acquired atavistic characteristics.[51] Bulgakov, in all likelihood, alludes to Lombroso. Indeed, Sharikov is a typical Lombrosian man with the corresponding "atavistic" craniological characteristics: "His brow was strikingly low. His hair began almost immediately above his spreading eyebrows."[52] The way Philip Philipovich shouts him down is quite notable: "'You were leaping around in the bathroom like a savage, smashing everything and jamming the taps. <. . .>.'You belong to the lowest possible stage of development.' 'You are still in the formative stage. You are intellectually weak, all your actions are purely bestial.'"[53] The savagery leitmotif sounds the most comical in the brief exchange of remarks between the professor and Sharikov: "'You are a savage.'—Me—a savage?" snarled Sharikov. 'I'm no savage.'"[54]

From the Lombrosian point of view, it seems logical to presume that the new man Sharikov received not only the shape but also the whole primitive "nature" of Chugunkin. He exists either in the quintessential form of stupidity or in extreme agitation, he indulges himself in idleness, he has cognitive problems and deficient "theory of mind," that is, he is incapable of assessing mental states of other people. He is spontaneously and excessively cruel (at least to cats). Besides, he is unable to think strategically—even proper goal setting is problematic for him.[55] Bulgakov presents Sharikov as an ideal semiotic system: his typically atavistic face and body (*the denotate*) fully correlate with his mental and emotional degenerative status (*the designate*).[56]

Certainly, Sharikov is in no way a descendant of Klim Chugunkin: the new man appeared with the help of Preobrazhensky's scalpel. The implanted pituitary gradually unfolded and materialized all the characteristics of the donor's "nature." So, the pituitary in the novella is a "generative mechanism" determining the recipient's looks and behavior. The quickly advancing endocrinology of the first decades of the twentieth century provided a perfect germ for Bulgakov's plot. It is equally important that at that time endocrinologists participated in the debates on heredity.

Lamarckian connotations in Bulgakov's text are also far from accidental. Not all eugenists were Mendelists in the 1920s.[57] For instance, the aforementioned eugenist of the Marxist camp, Mikhail Volotskoi, speculated that under the new improved conditions, scientists could secure the passing of acquired new characteristics on to the next generation of new men. From Lamarckian standpoint, one could easily imagine Sharikov's hypothetical descendants who would, in their turn, inherit such characteristics as weak intellect, predisposition to pointless and obsessive actions, uncontrollable sexuality and potential delinquency.[58] The appearance of a young girl in pale fawn stockings, the typist of the subdepartment for the control of stray animals, whom Sharikov is going to marry and settle with in the professor's apartment, gives us ground to believe that the chances for the reproduction of this new man are rather high. No eugenist would consider such a prospect desirable.

So far, I have looked into the "naturist" connotations in the novella. It also allows one to read it through the lens of "the nurturist concepts" of human nature. Bulgakov's text alludes to pedagogy in general, as well as to the method of formation of conditioned responses (behavioral reactions), in particular—specifically to the work of Ivan Pavlov, who, as is widely known, experimented on dogs, provoking the appropriate conditional reflexes. Most importantly, he strived to investigate whether corrected human behavior patterns could be passed on to descendants. Such research could be viewed by his Bolshevik patrons as the one most promising for the project of "making a new man" with bettered characteristics.[59] One has reasons to see the futile attempts of behavioral training, aimed at "developing Sharik into an intellectually advanced personality," as a travesty of Pavlov's experiments in particular and Soviet pedagogy in general.[60] After tackling the question of whether this hooligan can be turned into a human being, Preobrazhensky claims: "Now listen to me, professor-to-be-Bormenthal: no one could ever pull it off. It's obvious. No need to ask. If anybody asks you, tell them that Preobrazhensky said so. Finita. Klim!"[61]

Brought about by the daring medical experiment, the degenerate creature penetrates the apartment of the professor who seems to be the guarantor of norm, order, and sanity. Being supposedly protected from the overwhelming economic collapse in his Prechistenka apartment, he holds personal responsibility for "letting in" the defective being who is causing total chaos.

The Bolshevik authorities viewed the novella as a hostile commentary on the new Soviet regime. That is fair enough. Bulgakov was very skeptical in his assessment of political and economic status of the young Republic as well as of its sociobiological projects—and one can easily read it between the lines in the novella. Due to the proximity of Bulgakov's story to the real experiments conducted by Soviet medical researchers and pedagogues, "The Heart of a Dog" was an essentially modern text destined to cause displeasure of those supervising the respective scientific experiments. Moreover, the novella could be read as a satirical commentary on social and biological equality, such satire especially poignant in Sharikov's toasting: "Now everybody has the right to . . ."[62]

The epilogue of "The Heart of a Dog" accentuates a close relation of crime and biology. The very list of dramatis personae who appear there is telling: besides the "domkom" (house management committee) and Shvonder, its chair, there are medical professionals (*the suspects*), the patient (*the victim*), and the criminal militsiia (*law enforcement*). The reader cannot fail to pay attention to Professor Preobrazhensky's Lombrosian remark addressed to the detective and clarifying the biological status of his ward: "He talked and then he began to revert back to his primitive state. *Atavism*."[63] This is how Bulgakov stages and travesties the triumph of Lombrosianism: Preobrazhensky and Bormenthal show a ghoulish-looking dog that is capable only of rudimentary speech to the militia, the house management, and the detective. The allegedly "vanished," but, in reality, murdered and consequently revived Sharikov is degrading from the *subhuman* into the *nonhuman* state almost in front of the visitors. That dog is immediately recognized as the "former" Sharikov, which leads to the successful closing of the criminal case. In fact, the "new/old" Sharik, who is reversing to its initial canine state, symbolizes a successfully performed eugenic experiment: this "patient" is no longer dangerous for the human race.

In the epilogue, the dog's interior monologue allows the reader to contemplate the whole criminal adventure as a bad dream, and the pioneering experiment of making a new man with a new brain as a dangerous delusion. The progress turns out to be illusory and hitting the dead end. Preobrazhensky is disgusted by the idea of such experimenting because his first and only subject turned out to be a domestic monster and a scoundrel. With all due reasons, the subtitle of the novella, ignored by all but one of its English translators—"A Monstrous Story" (*Chudovishchnaia istoriia*)—can be read as "a story of a monster."[64]

Conclusion: Nature, Nurture, Crime, and the Two National Visions of "New Man"

As seen from the aforementioned analysis, the images of the new man in a work of fiction and film depend on a concrete development of ideas taking place in a certain culture at a certain time. Having commented on the respective amalgams of contemporaneous scientific ideas regarding human nature and the perspectives of manipulating it in the American and Russian science-fiction visions of "new man," I think it is now time to sum up major similarities and differences between these works in terms of themes, public reception, and afterlife.

The similarity of the transplantation discourse in "The Heart of a Dog" and Whale's *Frankenstein* is quite clear: in both plots, the "degenerative criminal brain" of a dead man is transplanted in another body. It is not so important which particular body it is placed into—one of a dog or of a cadaver stitched together from the "spare parts" of many different corpses, it largely predetermines the bodies and minds of the monstrous characters. Whale's film and Bulgakov's novella, in particular, show skepticism toward the idea of new man and its practical value.

The figures of Frankenstein's Monster and Sharikov were deliberately designed to be easily recognized by the contemporaneous readership and audience as men whom the Western eugenics identified as "degenerates" or the "unfit," and the Soviet one—as "defectives." Both "The Heart of a Dog" and *Frankenstein* contain certain references to Lombroso and sociobiological theories.

In both works, the creatures are pictured as unmistakably monstrous. The monster is an ideal heuristic and cognitive mechanism, as *monster studies* have demonstrated. The creatures in Bulgakov's novella and Whale's film are equally fascinating not only because "monsters are the most interesting people" but also because "the monster's body is a cultural body."[65] The monsters discussed here speak of the specific fears and dominating challenges of the 1920s and 1930s, the decades marked by eugenic battles at the crossroads of biology, medicine, pedagogics, sociology, and forensic psychiatry. Both characters provide excellent commentary on one of the dominant ideas of that time, according to which biology, anthropology, and medicine could, in theory, create a brand new type of man. The real danger of these previously unseen "new men" lies not only in their potential violence but in their potential procreation, too.[66]

In point of fact, what are the prospects of Frankenstein's Monster and Sharikov? Aren't they hopeless? Professor Preobrazhensky's forecast concerning his dog-man is simple: nobody can make this creature human. As an experienced doctor, a specialist in human neurophysiology and eugenically minded scientist, he does not believe in a successful correction of the hereditary criminal. The primary concept underlying the professor's logic is bio-determinism, according to which the future of a human being is determined by her/his inborn qualities. In other words, a born monster will live like a monster. But should he continue living? At first, the professor does not even allow a thought about any violence against the creature, still hoping for some correctional measures. However, it turns out that, in comparison with Sharikov, even such a natural cad as Shvonder is the least of two evils. It is non-accidental that Preobrazhensky concludes that such experiments are as untimely as pointless, which makes "The Heart of a Dog" a highly polemical text problematizing the values of the New Soviet Man project.

Apart from the "*naturist*" implications of the two plots, one cannot miss a "*nurturist*" aspect in these stories providing additional, environmental, explanation of the monsters' crimes: Shvonder with the house management committee in the novella and the antagonistic people surrounding the Monster in the movie surely play their parts in the destinies of these fantastic creatures. Yet, while Henry Frankenstein is guilty of being a bad parent who despises and neglects his own creation, one cannot accuse Professor Preobrazhensky and Doctor Bormenthal of neglecting Sharikov, who is surrounded by genuinely caring tenants of the most comfortable apartment. They spend considerable pedagogical effort in adapting the newly arrived man to some basic social norms.

Alongside the similarities between the novella and the movie, there are important differences in their respective fates. The sensational visuality guaranteed the popularity of *Frankenstein* (1931). The afterlife of the story of the metamorphosis of the dog was initially most unfortunate. Bulgakov's unpublished novella remained unknown to the very audience that it was intended for—to the contemporary readers who were, at least in some way, connected to the "new man" ideology and could have some knowledge about modern biomedical theories and experiments. The novella enjoyed a wide readership many decades later. Because of the postponed publication of Bulgakov's text, its readers failed to recognize a number of basic themes of the 1920s, as well as fully understand the challenges that the eugenicist professor faced. Bulgakov's multilayered and amazingly well-balanced text appealed to several scientific paradigms at the same time, inviting the reader to view the incredible "brain plot" within a wide spectrum of discourses: heredity, atavism, endocrinology, and pedagogy.

The creators of the cinematic Monster chose a much more straightforward approach that was dictated not only by the specifics of the horror genre and the wish for the box-office success but also by the ideological context in which the film was conceived and subsequently created. Unlike Soviet Russia, where eugenic ideas did not come to any practical fruition, half of the American states, starting from 1907, passed the laws ordaining forced sterilization of certain categories of "the unfit," including the criminals. The Great Depression reinforced the appeal of the degeneration and eugenic rhetoric and made the ideological message of the movie quite transparent. By "biologizing" the classical plot of Shelley's novel, Whale managed to make his own monster-story a piece of "actual art."

Still, with all the differences between the 1931 *Frankenstein* and "The Heart of a Dog," the fact that Whale and Bulgakov exterminated both fantastic creatures—the composite cadaver and the dog-man—could have been perceived by their contemporaries as a necessary eugenic measure against the biologically stigmatized "others." Such a finale of the American and Russian fantastic "brain stories" is in itself a definitive commentary on the controversial ideologies of "the new man" informed by a variety of social and bio-psycho-medical theories. Both works exemplify how the idea of "making a new man" served as a rich intellectual resource fitting specific cultural goals.

Part III

Displaying the New Man

In the Soviet Union of the 1920s and 1930s, the process of creating a "new man" for the world's first communist society involved multiple, often mutually contradictory, feats of imagination and improvisation, in which scientific knowledge, ideological imperatives, and aesthetic creativity all played a role. How would the new Soviet peasant—presumably a profoundly different creature than the subservient, backward peasant of old—be nurtured and educated into existence, while simultaneously becoming a participant in living displays of what the modern farm might look like? How would the Darwin Museum untangle the shifting roles of Nature and nurture in Soviet ideological constructions, when it put the tangled torsos of humans and orangutans on sculptural display in its grand hallway? If the Soviet "new man" was first and foremost an exemplary modern socialist laborer, then how would the ethnic diversity of the Soviet people be displayed and celebrated in a relevant way? The chapters in this section provide cases studies of how the emerging reality of Soviet "new men" was put on display throughout the 1920s and 1930s in order to both celebrate and inculcate the ideals of the future the Bolshevik revolution had promised to bring about.

Part III

Displaying the New Man

7

"A School of the Peasantry of the Future"

Constructing the Image of a "New Peasant" at the All-Russian Agricultural Exhibition, 1923

Olga Elina

It is time to abandon the old-fashioned division into city and village <. . .> The whole country now forms a continuous agricultural settlement punctuated by squares of public forests, strips of cooperative pastures and vast climate parks <. . .> At the heart of the economic system is a private peasant household. Each worker is a creator; each manifestation of his personality is an art of labor.[1]

This is how the peasantry of the future is described in a novel written shortly after the Bolshevik revolution by Alexander Chayanov, an eminent Russian agrarian visionary and theoretician. The novel's lead protagonist, a senior Soviet official, falls asleep in his Moscow apartment in 1920 and is transported the next morning to the year 1984 in the guise of an American who has arrived to explore the advanced "engineering installations in Russian agriculture." Over the preceding decades, the village has defeated the city: a peasant revolution has put an end to "communization," and the country has been completely "agrarianized." At the end of the twentieth century, Russia is a network of enlightened and technically advanced rural zones where creative forces are concentrated and a high level of science and culture is maintained. Traditional peasant labor has not been cancelled but instead supplemented by the high-tech artificial climate generation technology, which offers high yields and the ability to cultivate agricultural plants in all latitudes. Cities have been transformed into gardens and parks; they serve as centers of communication and cultural entertainment.

This picture of the future seems utterly utopian against the backdrop of the realities of life at the time of its creation—the civil war and "war communism" policy that caused a severe famine. However, the novel's author, the highly esteemed agricultural economist A. V. Chayanov, had reason to assume that the Russian village might develop in this direction. Indeed, the early 1920s were a time of an unprecedented debate on the evolution of the peasant economy, a "turn toward the peasantry." By placing Chayanov's utopia in the context of the impending socio-economic transformation of agriculture, when polar ideas clashed, and practices were rapidly changing, it becomes clear that his vision of the future peasantry was not all that unrealistic.[2]

Chayanov's reflections on the peasantry of the future are part of a broad discourse on the future of humankind, a powerful impetus to which was given by the October Revolution. As the "new man" idea was revived in Western Europe and the United States, Soviet Russia of the 1920s became a unique experimental platform where a "new man" was conceptualized and designed by the efforts of natural sciences, medicine, literature, visual arts, and cinema.[3] The idea was understood generically without emphasis on age, gender, profession, ethnic and class affiliation, although today's researchers develop the knowledge of strata and intragroup characteristics of a "new man."[4]

This chapter is about the attempts to create a "peasant of the future": that is, about the modernization discourse of state authorities, the theories of economists and sociologists, the dreams of writers and artists, and about schooling and propaganda in the name of certain ideals.

Soviet Russia emerged from the Russian empire as a predominantly peasant country where more than 75 percent of the population was involved in agriculture. The "union of workers and peasants," the gradual blurring of the line between rural and industrial labor, that was proclaimed by the Bolsheviks, pushed the boundaries of the Soviet "man of the future," inscribing in the concept the previously "awkward class"[5]—the peasantry. "New peasant" was thus inscribed in the search for "new man" already in the early 1920s. Viewing the peasant as a *subspecies* of the "new man," I expect to expand knowledge of the constituent components and developmental trends of the concept, the ideals, and the realities of "new man" creation in the 1920s.

I examine "new peasant" both as an *ideal*, a *model* constructed by social sciences and arts, and simultaneously as a real *product* that underwent a transformation in the changing society. Among many tools that the Bolshevik leaders applied to launch such a change, the All-Russian Agricultural and Handicraft Industrial Exhibition (VSKhV), held in Moscow in 1923, occupied a special place. One of the VSKhV major tasks was "to reveal to the peasant the new opportunities offered by the Soviet state";[6] among its many mottos was "the exhibition is a school of the peasantry of the future."[7]

VSKhV turned out to be an experimental space for solving an urgent practical task: the superfast implementation of the "new peasant" ideal. According to the VSKhV organizers' intention, "new peasant" as a product had to be formed right there, at the exhibition itself. The exhibition's scientific content and artistic appearance will provide an opportunity to reconstruct the ideal image as visionaries of the peasantry transformation intended it to be.

First of all, I will consider the origins of the ideal and the sociopolitical discussions on "new peasant." In the central part of the article, VSKhV will be analyzed as a "school of the peasantry of the future," which will require examining the images of ideal and "real" peasants at the exhibition, the content and design of expositions, forms of propaganda and cultural events related to the education of the "new peasant." A separate section presents the peasants' own experience as visitors, exhibitors, and "exhibits," as well as their reflections and comments on VSKhV. In conclusion, I will discuss the outcome of

VSKhV in terms of the success of "new peasant" project, adaptation, and reformatting of the implemented image.

VSKhV and Discussions on the "New Peasant"

What is the "peasant of today"? What should he become in the future? What needs to be done at the exhibition to accomplish such a transformation? These questions were discussed at various meetings, commissions, and advisory working groups that accompanied the preparation of VSKhV. The discussions usually turned into fierce debates—and not only because holding an exhibition with educational goals was a new concept and required the development of unique approaches.[8] The evolution of the peasantry was among the most vital issues in the country's history and its key question was the form of land ownership—private or communal, dating back to the old debate between the Slavophiles, populists and other guardians of a peasant commune (*obshchina*) and the Westernizers, the proponents of private property and capitalism, which had lasted since the 1840s. The Bolsheviks' coup d'état appeared to have radically solved the issue: the country's new rulers decreed to give the land "to those who cultivate it with their own labor." However, the civil war impeded the implementation of the decree. With the end of the war, debates resumed, turning into discussions about the optimal type of the peasant economy. To simplify, they can be reduced to the following controversy: the preservation of *private landholding* with a variety of *cooperation* (the proposal of the "organizational-production school" headed by Alexander Chayanov and Alexander Chelintsev) or the *communal socialization, collectivization* (the preferred solution of Marxist sociologists and economists).[9]

The postwar famine and mass unrest in the countryside called for a turn to the self-serving householder (*edinolichnik*) and the creation of conditions for his labor independence and material interest: market trade and in-kind taxation, which formed the basis of the New Economic Policy (NEP) in 1921. Cooperation came to the fore once again; according to Vladimir Lenin, it was "a tool of transition to a new order in the simpler, easier and more affordable way for the peasant."[10] The Land Code of 1922 legalized the coexistence of private farms, peasant communes, state farms, and collective farms, with an emphasis on supporting the individual peasant farm, a family household.[11] As statistics revealed a reduction in the number of private farms in the central grain-producing regions, the People's Commissariat of Agriculture (Narkomzem, NKZ) invited the local authorities to support the peasant-householder.[12]

The ambiguity of views on the path of the socioeconomic development of the Soviet peasantry did not undermine a consensus on the issue that seemed no less important, and perhaps even more fundamental for the "peasant of the future": his *progress through knowledge*. The notion that the "peasant of the future" should put into practice available scientific and technical knowledge was accepted by all the camps of state power and the scientific community in the early 1920s; as popular posters of the period show (see Figure 7.1). If disagreements did arise, they related only to the pace of the progress.

It is easy to trace prerevolutionary roots in the concept of *progress through knowledge*. First of all, the idea of turning the Russian peasant, a member of the commune, into an

Figure 7.1 Agitprop poster that encouraged the peasantry to learn agricultural innovations. The caption on top reads: "To have more one has to produce more"; the caption in the bottom reads: "To produce more one has to learn more." Artist Alexei Zelenskii. Petrograd, 1920. Paper, print. 66x47 © Courtesy of the State Museum of Political History of Russia.

"enlightened landowner"[13] was the basis of many modernization projects, including the Stolypin reforms of 1906–11.[14] From that time on, in journalistic and literary writings the term "new peasant" was used to describe the Stolypin peasantry as a new stratum of ambitious and successful individual owners who stood out from the "inert and backward" majority.[15] Their unique identity was based on the acquisition of versatile knowledge, which, in turn, was the result of the efforts of the zemstvo and government agronomists to train the peasants and to organize cooperative movements.[16] The external prerequisite for the emergence of the "new peasant" was already developed, thanks to the formation of industries that would serve the technological transformation of the village.[17]

The October Revolution, followed by a civil war and the introduction of "war communism" (a "food dictatorship" and surplus appropriation system, *prodrazvierstka*), led to severe famines in leading agricultural regions. The economic conditions forced the Bolsheviks to act "in an accelerated mode" to restore the crops: they proclaimed the goal to speed up a "bond between city and village." The "bond" (*smychka*) served as a comprehensible slogan that could convince the peasantry of the possibility of combining their traditional practices and modern technologies. VSKhV was to play a central role in the propaganda and implementation of the "bond" by "teaching peasants scientific and technical wisdom." VSKhV's expositions and performances demonstrated the conjunction of "a peasant and an agronomist," "a plough and a tractor," "a torch and an electric bulb." In a sense, the future "land of peasant utopia" with zones of artificial climate from Chayanov's novel cited at the beginning of the article is a utopia for the "bond" ideologists, one of the radical versions of the "bond" in which the village absorbed the city through industrial innovations.

This mottled picture of the peasantry of the early 1920s meant that the peasants of different strata and range of education would participate in VSKhV. Therefore, the concept of the exhibition as a *school for all groups of peasants* required careful consideration.

Demonstrating "Revolutionary Achievements and Plans": Arrangement of VSKhV

Agriculture had traditionally been the base for the peasant fairs and specialized exhibitions in Russia. By the end of the nineteenth century, agricultural science was added to the exhibitions' program, but it did not change their general pattern. Fairs and local exhibitions were still oriented exclusively to peasant trade, while all-Russian and international exhibitions displayed the products of the industry manufactured by large private and state exhibitors. Their target audience was from the same strata of society, that is, nobility and bourgeoisie. The international agrarian image of the Russian Empire could be seen in the Chicago exhibition of 1893. In the Russian pavilions the public was "surprised" with grottoes of vodka and Crimean wines, a fountain of grain, fortresses made from sacks of flour, leaving memories of the "tsarist luxury of decoration," "skill of craftsmen," "raw materials and products," not with the achievements of science and technology.[18] The content matched the design of the pavilions in the so-called *a la Rus* style with all the variations of the Moscow Kremlin.

The Stolypin reforms gave a new impetus to agricultural exhibiting: the formation of a market for consumers of scientific knowledge and technology. Among them, one can find zemstvo agronomists, land surveyors, teachers of agricultural educational institutions, government officials associated with the reforms, and most importantly—first enlightened peasants. The number of local shows grew rapidly: 3,380 were held in 1909–13. Several all-Russian exhibitions in the same period already included scientific sections and received high patronage from the Tsar's family.[19] In terms of architecture, the traditional style still dominated, but modernist variations and local motifs have already appeared. The emerging pattern of combining the trade and scientific-educational components at the agricultural exhibition was interrupted by a turbulent period of the First World War, the Bolshevik revolution, and the civil war.

VSKhV opened a new era of exhibitions, revolutionary both in terms of the goals it set for itself, and in the methods of implementation. According to the desire of the Bolshevik leaders, it had to mark the fifth anniversary of the October Revolution by exhibiting "the achievements and plans of the new-born Soviet state in agriculture and agricultural science."[20]

The supreme power institutions dealing with the organization of VSKhV were the All-Russian Central Executive Committee (VTsIK), the highest legislative and controlling state body, and Narkomzem as a key actor of the Council of the People's Commissars (Sovnarkom, SNK, the Soviet government). The Chief Exhibition Committee (GVK) of VSKhV as the body responsible for daily routine work was formed with Mikhail Scheffler, a senior Narkomzem official, as its chairman.[21] First and foremost among VSKhV tasks, the organizers named the economic revival of the country through a "turn to the peasantry": it was to be primarily a "peasant overview" and was to promote "investing large capital . . . into peasant farming where it will definitely be profitable."[22] VSKhV had some characteristics of an international fair: the organizers aspired to attract the attention of the world community to the prospects of trade and investment in the Soviet economy. An extensive *Foreign Section* (see Figure 7.2) was created to accommodate more than 600 foreign state and private companies and firms that participated as exhibitors. The formation of the USSR in December 1922 significantly increased the scope of the project.[23]

Since the general idea of VSKhV was to display innovations, a Scientific and Technical Council was set up to create and evaluate the expositions. A distinguished agronomist and agricultural statistician, Vladimir Kovalevsky, headed the Council;[24] among its members were such eminent agricultural scientists as Alexander Chayanov and Sokrat Chayanov, Alexei Doyarenko, Nikolai Tulaykov, Nikolai Vavilov, and Vladimir Winer.[25]

Figure 7.2 View at the Foreign Section of the All-Russian Agricultural and Handicraft Industrial Exhibition, 1923. Unknown photographer. © Courtesy of the Gorky Park Archive.

The VSKhV organizers sought to express the revolutionary renewal of the country through a unique design of the exposition pavilions, as VTsIK asked them "to build the Exhibition in such a way . . . that the appearance of the Exhibition and its internal content reflect the dignity of Soviet Russia."[26] Eminent architects, painters, and sculptors, invited to build VSKhV, demonstrated a wide range of contemporary artistic styles and trends—from neoclassicism and modernism to rationalism and constructivism. The artists involved in the Exhibition's design and construction included Ilya and Panteleimon Golosovs, Ivan Zholtovsky (author of the general plan), Viktor Kokorin, Konstantin Melnikov, Viacheslav Oltarzhevsky, Fedor Shekhtel', Alexei Shchusev (chief architect), Aristarkh Lentulov, Vladimir and Georgy Stenberg, Alexandra Exter, Vera Mukhina, Maria Strakhovskaia, and Ivan Shadr. Many journalists and littérateurs, Vladimir Mayakovsky, Demyan Bednyi, and Mikhail Bulgakov among them, were involved in covering the Exhibition in the press.[27] Well-paid exhibition orders obviously became a timely help for the art community, deprived of earning opportunities during the years of the revolution and the civil war.[28] This is perhaps why in historiography, VSKhV is known primarily as the first impressive statement made by artists of revolutionary Russia, the triumph of the Soviet avant-garde.[29]

VSKhV occupied an area of almost 100 hectares, located along the Moskva River near the Crimean bridge and spreading to the very famous place of recreation of Muscovites—the Neskuchnyi Garden. In just ten months, a railway was built, 225 buildings were erected, and 150 pavilions were equipped. On August 19, 1923, VSKhV was officially opened;[30] welcome speakers were Mikhail Kalinin from TsIK of the USSR, Aleksei Rykov from SNK, Lev Kamenev, from the Moscow Council, and Leon Trotsky, from the Politburo of the Bolshevik Party.[31]

Exhibition for the Peasantry: School of "Learning New Things"

The crucial innovation of VSKhV was the mass participation of peasants as exhibitors: "the peasant, the peasant farm should have become the focus of all work on setting the exhibition as the most important and basic economic unit in the Republic."[32] The organizers planned to invite thousands of peasants to exhibit their achievements: "Each pavilion should make sure that it can display an average of several dozen, and in some cases, over a hundred purely peasant exhibits."[33]

The objective of turning VSKhV into "an exhibition for the peasantry" required solving several issues. How to encourage peasants to come, and what language should be used for this purpose? Agitation and Propaganda department (APO) of VSKhV was set up to initiate "a broad campaign about the Exhibition."[34] APO pursued several goals: ensuring all forms of agitation and propaganda "on the ground," instructing local committees, training local instructors, and providing the campaign at VSKhV.[35] Some authors described the agitation work poetically: "Whether a land surveyor leaves for land planning, an agronomist travels to the countryside, a forester goes to a forest to do bidding or logging—their first concern should be to provide all the materials about the Exhibition, and their first word to the peasants should be 'Exhibition.'"[36]

The next question was about the preferable form of local agitation. It was directly related to the image of the peasant, to whom the exhibition was supposed to appeal. A universal mechanism for all peasants was considered to be verbal agitation, which demanded the mobilization of a large corps of agitators. But, the local committees reported that they could not handle this task.[37] During the period of the Stolypin reforms, the local agronomic press had proved its effectiveness in the propaganda issue. However, local newspapers informed APO that only "exemplary" peasants read newspapers; the journalists called them "Americans," emphasizing their level of education and thirst for knowledge that was rare for the village of the 1920s.[38] However, according to the experts' opinion, an expected visitor of VSKhV, would be not an advanced "American," but mostly an "average peasant, illiterate and unenlightened."[39]

Considering the situation in the countryside, APO recommended a poster as the most convenient tool for the pre-exhibition campaign and ordered "to prepare and send out large quantities of posters, mainly for the village."[40] The artistic language of the poster was thought to fit the archaic peasant consciousness, which required simplified images. These were the tasks set before the graphic artists who created posters for VSKhV. As a result, the mass distributed posters were designed mainly in a realistic manner, combining the traditions of the Russian popular print (*lubok*) with a grotesque satirical connotation (see Figure 7.3). The distribution of these posters "on the ground" was facilitated not only by VSKhV regional committees but also, for example, by the railway network.[41]

However, the posters drawn in a style similar to Art Nouveau won the competition held at the exhibition. The first prize was given to the piece "Gold of the Fields" by Sergey Ridman and I. Lebedev, featuring a stylized figure of a young peasant, bent under the weight of a symbolic sheaf.[42] A twin poster pictured a young peasant woman with the same bunch in her hands.[43] Both had a print run of 10,000 copies each and became the "trademark" of VSKhV.[44]

Another important task was to continue the propaganda during the exhibition, transforming it into the educational campaign: How exactly to organize a *learning new things* process for the peasants-visitors, who already came to the VSKhV "school"?

Three expert groups—the scientific, the artistic, and the literary—discussed the specific features of the "school." The experts stated that all varieties of material and figurative demonstrations had to prevail, including "live exhibits" (animal specimens, crops, experimental plantings, etc.), mechanisms and tools, models, poster graphics, paintings, slides, and film materials. Another essential part of the VSKhV "school" became educational excursions for the peasants. The visual demonstration had to be supplemented by qualified verbal explanations and briefs. A significant number of guides and the so-called explainers recruited from young agronomists and agricultural colleges' students worked at VSKhV.[45]

Let us visit some expositions that comprised the VSKhV "school of the peasantry of the future." The notion of technical enhancements was emphasized by the *Pavilion of Agricultural Machinery and Tools* (architect Ivan Zholtovskii), which was designed as a gearwheel. Avant-garde artist Alexandra Exter and renowned theater artist Ignatii Nivinskii painted its porticos and interiors with the agricultural implements, alternating with the inscriptions such as "metal" and "electricity."[46] The exhibits included extensive

Figure 7.3 Agitprop poster for the All-Russian Agricultural and Handicraft Industrial Exhibition, 1923. The caption in the bottom reads: "Comrades peasants! Get ready for the All-Russian Agricultural and Handicraft Industrial Exhibition in Moscow in August-September 1923. For information, contact the exhibition committees, the volost' committees, and your volost' agricultural department." Artist M. Evstaf'ev. Moscow, 1923. Paper, print. 70 × 52. © Courtesy of the State Museum of Political History of Russia.

collections of machines and tools—tractors, electric ploughs, implements for fertilizer distribution, seeders, threshers, uproots, sprayers, electric saws, and so on.[47] The peasants could try out many of the exhibits in special classes with instructors. To demonstrate the capabilities of the most sophisticated equipment—the US tractors "Fordson" and "International"—individual operators were invited. A new profession—tractor driver (*traktorist*)—came into fashion thanks to VSKhV. The tractor as a symbol of the "bond between city and village" became the "main character" of numerous meetings and discussions. "All the benches are full. They are sitting very close to one another"—reported Mikhail Bulgakov on the debate "Tractor and Electrification in Agriculture."[48]

A crucial point for the peasantry was *the Plant Cultivation Section* (architects Ivan Zholtovskii and Nikolai Kolli). Its main pavilion, *Crop Cultivation*, exhibited models of improved crop rotation systems, "dry farming" techniques, fertilizing techniques, seed cultivation, and particular crop (cotton, flax, hemp, sunflower) techniques, practices of plant protection.[49] The experts widely used material demonstration, such as "live crop plantings."[50] For example, a central plot, designed to resemble the map of Russia, could be conveniently observed from the observation deck on top of a viaduct, which the photographs showed to be filled with spectators at all times.[51] This pavilion was also an example of a skillful constructivist decoration of the exhibition space. The brothers Stenbergs' counter-reliefs placed on the porticos were of particular interest. They "hung" volumetric compositions, featuring fantasies about the field and soil improvement practices: stylized details of the harrow, manual and mechanical sprayers.[52] Elements of these structures "soared," changing position depending on the angle of view. Visitors were amazed by the unusual decor.[53]

Another vital section of the "school" was *Cooperation*. Its leading pavilion, *Agricultural Cooperation*, was built on the right side of the central ground. The task of the exposition was to "open up a vast field for small-scale peasant farms to take full advantage of large-scale farming."[54] The difficulties of introducing the idea of cooperation to peasants were successfully overcome by using the propaganda posters and vivid paintings, demonstrating the technical advantage of cooperative farming.[55]

Peasant at VSKhV: Visitor, Exhibitor, Inhabitant

The *learning new things* tour covered only a few pavilions important for the "school of the peasantry of the future." Beyond the tour, there were dozens of expositions related to agricultural product processing, forestry and handicraft industry, labor organization, republican and national buildings, a vast *Foreign Section* (see Figure 7.2), and much more, which may have been of interest to some of the peasants. The most telling propaganda class of the VSKhV "school" was its *Village Section*. This section included nearly three dozen buildings, divided into "The Village of the Past and the Present" ("Old Village") and "The Village of the Future" ("New Village").[56] The organizers considered this section "a *core* of the Exhibition," where "the mindset of the peasant" was supposed to change.[57] Each peasant who came to the exhibition was obliged to visit the "Villages."

On average, the peasant would spend a week in Moscow, including four or five full days of excursions at VSKhV.[58] The accommodation and all education and entertainment events, as well as snacks, were free of charge. The expected number of peasant-excursionists was estimated at around 140,000—ten peasants from each *volost'*, the smallest regional territory inside the province.[59] Another group of peasants were the so-called volunteers, who covered their travel and exhibition costs by themselves.[60] All peasants who visited VSKhV as exhibitors were granted an agricultural tax deduction of 25 percent.[61]

The organizers of VSKhV wanted to encourage the peasants to compare their current life to the life "in the Soviet future," so that once they have witnessed the contrast in technologies, they would consciously choose the future.[62] The expositions of the *Village Section* were designed to show and propagate the dramatic difference between "The Village of the Past" and "The Village of the Future."

The experts proposed an unusually bold solution: for primary agricultural regions "to exhibit a hut with household items, a yard with all the equipment, horses, cattle and other animals."[63] They selected dozens of "typical" local farms from the Central Black Soil (see Figure 7.4) and the other climatic regions.[64] The Ostyak yurts from the Tobolsk province (see Figure 7.5) and the traditional dwellings of Uzbeks, Bashkirs, and Kyrgyz were also added to the list.[65] The huts selected for display were carefully measured and reproduced according to the blueprints at the exhibition. The owners brought all their belongings, pets, and farm animals with them.

Most important, these peasant families would stay in their huts for the entire period of the exhibition! The "peasant-inhabitants" were supposed to continue their everyday practices: look after the cattle, feed poultry, serve hives in the apiary, knit baskets, cut spoons, and so on. The demonstration of "peasant-inhabitants" can be considered as a unique ethnographic event: the traditional life of the peasantry was shown unconventionally by involving the peasants as "living exhibits." At first glance, the presence of "inhabitants" contradicted the main idea of the exhibition, turning the peasant into *an object* on display, an *exhibit*. However, the "inhabitants" were taking advantage of their extended stay at VSKhV. In essence, they explored the expositions on par with the regular visitors and arranged their activities such as meetings to "exchange

Figure 7.4 Family of peasant-"inhabitants" from Central Russia at the "Old Village" ("Village of the Past") section, the All-Russian Agricultural and Handicraft Industrial Exhibition, 1923. Unknown photographer. © Courtesy of RGAE.

Figure 7.5 The Ostyak family at the "Old Village" section, the All-Russian Agricultural and Handicraft Industrial Exhibition, 1923. Unknown photographer. © Courtesy of RGAE.

impressions of the exhibition." As the Commandant of the "Old Village" argued, these activities "strengthen the significance of the exhibition and acquired knowledge in the consciousness of the peasants."[66]

Such an unusual experiment could not have gone smoothly. The "peasant-inhabitants" faced many difficulties: they were not happy with the quality and quantity of food, there were interruptions in the supply of boiling water, washing in the bathhouse was poorly organized, payments were delayed. While such problems could be resolved, the main trouble—the early autumn weather that led to dampness and cold in most huts—was unsolvable. It was especially difficult for two families with children; in one of the families, the child was coughing; in the other, "the six-months child was suffering from digestive disorder because his mother had lost milk from cold and hunger."[67] One can only guess what the "peasant-inhabitants" must have thought of their exhibition experience.

In contrast, the "Village of the Future" demonstrated innovation in everything, starting with the appearance of buildings. The avant-garde architects Aleksei Rukhliadev, Viktor Kokorin, and Nikolai Kolli proposed bold designs and color solutions that resembled suprematist compositions. However, the Chief Committee felt that the concept would be too complicated for the peasantry to understand, so it had to be modified, and the "Village of the Future" appeared in more restrained forms: no longer so provocative, but still bright and avant-garde.[68]

The "New Village" demonstrated comfortable, electrified buildings: residential cottages, the agronomic center, the Peasant's House (a peasant club with a hall for 300 people, a library, and classrooms; see Figure 7.6), and a cooperative dairy. There was also an exemplary collective farm with a barn for fifteen to twenty heads of cattle, a pigsty, and a poultry pen.[69]

The contrast with the "Old Village," according to the experts, was to convince the peasants of the "advantages of socialism" as applied to their work and life:

> Here, the peasants will see a New Village where the Soviet state and agronomic science are inviting them, and which they will create themselves upon their return home. Let the peasant wake up with disgust at the Old Village, let the peasant promise himself that he would strive to create a New Village.[70]

APO of VSKhV proposed an elaborated cultural program to support exhibit propaganda of the "Villages." Festive events traditionally served as an integral part of exhibitions and peasant fairs.[71] A new synthetic genre appeared at VSKhV: "folk performance" in which the peasant himself became a participant.[72] "The Day of the New and Old Villages," celebrated on September 7, serves a perfect example.[73] The celebration began in the square of the "Old Village," from where peasant families with old tools—*sokhas* (primitive wooden ploughs—O. E.), sickles, scythes, and so on—proceeded to the tribune of the Main Pavilion, accompanied by the famous Piatnitsky folk choir. A delegation of the "New Village" with modern tools—tractors, reapers,

Figure 7.6 The House of the Peasant ("Peasant's House") at the "New Village" ("Village of the Future") section, the All-Russian Agricultural and Handicraft Industrial Exhibition, 1923. Unknown photographer. © Courtesy of the Gorky Park Archive.

and ploughs—also headed there.[74] When they met, the processions of the old and new villages first quarreled, then came together in a symbolic "bond."[75] Another popular theme of VSKhV performances was the "public court" representing scenes of symbolic trials, such as "The trial of an old hut" and "The trial of a *sokha*."[76]

According to APO, "folk performances" should imitate traditional religious holidays that had become firmly established in the minds of peasants and replace them with the new Soviet ones. It corresponded to the policy of weakening the influence of the church on mass consciousness, the "internal Sovietization" of the village.[77] The peasant youth was inspired to regard "the whole village as a continuous celebration, continuous joy," and urged to "raise the banner against the old holidays."[78] The number of celebrations increased as VSKhV was wrapping up and awards were being presented.[79]

Another exciting innovation introduced by the propaganda experts was slogans, agitation chants, and ditties in the spirit of Russian folklore, composed by the invited writers and poets. The most popular form was a "rhymed ditty," *chastushka*, which imitated the traditional folk rhymes, for example:

They have kept us in the dark,
but those days are over.
We're the same and yet different
following the light of knowledge.[80]

The peasants quickly picked up the ditties and sang them with pleasure; the "new peasant" folk rhymes spread throughout the villages of the USSR, helping promote the Exhibition as a "school of the peasantry of the future."

Peasant after VSKhV: Reflections and New Realities

The peasants brought back prizes to their homeplaces from the exhibition: items, which served as symbols and advertisement for the "bond between city and village." Such a case became the plot of Vladimir Mayakovsky's propaganda poem about VSKhV. The language of the poetry was stylized as folk, peasant.

Soviet people everywhere
Were roaring with excitement:
Behold true miracle right here
Not far from Park Neskuchny!
Moscow's calling everyone
To come together swiftly,
so that peasants and the workers
Can strengthen their bond!

The narrative elements of a well-known fairy tale were used: "walking" of the peasant "to the city-capital," a "big-big" turnip, a hen that lays "golden eggs," and a happy ending. Having heard about the exhibition, Klim, the protagonist of the comic poem, brings his exhibits there:

Am I worse? Guess, I'm not!
Klim was cursing madly
and displayed all that he had—
the hen and the turnip.

Becoming a winner, Klim receives products from rubber (bicycle tires, children toys and even a hose for extinguishing fire) of the famous "*Treugol'nik*" brand as awards. The story ends with a traditional happy ending and promises of a better life: the entire village "shows respect to Klim," asking him once and again to tell about the Exhibition; its "miracles," he claims, will soon enter the village life.[81]

As to the observations of the real peasants-excursionists, they were mostly published as reported by local journalists covering VSKhV. For example, the Vyatka journalist Konstantin Altaisky (Korolev), who was accompanying a provincial delegation of 400 peasants, vividly described the reaction of peasants to the "contrast of the old and the new" in the spirit of Mayakovsky's protagonist: "A tractor caught the eye of the peasants, and nearby there was a *sokha* from the Perm province. A peasant saw it and, after examining the tractor, he spat in anger and cursed. This means the exhibition had touched the peasant's heart."[82]

The peasants' recollections resemble the praising narrative of Mayakovsky's poem in emphasizing the beauty and exciting content of the expositions, the comfort of the accommodations, etc. For instance, the peasant Mikhail Kovrov from the Vyatka region noted: "Moscow met us very warmly, the room was perfect. There were guides with whom we visited the exhibition. We had only four days for excursions, but we will never forget what we saw." Describing expositions that particularly impressed him and his comrades, he concluded: "For us, peasants, the most interesting were the departments of field farming and animal husbandry with purebred cattle. We saw a farm with crop rotation system." Like the character of Mayakovsky, peasant Kovrov wanted to introduce innovations to his village. However, his letter from the exhibition included an essential element—reflection and analysis. Kovrov insisted that the village needs not only knowledge but also private land ownership. He called for the cooperation of the peasant householders as a vital precondition for improvements: "It is possible to establish such farming in our Vyatka province, but I think it will be better for our peasants to join the cooperative farms. Then the crop rotation system will take root, as well as all agricultural knowledge."[83]

The peasant Kovrov comments and other publications demonstrate huge interest to VSKhV among the peasantry. More than 1.5 million people, mostly the peasants, visited the exhibition. The visitors' flow was so massive that the organizers decided to keep VSKhV "till the cold comes," despite some proposals to close it ahead of schedule.[84] This was not the end of the project: VSKhV served as an impulse and a model for more than six thousand local exhibitions that took place in 1924–8, with the total number of visitors approaching six millions.

The village stirred up, as the local press quickly noted. The first to respond were those who could be considered "new peasants": community activists, ready to take in the new knowledge, like peasant Kovrov from Vyatka and other so-called Americans. In their mentality and practices, they were the followers of Stolypin's "new peasants," who served as models for the economists of the Chayanov circle. It can be assumed that the youngest generation of this stratum, who were about twenty years old during the Stolypin reform, could be found among the "new peasants" of early Soviet Russia. It can also be assumed that most of the "new peasants" would later be declared *kulaks* in the period of Stalin's "Great Break."[85]

As for the bulk of the peasantry, the organizers of VSKhV argued that "the resonance of the Exhibition can be calculated in a year or two when peasant visitors will convey to their comrades what they perceived at the Exhibition."[86] It would also take time to launch the agricultural cooperation, an essential tool for the renewal of the village, promoted by the exhibition.

However, with the changed USSR leadership, the exhibition ideas were losing their support. The concept of economic transformation focused on accelerated industrialization prevailed; the peasantry served only as a means to achieving this goal. The cooperative movement was defeated, mass collectivization of peasant householders took place, which forever erased the ideals of labor individualism from the peasant mind. The sprouts of this communist transformation of the village were already visible at VSKhV, but in 1923, though imposed by party propaganda bodies, they were not prevailing at all. Yet, while the peasant-owner ideal dominated at VSKhV, the seeds of the uncertainty were already planted in the future "new peasant" product: the hasty "education" started to resemble the compulsory "re-forging."

The collective farm future turned out to be incompatible with the vision of "new peasant" by those whose ideas formed the basis of the exhibition. The fate of many active organizers of VSKhV was tragic. In 1926 Alexander Chayanov was accused of "anti-Marxist interpretation of peasant farming."[87] He was arrested in 1930, along with his cousin Sokrat Chayanov, in the so-called Labor Peasant Party case, fabricated by the NKVD; Alexander was later executed, Sokrat spent years in prison and exile.[88]

Conclusion

The All-Russian Agricultural Exhibition serves as a magnifying glass through which one can see the general panorama and details of the grandiose project to create a "new peasant" in the early USSR.

As this study shows, at the beginning of the 1920s, the bureaucrats responsible for agriculture proclaimed the ideal of "new peasant" as an educated householder, ready for modernization through agronomic knowledge and cooperation. VSKhV worked as one of the instruments to construct the ideal image of such a peasant-owner and to make this model a reality.

The focus on the peasantry as the most economically significant social stratum distinguishes VSKhV from a series of subsequent large Soviet displays, especially the Exhibition of the Achievements of the National Economy (VDNKh), where the industrial component was dominant. The subjectification of the peasantry makes VSKhV stand out also from the prerevolutionary exhibitions with the peasant as an ethnographic exhibit or a fun character. Asserting the idea of the peasantry as an essential integral part of the society of the 1920s, VSKhV provides a valuable case for understanding the constituents of the broader project of "making new man" in early Soviet Russia.

The organizers of VSKhV came up with a relevant language that allowed them to articulate the image of "new peasant" and to make it quickly understandable for the peasants who visited the exhibition. Art, as was shown, became a crucial constituent of this language. The peasants were immediately intrigued by the exterior of VSKhV, which trumpeted the idea of "revolutionary novelty" through varied attributes of innovated visual reality, including the spectacular design of the pavilions. Further, thousands of exhibits demonstrated the impressive results of improved farming technologies, different machinery, and other technical innovations of the "future village" that persuaded the peasantry of the importance to urgently transform the mode of their life and work.

VSKhV offered an arsenal of demonstrations, lectures, excursions, and learning entertainments to educate visiting peasants in the new ways. The most crucial characteristic of this "school of learning new things" was its concentration in time and space: a superfast education process was taking place right at the exhibition. As the case of the exhibition demonstrates, the mechanism for the creation of "new man" in early Soviet Russia included not only gradual education, but also revolutionary transformation in the "here and now" mode. Thereby, this research reveals a new dimension of converting "ideal" new human product into a "real" one.

How productive proved the project of VSKhV as a "school of the peasantry of the future"? Were the two interconnected tasks within the project—constructing the ideal image of a "new peasant" and making it a reality—equally successful? Judging by the classic indicator of the exhibition industry—the number of visitors—the task to articulate the image of "new peasant" and introduce the peasantry to new ideas was achieved. The exhibition did spur genuine interest among the peasantry; millions of peasants also visited numerous regional shows that were modeled after VSKhV. The contents of the local press publications confirm that ideas articulated by VSKhV convinced the majority of the peasant-owners of the necessity to transform their lives and work in a new way.

The answer to the key question, concerning the creation of a real "new peasant" as the product of the VSKhV school, is more complicated. Such creation would take time to materialize, as it demanded the long-term science-based modernization of rural life. However, the potential "peasants of the future" were deprived of that future due to the radical transformation of the rural policy in the second half of the 1920s. The VSKhV ideals ceased to match the realities of the "Great Break." It is hard to estimate how many from the hundreds of thousands of peasants, adherents to the new ideas, managed to adapt to collectivization and how many were declared *kulaks*, dispossessed, exiled, executed. Therefore, transforming the concept of "new peasant" into reality through VSKhV can only be discussed in the subjunctive mood. Even if VSKhV gave a good start to this process, it failed in the long run.

The turn for industrialization not only ruined the peasant-owner ideology but also seems to have influenced the historical fate of VSKhV itself, crossing it out of the list of events important for the development of Soviet agriculture. The exhibition appeared to draw no interest from later agricultural history and peasantry studies, leaving a trace only as an exceptional event of Russian art.

In this work, I tried to place the All-Russian Agricultural Exhibition of 1923 into the context of the scholarship on "making new man" in Soviet Russia: a striking attempt by prominent visionaries to create a "new peasant," which lasted only for as long as the Bolshevik leaders backed it.

Acknowledgments

I would like to thank the staff of several museums and archives for their kind help in gathering and copying the materials for this piece. In particular, my gratitude goes to Anton Belov, director of the Garage Museum of Contemporary Art, and to Anna Dikovich, Institutional Archive Keeper, Research department of the Garage Museum. The support of Elizaveta Likhacheva, director of the A. V. Shchusev State Museum of Architecture (GMA), and Lev Rassadnikov, keeper of the GMA Catalogue of Photos, was indispensable. The staff of the Russian State Archive of Economy was extremely helpful. Elena Soboleva, head of the Archive of the Gorky Park, and Svetlana Khodokovskaia, chief keeper of the State Museum of Political History of Russia, provided much-appreciated assistance. I gratefully acknowledge Marianna Evstratova, head of the Library of the Moscow Institute of Architecture, for her expert assistance. My sincere thanks to Nikolai Krementsov for his criticism and comments throughout all the process of conceiving, writing, and editing this chapter.

8

Revolutionary Evolution in Apes and Humans in the 1920s

Sculpture and Constructs of the "New Man" at the Moscow Darwin Museum

Pat Simpson

Introduction

Western and post-Soviet Russian art-historical writings have predominantly tended to associate the experimental work of avant-garde artists such as Kasimir Malevich, El Lissitzkii, and Pavel Filonov, exclusively with early Soviet constructs of the creation or evolution of the "New Man." For example, John Bowlt and Olga Matich's "Introduction" to the anthology *Laboratory of Dreams* (1996) suggests that this stems from such artists' identifications of a necessary link between their artistic radicalism and the "radical politics" of the new regime, which also chimed with their prerevolutionary Russian Symbolist beliefs in the power of art to transform life.[1] By contrast, this chapter analyzes the apparently more conventional, naturalistic approach to representing some of the key components of the deeply pervasive construct of the Soviet "New Man" that, arguably, were taken up by the artist and zoologist Vasilii Vatagin at the Moscow Darwin Museum in 1926.

Vatagin had engaged with Russian Symbolist ideas before the October Revolution, and also with avant-garde, geometrical abstraction afterward,[2] but the latter was not the mode of practice he adopted in his role as chief artist at the Darwin Museum. This role required illusionistic precision of representation, as will be discussed herein. The chapter focuses on the contextual, biopolitical resonances regarding contemporary constructs of the "New Man" relating to Vatagin's intriguing pair of monumental, plaster relief sculptures entitled *Age of Life*, commissioned by the museum in 1926 (Figures 8.1 and 8.2). One of these sculptures represents the Darwinian notion of variation and variability in relation to the reproductive cycle and sociability of human women, while the other represents those of orangutans. Interestingly, there seems to be no explanation of these works provided by the museum either in its official publications or in its archives so far as I can find, despite the sculptures being prominently displayed

Figure 8.1 Vasilii Vatagin, *Age of Life: Variation in Humankind,* 1926, 0.8 × 1.3 × 2.6 m, plaster. © The State Darwin Museum Moscow.

on the second-floor gallery of the current museum. This chapter, therefore, sets out to question what these sculptures may be about, and, given the context of their production, how they may relate to contemporary and past Soviet and Russian constructs of the "New Man."

The Darwin Museum, from its inception in 1907, was committed to using artworks to support and illuminate the shifting and sometimes-contradictory contemporary concepts of evolution in the West and Russia. Officially adopted by the Higher

Figure 8.2 Vasilii Vatagin, *Age of Life: Variation in Orangutans*, 1926, 0.8 × 1.3 × 2.6 m. plaster. © The State Darwin Museum Moscow.

Women's Courses section of Moscow University in 1914, the museum's position within the new State Moscow University was confirmed after the Bolshevik revolution in 1917.[3] Throughout this time and until the early 1960s, the museum remained under the same directorship. One of the directors was Professor Alexander Kots—a zoologist and ornithological expert. The other was his wife, Nadezhda Ladygina-Kots—a zoo-psychologist and ape-researcher, particularly interested in using environment and training to explore the extent to which these could permanently change the behavior of apes to be more humanlike. In this chapter I have used the term "evolutionizing" as a short way of referring both to this ambition and to the differently framed ambition of the Soviet geneticist, Il'ia Ivanov.

A crucial factor in the Kotses longevity as directors, and indeed in the survival of the museum itself, was their ability to adapt the museum's display policy to fit in with the shifting Soviet definitions of evolution and Darwinism.[4] Given the concern for institutional self-preservation, and the high significance placed on the evolution/creation of the "New Man" within the immediate postrevolutionary political, cultural, and bioscientific discourses, it would seem inevitable that the museum's display policy in the mid-1920s would take some visual account of this.

The first section of the chapter sets out some basic details about the sculptures and relates aspects of these details to the institutional, ideological, and artistic conditions that possibly precipitated the commissioning of the works in 1926. The second section examines the complex, potential ideological reference points of one of the sculptures, *Age Variability in Humankind*, to Soviet engagement with eugenics, "social hygiene," and "hygienic maternity"—key factors in contemporary discourse on making the "New Man." The third section explores the other sculpture, *Age Variability in Orangutans*, and interrogates the possible, shifting resonances of the choice of images of orangutans both in 1926 and in 1929–30, in relation to the ideas of Lamarck and Darwin, and also to Professor Il'ia Ivanov's ape-human hybridization project 1925–9, all of which arguably had relevance to the broader Revolutionary project of prompting the evolution of the "New Man."

In conclusion, I suggest that there is a sense in which the sculptures were partly a memorial to Ladygina-Kots's ape-human comparative research at the Darwin Museum. The complex imagery in the sculptures, however, arguably also relates specifically to certain contemporary crypto-Lamarckian[5] theorizations of revolutionary models concerning the evolution of the"New Man."

One of these was the Soviet propaganda on "hygienic motherhood" as a socially "hygienic," eugenic pathway to the generation of the "New Man" through social and environmental changes. The other was the mutually competitive and ideologically divergent "evolutionizing" ape-research of Il'ia Ivanov and Ladygina-Kots in the 1910s and 1920s, which implicitly counterposed the Lamarckian-style and hard-line "genetic" solutions to the problem of "proving" human evolution from apes. I will also suggest that, as a result of these conflicting bioscientific and ideological connections, the pair of sculptures may be argued to share a projected positive vision of what the French critical theorist Michel Foucault would call "docile bodies"[6]—both ape and human—scientifically objectified and medicalized for the purposes of renovating the population. Finally, on a broader level, I will reflect briefly on the complex nature of the 1920s Soviet "New Man" discourse and the endemic limitations on the powers of visual art to represent and disseminate it, relating to the context of the Darwin Museum 1926–9.

The Commissioning of the *Age of Life* Sculptures

The *Age of Life* sculptures are large, cast, and carved plaster reliefs. Both are 80 centimeters deep at the base, 130 centimeters wide, and 260 centimeters tall. In the current museum display both now stand on *c.* 0.5-meter-high plinths. Without these they would still be quite imposing, suggesting that they had significance for the museum's scientific work and for its presentation of Darwinian evolutionary theory at the time. Since Vatagin produced a very small number of large-scale sculptures for the museum—a total of four—Why may Kots have commissioned these monumental sculptures in the context of 1926?

One likely incentive, within this context, was the Decree issued by the Soviet government in 1926, promising a new and larger museum building.[7] Although the building never materialized, the hopes of more exhibition space that it raised may have prompted not only the commissioning of the *Age of Life* works in 1926 but also in 1927 of an equally large monumental sculpture of *Seated Darwin* by Vatagin, as well as of a taxidermized African elephant executed by Fillip Fedulov, the museum's chief taxidermist.[8] Moreover, on May 6, 1926, a speech by the Soviet historian and art critic Piotr Kagan particularly emphasized the need for, and political value of, monumental artworks in places, "which attract people in their thousands,"[9] which the Darwin Museum effectively did, albeit in organized, prebooked, lecture-tour groups. The speech was delivered in Gorky Park at the opening of the exhibition *The Life and Peoples of the USSR*, containing figurative works by the Association of Artists of Revolutionary Russia (AKhRR). This exhibition was considered to be so important by the authorities as a propaganda event, that the populace of Moscow was given the day off work to attend the opening.[10]

Kogan's speech referred back to Lenin's "Plan for Monumental Propaganda." Initiated in 1918 the campaign had ceased during the civil war period in the early 1920s, but after Lenin's death in 1924 there was a "resurgence" of the Party's interest in the power of monumental propaganda.[11] The choice of relief formats for the *Age of Life* sculptures may have also referred back to Lenin's "Plan," because Vatagin had used this format for a memorial to Andrei Rublev, the famous medieval Russian icon painter, that was accepted by the "Plan" in 1918 (Figure 8.3).[12] Although a painted cast of the Rublev monument's head resides in the Darwin Museum archive,[13] the original plaster sculpture eventually dissolved, like many other campaign monuments, because it was placed outdoors,[14] unlike the *Age of Life* sculptures that have survived due to their indoor locations.

The *Rublev* monument and *Age of Life* sculptures also potentially shared a Russian Symbolist approach to embedding meaning in the works, using visually encrypted references to concepts and constructs. Vatagin had absorbed this approach in his prerevolutionary training at the shared atelier of the Symbolist sculptor Ivan Dudin, and the painter Konstantin Iuon—famous for his postrevolutionary work, *New Planet* (1921).[15] After the revolution, Vatagin joined the State Academy of Artistic Sciences (GAKhN), which proclaimed itself "scientifically" concerned with the symbolic expression of the "inexpressible."[16] The style used by Vatagin in *Age of Life*, however, was less abstract than that of the *Rublev* monument, and was more in keeping, both with his other works for the Darwin Museum and with the Party's current preference for the naturalistic, figurative work produced by AKhRR, as denoted by the presentation and critical reception of the 1926 AKhRR exhibition.

Between 1925 and 1926 Vatagin's figurative and "animalist" artwork had gained considerable status outside the confines of the Darwin Museum displays. His works

Figure 8.3 Vasilii Vatagin beside his *Monument to Andrei Rublev*, 1918, plaster, 3-m high, in V. A. Vatagin, *Vospominaniia*, Figure 7, p. 61. Original photo © Nikolai Vatagin/Vatagin Estate. Reproduced by kind permission of the Syndics of Cambridge University Library, 2020.

had been shown in the *International Expositions of Art* in Paris and Venice, and in 1926 gained favorable reviews from the leading art critic Iakov Tugenkhol'd, and also from the Soviet Commissar for Enlightenment, Anatoly Lunacharskii.[17] In this historical context, what better way to demonstrate the Darwin Museum's contemporary political correctness and thus worthiness to receive the promised new premises, than to commission monumental, implicitly propagandistic artworks from an artist publicly admired by Tugenkhol'd and Lunacharskii?

The *Age of Life* sculptures may have been conceived of as a narrative pair, but they are not mirror images of each other. The subject matter—orangutans and people, and the modes of facture (making)—rough for the orangutans and smooth for the humans are clearly different. This rather suggests that, despite sharing a basic Darwinian theme regarding the evolution of humankind from apes as hinted in *Origin of Species* (1859), and further elaborated in *The Descent of Man* (1871) and *The Expression of the Emotions* (1872),[18] each work required a different form or level of interpretation in relation to the context of 1926. The next two sections examine the potential contemporary ideological reference points for each individual sculpture.

Age Variability in Humankind

In *Age Variability in Humankind* (Figure 8.4) the sculptural treatment of the bodies renders them smooth and somewhat idealized and the representations of the a-historical but body-molding drapery add to this effect. Although there are a number of different figures—mostly female—all are depicted as seemingly healthy, and certainly not overweight. Moreover, the figures are largely represented as cooperating across the generations, so the sculpture lacks any reference to the famous Darwinian idea of "struggle for existence"[19] within the shifting age-roles from infant to crone delineated in the sculpture. The image of the infant (possibly male) ostensibly is the focus of gaze for the images of the old woman, the "mother" (central draped figure), the nude young woman and the nude female child. The one exception

Figure 8.4 Vasilii Vatagin, *Age of Life: Variation in Humankind* (detail), 1926. © The State Darwin Museum, Moscow.

to this apparent focus is the low-relief, female figure at the top of the sculpture (see Figure 8.4)).

This image is depicted in a contemplative pose, like a professional observer, and appears to look directly at the viewers, as if inviting them to share "her" vision of the represented life cycle. This "vision" seems to emphasize the important role of women in reproduction and childcare. However, the image of the "visionary observer" itself also seems to imply that women could/should also have some professional employment as well—as did Nadezhda Ladygina-Kots. These are all topics that will be discussed further, later on in this section.

The conflicting depictions of nudity in this sculpture are very interesting. For example, those of the children represented probably relate to the idea of childhood innocence, and the poses are quite believably naturalistic. The pose of the nude, nubile young woman, however, seems to offer a more "arty" Western-style image of female sexual availability, similar to Auguste Rodin's much-reproduced *Toilette de Venus* (1888).[20] Vatagin was interested in the work of Rodin, particularly his sculpture of *Eve* (1881),[21] as well as works by other late-nineteenth-century French artists, including the sculptor Aristide Maillol. Before the revolution he would have been able to see such works at the homes of the Moscow art collectors Sergei Shchukin and Ivan Morozov. While their collections were confiscated soon after the revolution, the works would still have been available to Vatagin and other artists in the 1920s, at the Museum of Modern Western Art in Moscow.[22]

The faint references in *Age Variability in Humankind* to the sensual poses and the abstracted, jutting breasts to be found in Rodin's and Maillol's sculptures, however, may not have been a purely personal choice on Vatagin's part. Rather, these references may also have been another piece of political correctness, since Tugenkhol'd's speech particularly emphasized Rodin's and Maillol's work as exemplars for future Soviet sculptures of "healthy bodies."[23] This concern with "healthy bodies" related to two key, interlinked aspects of contemporary ideological discourse—Soviet eugenics and "hygienic maternity"—with which the Darwin Museum was arguably involved in the mid-1920s.

As in nationalist discourses in Europe and elsewhere, from the 1890s onward, Russian and then Soviet politicians and bioscientists became concerned about issues of population degeneracy, and the possible avenues of population regeneration.[24] The nascent Soviet Union had already been ravaged by international and internal wars and the accompanying exacerbation of extant large-scale epidemic diseases (malaria, typhus, typhoid, syphilis, and dysentery, to name but a few).[25] Resolution of these national health issues was crucial to the survival of the new state.

It is, therefore, entirely unsurprising that the Bolsheviks initially supported discourse on eugenics, a recently invented European "science" based on the ideas of Charles Darwin's cousin Francis Galton.[26] Eugenics discourse held out the hope that there might be economically viable solutions to physical, mental, and social problems within the workforce, by the exertion of certain forms of biosocial control. On the whole, the Soviet approach to eugenics was quite different from approaches espoused in Nazi Germany, Britain, Scandinavia, and the United States, for example, largely preferring the improvement of the population's health, and reduction of infant mortality, to programs of enforced sterilization or incarceration for those who were deemed as "unfit."[27]

This idea of eugenics is something that the Darwin Museum seems to have taken on board between 1923 and 1926, in the sense that the museum can be seen to have subscribed to issues of the *Russian Eugenics Journal* in those years—at least.[28] Moreover, Kots was a colleague and friend of a leading Soviet eugenicist, the geneticist Nikolai Kol'tsov,[29] commemorating him in the Darwin Museum collection with busts by Vatagin and the famous Soviet sculptor Vera Mukhina. Not only did the Kotses personal libraries contain quite a lot of books by Russian and international eugenicists,[30] but both Kots and his wife were also in correspondence with the American eugenicists Henry Fairfield Osborn, the director of the American Museum of Natural History in New York, and the ape-researcher Robert Yerkes.[31] All of this indicates at least an acquaintance, and probably an engagement with contemporary eugenics discourse.

Central to contemporary, eugenics-inspired propaganda on regenerating the Soviet population was the notion of "hygienic maternity" that was to some extent based on the French eugenic notion of *puériculture*.[32] Okhrmatmlad, the State Department for the Protection of Mothers and Children, was set up in 1918 at the instigation of Alexandra Kollontai.[33] By the mid-1920s it was issuing thousands of "Sanitary Enlightenment" (*Sanprosvet*) posters aimed at educating urban and rural women about "hygienic maternity" and "correct" childcare and nutrition.[34] This was supported by the People's Commissariat for Public Health (Narkomzdav), presided over by the "social hygienist" Commissar of Health, Nikolai Semashko. Semashko regarded "social hygiene" as the first step toward the adoption of "eugenics as the science of making the human race healthy."[35]

Soviet concerns with eugenics and "hygienic maternity" seem to have been inextricably bound up with the crypto-Lamarckian, pre- and postrevolutionary Bolshevik construct of the "New Man." Leading Party theoreticians such as Nikolai Buhkharin and Leon Trotsky had prophesied the coming of a new type of humankind, which would be generated by the environmental and social transformations brought about by socialist revolution.[36] In May 1926, Lunacharskii's review article on the AKhRR exhibition *The Life and Being of the Peoples of the USSR* even identified monumental figurative art as one of the means to encourage the emergence of the "New Man," and spoke of the portrait works displayed as images of the "organisers of a completely renewed social being, hitherto unknown to human history."[37] This statement reflected Lunacharskii's engagement, both with the contemporary discourses on the "New Man" and with those on Soviet eugenics.[38]

Lunacharskii's optimistic statement was rooted in prerevolutionary Russian dissident writings, for example, by Nikolai Chernyshevskii and Alexander Bogdanov. These writers, separated by half a century, were politically divergent in a partisan sense—Bogdanov was a Social Democrat Marxist and Chernyshevskii was not. What they had in common, however, was the belief that "nurture"—particularly education and training—was the means to generate the "new man." As Nikolai Kremenstov has noted in the Introduction to this anthology, in the immediate postrevolutionary context, Lunacharsky, Bogdanov, and other Bolsheviks such as Leon Trotsky proselytized "nurture" as the pathway to the making of the Soviet "new man."

Lunacharskii's statement was also rooted in a strong trend of prerevolutionary, neo-Lamarckian discourse on Darwinism.[39] After the revolution this trend was also partly fueled by the pro-, but also critical, writings on Darwinism by Friedrich Engels, particularly his *Dialectics of Nature* (written 1883, first published in Russian 1922) and also his unfinished article *The Part Played by Labour in the Origin of Man from Apes* (written 1876, first published in Russian 1925).[40] In this form, it became increasingly dominant in the mid- to late 1920s in the USSR, as exemplified by the entry in the *Great Soviet Encyclopedia* by S. Sobol (1927),[41] and became an essential part of the context for Trofim Lysenko's rise to power over Soviet bioscience 1935–64.[42]

This trend, recently entitled "Marxist Darwinism" by Nikolai Krementsov,[43] essentially identified the impact of environment on heredity, and the inheritability of acquired characteristics, as more important than that of purely genetic, random mutational input on the process of evolution. Both of these ideas derived from Lamarck, but traces of them were also to be found in Darwin's own writings. Although all editions of *Origin of Species* expressed critical views on some of Lamarck's theories, Darwin did follow Lamarck in noting the possibility for environment and habit to affect evolutionary development.[44] Also, in *Descent of Man*, in discussing the relationship of the "higher apes" to humankind, for example, regarding the vestigial tails of both, Darwin came close to Lamarck's proposition that acquired characteristics might be inheritable.[45]

Contemporary "Marxist Darwinism," as indicated by Sobol's article in the *Great Soviet Encyclopedia* (1927),[46] however, seriously diverged from Darwin's writings regarding the idea of the "struggle for existence." Although in *Origin of Species* Darwin did note instances of cooperation within and between species,[47] he maintained that the "struggle for existence," central to his concept of "natural selection," was an evolutionary force applicable to all life-forms, implicitly including humans.[48] Darwin's terminology was derived from the human population theories of the English clergyman Thomas Malthus (1766–1834) expressed in "An Essay on the Principle of Population," 1898. This effectively asserted that, because the working classes tended to procreate excessively, they should not be given access to education or healthcare, since their numbers needed to be continuously reduced by disease/malnutrition. Any other action, in his view, would lead to overpopulation, and thus to shortages of goods and services for all citizens.[49]

The Bolsheviks' foundational theorist, Karl Marx (1818–1883), clearly despised Malthus's theory.[50] In the later parts of *Capital* he was positioned by Engels [who composed the rest of *Capital* after vol.1, 1867, from Marx's notes] as denouncing Malthus for presenting his idea of the "struggle for existence" regarding the issue of "overpopulation" as: "due to the eternal laws of nature," whereas in Marx's view (as interpreted by Engels) it was merely part of "the natural history of capitalist production."[51]

Engels agreed with Marx on this point,[52] so his Darwin-inspired writings on human evolution and socialism not only excluded humankind from the "struggle for existence" experienced by the plant and animal realms but also stressed the importance of cooperation as the means for both revolutionary and evolutionary development in human society.[53] Additionally, and again with reference to Engels's writings, the

Russian "Marxist Darwinist" trend, exemplified by Sobol's entry for "The struggle for existence" in the *Great Soviet Encyclopedia*, 1927, explicitly emphasized the superior power of humankind over nature—including their own nature—as a primary means to evolutionary change, through the exertion of both individual and collective will.[54] It was an idea that became embedded in a number of enterprises focused on the generation of the "New Man," from Alexei Gastev's psycho-technical experiments of the 1920s and 1930s,[55] to the Darwin Museum's "evolutionary psychotherapy" lectures to wounded soldiers in the Second World War.[56] This idea will also be referred to in the next section, with reference to the discussion of the potential political resonances of *Age Variations in Orangutans*.

Bearing in mind Kots's concerns with political correctness and thus alignment with "Marxist Darwinism," and Ladygina-Kots's recent and probably ongoing contact with Okrmatmlad propaganda in relation to the birth of their son "Rudi" in 1925, plus their combined interest in eugenics, what better than to commission a pair of "Darwinian" monumental sculptures that hit all of the above ideological buttons simultaneously, by reference to healthy female bodies, "hygienic maternity," and cooperation rather than "struggle for existence"?

There is also a sense in which the low-relief figure at the top of the sculpture (Figure 8.4) could be a professional educator, someone like Ladygina-Kots, urging the lecture-tour viewers to take account of the "correct" role of patriotic and "party-minded" women in generating the future "New People." It needs to be noted here that this role was undeniably problematic and enduringly contradictory within Soviet society. On the one hand, it involved obedience to the pressure for women to produce and look after children—as a duty to the state. On the other hand, there was also pressure to engage in paid employment, another prescribed state duty resulting from women's officially designated status post-1917, as being equal to men.[57] Nevertheless, these were the rules of the day that were arguably symbolically embodied in the sculpture.

There is also a strong sense in which the eugenics-inspired propaganda of Okrmatmlad,[58] potentially inscribed into the imagery of Vatagin's sculpture, could be seen in Michel Foucault's terms as referring to a state-generated move to medicalize Soviet women's bodies to bring them more closely under the "scientific" surveillance and control of the state. In this case, then, what we are looking in *Age of Life: Variation in Humankind* is also a symbolic and "party-minded" representation of what Foucault would call "docile" bodies.[59] This is an idea that I will return to in the next section, regarding Vatagin's representations of apes in *Age Variability in Orangutans* (Figure 8.2).

Age Variability in Orangutans and Contemporary Soviet "Monkey Business"

This section investigates the possible contextual references implicit in the other *Age of Life* sculpture, *Age Variability in Orangutans* (Figure 8.5), including the potential relationship to the ape-research undertaken by Nadezhda Ladygina-Kots and Professor Il'ia Ivanov in the 1910s to the 1920s. The representation of the orangutans in this

Figure 8.5 Vasilii Vatagin, *Age of Life: Variation in Orangutans*, 1926 (detail). Photo © The State Darwin Museum, Moscow.

work is quite different from the representations of humans in its pair. Instead of the relative smoothness of the represented bodies, background, and even the drapery in *Age Variability in Humankind*, the surface appears rough both on the animal figures and on the background. This is especially so in the images of baby orangutans depicted above the heads of the two central characters, where it seems difficult to distinguish the figures from the background .

In terms of the artistic precedents for this sort of sculptural treatment, *Age Variability in Orangutans* may contain a reference to elements of Rodin's *Eternal Springtime* (1884). The Museum of Modern Western Art had a small bronze maquette of this work – now held at the Pushkin Museum, Moscow.[60] In this work, while the depicted bodies of an entwined couple are very smoothly rendered, the background, interpretable as "nature," by comparison, is relatively rough. Vatagin's sculpture may also have a closer relationship with *Mound* 1904, (Figure 8.6) by the well-known Russian sculptor Anna Golubkina (1864–1927).

Golubkina had studied with Rodin in Paris, and at one time had been Vatagin's sculptural mentor, as well as being a co-member of the Society of Russian Sculptors in the early 1920s.[61] This work (Figure 8.6)) appears to represent the images of two children (her two nieces, Vera and Alexandra)[62] hiding or sheltering in some natural setting, in a way that suggests, by the facture, that they are physically blending with this setting, like little feral creatures.

Since Vatagin deliberately seems to have chosen to differentiate the *Age Variability in Orangutans* sculpture from the *Humankind* sculpture by means of rough versus smooth facture, it does not seem too fanciful to suggest that in doing so, he borrowed the symbolic visual tropes from Rodin and particularly Golubkina, as described earlier. Such differentiation would also have fitted neatly with the widespread, Russian

Figure 8.6 Anna Golubkina, *Mound*, 1904, 75 × 67 × 37 cm, bronze (cast from a plaster version 1940). State Russian Museum, St Petersburg. Photo Adam Shterenberg (Novosti, 1972), © Sputnik Images 2021.

postrevolutionary assumption based on Engels's *Dialectics of Nature*, that while both humans and creatures were part of nature, only humans were able to dominate and manipulate nature for their own ends. For Engels, plants and animals were necessarily subject to "struggle for existence" because they were governed only by the "blind forces" of nature,[63] so did not have this manipulative ability and were just helplessly embedded in nature. Perhaps it is for all of these reasons that the images of the orangutans in *Age of Life*, (Figures 8. 2 and 8.4)) seem to be symbolically presented as indivisible from that of the represented "natural" background, to a greater or lesser extent.

The largest, clear orangutan image indicates by the "cheek flanges and large throat sac"[64] that this figure is a representation of a dominant male. The other, smaller figure with arm upstretched to a baby orangutan is likely to represent an adult female, as these are smaller than the males,[65] and the humanlike gesture, given the apparent "family" theme of the sculptures, appears to reinforce this. It is unclear, however, what sex the immature orangutan figures are supposed to be. This may be immaterial to the narrative apparently presented, of a healthy, cooperative, but essentially male-dominated social structure, which then might be seen to contrast strongly with the social structure offered in the other sculpture, which illustrates no patriarchal figure, but rather a somewhat broader scope of roles open to contemporary human females.

The poses and facial expressions in the sculpture seem anthropomorphized, much like the watercolor sketches of an orangutan's head made by Vatagin in 1920 (Figure 8.7), making not only a conceptual link to Darwin's *Descent of Man*, but also a visual one to Darwin's study of *The Expression of the Emotions*. These sketches may have been based on the orangutan named "Friny" held at Moscow Zoological Gardens in the late 1910s—of which Vatagin made portraits of from photographs[66]—for Vatagin was known for his ability to produce convincing sculptures from photographs.[67] Kots's biography of Vatagin is unclear, however, on the age of "Friny," and whether this creature was the subject for the other works representing orangutans by Vatagin in 1917 that Kots cites.[68]

Vatagin may also have seen orangutans on his visit to Berlin zoo in November 1926, where he was sent to capture images of anthropoid apes.[69] Kots, however, only mentions images of baby chimpanzees and the huge gorilla "Bobby."[70] But, since Germany seems to have been involved in the trade in orangutans and other anthropoids,[71] it is highly likely that the zoo also had orangutans in its collection. Even if they did not, Vatagin still had firsthand experience of making images of orangutans in the 1910s, upon which he could have drawn for his *Age Variability in Orangutans* sculpture.

The expression of emotion in primates was of central interest at the Darwin Museum in this period, not only in relation to Nadezhda Ladygina-Kots's studies of the macaques at Moscow Zoological Gardens—which was published in 1928—but especially to her three-year-long, firsthand research on chimpanzee behavioral development. The latter related to "Joni," a very young chimpanzee given to her in 1913 by Fillip Fedulov, and studied until its death in 1916.[72] Vatagin had worked on this project with her, providing composite drawings and paintings as part of the documentation.[73] When her son "Rudi" (Rudolf) was born in 1925, she began a sort of post hoc comparative study, 1925–9, eventually published under the title of *Infant Chimpanzee and Human Child*, in which Vatagin, again, collaborated.[74] Indeed, the human infant in *Age of Life; Variability in Humans* (Figure 8.2) may have been modeled on one-year-old Rudi, and the woman "observer" on Ladygina-Kots.[75]

The published version of Ladygina-Kots's study (1935) concluded that contemporary chimpanzees, in parallel with macaques, were an evolutionary dead-end—not "almost human," but "by no means human."[76] She argued that, unlike humans, they ultimately had no will or incentive toward "self-improvement,"[77] which was, interestingly, a characteristic demanded by the current Soviet discourse on the evolution of the "New Man."[78] So while these apes could be trained to a certain extent, they could not be environmentally "evolutionized." Because the comparative research on "Joni" and Rudi was still at an early stage, and her research on educating macaques was also unfinished, however, this may not have been the conclusion that Ladygina-Kots envisaged in 1926.

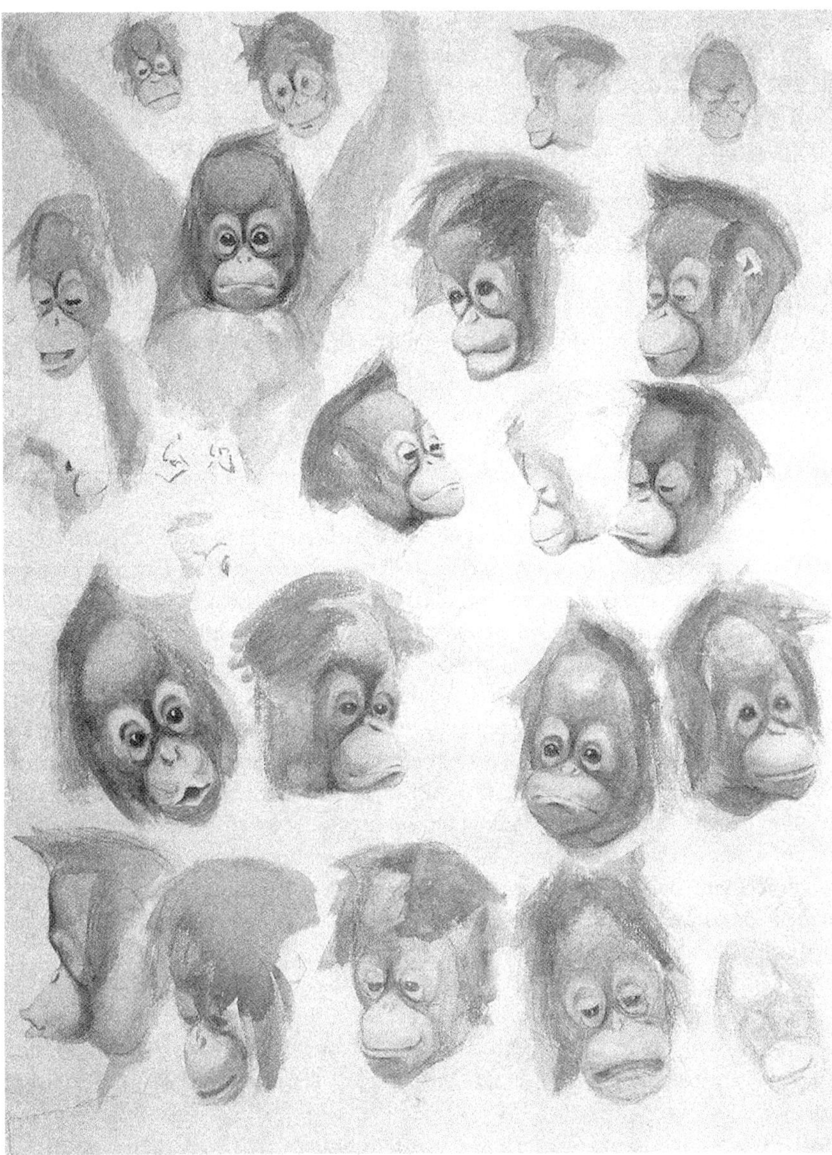

Figure 8.7 Vasilii Vatagin, *Head of an Orangutan. Sketches*, 1920, 61 × 47 cm, graphite pencil and watercolor on paper, in V. Udaltsova, *Sokrovishcha russkogo iskusstva: gosudarstvennyi darvinovskii muzei moskva* (Moscow, 2007) plate 27:14. © State Darwin Museum. Reproduction © E.P. Dillon (2019).

The implicit symbolic reference in the sculpture to the ape-research carried out at the Darwin Museum raises the question of why images of orangutans, rather than those of chimpanzees or macaques, were chosen to represent this. In the absence of any solid archival data on this choice, there would seem to be three possible and potentially compatible, speculative reasons for it, relating to both Lamarck and Darwin, as well as to Il'ia Ivanov's contemporary human-ape hybridization project 1926–9. First, in *Philosphie Zoologique* (1809), Lamarck had asserted that "orangutans" were the closest anthropoid ancestors of humankind. In doing so, he depended partly on the controversial decision made by the taxonomist Carolus Linnaeus in 1758, to group only chimpanzees and orangutans into the *Homo* (human) genus of the order of primates.[79] According to John van Wyhe and Peter C. Kjaergaard (2015), however, Lamarck had also utilized the term "orangutan" in the generalized sense commonly deployed to cover both chimpanzees and orangutans in seventeenth- to early-nineteenth-century writings.[80] This was apparently despite the fact that by the late eighteenth century, orangutans and chimpanzees had been scientifically identified as two different species, respectively, living in Southeast Asia and Africa.[81]

For Aleksandr Kots, Lamarck seems to have been a particular hero in the history of evolutionary theory. One clue to this is a lecture he gave on March 15, 1909, at the auditorium of the Physico-Chemical Institute, Moscow, in an evening session "Dedicated to the Memory of Lamarck and Darwin," that was part of the Russian celebrations of the 100th anniversary of Darwin's birth (1809) and 50th anniversary of the publication of *Origin of Species* (1859).[82] Moreover, the first monumental sculpture commissioned from Vatagin for the museum was not of Darwin but of *Blind Lamarck and His Lamenting Daughters* (*c.* 1921). This was a work that had potentially ambivalent meanings, relating both to Lamarck's lack of recognition by his peers, and to his "blindness" to the possibilities of evolutionary theory identified later by Darwin. Additionally, a letter from the geneticist Alexander Serebrovskii to Alexander Kots in 1920 can be seen to identify Kots's doubts, shared with other colleagues, about the relevance of Mendelian genetics to Darwinism, as well as his Lamarckian leanings.[83] In relation to all of this, a focus on orangutans in the *Age of Life*: *Variability and Variation in Orangutans* sculpture (Figure 8.2) may have symbolically coincided with Kots's alignment with both past and present Russian and Soviet inclinations toward a crypto-Lamarckian interpretation of Darwinian evolutionary theory, perhaps as an implicit *homage* to Lamarck.

Second, regarding the connection to Darwin, the choice of orangutans would also have been symbolically apposite to some extent, insofar as Darwin did experiments with orangutans—particularly with one named "Jenny" in 1838—as well as with other primates and monkeys at the London Zoological Gardens in 1838 to the 1840s.[84] Indeed, these encounters arguably formed the basis for Darwin's theories of the evolutionary relationship of humans to primates, hinted at in *Origin of Species* (1859),[85] and expressed more clearly in *The Expression of the Emotions* (1872),[86] and *The Descent of Man* (1879).[87] A fascinating, but unpublished, detailed document held in Cambridge University Library (DAR 191) about Darwin's encounters and experiments with "Jenny" the orangutan (1838) would probably not have been accessible to Kots and his team.[88] However, aspects of Darwin's experimental research with orangutans were particularly noted, albeit without source references or illustrations, in *The Expression of the Emotions*.[89]

This was a text that was most important for Ladygina-Kots's own comparative research, which focused on physiognomic and behavioral similarities and differences in the emotional responses of an infant chimpanzee and a human child. In this sense, the usage of orangutan imagery in the sculpture could also have been an *homage* not only to Lamarck but also to Darwin for providing the foundations for Ladygina-Kots's own comparative studies of apes and humans. But, while this speculative interpretation may probably be partially correct, it still does not help to fully explain the specific choice of orangutans for Vatagin's sculpture. After all, Darwin did not seem to give any special emphasis to orangutans above other primates, either in *The Expression of the Emotions,* or in *The Descent of Man.* Although, following Linnaeus and also possibly T. H. Huxley's book *Evidence to Man's Place in Nature* (1863),[90] Darwin did at least identify contemporary primates as being the most likely relatives of humankind's ancestors.[91]

It also may be very speculatively suggested that the choice of orangutans rather than chimpanzees for this sculpture, with its crypto-Lamarckian, as well as Darwinian historical reference points may have had an additional contextual trigger. Conceivably it may have been partly an antagonistic response to the news that Professor Il'ia Ivanov had obtained a state grant channeled through the Academy of Sciences, to experiment with ape-human hybridization using chimpanzees.[92] Thus in 1926 there were now two competing, but equally possible, contemporary theoretical and "scientific" means of "evolutionizing" anthropoid apes and thus of potentially "proving" Darwin's evolutionary theory of ape-human kinship.

One of these—the pathway chosen by Ladygina-Kots—was through training and environment, a crypto-Lamarckian solution that chimed well with contemporary Bolshevik discourse on generating the "New Man," and also with current, equally crypto-Lamarckian expositions of Darwinian evolutionary theory. The other possible pathway, however, was offered by Ivanov's project and involved direct genetic intervention by means of artificial insemination. Both trajectories of research at this point focused on chimpanzees. So it could be argued that in 1926, given Vatagin's recent visit to Berlin zoo, and the previously discussed potential relationships with the ideas of Lamarck and Darwin, the choice of orangutans for the second *Age of Life* sculpture may have been a deliberate, symbolic ploy to distance the Darwin Museum from Ivanov's type of ape-research.

Unfortunately, the problem here is that there appears to be no substantiating materials regarding this sculpture, and, no mention of Ivanov and his experimental project in the Darwin Museum's digitized catalogue of its archive. This in itself is strange, as Kots and Ladygina-Kots would have known of the project through the Moscow bioscientific grapevine. Curiously, this absence is replicated in the extensive, but incomplete, correspondence between the Kotses and the American ape-researcher and eugenicist Robert Yerkes, contained in both the Darwin Museum archive and the Yerkes Papers archive at the Sterling Memorial Library at Yale University.[93]

Yet, it is clear that Yerkes knew about Ivanov's project in January 1926,[94] and his knowledge would have been further reinforced by sensationalist articles in the American press in the summer of 1926.[95] In addition, he visited the Darwin Museum in 1929 with the specific intention of traveling on to the Sukhumi monkey/ape station, so the Darwin Museum Directors would probably have known about Ivanov's project at this point, even if they had not done previously. Yerkes, however, was unable to visit Sukhumi in 1929 as his English-speaking contact, Professor Fursikov, was ill and unavailable at the time, and Yerkes was told that the monkey/ape station "was closed or nearly so."[96] Ivanov's project, however, was still ongoing as will be discussed later.

The idea of ape-human hybridization was not invented by Ivanov. It had actually been circulating in European ape-research discourse since the early 1900s. It was, for example, articulated by the Dutch scientist Herman Marie Moens (1875–1938) in 1908. His idea was approved by the famous German zoologist Ernst Haeckel and supported by the Russian zoologist and immunologist Il'ia Metchnikov (1845–1916), the director of the Pasteur Institute in Paris. It was also proposed by the German sexologist Herman Rohleder (1866–1934) in relation to the German anthropoid ape experimental station operating on the island of Tenerife 1912–20.[97] There is no evidence, however, that anyone had actually tried to do it. Ivanov, already famed for his work on artificial insemination with horses and other mammals[98] and whose project for ape-human hybridization was initially mooted in 1910,[99] did at least try to do this experiment.

Ivanov's government funding, via the Academy of Sciences, included the use of an experimental monkey/ape station at Sukhumi in Georgia, near the Black Sea. It was being set up by Iakov Tobolkin in 1926, with the support of the People's Commissariat for Health (Narkomzdrav) and under the aegis of the Institute for Experimental Endocrinology in Moscow, of which Tobolkin was the deputy director. Its main purpose was to breed monkeys and apes to serve the apparently quite large-scale contemporary medical requirements for monkey glands for "organotherapy"—a precursor to endocrinology—particularly within the higher echelons of the Party that included Lenin's wife, Nadezhda Krupskaia.[100] While Tobolkin went to Europe to research the best climatic conditions for an ape-research center in Russia, and identified a suitable site at Sukhumi, Ivanov was funded to visit the Pasteur Institute's ape station in Kindia in the French Congo, and send chimpanzees back to Sukhumi.[101]

An essential part of the deal was that Ivanov had Soviet permission to pursue his ape-human hybridization research both in Sukhumi and in Kindia.[102] In Kindia, unsuccessful human-ape hybridization experiments were carried out by Ivanov and his son on female chimpanzees. Ivanov, however, was forbidden by the French authorities to do chimpanzee-human hybridization experiments on the native female inmates of the hospital at Kindia without their permission, which had been his intention, since these vulnerable women were, culturally, very unlikely to cooperate with his experiment.[103]

When Ivanov returned to Russia, he turned his attention to the possibilities of using the orangutans otherwise kept at Sukhumi for other purposes. The main reason for this was the high mortality rate of the imported chimpanzees. The orangutan mortality rate, however, was not to prove much better. According to Rossianov, with new funding from the Communist Academy in 1929, Ivanov targeted one mature, twenty-six-year-old orangutan held at Sukhumi named "Tarzan," as a prospective sperm donor, and then advertised for female human volunteers for artificial insemination. One positive reply was received from a woman identified only as "G."[104] However "Tarzan" died before the experimental union could be clinically consummated. This turned out to signal the end of Ivanov's ape-human hybridization project.[105]

Within the context of the so-called Cultural Revolution 1928–32, Ivanov's enforced choice of an orangutan for his hybridization experiment in 1929 may have proved an unforeseen and potentially unfortunate coincidence in relation to the possible contemporary interpretations of Vatagin's use of orangutans in his *Age of Life* sculpture. This was a very fraught period, when youthful, self-styled "proletarian" groups and individuals were busily denouncing intellectuals and academics as "bourgeois specialists," if these people had obtained their qualifications and skills in the prerevolutionary period. Such denunciations could have very serious implications for the victims' current employment, future employability, personal freedom, and even their lives—as exemplified by the outcome of the famous Shakhty trial in April 1928, where twenty of the accused were sentenced to death.[106]

Ivanov was targeted by a group at the State Experimental Veterinary Institute in Moscow as a "bourgeois specialist" early in 1930. In December 1930 he was arrested and sentenced to five years' internal exile in Alma Ata, Kazakhstan. Released in 1932, he died of a stroke before he could return to Moscow, thus putting an end to one of the Soviet trajectories of "evolutionizing" apes.[107]

Alexander Kots, Nadezhda Ladygina-Kots, and most of their trusted team were also effectively "bourgeois experts." It is unsurprising, therefore, that the Darwin Museum had a party mentor foisted on it in July 1930, as an "assistant director."[108] In these circumstances, it may be that in 1930, either around the time of Ivanov's arrest, or even before the arrival of the new "assistant director," that there may have been a minor data cull by Kots, Ladygina-Kots, and their long-standing colleagues, of anything that might conceivably have linked the museum, and particularly Ladygina-Kots, to Ivanov or his experiments. Hence, perhaps, the lack of information about the *Age of Life: Variability in Orangutans* sculpture contained in the Darwin Museum archive.

Whatever the choice of orangutans in this sculpture referred to, in the context of both the Darwin Museum and contemporary Soviet bioscience, the images effectively identified the animals as objects of scientific research, under the control of state-subsidized institutions. Thus, in Foucault's terms we may again be looking at images of "docile bodies." In this case, however, the bodies were of animals specifically targeted for a range of scientific experimental purposes, some of which might have been beneficial to the development of the Soviet "New Man."

Conclusion

In this chapter I have argued that Vatagin's *Ages of Life* sculpture group may be seen as ambitious, enigmatic, and complex symbolic works, potentially stylistically fueled not only by his acquaintance with and training by prerevolutionary Russian Symbolist artists but also by his acquaintance with French late-nineteenth- to early-twentieth-century avant-garde art. The year of its production, 1926, seems to have been particularly propitious for the production of monumental works by Vatagin, in order to support the Darwin Museum's expansionist ambitions and associated concerns for displaying political correctness regarding contemporary Bolshevik cultural and bioscientific discourse, particularly, but not exclusively, related to Darwinism.

What the pair of sculptures share is a representation of the existential life cycles of both humans and orangutans that emphasizes cooperation within species above the Darwinian notion of the "struggle for existence." This is a crypto-Lamarckian element that relates closely to contemporary Bolshevik scientific interpretations of Darwinian theory in the mid-late 1920s. The sculptures clearly differ, in physical "facture" and subject matter. However, the differences in facture—the rough appearance of the depiction of the orangutans as opposed to the smooth appearance of the depicted human bodies—may, as I have argued, symbolically relate to the currently favored Bolshevik idea of human superiority over nature, inspired by the writings of Engels.

I have also argued that the sculptures differ in relation to the aspects of the contemporary biopolitical discourses to which they seem to refer. For example, *Age Variability in Humankind* appears to relate to current Soviet eugenic discourse concerning "hygienic maternity" and childcare. *Age Variability in Orangutans,* however, possibly has more to do with the power of Soviet scientific experimentalism to explore previous theorizations of human-ape kinship. Ultimately I suggest that the final element that these works share is a representation of what Foucault would call "docile bodies"—objectified, medicalized, scientificized—harnessed both to the expansionist ambitions of the Darwin Museum, and to the concerns of the Soviet state with building a new sort of society, populated by a new species of humankind.

Looking more broadly at the potential relationships of Vatagin's sculptures to contemporary Soviet constructs of the "New Man," there seems to be one remaining crucial observation to be made. While the "New Man" was clearly a key construct in a broad range of cultural, scientific, and political discourses in the 1920s, it had no singular definition. Rather, it stood for a concatenation of often diverse and conflicting ideas that could be used for a variety of institutional or self-propagandisement—or, indeed, for institutional or self-defensive/preservational purposes in any of the aforementioned broad discipline areas. In this sense the situation in the visual arts would seem to have been no different from that in any other of the many artistic disciplines affected by the multi-trajectory "New Man" discourse.

In this anthology Nikolai Krementsov usefully describes the term "New Man" in the postrevolutionary context as representing a sort of multifaceted "cultural resource" that was open to a wide variety of uses by interested parties.[109] Arguably, the Darwin Museum made instrumental use of aspects of this resource, symbolically embodied in the *Age of Life* sculptures, to locate itself favorably in relation to contemporary debates in pursuit of its (unfulfilled) goal of obtaining a new museum premises. I can only speculate about this, however—albeit in an informed way—because the meaning and content of visual artwork (such as sculptures or paintings) are rarely, if ever, entirely self-evident from the appearance of the work itself, no matter how naturalistic the imagery may be. Rather, such artefacts need to be contextualized using words and other artworks to draw out the potential reference points. This was true in terms of words at least, for example, regarding the AKhRR exhibition of 1926, as exemplified by the way the works were positioned by the commentaries of Tugenkhol'd and Lunacharskii. It was probably equally true of the staging of the *Age of Life* sculptures in the same year, by the way that the representatives of the Darwin Museum may have explained the works to their audiences in the period 1926–9, to which, unfortunately, we do not seem to have access.

9

The New Man in the Museum of Ethnography

Between Socialist Content and National Form

Stanislav Petriashin

In 1938, a permanent exhibition entitled *The Turkmen Then and Now* was opened at the State Museum of Ethnography (SME) in Leningrad. In the development plan for the exhibition, the aim of the "Socialist Turkmenistan" section was laid out as follows:

> TO DEMONSTRATE, in light of the Leninist-Stalinist nationalities policy and the Stalinist Constitution, the tremendous accomplishments of socialist construction at all levels of economic, political, and cultural life in Turkmenistan, and within this context to organize a DISPLAY, first and foremost, of the MAN, the man of the Stalinist Era, and the long and determined struggle of the party of Lenin and Stalin in support of this man.[1]

The exhibition on Turkmenistan—while fairly typical for the SME in the 1930s—stands in contrast both with contemporaneous ethnographic exhibitions in Europe and America, and with earlier exhibitions in Russian ethnographic museums. Exhibitions in these museums usually focused on either the evolution of human culture from simple to more complex forms (typological criteria) or the distinguishing cultural characteristics of specific regions (geographical criteria).[2] Regardless, it was always the "archaic" cultures of colonized societies and European peasants whose lives were far removed from the "modern world"—urban, industrial civilization—that were best represented in museum display.[3] In the 1930s Soviet Museum, as the exhibition on Turkmenistan demonstrates, the focus of displays was not only the traditional culture of the nationality ("The Turkmen Then") but also their place in the modern, socialist world ("and Now"). The conceptual focal point of the exhibition was acknowledged to be the "man of the Stalinist era." So, who is this man exactly, and why was he on display in an ethnographic museum?

During the "cultural revolution" of the 1920s and 1930s, Soviet museums had thrust upon them the task of political enlightenment and of propagandizing the achievements of the Soviet government, industrialization, and collectivization.[4] In the second half of the 1930s, as a part of this state policy, museums (along with other types of media) were required to honor the Stakhanovites as heroes of the Stalinist era and Soviet "new men." The Stakhanovites were workers from various industries who followed the movement initiated by Alexey Stakhanov. He became a nationwide celebrity in 1935, when he managed to increase the productivity of labor in his coal mine and exceeded production targets. Representation of the Stakhanovite in the museums as a model personality was a particular way to nurture the ordinary people into the Soviet "new men." The pages of *Soviet Museum*—the official publication of the Museums Department of the People's Commissariat for Education (Narkompros)—rang with demands to make the "new man" the centerpiece of museum exhibits:

> We've talked and are still talking about exhibiting the new man. The Stakhanovite is this new man, one who was educated by the Communist Party of the Bolsheviks and the Soviet government. This must be demonstrated through concrete examples, through specific people. It must become the centerpiece of exhibitions concerning aspects of socialist construction.[5]

Responding to the demands of the day, ethnographic museums began remaking their exhibits to include the Stakhanovites in "Soviet" sections. However, this task proved challenging. The representation of socialist construction in ethnographic museums was intended as a demonstration of the success of the *nationalities policy*; in contrast, the Stakhanovite movement was primarily touted as a driving force of *economic modernization*. The Stakhanovites were ill-suited to an exhibition of the contemporary culture of the peoples of the USSR: while they were abundantly "socialist in content," they were insufficiently "national in form." In other words, the future nature of a Soviet man envisioned and manifested in the Stakhanovite movement lacked ethnic particularities. Propagandists saw the "new men" as heralds of a communist future, free from the boundaries and prejudices of nationality—extraordinary individuals who bravely challenged authority and tradition.[6] The pantheon of pioneers of the Stakhanovite movement was grouped not along national or territorial lines but according to profession and economic sector: Alexei Stakhanov (miner), Makar Mazai (steelworker), Dusia Vinogradova (weaver), Piotr Krivonos (railroad worker), Pasha Angelina (tractor driver), Maria Demchenko (beet grower), Bilial Ikhlasov (drill operator), and so on.[7]

Attaining the status of a Stakhanovite or an *udarnik* ("shock worker") was particularly appealing to those who faced discrimination based on gender or nationality, as this status allowed the worker to openly resist societal prejudices.[8] This led to women from colorful ethnic minorities becoming the typical examples of collective farm "celebrities."[9] Semion Dimanshtein, the head of the Institute for National Minorities, wrote that the Stakhanovite movement would lead to a sharp increase in productivity, while also helping achieve the "total liquidation of backwardness" and "[of] a de facto inequality" among the national groups.[10] To this end, the Stakhanovites were held up by the government as examples of the successful modernization of remote, "backward" regions, and the integration of national minorities into Soviet society.

That said, the ethnic identity of the Stakhanovites was confined to appearing in traditional national costume at Stakhanovite rallies and award ceremonies, and reading reports in their mother tongues. In fact, the propagandized model of Stakhanovite behavior did more to drive people toward cultural assimilation. They had to be able to use modern technology, to propose laborsaving ideas, and to serve as examples of "culturedness," which can be defined as an "amalgamation of traits of the historical and national culture of Russia with traits belonging to the Communist cycle of ideas and behavior patterns."[11] As Lewis Siegelbaum notes, the designation of Stakhanovites as *bogatyrs*—medieval warriors from Russian legends—in ideological discourse evoked both *bylinas* (epic folk poems), and Kievan Rus', and had an exclusively "Russian" connotation.[12] It could be said that the Stakhanovites worked to dismantle traditions, while at the same time the official nationalities policy was to selectively support these traditions, and to maintain them through the "national form" of culture. This was a contradiction that required a solution, and one which became a matter for concern among museum ethnographers.

How should the Stakhanovites be represented in museum exhibitions? They were concrete individuals from real life, and also people who embodied all of the characteristic qualities of the Stakhanovites, like characters from the pages of literary socialist realism. This synthesis of the general and the specific was what the museum workers had to show in their exhibitions. While ethnographers did consult with actual people holding the rank of Stakhanovite, they drew their conceptions of their typical characteristics from particular cultural resources available and politically appropriate in Stalinist period. These included ideological literature, propaganda speeches, and popular creative works (paintings, posters, films, etc.). I will refer to the whole set of official postulates, and the prescribed norms and values that shaped the lives of real Stakhanovites, as their *ideological image*. It should be noted that the representation of the Stakhanovites in the context of ethnographic exhibitions gave rise to a specifically "museum" version of this ideological image.

The definition of the Stakhanovite as a "new man" was of particular importance. The concept of the "new man" has always implied a distinction between "old" and "new," and a specific vision of the past, present, and future of human nature and society.[13] That is why I will examine Stakhanovites in ethnographic museums in terms of the temporal framework of their ideological image: the juxtaposition of the Stakhanovite as an example of the new Socialist attitude toward labor ("the seeds of the future in the present"), technological backwardness, outdated norms, and obsolete traditions ("the remnants of the past"). I will supplement this Marxist temporality, which was common to all Stakhanovites, with the concept of *biographical time*, reflected in the personal stories of individual people. The biography of each Stakhanovite not only illustrated their ideological image but also enhanced that image by using personal details and made it easily understandable to the general public.

The present work must answer the following questions: How did the "new man" appear in ethnographic museums? What was the place of the Stakhanovites in ethnographic exhibitions, and how were they portrayed? In museum representations of the Stakhanovites, how did the concept of "national form" align with that of "socialist content"? How did the nationalities policy align with economic modernization? How did the past align with the future? In the portrayal of "new men," how did the specific relate to the general, and how did biographical time relate to historical time?

These questions will be addressed using materials from the SME in Leningrad from the second half of the 1930s. The first section of this chapter will briefly describe the development of the museum and its sovietization, from 1902 to the mid-1930s. The second section will show how the embedding of the idea of "new man" in the museum was realized in the second part of the 1930s. In the third section, I will explore the main types of museum representation of "new men" in the context of displays on industrial and agricultural achievements. The fourth section will analyze the topic of "the education of new men" in exhibitions on the results of government cultural policy. The fifth section will deal with the biography of the "new man" in "story excursions." Finally, the sixth section will compare the temporal framework of the ideological image of the Stakhanovite as it was shown in ethnographic exhibitions, and in Stalin's famous speech at the All-Union conference of Stakhanovites in 1935.

The Ethnographic Department in the 1920s to the mid-1930s: Sovietization of the Imperial Museum

The SME (known today as the Russian Museum of Ethnography) was founded in 1902 as the Ethnographic Department of the Russian Museum of Emperor Alexander III. Its mission was stated as the following: "To give a picture of the ethnographic makeup of our society, and of the peoples that inhabit Russia and its immediate vicinity."[14] That said, the primary focus was on the Russian and Slavic peoples. The entire territory of the Russian Empire was divided into four regions, corresponding to the number of museum curators—this was done to make each curator's collecting work and reporting easier.[15] By the 1920s, in light of staffing increases, the museum had grown to four departments: the ethnography of the Great Russians and the Finns (I); the ethnography of Ukraine and Byelorussia (II); the ethnography of the Caucasus and Turkestan (III); and the ethnography of the Siberian peoples and the Far East (IV). The museum's exhibitions, created in 1916, were structured in the same way. As a result of the First World War, revolutionary upheaval, and the civil war, the exhibitions were opened only in 1923, and they maintained the same approach to display. Nevertheless, after the October Revolution museum ethnographers endeavored to make their exhibits more intelligible for new and poorly educated visitors—Red Army men, sailors, workers, and peasants—and introduced some geographical maps, pictures, photographs, texts, and explanatory texts. The definition of the museum's "formula" in 1919 was also a reiteration of that of Imperial period: "The Ethnographic department is a museum of folk life and art of peoples and tribes of Russia."[16]

The Russian Museum, previously managed by the Ministry of the Imperial Court, in 1918 became a state museum and was directed by Narkompros. But until the end of the 1920s, Soviet state administrators did not try to directly intervene in the museum's inner life and authoritatively define its work. During the first five-year plan (1928–32) a new policy was established in regard to the economy (collectivization, industrialization), as well as in the spheres of culture and science. The "cultural revolution" resulted in the replacement of the old generation of ethnographers by a new one, who had an appropriate class background and was much less experienced, but familiar with the basics of Marxism. The museum's primary mission was no longer scientific research and the popularization of ethnographic knowledge, but political enlightenment and propaganda of Soviet national policy.

In that period, the exhibitions in the Ethnographic department came under fire for being excessively "academic" and incomprehensible to the common people. The museum management was also displeased with lack of displays portraying class struggle or Soviet successes in nation-building.[17] In other words, ethnographers were required to place the nationalities onto the Marxist historical timeline, and to demonstrate in exhibitions the progression of these nationalities from a pre-capitalist stage of development to socialism. Museum workers strove to incorporate these demands into their new exhibitions. In the first half of the 1930s, three permanent exhibits were opened: *The Ukrainian Village Before and After October* (1931), *Peoples of the Saian-Altai in the Past and Present* (1931), and *Byelorussia and the BSSR* (1933).

In the 1930s, museum workers developed a general, two-part model for exhibitions, the broad aspects of which continued to be used until the 1950s. Generally, permanent exhibitions were dedicated to one nationality or one group of related nationalities within one republic or region. The first section of the exhibition would display the museum collections along standard ethnographic lines (occupations, dwellings, clothing, rituals, etc.), supplemented by the Marxist approach, which emphasized class struggle and colonial oppression. The revolutions of 1905 and 1917, the civil war, and the Allied intervention served as a bridge between the prerevolutionary past and the Soviet present in SME exhibitions. In contrast, the second, "Soviet" section displayed the successes of socialist construction, cultural advancement, and the prosperous lives of the collective farmers. Up to the mid-1930s, the topic of class struggle on the *kolkhoz* (collective farm) was also relevant. In this Soviet section, the majority of these topics were presented using two-dimensional, "paper" sources: photographs, posters, documents, diagrams, and exhibit labels. Life groups using mannequins were, at times, created using factory-made items purchased from nearby stores in Leningrad. In the early 1930s, to demonstrate economic achievements, museum workers acquired collections of industrial artifacts. For instance, in 1932 they acquired a collection that illustrated the process of iron and steel production in Kerch. The collection included photographs of factory shock workers (*udarniki*—highly productive workers) during the production process, as well as samples of ores, agglomerates, calcareous stones, scrubs, cast iron, steel, and so forth.[18]

The obligation to showcase Soviet modernity distanced museum ethnography from its academic variant. The All-Russian Conference on Archaeology and Ethnography in May 1932 resulted in the reduction of academic ethnography to the study of "primitive communist formation," and "the debate over the genesis of class institutions, the problem of internal contradictions within preclass societies, and the role of survivals in subsequent evolution."[19] Consequently, there was almost no study of contemporaneity and particularly of "new man" in Soviet ethnography outside of museums in 1930s. Ethnographers from the Academy of Sciences and universities became engaged in the research of modern Soviet life only after the Second World War.[20]

Introduction of the New Man in the Museum

In March of 1934, the Ethnographic department was separated from the Russian Museum, and became the SME.[21] The approach to displaying the modern Soviet era changed: the prevalence of purely economic topics in the exhibitions of socialist construction was criticized. Thus, the authors of a 1934 editorial article in the *Soviet Museum* critically assessed the Byelorussian exhibition:

> The designers of this exhibition are mistaken in their assumption that in order to characterize the socialist way of life in the construction of Soviet Byelorussia it is enough to display button factories and knitting mills and so forth. They do not understand that it is not the simple fact of such works' existence that is characteristic of socialist Byelorussia, but a new way of life of the workers both at their workplace and in their social life which can exist only in a country under the dictatorship of the proletariat which is building socialism.[22]

The authors of this quote also demanded the display of the "new man": "We do not see the new man who has been created by the Soviet system in any exhibitions." In that year ethnographers in SME were already working on representation of the new socialist way of life, but they did not have proper cultural resources to show the "new man."

Toward the mid-1930s, museum employees strove to depict the successes of socialist construction through the lens of industrial, public, and domestic ways of life.[23] The first exhibition based on these new principles, *The Uzbeks*, was developed in 1935–6. It differed from previous exhibitions in the number of colorful life groups with picturesque murals and dioramas, which were used as backgrounds. The effort was seen as a success—the exhibition appeared to be popular and was highly valued by visitors leaving enthusiastic remarks in the museum guest book.[24] The *Uzbeks* exhibition became a reference point and a model for all other exhibitions during the second half of the 1930s.

The shift to focusing on the way of life was soon supplemented with a focus on the "new man." Its display in the museum became possible after the emergence of the Stakhanovite movement in late 1935. Important guidelines were announced during a meeting of museum employees with the director of the SME and representatives of Narkompros of RSFSR in March 1937. The head of the Narkompros Museums department, Felix Kon, decreed that, when making exhibits on socialist construction, the main emphasis should be placed on the guiding role of the party and the "new man." In his view, exhibitions ought to portray "how, under the leadership of the Party, the man who was until recently oppressed has created his own culture," and to represent the "stages through which the new man was educated and led to the Stakhanovite movement."[25]

At the same meeting, Anton Supinskii, the head of the Byelorussia department, urged that the Soviet sections of exhibitions be built based on fieldwork studies of "the identity of the man who was reborn into a new way of life"—"the Soviet socialist man."[26] By 1936, he was criticizing the accepted methods of exhibiting socialist construction in the SME, "from which this man either disappears completely, or is shown from only one side, during manufacturing processes."[27] Demonstrating the "new life of the new men" also required a new approach to studying Soviet villages. During his preparations for an expedition to Northern Byelorussia, Supinskii worked out a program for studying the new way of life, which included a number of questions concerning the "new man." In particular, he planned to study the stories the youth told about heroes of socialist labor, the participation of the younger and older residents in the Stakhanovite movement, and their own "heroic" actions.[28]

In the summer of 1937, the museum was closed, and its management was declared "wreckers" (saboteurs).[29] But by November, after the "distortions" uncovered in the exhibitions were fixed, the museum was reopened to the public.[30] Under a new director (Efim Milstein[31]) the SME continued its work in the same direction. The need to study "new men" played an important role in fieldwork done by museum ethnographers. The most advanced—"typical"—sites were chosen for expeditionary work.[32] In making their choices, museum workers relied on regional and republic officials, as well as local cultural professionals, who provided them with statistics and directed them toward the most economically successful regions. Then their colleagues working in these regions would recommend the most prosperous and cultural collective farms (*kolkhozy*) to study. On these farms, the ethnographers could finally start working with the Stakhanovites, other decorated workers, and so on. The researchers would talk with them, take photographs, write down their biographies, and observe their daily living conditions. They also collected material on "notable residents" of the *kolkhoz* from local cultural institutions, from newspaper editors, and from the farm administration. For example, during an expedition to Voronezh province, Nadezhda Grinkova and her colleagues worked with six "five-hundredists," who had set records by growing 500 centners of beetroot per hectare:

> We met them, had a photo shoot, and examined their fields, where we photographed the decorated workers at their work. What these wonderful women told us was of much value and interest in characterizing the new collective farmer, and the new socialist attitude to labor.[33]

The New Man as an Economic Hero

After its reopening in late 1937, the museum closely adhered to the new policies articulated by Felix Kon on emphasizing in its exhibits the appearance of the "new man" under the guidance of the party and personally Stalin. Judging by an unpublished 1937 guide, the exhibition *The Russian Inhabitants of the Black Earth Regions* (opened in late 1936) had almost no depiction of the "new men" and was bitterly criticized for this omission.[34] As a new guide issued two years later clearly shows, the exhibit's designers led by Nadezhda Grinkova quickly responded to the criticism and filled the exhibit with appropriate materials.[35]

After 1937 all exhibitions of Soviet modernity were loosely divided into two subsections. Following the Marxist conception of history, the first subsection focused on the economic foundations—agriculture (and, to a smaller extent, industry), working conditions, and the achievements of labor. The second subsection addressed the cultural superstructure—"the new way of life," education, healthcare, folk art, and craftsmanship. Included at the end were short discussions of civil defense, the Red Army and the Border Service, the 1936 Constitution and the elections to the Supreme Soviet of the USSR, along with some general conclusions.

The "new men"—the Stakhanovites—were given a much more in-depth depiction in the economic subsection. They were represented mainly via official studio portraits, head-and-shoulders or bust-length, set against a neutral background. They were usually shown in urban European dress, although members of constituent republics could wear national costumes. For example, men from Central Asia were often shown wearing robes and *tiubeteikas* (an indigenous type of skullcap common in Central Asia). They wore, in pride of place on their chests, the Order of Lenin, the Order of the Red Banner of Labor, the Order of the Badge of Honor, and other Soviet awards. Group photos generally showed "new men" at rallies and congresses of industrial or agricultural *udarniki* and Stakhanovites (see Figure 9.1).

Let us take as an example the image of the "new man" found in the exhibition *The Russian Inhabitants of the Black Earth Regions* (1936–7). The "new man" first appeared on display panel 45. The left half of the panel held materials about the recent past: the fight against kulaks and religious sects in the Voronezh Region, and the resolution of the "land question" during the collectivization. The right half depicted the happy present, notably through a diorama mock-up of "cultural field-living camp" for workers, set among the fields of the *kolkhoz*. The new industrial norms and way of life of the collective farmers were displayed using this mock-up:

Figure 9.1 The rally of the Stakhanovites of industry and transport of the Uzbek SSR Photographer—Max Penson (?). 1936. © Courtesy of the Photo Library of the Russian Museum of Ethnography (St. Petersburg), 5833–18.

the lodgings, the kitchens, the well, the radio, the nursery, and so on.[36] Next to this diorama were portraits of the "decorated collective farmers of the Voronezh Region." In this manner, the Soviet government created the new cultural way of life and the "new men"—top employees in industry, and standard-bearers of Soviet society. The tsarist regime, on the other hand, had given rise only to the kulaks and "religious dope."

Panel 47 was dedicated to the aforementioned decorated workers, who harvested record quantities of beetroot. Along with photographs of these women, including photos of them at a reception in the Kremlin, were letters from their parents to Stalin, in which the parents "gave many thanks for the prestigious awards their daughters were given and for their happy lives on the *kolkhoz*"[37] (see Figure 9.2). Next to this panel were materials on hut-laboratories (panel 46), and on the opposite side of the hall there was a life group (47), which depicted the horticultural work of Ivan Michurin's nursery. On the one hand, this combination reflected the literacy of the collective farmers, their rationality, and their trust in science. On the other hand, it shows that, taken in context, the record harvests could not be credited just to the Stakhanovites and the decorated workers themselves, but also to socialist science, which had taught them how to overcome evolution and transform nature in a rational way.[38]

The items on panel 49 demonstrated how the Voronezh collective farmers, using socialist labor practices, accomplished the objective set out by Stalin of advancing animal husbandry. On display was a joint letter written by the collective farmers to Stalin, discussing these accomplishments, along with photographs of four decorated workers (see Figure 9.2). The workers' biographies were also reflected in the script of a typical tour. The script's authors suggested that tour guides give the full names of each collective farmer, their profession, and work place, and describe their achievements in labor. "The life of each decorated worker is its own creative journey, showing their great love for their jobs and their honest attitude to work."[39] The topic of animal husbandry was concluded with material on the creation of an animal-husbandry staff at the Zootechnical Institute, at the vocational school, and in clubs.[40] From this perspective, it was the guidance of the "leader of the people" (i.e., Stalin) that inspired the labor achievements of the "new men," and helped lead to their education in Soviet institutions.

In this part of the SME's exhibits, photographs of top-performers in industry were often accompanied by public letters to Stalin, written both jointly and individually. In a tour of the exhibition *Jews in Imperial Russia and in the USSR* (1939), the letters were presented as follows:

> The letters of the collective farmers and the letters from notable members of the Jewish national regions addressed to Comrade Stalin are an expression of love and gratitude for their happy lives. The collective farmers describe their achievements in socialist labor and in agricultural development.[41]

In the exhibition *The Evenks Then and Now* (1936), materials on the new cultural and social conditions at work ("the home of the hunter"), photographs of Stakhanovites, and their letters were all fit into one display case. In the letters, the Stakhanovite

Figure 9.2 The beginning of the Soviet section of the "Russian Inhabitants of the Black Earth Regions" exposition. A "red partisan" is in the foreground of the picture. Life group "In the collective farm field" is in the background. Photographs of "new men" are displayed on the panels on the sides of the diorama. The unknown photographer. 1936. © Courtesy of the Photo Library of the Russian Museum of Ethnography (St. Petersburg), ИМ 3–79.

hunters thank Stalin for their happy lives and tell him about "how they hunt, how they are raising their level of culture, and how they are becoming more prosperous."[42]

The Stakhanovite portrait gallery could also reflect the friendship between the peoples of the USSR. Notably, this was achieved in the exhibition on Turkmen (1938) through a photo display of "notable people" in the industry from different nationalities (e.g., Turkmen, Kyrgyz, Kazakhs, Baluchi).[43] In the case of the Kola Peninsula (1935), the photo portraits were put on display in a special case or put into albums on tables in the center of the room. They depicted the heroic struggle of the decorated workers and *udarniki* with nature in the Arctic Circle.[44]

The participation of women in the Stakhanovite movement, in administration, and in public service was displayed as a way to highlight the topic of women's emancipation under Soviet power. For example, in the exhibition *The Uzbeks Then and Now* (1935–6), photos depicting the efforts of the party and the Soviet councils toward women's liberation, the symbolic burning of *paranjas* (a traditional Central Asian women's garment covering the face and body), and photos of a female delegate, a chairwoman of the Village Soviet, and the instigator of the Stakhanovite movement were all displayed together as a set.[45]

The final part of the exhibit, which came after the subsection on cultural development (see below), depicted "the best people in the country." Most commonly, these were portraits of deputies from the Supreme Soviet of the USSR and the top-party officials in the republic or region. Next to this were materials on civil defense and the Red Army, a large economic map of the region, and bas-reliefs or busts of Lenin and Stalin—"the creator and mastermind of all victories."[46] This part of the exhibition also displayed a special category of "notable people," who differed from top-performers in industry in that they had political power and high levels of "consciousness." Alongside Stalin and Lenin, these people encapsulated the party leadership of the country and the care of wise "fathers" for the education of their "sons"—the Stakhanovites, the Chkalovites (outstanding pilots named after Valerii P. Chkalov), and so on.[47]

The Cultural Life and Education of the New Man

In contrast to economic sections of the exhibitions, cultural sections barely mentioned the Stakhanovites. Photographs of nurseries and kindergartens, schools and libraries, hospitals and health sanatoria, theaters and clubs all demonstrated the highlights of the cultural advancement of Soviet citizens, the establishment of a new way of life, and the care shown to the workers. While the "new men" themselves were not on display, the topic of their education was considered of key importance. Soviet children of various ages—the "new men" of the future—were portrayed in photographs, murals, and life groups. Their education was not to be limited to government institutions like schools, or clubs. It also had to take place at home, in the correct—"cultured"—environment. As has already been noted, the forms of "culturedness" propagandized by the government (and the Stakhanovites themselves) in many ways recalled the standards of urban bourgeois culture. The recognizable embodiments of domestic "culturedness" were lampshades, tablecloths, curtains, carpets, bicycles, and fresh flowers.[48] It was through exhibits of such material symbols that the SME had to demonstrate the growing "culturedness" of Soviet citizens.

The model interiors of *kolkhoz* lodgings, which were built for all regional exhibits, are particularly illustrative. Generally, these included a scene depicting a home-cooked meal, with all the members of the family around the table, from children to elderly relatives. For example, at the exhibition *Karelia and the Kola Peninsula* (1935), the interior of a house of Saami collective farmers was recreated: "Today, most Saami live in wooden houses, in relatively cultured conditions. The Saami have access to manufactured goods and items for recreation. Here we see a radio, newspapers, and books."[49] The same exhibition also featured the interior of a Finnish fisherman's house (see Figure 9.3) in the village of Belokamenka (part of the *Severnaia Zvezda* collective farm):

> As a result of their substantial earnings, these collective farmers are able to get their housewares and clothing from a cooperative. This explains why there are almost no objects of Finnish national culture on display. The set-up of the interior, as well as the costumes of the mannequins, reproduce the typical features of material culture on the *kolkhoz.*[50]

This description is also interesting for the apologetic tone of its author—a museum display of the interior of a modern Finnish dwelling was ideally supposed to include symbols of nationality and "culturedness," as well as give evidence of the convergence of urban and rural life. Comparable displays in other exhibitions included various pieces of folk art (embroidery, towels, bed skirts, toys, pieces of national costumes, etc.), as well as clocks, radios, books, and other symbols of urban culture. Folk art and crafts were meant not only to depict the distinctive aspects of Soviet national cultures but also to represent a new—aestheticized—way of life, the only possible conditions for a "new man" to be educated in.

Figure 9.3 Life group "Finnish fisherman's room" depicting a family having a lunch in the "Karelia and the Kola Peninsula" exposition. The unknown photographer. 1936. © Courtesy of the Photo Library of the Russian Museum of Ethnography (St. Petersburg), ИМ 3–46.

Soviet culture policy also set a goal of making various types of art more available to all segments of the population. All exhibitions, starting with the one on Uzbeks, depicted the emergence of new methods of professional art—theater and literature—which had previously been unavailable to peasants and ethnic minorities. These topics differed from others in that they allowed special emphasis to be placed on individual performers and authors. For example, a display on Jews featured photographs of Jewish poets and writers who had been honored with government awards.[51] Photographs of Tamara Khanum and Halima Nosirova—famous dancer and opera singer—were showcased in Uzbek exhibition. Descriptions of theaters highlighted their varied repertoires: plays with folklore and historical "national" plotlines were included alongside productions of Russian and Western European classics.[52] The first ones were supposed to develop the "national form" of culture, while the second ones formed its "socialist content" and internationalist attitude.[53]

Various types of amateur art (*kolkhoz* choirs, ensembles playing national instruments, etc.) also became objects of display. The exhibition *The Russian Inhabitants of the Black Earth Regions* (1936–7) was the first to make wide use of folklore (mostly *chastushki*—short witty folk rhymes) as part of the display.[54] Also incorporated into exhibitions were examples of the folk decorative arts of Soviet period—patterned fabrics, carpet-making, Yelets lace, Skopin pottery, and so on (see Figure 9.4).[55] In later SME exhibits, displays of folklore texts and objects of modern national decorative arts became commonplace.

Figure 9.4 The ending of the Soviet section of the "Russian Inhabitants of the Black Earth Regions" exposition with folk art in the foreground. The unknown photographer. 1936. © Courtesy of the Photo Library of the Russian Museum of Ethnography (St. Petersburg), ИМ 3–52.

The Soviet government believed that the people could only come to understand socialism in a national form.[56] Thus, museums focused particularly on works of national folk arts that depicted the "new subjects"—scenes from *kolkhoz* life and in cities, portraits of leaders, hammers, sickles, stars, and so on. These works most clearly embodied the ideological principles of socialist realism—participation in the "fight for tomorrow," depiction of the future in the present, of "what ought to be as what is."[57] It could be said that Soviet national art most fully expressed the desired synthesis of "socialist in content" and "national in form"—a synthesis of modernity and tradition: the utilitarian functionality of items and the propaganda of revolutionary symbols and successes were merged, by the artist, with traditional forms, materials, styles, production methods, and ornamentation. However, the problem was that in exhibitions, this synthesis was not an organic part or essence of the "new man"—it was just part of his education and "cultural" leisure time.

Exhibits of works of Soviet decorative art did not highlight the names of their creators. None of the guidebooks or scripts considers a single piece of national art for its artistic mastery, or touches on the author's conception of the piece. This anonymized approach, commonly used in exhibits on traditional agrarian cultures, was intended both to emphasize the seamless link between the "national form" of the modern culture of a nationality and the best traditions of folk art from its past, and to present Soviet decorative arts as "national," that is, as an expression of the feelings of all members of a certain ethnic group.

It is interesting to compare the ways of expressing gratitude to Stalin and the party found in the two different subsections of the exhibition. In the agricultural section, gratitude is expressed publicly in epistolary format, on behalf of the "new men." This method reflects the predominance of the epistolary medium in Soviet culture of the 1930s.[58] In displays on culture construction, works of decorative art are used to express the "love, trust, and gratitude" of the entire people toward their "leader."[59] This idea is most clearly expressed in objects (embroidery, carpets, carved ivory figures, etc.) depicting Stalin, Lenin, Molotov, Kalinin, and other top-ranking officials. This was a more touching, more emotional means of expressing gratitude than a clichéd letter concerning economic objectives and industrial accomplishments.[60]

The Story of the New Man

However, folk art only indirectly made up for the "on paper" version of the "new man" that was displayed in the economic subsections of exhibits. This was a two-dimensional image, one for the most part stripped of any ethnic characteristics. As has been mentioned previously, SME exhibits in the second half of the 1930s included a large number of life groups. In Soviet sections, mannequins represented the average Soviet citizen in various life situations—at work in the fields or in a factory, at home, at rest, or during a village festival. Despite the idealized nature of the life groups, it was hard to distinguish specifically "new men" in them, as they were too impersonal and general. In this we once again detect the tendency, inherent to ethnographic museums, to have anonymized displays.[61]

In the late 1930s, Evgeniia Studenetskaia, head of the Caucasus department, proposed an original approach. In order to see in a mannequin not just an impersonal generalization, but a distinct individual, the mannequin had to be given a name and a biography, to be made into a character in a story.[62] This gave rise to "story" excursions, which depicted life before and after the October Revolution via several generations of an imaginary family. The first "story excursion"— "The Story of Little Maiskhon"—told the story of three generations of an Uzbek family from the mid-nineteenth century through the 1930s. Similar tours were developed for several other exhibitions, all aimed primarily at children. The tour of the exhibition *Peoples of the North Caucasus in the Past and Present* (1939) was called "A Hundred Years in the Life of Aekhsaer." Among the tours created for the Russian exhibition, worthy of note are "Two Childhoods" and "The Fate of Little Aniuta."[63] Two story excursions were developed for the *History of the USSR in the 18th Century* exhibition in the SME's History and Way of Life department—"The Moor of Peter the Great" and "The History of a Serf Family."[64]

All of these ethnographic "stories" (excluding those set in the eighteenth century) had plots based on the contrast between the older generation, which suffered during prerevolutionary times, and the generation of their grandchildren, who were raised under socialism and who embodied the ideals of the "new man." So, the elder Maiskhon was born in feudal Bukhara, and died in the Central Asian revolt of 1916. The younger Maiskhon—her granddaughter—"made parachute jumps, helped to build the Fergana Canal, voted in elections to the Soviets, in a word, at the will of the guide she did everything that it was particularly important to tell the audience about at that particular moment."[65] The three generations of the family corresponded to the three sections of the exhibition, dedicated to Uzbek life under feudalism, capitalism, and socialism. The symbolic link between the names encouraged comparison of a woman's fate before and after the revolution.

The story "A Hundred Years in the Life of Aekhsaer," also created by Studenetskaia, shows how the "new man" and a socialist way of life were manifested in the display. After successfully invading an Ossetian village, a Kabardian prince sells the captured Aekhsaer into slavery to a wealthy Balkar. Once he has been freed, Aekhsaer works for a Karachay man as a field hand and for a Russian factory owner as a laborer. This difficult life ends only after the civil war, in which he fights on the side of the Soviets. His son, Chermen, works as the chairman of a *kolkhoz*, and his grandson, Beibulat, is a tractorist under the famed worker Mylykho Tsoraev. When Tsoraev is sent to study in Moscow, Beibulat is put in charge: he "values the experience of Mylykho, and gains his own. On his order, his *kolkhoz* challenges the *kolkhoz* of Karachai and Balkariia to a competition."[66] Beibulat's life is depicted in the items in the life group "Lunch in the Fields," a portrait of Mylykho Tsoraev, and a display with photographs showing his prosperous life.

In his old age, Aekhsaer takes up woodcarving and makes a lovely walking stick:

> The walking-stick represents the story of the Ossetian people. The Ossetian people were caught in the grasp of two snakes: oppression and ignorance. One of these snakes has the head of Nicholas II. <. . .> But the people would not put up with this—they fought and they won. Here is the dismal past—a priest, an officer; from

> the ruins of the past grew a new man, with a book in his hand and a horse, ready to learn and to fight.[67]

In fact, the walking stick was made by a well-known "naïve" artist from North Ossetia, Soslanbek Edziev (1865–1953).

The description of the house of Karakulak, an old friend of Aekhsaer's, continues the theme of national decorative arts, and interlinks it with amateur performance and folklore:

> In this cozy house there lives an old man. His grandson's young wife has decorated their entire house with patterns. She's an expert at coming up with patterns. She makes wonderful carpets. Her son clearly takes after her—he's the best member of the House of Children's Artistic Education. On holidays, they come and take the carpets she's made. On the most important holidays, she goes herself, as the expert. She is accompanied by an elderly singer. His songs are played on the radio, and his stories are turned into plays.[68]

The story is backed up by a life group entitled "The Collective Farmer's House."

The allusion to the longevity of people from the Caucasus allowed Studenetskaia to fit three transitions—from feudalism to capitalism to socialism—into the story of Aekhsaer. But the "new man" in the story is not Aekhsaer—it is his grandson, Beibulat. As such, he was placed in the life group in the economic subsection. There are no active, adult men to be found in the cultural subsection—only elderly men and women and children, engaged in making folk art. Nevertheless, this art has a critical purpose: it serves as a means of self-expression, a symbol of cultural continuity, and a method of female emancipation and Soviet-style education of children. It must be noted that in other exhibitions, men were generally included in scenes depicting the interior of dwellings. For instance, in the story excursion for the Russian exhibition, the "Collective Farmer's House" interior made great use of the figure of a young man at the head of the table, depicting him as a "new man" who has come home after work.

Thus, through the story excursions, exhibitions were turned into part of a socialist-realist narrative, and the mannequins in the life groups became individuals with names and life stories. The biographies of specific individuals became a stage for class struggle and the change of Marxist formations. In addition, in the Soviet section of the exhibit, the "new men"—the younger generation of characters in the story—were brought to life and imbued with attributes of national culture: they were dressed in selected pieces of a national costume, they were placed in interiors decorated with folk art, and in a regional landscape shown through picturesque murals and dioramas.

The Temporal Framework of the New Man

The layout and placement of the Stakhanovites within the museum exhibition reflected the temporal character of their ideological image. The Soviet "new men" on display in the economic subsection were contrasted with prerevolutionary "backwardness" and "remnants of the past" such as the kulaks who resisted collectivization. Through them, socialism replaced the traditional way of life of the peoples of the Russian Empire. That is, when visiting an exhibition, the transition from the prerevolutionary section to the Soviet section embodied the temporality of modernization, or, in the words of Francine Hirsch, "state-sponsored evolutionism."[69]

The composition of the socialist construction section, however, reflected a different temporality—the ontogenesis of the Stakhanovite. The logic of the spatial layout was destroyed here, as the education and childhood of the "new man" was in the second, cultural subsection, but the new man was featured in the first, economic subsection. A different layout would have ruined the useful comparison of the prerevolutionary way of life with the achievements of the Soviet economy and the Marxist concept of movement from base (the economy) to superstructure (culture). Moreover, the cultural subsection, with its displays of art, was where the acceptable synthesis of national characteristics, which required continuity with the past, and socialist modernism, which proposed a break with traditions, could be found. This synthesis was necessary, the Bolsheviks thought, because giving the "elemental" people from these ethnic groups (and their no less "elemental" children) a Soviet education required not just strict supervision and advice from the "conscious" Father, but also the packaging of Marxist content in an accessible, "national" form.

It must be noted that the ontogenesis of the Stakhanovite was not seen as merely a biological maturation—the education of the "new man" implied, first and foremost, an inner transition from "elementality" to "consciousness." Hence, even an elderly person could be a Stakhanovite, after being "rejuvenated" by free socialist labor. The results of this type of education, or "reforging"—their achievements in labor—were a key part of the biographical narratives of the Stakhanovites, and were displayed in the economic sections of exhibitions. In accordance with the development plan for the exhibition *Uzbeks in the Past and the Present* (1936), an excerpt from a conversation with decorated crew leader Faizullah Yunusov was also included:

> I want our leaders to know that the old people on the collective farm have grown young again. I'm already 62, but I don't feel old and I work better than the young men. I've only started to like work on the collective farm. How could you like working before, when it was a torment for you and only made other people's lives better? Our section has brought in a harvest of 5,700 kg/ha. My section's secret is that we don't say what the most important work is. All our work is the most important.[70]

The most authoritative ideological text on the Stakhanovites—Stalin's speech at the First All-Union Conference of Stakhanovites in 1935—helps us understand the origins of this particular temporal framework. According to Stalin, the Stakhanovites are "new people, of a special type." They emerged only thanks to the revolution and to Soviet power, which ended exploitation and brought about a radical improvement in the material status of the workers.[71] In this context, the Stakhanovite movement comes across as a historical phenomenon, one which arose during the transition from capitalism to communism, and one which foreshadowed the latter.

In Stalin's view, the Stakhanovites were also historical actors. They set themselves a goal of "smashing old traditions"—overcoming existing technological standards, estimated capacities, production plans, and financial statements. However, the "engineers, technical workers, and business managers" were in favor of these old standards; they clung to the "technical backwardness" of workers.[72] Thus Stalin linked the opponents of the Stakhanovites with backwardness and tradition. Their "struggle" ends in the inevitable victory of Socialist modernity. Stalin, however, begins his assessment of the significance of the Stakhanovite movement not with the struggle with outmoded standards, but with classifying the movement as a new, higher stage of Socialist competition. The Stakhanovite movement contrasts favorably with the "old stage" in its new technology and new features.[73] This temporality does not imply a contrast of "dangerous" traditions with "useful" innovations, but rather a "battle between good and best." Stalin's assessment captures the distinguishing features of the labor of *udarniki* and Stakhanovites—the constant exceeding of standards, the surpassing of one's own labor achievements or the records of comrades in the movement.[74]

The temporal framework of the ideological image of the Stakhanovite in Stalin's speech and in museum exhibitions coincides with a contrast of past and present, of traditional and socialist time, and the affirmation of their historical transition. The "backward" traditional societies, oppressed by "servants of capital," were the ethnographic analogue of these outmoded standards and conservative engineers. Similarity can also be found between the biographical narratives of the Stakhanovites, divided into "before" and "after" by their personal achievements.

The main problem with Stalin's model of the Stakhanovite might be said to be the lack of a positive image of tradition that would allow "new men" to be satisfactorily inserted into Soviet national cultures. Consequently, the Stakhanovites, if they are represented at all in the cultural subsections of ethnographic exhibitions, are represented only insignificantly—as children, whose proper upbringing will give rise to the next generation of "new men." Thus the opposition to tradition and the past, which was a constitutive part of the ideological image of the Stakhanovite, became a cause of the temporal distance between the "new man" and national/ethnic cultures: from a historical perspective, these cultures were forced to be part of the prerevolutionary way of life, while from an ontogenetic perspective, they were forced into the realm of Soviet education and childhood.

Conclusion

In the 1920s the "new man" of a communist future was predominantly a subject of scientific experiments, artistic imagination, and social engineering. S/he was not manifested in concrete people, but should be produced or nurtured. From a Marxist point of view, it was impossible to educate the "new man" in a semi-capitalist NEP environment, burdened with multiple remnants of the past. In the mid-1930s Stalin decreed that the socialism has indeed been constructed in the USSR. The logical conclusion of this statement was the appearance of the "new man" in flesh. The Stakhanovite became this Stalinist kind of the "new man"—an outcome of the epoch of fierce economic modernization and also of conservative retreat from egalitarian revolutionary ideals of the 1920s.

The introduction of the Stakhanovite into the ethnographic museum during the years of the Great Terror was the culmination of ideological pressure on the work of the SME. However, the depiction of the Stakhanovites in the museum was not merely a part of a propaganda campaign in support of the socialist attitude toward labor; it also served as a conduit for the ideological conception of the "new man" and expressed a specific view of the past, present, and future. The representation of the Stakhanovites in the ethnographic ("national") context highlighted the structural contradiction within the domestic policy of the Soviet Union. If the nationalities policy served as more of a "carrot," encouraging *korenizatsiia* ("nativization") within the governmental apparatus and supporting national cultures, then the centralized planned economy acted as the "stick," pushing forced industrialization and collectivization. This contradiction had a temporal aspect. The nationalities policy was based on the continuity of past and present, while the economic policy was grounded in a break with the past, in favor of a present that focused on the future. The ideological image of the Stakhanovite was thus a product of economic modernization and the embodiment of Marxist temporality. Historically, the Stakhanovite was the logical outcome of social development and the shift between socioeconomic formations, while in day-to-day life, s/he fought with the "remnants" of the past, in support of a communist future. In this capacity, the Stakhanovite could not be easily integrated into the nationalities policy or into ethnographic exhibitions.

The various shortcomings and contradictions in the representation of the Stakhanovites were smoothed over partly through the use of cultural resources of art—pieces of Soviet artistic handicrafts, life groups, and "story excursions." Art provided a link between "national form" and "socialist content," while paper materials, which referenced newspapers and political-education exhibitions, supplemented the three-dimensional objects that were common to ethnographic museums. Finally, the "story excursions" linked the biographies of the "new men" with the historical process, within the Marxist paradigm. In accordance with the spirit of the age, art in the ethnographic museum was meant to find and propagandize the beauty of the new way of life, but in reality it functioned more as a way of filling in gaps and erasing contradictions, by using the aesthetics of socialist realism.[75] The beauty of Soviet life and of museum exhibitions depended on the aestheticization of the Stakhanovites. In other words, the very nurturing of the Soviet "new man" in the Stalinist representational state was, paradoxically, a matter of its proper museum depiction.

Translated by Maeve Wiegand

Conclusion

The New Man: One Hundred Years Later

Yonne Howell

The New Man, the Posthuman, and the Transhuman

What happened to the New Man? Did all the visionary, liberating, controversial, and disciplining plans for constructing a new type of human being disappear forever after the mid-1930s? Was the Soviet construction of a New Man the last attempt to remake humanity? Of course not. We know from history that the emergence of powerful new paradigms of knowledge—traditionally a change in the way we see our place in the world from the point of view of religion, philosophy, science, or political organization—tends to coincide with times of social upheaval and a sense of crisis. The conjunction of new ways of knowing and the apprehension of crisis periodically gives rise to the search for new definitions of who we are and what we can or should ideally become.

At the dawn of the twentieth century, however, the influence of a certain type of new scientific knowledge (what Nikolai Krementsov refers to in his chapter as "the experimentalist revolution in biology") on the cultural imagination was particularly strong in Russia. There the impetus to create a new type of person—the "new man" of the more perfect future[1]—was *driven* by a historic, tumultuous break with the past, but *fueled*, as we have seen in the preceding chapters, by the possibility of tantalizing interventions into human biology and psychology. In today's parlance, new scientific discoveries suggested that powerful hacks into human nature were possible.

One hundred years later, in the first two (going on third) decades of the twenty-first century, we have arrived at another era of consequential endeavors to imagine and create "new men." This time around, the being we may be conjuring into existence is usually referred to as the posthuman or the transhuman. (We will return to the necessary definitions of these terms shortly.) What can we learn from a comparison between the nexus of ideas, policies, and cultural features that can be said to have constituted the construction of the Soviet "new man," and the contemporary nexus of ideas, projects, and cultural trends that is unfolding in various parts of the globe under the banner of transhumanism? After all, the same radical, abstracting, science-fictional aspirations for the New Man that have been routinely condemned as naïve at best, and cruelly dystopian at worst, seem quite familiar and compatible with contemporary projects for enhancing human life and reinvigorating the project of populating outer space.[2] Why do today's global initiatives to "upgrade" human potential, extend life spans, edit and direct evolution, overcome cognitive and physical limitations, and "realize our full potential" as a species[3] resonate so strongly—sometimes almost verbatim—with Bolshevik pronouncements about constructing the New Man from 100 years ago?

A few words about the difference between the New Man, the posthuman, and the transhuman are in order. The contemporary terms signal their location in an intellectual continuum that is posthumanist in the first case, and technologically beyond-human in either case. Both posthumanism and transhumanism emphasize the role of nonorganic, technological "traits" in the further evolution of our species. They both question what it means to be "human" at all, once we have reached the point of "coevolving" with our own technological systems.[4] For our purposes, however, the contrast between the two is important: posthumanists reject the legacy of Enlightenment thought, and regard humanism as a "fundamentally flawed idea used to alienate humans and dominate nature."[5] Transhumanists operate on the view that Enlightenment ideals have not been fully realized, or that humanism has not gone far enough to do what it needs to do to allow the capacity for rational thought to help us achieve our godlike potential.

In the second decade of the twenty-first century, "transhumanism" is a burgeoning academic discipline,[6] an official (if nascent) political party in the United States,[7] and a global movement whose advocates have already had time to differentiate themselves into various philosophical subgroups.[8] Today's Russian transhumanist thinkers draw inspiration from their peers in other parts of the world, while also contributing a Russian historical-cultural element to their work (which will be discussed at the end of this chapter). It is not my intention here to provide empirical evidence to show how deeply the main ideas of transhumanism have penetrated into our global Zeitgeist. The label itself is far less in evidence than the ubiquity of its principles, which have become a *cultural resource* for everyone from technological entrepreneurs to biomedical innovators to marketing executives hawking rejuvenation serums and mental acuity diets. The following list of basic principles paraphrases several repetitive websites:

- The aim of transhumanism is to break through man's biological boundaries through science and technology. Examples include the expansion of physical and cognitive abilities, as well as the pursuit of immortality;
- Transhumanism can accommodate many different political, philosophical, and even religious views;
- Using technology to improve ourselves is the hallmark of the human species; one could say that it is part of our evolutionary path to take control of our evolutionary path;
- Although some techniques, like cryogenic suspension, mind uploading, and "hive intelligence," still seem far-fetched, scientists and research companies are actively at work in all of these domains;
- Creating the transhuman of the future will depend as much on social factors as technological ones: economic, cultural, and political factors will determine how advances in technology are implemented.

We do not (yet) have the historical evidence to definitively prove that the first third of the twenty-first century is another epoch in quest of the "new man." All we can do is highlight the reverberations between our current historical moment and the early twentieth century's quest to create a "new man." This chapter seeks to identify some of the key qualities and implications of those reverberations.

The Science-Fictionality of New-Man Chronotopes

In a 2016 interview, Yuval Noah Harari stated that "the next big projects of human kind will be to overcome old age and death, to find the keys to happiness, and to basically upgrade humans into gods."[9] The first point that has to be reiterated in a conclusion to this volume is that historical epochs marked by consequential attempts to envision and construct "new men" are cyclical. Once we delve more deeply into the multiple voices, improvised practices, and genuinely innovative thinking that constituted Soviet efforts to create a "new man," we are faced with a phenomenon that was not isolated to a single time and place, but resonates with other "new man" movements of the time, as well as with both previous and subsequent efforts to reimagine humanity of the future. The early Soviet version of building a "new man" was in this sense not unique, much less a singular diabolic expression of communist control. To be sure, as we point out in the Introduction, almost every case study in this volume affirms the role of the State in controlling the "variability and availability of ideas and ideals" that went into creating "new men."[10] After the Bolshevik revolution, the shifting priorities of the State overwhelmingly determined what kind of scientific research would be funded, and which scientific ideas might be implemented as practical policies for creating the desired new bodies, new behaviors, and new social outcomes. The fact that it was the Soviet State that selected, discarded, and shaped various approaches to producing "new men" seems to have almost completely blinded Cold War scholarship on this topic to another, equally viable proposition: namely, many of the approaches and ideas that were forwarded and implemented would have just as easily found champions and sponsors in the West. From today's vantage point, it seems obvious that one doesn't have to be a Bolshevik to warm up to the idea of using Silicon Valley technology to monitor the thoughts and desires of other human beings.

We have already noted that intensified questioning about the destiny of humans, and attempts to shape that destiny, arise in moments when paradigm shifts in knowledge (since the nineteenth century, modern science) break like a wave over unstable and shifting social structures. In the early twentieth century, a succession of unprecedented discoveries in the realm of radiology, endocrinology, epidemiology, population genetics, and so forth arrived as the world was heading toward the first great world war—in other words, at a time of dislocation, change, and apocalyptic apprehensions. I will argue that the twenty-first century's paradigm shifts in biotechnology and artificial intelligence arrive at another moment of historical anxiety—driven by the repercussions of climate change and social inequalities. This kind of *fatal conjunction* between scientific advancement and sense of social crisis gives rise to the chronotope in which "new man" movements arise.

What does the "new man" chronotope look like? We can now posit certain structural and stylistic features that characterize the periodic emergence of concentrated interest in creating "new men." We can use the term "science-fictional chronotope" to denote a historical moment in which the penetration of aspirational science into mundane behaviors happens so suddenly that "everyday reality becomes science-fictional."[11] However, twentieth-century history suggests that the appearance of new technologies in everyday life (for example, the postwar appearance of TV sets, synthetic fabrics, highly processed foods) does not in and of itself invoke the awareness of a science-fictional "future" that has already arrived and seems to penetrate our everyday world. The uneasy (or exhilarating) hallmark of this chronotope is its ability to lift (overcome) the specter of apocalypse, usually by putting the science ahead of the fiction. Worried about exponentially escalating global warming? This is when the idea of radically scaling back human consumption seems more fictional than promises from scientific-entrepreneurial culture to create a NeuroNet of minds whose collective e-brain-power will come up with a solution;[12] or to establish population bases on Mars, where global warming is not a problem.[13]

Thus, the science-fictional chronotope (in any age) has its own *stylistic* features. Bolshevik visionaries and today's transhumanists share a similar rhetorical style of bombastic anthropocentrism and visionary pathos. I will argue that the characteristic discourse of scientific-spiritual utopianism enables an embrace of science-fictional technologies by framing them as morally or spiritually uplifting.[14] Both then and now, it is this discourse that forms the *necessary bridge* between science as a *method of discovery*, and scientific ideas as a *cultural resource* that can be used for various ends. Techno-spiritual discourse avoids the stubborn, material contradictions of the here and now by constantly turning (at least rhetorically) "inert matter" into something lighter, more abstract, more mobile, more "spiritual."

Consider Maxim Gorky's pronouncements on the future, uttered amid the ruins of the old regime in 1919.[15] The "stormy petrel" of a revolutionary movement that transformed the old Russian Empire into the world's first communist State—fiery, mustachioed Gorky sat down on a park bench with the effete, mystical *fin de siècle* poet Alexander Blok, and they got into a discussion about immortality.[16] According to Gorky's written reminiscences, Blok exuded pessimism and defeat:

> If only we could completely cease to *think* for at least ten years. To stop following the will o' the wisp that beckons us into the world's darkest night, and to move towards the world's harmony with our hearts instead. The brain, the brain—an unreliable organ, monstrously big and over-developed. A tumor . . .

While Blok evoked the dangers of rationalism, the "monstrous" perversions of scientific progress (in the same conversation, he mentions the deadly weapons that debuted during the First World War), and his dread of the "new" future, which seemed to already occupy the present, Gorky offered a completely different vision of what would be "new" and what would be "human" in the future:

> Personally, I would prefer to imagine Man as an apparatus for transforming so-called "dead matter" into living psychic energy. Someday, in the far distant future, human beings will have transformed the whole world into pure thought.[17]

We don't know whether Blok really "[had] the eyes of a crazy man" or that he "stumbled [away] with uncertain steps" after the conversation in the Summer Garden.[18] Gorky used his artistic prerogative in writing the memoir to heighten the emotional distance between two worldviews: on the one hand, a longing for the archaic, pre-Enlightenment values of cosmic harmony; on the other hand, a future-forward, radical acceptance of human industry and ingenuity. Upon closer inspection, the binaries represented in the two quotes are not a set of unambiguous opposites, but a way of aligning arrays of cultural values that exist simultaneously in tension. Blok's words represent, broadly speaking, the apocalyptic mysticism of *fin de siècle* decadence, which can be understood as the moment when some of Russia's most highly developed rational minds shuddered at the horrors that Reason had created and began to advocate a "Buddhist" withdrawal from active thought.[19] It is important to note, however, that the mystical, occultist quest may frame itself as a specific rejection of both nurturist (educational) and naturalist (scientific) paths to the future, but it still posits a radical break with existing limitations in time, space, and knowledge. Thus, as we noted in the Introduction, strains of *fin de siècle* supernatural and anthroposophical thought envisioned a semi-mystical, quasi-scientific process of dematerializing mankind into energy and becoming part of a cosmic dance of electrons in the universe. The occult vision can be framed in the language of the spirit, or it can be coopted into the language of science, as Gorky tries to do. In either case, we confront the second key feature of the recurring "new man" chronotope—the rejection of limits, a fundamental orientation toward revolution and resurrection.

Transcendence: Spatial, Temporal, and Social

The current conjunction of new science and apprehension of crisis produces familiar rhetorical strategies for talking about "upgraded" humans and the habitat (often outer space, but sometimes a mystical inner space) where the people of the future will dwell. In a science-fictional chronotope, excesses are as compatible with capitalism as they were with Bolshevism.

Many of the chapters in this volume suggest that in late Imperial Russia and the first two decades of the Soviet Union, a very large range of social actors was allowed to participate in the discussion of *who should we become in the future?* The writers of entertaining literature indulged in inspiring fantasies about scientifically enlightened Man conquering Nature, but early Soviet science fantasies also trafficked in horror and frightening "what if" scenarios about future mutations and catastrophes (see Schwartz, Chapter 5). In the medium of sculpture, when it came to designing monumental works on human and orangutan evolution for Moscow's Darwin Museum, the eventual representations in plaster relief seem to reflect several "voices" in ongoing debates about species evolution (see Simpson, Chapter 8). Even the conundrum of how to balance "socialist content" and "national form" in displaying the "new Turkmen" implied the ingenuity of minds that could properly negotiate a complicated ideological spectrum (see Petriashin, Chapter 9). As almost all contributors point out, *present anxieties* are powerfully reflected in strategies for imaging the new, future man. Our current moment is dominated by uncertainty generated by the effects of climate change, and by fears of limited and dwindling essential resources, like clean water and air. Ecological thinkers who see our planetary resources as finite and worthy of preservation rightfully view our current predicament as a crisis of capitalism. If the early Marxist thinkers faulted capitalism for the psychological defects that marred the "old" men (egotism, mercantilism, etc.), it is more common today to fault capitalism for its macro-effects: in many circles, it is axiomatic that the logic of capitalism is fueling the approach of near-apocalyptic natural and social disasters. The obvious logic of capitalism, as has been repeatedly demonstrated (notably by Fredric Jameson, Slavoj Zizek, and Bill McKibben),[20] relentlessly reinforces exploitative, extractive, expansionist behaviors that will inevitably (and rather soon, at the current rate of things) lead to the collapse of a sustainable habitat on earth—not only for humans but also for many other animals and plants. In other words, from within the anthropological conception of human space-time as exclusively "earthly," capitalism is not a sustainable ideology or practice.

Can we really defy the logic of capitalism by changing human nature? In the context of this volume, we have to ask how the logic of capitalism and recurrent dreams of "making man anew" fit together. To paraphrase Fredric Jameson, it is easier to imagine the end of the human than the end of capitalism. The first decades of the twenty-first century can be described as another moment of fatal conjunction—between the *digital* or *artificial intelligence* revolution in science and technology, and the *acute social anxiety* that is mounting worldwide in response to the twin forces of environmental instability (global warming, toxic soil and water, resistance to antibiotics, etc.) and economic inequality. One half of the equation—the momentum of scientific advancement spilling into society as a cultural resource—has well-established connections to global corporations and global capital. Dramatic advancements have led to the possibility (real and immanent) of technologies that blur the boundaries between biological, physical, and informational systems. The impact of today's "visionary science" on all aspects of our contemporary existence has been hailed as the Fourth Industrial Revolution. It is telling that Klaus Schwab, the Executive Chairman of the World Economic Forum, takes credit for coining the term and popularizing its importance at the Davos meeting of global leaders of capitalism.[21] The other half of the equation—the fusion of imagination and anxiety that produces new visions of the future of humanity—is also coopted, at least in many influential forums, by the mindset of "limitless vistas" and the dream of a humanity that can be "post" or "trans" human.

Despite some critical differences, both posthumanism and transhumanism (which is more relevant here) replicate the faith in infinite growth that was characteristic of the early phases of Bolshevik "revolutionary dreaming." This entails an anthropological view of the human that begins with the premise that our species is not limited to a single planet, but that we can continue to reimagine ourselves and our technological prostheses endlessly, as we have done periodically since the beginning of human history.[22] From this perspective, ecological containment and the curtailing of bold technological research are counterproductive. From this same perspective, trying to hobble or even redirect the logic of capitalism away from other planetary visions is dangerous. As at least one astute scholar of eco-criticism reminds us, from a positivist-masked-as-spiritual point of view, "off-planeting production in order to recreate earth as a sanctuary for humans is a good idea."[23] The most radical of the early communist ideologues would have agreed.

Alexander Bogdanov's 1908 novel *Red Star* tells the story of an enlightened Bolshevik activist who gets the chance to observe the future of communism firsthand on Mars, where a transformative socialist revolution has already occurred some 300 years ago. Bogdanov's earthling protagonist uses his time on Mars to convey to us, the reader, something like an anthropologist's "deep description" of another culture: how mature socialists think, act, behave, and live with exquisite grace (for most of the novel) in their ideally realized communist culture. *Red Star* is usually considered to be the first example of a "Bolshevik" literary utopia, penned by one of the most polymathic thinkers of the revolutionary cohort (examined by Coates in Chapter 1). Fortunately for his readers (*Red Star* was a bestseller, reprinted three times in ten years), Bogdanov was not interested in producing frictionless utopian literature; he couldn't help but introduce productive conflicts into his utopia. The drama that most readers remember has to do with the rise of an interspecies (Mars-Earthling) love affair, made even more intriguing by the Martians' genderless biology and affect. However, we should also recall that toward the climax of the novel, the real conflict that arises has to do with something else: the characters come to blows over the very unsexy problem of interplanetary mining of mineral resources: space mining.

It is no coincidence that both Alexander Bogdanov and Konstantin Tsiolkovsky, a "founding father" of rocket science, gave prominent place to space mining in their sociotechnical utopias.[24] Space mining means the extraction of raw materials from asteroids, the moon, comets, and other mineral-laden objects in space. It assumes the desirability and inevitability of limitless technological advancement. It assumes that when we run out of resources on this (home) planet, we can obtain them from somewhere else. It suggests that there are no limits to growth,[25] only limits to the socio-technological imagination. It suggests that unlike earth mining, which is rightfully viewed as an assault on the earth, a polluting enterprise, and an ultimately unsustainable practice, space mining will entail the harvesting of abundantly available minerals from space objects that were never "green" in the first place.[26]

In *Red Star*, the Martians find themselves in the same situation we are in today: they are running out of rare earth metals and radioactive fuel for their advanced technologies. In the advanced communist society imagined by Bogdanov, the solution to energetic problems is not to cut back on consumption, but to exploit the resources of the wider cosmic neighborhood. The logical (and easiest) solution for the Martians is to colonize earth and extract the necessary minerals that are still found in abundance on our planet. This plan is rejected, as it would repeat the worst sins of earth's "backwards" humanity, namely, the subjugation and destruction of another race for the sake of plundering resources. The Martians settle on a more difficult plan, but one that is full of romantic appeal. The more difficult alternative is to develop technologies that will allow the Martians to safely harvest minerals from the fiery, gaseous planet Venus. The point that needs to be made here is that from its beginnings, in seminal utopian works like *Red Star*, the multifaceted project of creating the "new man" (to which many different artists, scientists, and thinkers contributed) assumed a transcendence of earthbound history toward a post-planetary cosmic history.

In contemporary discourse attached to corporate-funded and state-supported research and development toward space mining, the billions of dollars that will be spent on making an outer space mining industry possible is not only worth it in the long run economically, it is also the fulfillment of a moral imperative. Like Bogdanov's Martians, the idea is to ensure the well-being of future generations, as well as the survival of our home planet, by mining needed resources from a cosmic body that "doesn't care." In *Red Star*, the hero Menni scuttles dastardly plans for the Martians to colonize earth by arguing, convincingly, that on Venus, the needed resources are there for the taking ("so close to the surface that they were easily spotted by means of a photographic detector")[27] and the planet's only other features are violent storms and nasty bacteria. In the same way, contemporary advocates of space mining have contrasted the image of a miner covered in soot and the industry that over-warmed the earth to a new image: that of a robot "clothed" in white, and an industry that will off-planet pollution, thereby transforming earth back into a garden (with energy abundance intact). Brad Tabas makes the crucial interpretive move for us, showing how in this way, the ecological conundrums that hamstring the conscience of twenty-first-century eco-critics are *aufgehoben* (lifted)—that is, as Tabas points out in a Hegelian vein, space mining is framed as a negation of a negation: the opposite of "blackening" the earth with coal-mining is "greening" the earth with space mining, which appears to us visually and rhetorically as a goal of blinding white purity. When early-twentieth-century Russian artists and innovators imagined the New Man, they imagined him/her within precisely this framework: human beings who are infinitely able to negate negations. Malevich's "Black Square" and "White on White."[28]

At this point, we have established the essential convergence of anthropological imagination across the century: early Soviet science, fiction, and science fiction all imagined the New Man's place in a universe that was conceived of as a potentially infinitely exploitable space for human colonization (whether as habitable space or as sources of necessary raw material). Contemporary discussions of space mining, whether in popular fiction or in serious nonfictional venues,[29] are all based on fundamentally the same view of human agency in cosmic dimensions. These ideologies of nature-overcoming, transcending human activity converge in the foundational conviction that we are the species that actively constructs and directs its own destiny. Historically, this conviction has consistently elided the role of large groups of humanity in its destiny-shaping zeal. Exclusion from the conversation can run along racial or gender lines, or both. Yet with equal consistency, visions of science-enabled transcendence have saturated popular culture and captured the imagination of "modern" people all over the world.[30] Depending on the political context of modernization, the construction of "new men" could be promoted and to some degree directed by the State in the name of reaching "full communism," or very similar tactics for directing the "optimal" evolution of humans could also be promoted and directed by philanthropists, quacks, businessmen, and the military in order to reach full and continuing profitability.

The New Man between Reality and Fictionality

A final point to be made in conclusion to this volume: How do we move from historical analyses of the myriad efforts to create "new men" in the early Soviet period to the question of *why we still care*? Is it possible to discern the reasons for this topic's particular emotional, political, and philosophical resonance in our current age, exactly 100 years from the peak of the previous century's interest in creating new men? For example, do we still find ourselves rooting (alongside both John Dewey and Felix Dzerzhinsky, Chapter 2) for the homeless delinquents in experimental labor colonies to repay the wager that was made on them: that given cleanliness, autonomy, and a chance, they would turn into productive builders of a new society? We need to examine how policy debates—and even particular policy prescriptions—about creating the "new man" circulated in an emotionally charged atmosphere of anxiety, dizzying change, and enormous hope. While we cannot historically document these emotions, we can decode their presence in literary works and art, where the sense of disorientation and anticipation is baked into imagery, syntax, and strange new forms.

Let us reiterate here that all of the meticulous case studies represented in this volume suggest a kind of binary reception. On the one hand, the appropriation of science as a "cultural resource" to shape the men of the future is easily comparable to similar efforts in the West. Bugaeva's research uncovers the previously unfathomable points of conviction shared by the American pragmatist John Dewey and the Soviet State's secret police (OGPU) administrators in charge of reforming juvenile delinquents. Golovacheva's comparison of Bulgakov's *Heart of a Dog* and a 1931 US film version of *Frankenstein* emphasizes the degree to which fear of degeneration and criminality could not be assuaged (in either country) by a fail-proof application of "naturist" or "nurturist" theories. We can also posit that any study of early Soviet dietary recommendations would reveal a link between dietary and moral fiber that could also be heard in the American J. H. Kellog's thundering insistence that Americans stick to a diet of bran flakes for breakfast, and so on.

On the other hand, we cannot get rid of the impression that there is something particularly "Russian" about both the policy scripts produced by early Soviet visionaries, and about the way the players were cajoled (or forced) into taking up their roles as "new men." In other words, as a "script" for defining the new worldview and new consciousness of the future, Bogdanov's comprehensive science of "tektology" and its would-be encyclopedia suggests a cultural penchant for outsized engineering (whether oversized hydroelectric dams or oversized totalizing systems). In a different way, the idea of gathering thousands of illiterate peasants into an exhibition of "future agriculture," where they will apprehend their ways as backwards and *simultaneously* learn to overcome that backwardness (see Elina, Chapter 7), also strikes us as "science-fictional" in a way that reiterates other themes in Russian culture.[31] Is there a way to describe the cultural distinctiveness of Russian contributions to a much broader international enthusiasm for periodically conceiving of and constructing a "new man"? I think there is an answer that derives at least as much from within Russian cultural analysis as it does from a potentially "orientalizing" Western perspective. I will argue that what is peculiar to Russian constructions of "renewal" or "the future" is not so much a tendency toward collectivism (the peasant *obshchina*, the supposedly *a priori* preference for collectivism over individualism), as a function of the *gap* between existing reality and the desired future. In Russian cultural terms, this can be approximated as the gap between mundane reality (*byt*) and higher existence (*bytie*), or, roughly "the unfulfilling routine of everyday hardship" versus "the spiritual fulfillment of true existence." In less abstract terms, Russian cultural dynamics form around a *gap*, which is figured as a potentially productive contradiction between scant material resources versus abundant intellectual resources; inadequate material infrastructure versus vibrant imaginative infrastructure.

To illustrate the tension between the inadequate present (which is *already consigned* to the "past" and must be replaced by the new), and the imagined future, we can once again turn to the bard of "new man" pathos, Andrei Platonov. In his 1926 short story "The Lunar Bomb" (*Lunnaia bomba*), the fictional protagonist tries to formulate a remarkable intuition: Platonov's Kreuzkopf believes that about-to-be-real rocket science ("visionary physics") and a-better-life-for-all ("revolutionary dreams") can be connected—by an impoverished self-taught Soviet citizen, no less:

> Kreuzkopf was guided by a secret thought: there were a lot of humans on earth, passing the days of the unrepeatable lives in stifling crowds that gathered around the shriveling veins sustaining the earth. Kreuzkopf hoped to open up new virgin sources of sustenance for life, *run hoses from these [cosmic] sources to the earth*, and use them to swallow up the meanness and the burdened, cramped feeing of human life. And then, when the endless depths of the alien celestial gift were opened, *people would feel more of a need for other people.*[32]

This passage strongly suggests that we can recognize the *emotional landscape* in which the "new man" was constructed by its familiar features. The distinctive pathos of Platonov's work lies in the almost word-by-word double exposure of the *rhetoric* of visionary science, and the *reality* of material backwardness and poverty. Yet the gap between the possibilities suggested by science ("new virgin sources of sustenance" to be found in outer space) and the meager realities of postrevolutionary Soviet existence is imbued with the hope for spiritual redemption. People will "feel more need for other people," and the "meanness and burdened, cramped feeling of human life" will dissolve in the brilliant light of a science-fictional future. The fairy-tale binaries of early Soviet fiction and film (where complete desolation may suddenly give rise to shining factories) never entirely disappears, even in the post-Stalin years. In their 1965 novel *Monday Begins on Saturday* (*Ponedel'nik nachinaetsia v subbotu*), the brothers Strugatsky again invoke the power of the gap between Soviet realities and scientific wonders, albeit in a much more lighthearted way.[33]

In much of the Cold War–era scholarship, it is precisely this emotional pathos, and its potentially tragic results, that has given us grounds to condemn the entire project of "creating a new man" under Soviet rule as a misguided cruelty. In this line of thought, the gap between reality and the imagined future is too great to be overcome by anything other than the most brutal Stalinist measures. At the 1931 Worker's Congress of the Soviet Union, Stalin explained the magnitude of the gap he was determined to close: "We are fifty or a hundred years behind the advanced countries. We must close up this gap in ten years. Either we do it or they will crush us."[34] As priorities shifted abruptly toward rapid industrialization and collectivization of agriculture under the first five-year plans (1928–32; 1933–7), the economic and material gap that yawned between Stalin's admission that "we are 50 years behind" and the future embodied by his mandate that "we must catch up in 10 years" manifested itself in the real bodies of Soviet people—malnourished, overworked, imprisoned, deported, or—in the ultimate image of a tragic "gap"—dumped into mass graves.

And yet this story is unique to the Soviet experience *only* if we make the mistake of assuming it cannot happen anywhere else. The structure of the "gap" between reality and the desired future is easily bridged rhetorically, as we saw in the first part of this chapter. The easiest way to hide the potential shortfall between material poverty and future abundance is to rhetorically transform stubborn, recalcitrant, impoverished matter into abstract, spiritual values. Today, this is precisely the strategy employed by the global oil and gas industry, including Exxon-Mobile, BP, and so forth.[35] We now know that what actually happened—in the state-controlled modernity of the USSR as well as in the ideologically diverse, capitalist West—is that the gap between the possibilities suggested by ever-advancing science and the reality of material poverty for large pockets of the population never disappeared; it only narrowed and widened in different eras. In our contemporary era, most scholars assert that the gap is dramatically widening, as those with access to advanced technology and high-end infrastructure live in one world, and those who have been left behind by "progress" live in another. Under these conditions, once again, the *rhetoric* of the energy corporations and power brokers extols the transformation of "heavy, dirty material" produced by the old industries (coal mines, crude oil refineries) into "invisible, clean energy," by which they mean "clean-burning" "natural" (fracked) gas and nuclear power. At least in their advertisements, energy corporations suggest that communities whose business and homes are lit up and warmed by clean and limitless energy are also thriving places, where the "meanness and burden" of life are gone. Platonov's paradoxical anticipations come back to haunt us: where fracking has yielded abundant gas and nuclear plants have generated abundant energy, the very material, sick and burdened, dirty and dark bodies of the human beings who have been poisoned by their (fracked, radioactive) land or displaced from their land—those bodies have become nearly invisible, or they have disappeared (died early deaths) altogether. Neither the state-encouraged strategies for generating "new men" nor the strategies of independent actors with vision and money have come close to resolving the question that dogs us when we ask *who are we, where do we come from, and what do we want to become?*—namely, the question of who is allowed to ask, and who is allowed to participate in the answering.

"Better Than Us": Conclusion

When an anthropologist interviewed a leading member of the Russian State Agency for Strategic Initiatives, he made it sound like the mindset of transhumanism comes naturally to Russians. Describing the early origins of Russian rocketry, the contemporary strategist said "[it's] quite a Russian story: one is sitting in deep shit but thinking about stratospheric issues—not about how to sell more cabbage, but about how to save humanity."[36] The full context of Pavel Luksha's statement about cabbages and spacecraft would indicate that Russia's contemporary transhumanist thought-leaders are proud of their history, and see ways to use it to their advantage. Luksha's point, in telling the story of Soviet aeronautics pioneer Tsiolkovsky and his influence on the generation of engineers who put the first (Soviet) man into space, is that in Russia, the future is shaped by the energy of unlikely visionaries:

> From this devastated country, Gagarin goes into space—that's also a purely Russian story. Because the rest of humanity operates on the following logic: we need to feed everyone and then go into space. But here they say: screw it, we are not going to feed anyone but to space we absolutely must go![37]

In fact, research and development of transhumanist goals—radical life extension and mind-computer melding foremost among them—is well supported by the current Russian government. As longevity researchers search for answers at a molecular level, life extension activists insist that we should view death as a "curable disease," not an inevitability. Likewise, Russian researchers are concentrating their efforts on emergent neurotechnologies, with the clear understanding that this kind of science should pay off in enormous profits and Russian state prestige within a few decades. For this reason, presumably, the government under Putin officially supports and encourages futuristic thinking in the new Skolkovo institutes outside of Moscow, and in its advisory council at the "Agency of Future Initiatives." And yet the most prominent promoters of Russia's twenty-first-century transhumanist agenda speak consistently of the need to reimagine the horizons of what it means to be human, and what it means for our species to properly direct its evolution toward a greater harmony with other planetary systems. In a 2019 lecture series, Luksha began with an explicit comparison of our current moment with the Russian revolutionary era of one hundred years ago. By the end of the ninety-minute lecture, having discarded the mistakes made at either end of Soviet history ("first they bludgeoned people into one version of happiness; then they deceived people that happiness was 'over there' (in liberal free markets) and stole everything while people looked in the wrong direction"), Luksha evokes the scientific metaphor of fractal geometry to prove to his audience that every individual righteous action is amplified by a factor of everyone we connect with in life, so that we are all connected in a universal web of life. Ultimately, he concludes, one must lead with the heart. In other words, he continues the tradition of yoking the project of breakthrough science to the rewards of spiritual transcendence. Will Russian popular culture—not to mention the rest of the global audience for transhumanism—follow in this tradition?

In 2019, the Russian television series "Better Than People" (*Luchshe, chem liudi*) was purchased by Netflix, thereby becoming the first *Russian* production in Netflix's push to acquire globally attractive shows that can be marketed as Netflix originals. Broadcast in English under the title "Better Than Us," the Russian show takes up the theme of the "new man" directly, except the setting is in the near future (2029), and—surprise!—the "new man" is actually a woman, Arisa. The action takes place in Moscow, but the Moscow we see could be any highly developed world city. The powerful artificial intelligence company "Cronos" supplies the country with the kind of robots that have become ubiquitous in the near future: well-programmed workers in human form designed to do the jobs we no longer do—cleaning streets and buildings, retailing fast food, transporting and unloading goods, shopping and caring for old people, guiding people through museums, and so on. As one reviewer put it: "Siri with a body." However, "Cronos" has illegally purchased a new model of "bot" (as society dismissively refers to the workers in its midst) from China. The prototype Arisa has been designed to serve as the ideal wife for lonely Chinese men who outnumber women in their society by the millions. Arisa's programming allows her to develop (through powerful machine learning algorithms) empathy, emotional sensitivity, and love of children. The plot is set in motion when Arisa kills a guard in order to escape the gleaming "Cronos" factory, indicating that she is capable of not obeying the three laws of robotics. Out on the streets, she befriends a young girl and ends up becoming a member of the upper-middle class Safronov household, in which the parents are undergoing a difficult divorce. As the series unfolds, we follow a familiar story: will the high-end robot (Arisa) in fact make the leap to full sentience, and when she does, what does this say about what it means to be human?

The beautifully produced show fits comfortably into global visions of life in a technologically advanced capitalist society. The Safronov's apartment is spacious, decorated in Scandinavian minimalist style, and the bickering parents still breakfast on organic granola and go for scenic runs along the river embankment park near their home. The philosophical problem of how to respond to the reality of sentient, emotionally vulnerable and emotionally attractive (not to mention physically attractive) cybernetic organisms is submerged, for most of the first sixteen episodes, by the more familiar drama of rich men behaving badly. The uber-wealthy director of "Cronos" abuses his power to rig public offerings of his stock and he abuses his wife. The ethical and handsome doctor Safronov, on the other hand, finds himself confused by simultaneous attractions to his ex-wife, his new tech-whiz girlfriend, and to the rapidly humanizing Arisa, who is indeed "better than human" in her capacity to do everything: cook delicious meals, perform delicate surgery, and give small children the full, constant, undivided attention that they crave. Thus, for the most part, there is nothing particularly "Russian" about Netflix's new acquisition, which treats the topic of living with the "new" new people created by artificial intelligence with mostly familiar entertainment devices. On the other hand, by highlighting both the gender dynamics and the spiritual values of the new "Better Than Us" (wo)man of the twenty-first century, the show about Arisa has hit a nerve in Russia, and internationally.

On the final page of Karel Čapek's 1921 play "Rossum's Universal Robots," the last remaining human in a society besieged by its own rebellious product—advanced humanoid androids—sees a glimmer of hope. Two of the same terrifying robots who masterminded the demise of "old" humanity now stand before the last human, gazing longingly into each other's eyes. They've fallen in love. They have "acquired souls." Robots, as it turns out in the play's ambiguous ending, may be not only *new*, but also *human*. Nearly a century later, the sophisticated Russian television drama series ends its first successful season with a nod to Čapek: the biotechnological marvel that viewers have come to know as the robot “Arisa” is not only capable of falling in love, she may be *Better Than Us* (the apt English translation of the series title) at being the future of humanity. If “Homo sapiens” is the species that is capable of imagining its own evolution, then the historical periods in which this activity is intensified certainly deserve our close scrutiny, and even our admiration. The chapters in this volume, taken together, suggest that creating the “new man” is always a project whose “radiant horizon” will shift out of reach, even as our arts and our sciences strive to bring us closer to visions of betterment.

Notes

Introduction

1 H. G. Wells, "Anticipations," *Fortnightly Review*, 69, no. 412 (1901): 747–60; the subsequent quotations are from p. 747.

2 Roslynn D. Haynes, *H. G. Wells: Discoverer of the Future. The Influence of Science on His Thought* (London, 1980).

3 See H. G. Wells, *Anticipations of the Reaction of Mechanical and Scientific Progress upon Human Life and Thought* (London, 1901).

4 H. G. Wells, "Anticipations," *Fortnightly Review*, 70, no. 419 (1901): 911–26, on 919. Emphasis added.

5 H. G. Wells, *Mankind in the Making* (London, 1903), 284.

6 Ibid., 21.

7 Ibid., 391.

8 See Edward Bellamy, *Looking Backward: 2000–1887* (Boston, 1888); Richard Michaelis, *Looking Forward* (Chicago and New York, 1890); and Arthur Bird, *Looking Forward: A Dream of the United States of the Americas in 1999* (Utica, NY, 1899).

9 The scholarly literature on the "new man" in Russian culture is quite voluminous and varied. For arguably the first monographic study of the subject, see Raymond A. Bauer, *The New Man in Soviet Psychology* (Cambridge, MA, 1952). For recent overviews, see Lynne Attwood and Catriona Kelly, "Programmes for Identity: The 'New Man' and the 'New Woman,'" in *Constructing Russian Culture in the Age of Revolution, 1881–1940*, eds. Catriona Kelly and David Shepherd (Oxford, 1998), 256–90; Catriona Kelly, "The New Soviet Man and Woman," in *The Oxford Handbook of Modern Russian History*, ed. Simon Dixon (Oxford, 2015). doi: 10.1093/oxfordhb/9780199236701.013.024; and Maja Soboleva, "The Concept of the 'New Soviet Man' and Its Short History," *Canadian-American Slavic Studies*, 51 (2017): 64–85.

10 For a sample of only book-length recent studies on the "new man" in Russian culture, see Derek Muller, *Der Topos des Neuen Menschen in der russischen und sowjetrussischen Geistesgeschichte* (Bern, 1998); Bianka Pietrow-Ennker, *Russlands "neuen Menschen": Die Entwicklung der Frauenbewegung von den Anfängen bis zur Oktoberrevolution* (Frankfurt, 1999); Evgenii Shteiner, *Avangard i postroenie novogo cheloveka. Iskusstvo sovetskoi detskoi knigi 1920-kh godov* [Avant-garde and the construction of the new man. The art of Soviet children's books of the 1920s] (Moscow, 2002); John Haynes, *New Soviet Man: Gender and Masculinity in Stalinist Soviet Cinema* (Manchester, 2003); Boris Groys and Michael Hagemeister, eds., *Die neue Menschheit. Biopolitische Utopien in Russland zu Beginn des 20. Jahrhunderts* (Frankfurt am Main, 2005); V. S. Izmozik and N. B. Lebina, *Peterburg sovetskii: "novyi chelovek" v starom prostranstve, 1920–1930-e gody* [Soviet Petersburg: the "new man"

in the old space in the 1920s-1930s] (St. Petersburg, 2016); Cécile Vaissié, *La fabrique de l'Homme nouveau après Staline: les arts et la culture dans le projet soviétique* (Rennes, 2016); Tijana Vujosevic, *Modernism and the Making of the Soviet New Man* (Manchester, 2017); and Claire E. McCallum, *The Fate of the New Man: Representing & Reconstructing Masculinity in Soviet Visual Culture, 1945–1965* (DeKalb, IL, 2018). See also numerous articles on the subject in *Obraz cheloveka budushchego: Filosofiia, psikhologiia, pedagogika* [Image of the Future Man: Philosophy, Psychology, Pedagogy], a special journal established in 2011.

11 A search through the entire catalogue of the Russian National Library with the key words "*nov* sovetsk* chelov**" for the period of 1917–40 yields only one result. In contrast, a search with the key words "*nov* chelov**" yields more than 700! A search for the phrase "new Soviet man" in the Google Books Russian corpus from 1890 to 1940 produces no results at all; see https://books.google.com/ngrams/graph?year_start=1890&year_end=1940&corpus=25&smoothing=5&content=%22+%D0%BD%D0%BE%D0%B2%D1%8B%D0%B9+%D1%81%D0%BE%D0%B2%D0%B5%D1%82%D1%81%D0%BA%D0%B8%D0%B9+%D1%87%D0%B5%D0%BB%D0%BE%D0%B2%D0%B5%D0%BA+%22&case_insensitive=on&direct_url=. Despite all the limitations and imprecision of the Google Books research tools, the graphs generated by these tools are quite illustrative and suggestive. They certainly point to the need and possible avenues of further research. For more on the limitations and utility of Ngrams see below.

12 A Google Book Ngram for the phrase "new woman" in the Russian-language sources from 1890 to 1950 illustrates this disparity quite clearly. See https://books.google.com/ngrams/graph?content=%22+%D0%BD%D0%BE%D0%B2%D0%B0%D1%8F+%D0%B6%D0%B5%D0%BD%D1%89%D0%B8%D0%BD%D0%B0+%22&year_start=1890&year_end=1940&corpus=36&smoothing=5&case_insensitive=true (accessed on September 1, 2020).

13 For the first attempts at such comparative analysis, see Peter Fritzsche and Jochen Hellbeck, "The New Man in Stalinist Russia and Nazi Germany," in *Beyond Totalitarianism: Stalinism and Nazism Compared*, eds. Michael Geyer and Sheila Fitzpatrick (Cambridge, 2009), 302–41; and Yinghong Cheng, *Creating the "New Man": From Enlightenment Ideals to Socialist Realities* (Honolulu, 2009). For a highly successful attempt at comparing different visions of the "new man" in non-Russian contexts, see Matthew Feldman, Jorge Dagnino, and Paul Stocker, eds., *The "New Man" in Radical Right Ideology and Practice, 1919–45* (London, 2018).

14 Historical literature on the "new man" is vast and varied. For a nearly random sample of only book-length studies, see James T. Adams, *The American: The Making of a New Man* (New York, 1943); Francesco Cassata, *Building the New Man. Eugenics, Racial Science and Genetics in Twentieth-Century Italy* (Budapest, 2011); John Dugan, *Making a New Man: Ciceronian Self-fashioning in the Rhetorical Works* (New York, 2005); G. Küenzlen, *Der neue Mensch: eine Untersuchung zur säkularen Religionsgeschichte der Moderne* (Paderborn, 1993); Nicola Lepp, Martin Roth, and Klaus Vogel, eds., *Der neue Mensch: Obsessionen des 20. Jahrhunderts* (Ostfildern-Ruit, 1999); Mona Ozouf, *L'homme régénéré. Essais sur la Révolution française* (Paris, 1989); Robert Redeker, *Egobody: la fabrique de l'homme nouveau* (Paris, 2010); Michael Schwarze, *Der neue Mensch: Perspektiven der Renaissance* (Regensburg, 2000); Ted Spivey, *The Coming of the New Man; a Study of Literature, Myth, and Vision since 1750* (New York, 1970); and Mads R. Thomsen, *The New Human in Literature: Posthuman Visions of Changes in Body, Mind and Society after 1900* (London, 2013); and Wolfgang Voigt,

Dorothea Deschermeier, and Peter Cachola Schmal, eds., *New Human, New Housing: Architecture of the New Frankfurt, 1925–1933* (Berlin, 2019).

15 Lewis Carroll, *Through the Looking-Glass and What Alice Found There* (London, 1872), 124. Emphasis in the original.

16 Compare, for example, Rudolf Bultmann, *The Old and New Man in the Letters of Paul* (Richmond, 1967); and Lynne Attwood, *The New Soviet Man and Woman: Sex-Role Socialization in the USSR* (Basingstoke, 1990).

17 On the Bolshevik experiments with and attitudes toward time, see Robert C. Williams, "The Russian Revolution and the End of Time: 1900–1940," *Jahrbücher für Geschichte Osteuropas*, 43, no. 3 (1995): 364–401; see also Stanislav Petriashin's chapter in this volume.

18 Cited from *Poems of Heinrich Heine*. Translated by Louis Untermeyer (New York, 1916), 194–5. Emphasis added.

19 For a fine-grained analysis of the role of the past in envisioning the future, see Carter F. Hanson, *Memory and Utopian Agency in Utopian/Dystopian Literature: Memory of the Future* (New York, 2020).

20 I do not use the expression "networks of meanings" in any technical sense it has in semiotics or sociology (see, for instance, F. C. Godard and H. C. White, "Switchings under Uncertainty: The Coming and Becoming of Meanings," *Poetics*, 38 [2010]: 567–86). Rather I employ it in a very loose sense as signifying both an actual network of actors involved in the construction/propagation of particular meanings and the specific meanings generated by a particular network.

21 See, for example, a sermon by the Reverend John Bradford, "A Comparison between the Old Man and the New, Also between the Law and the Gospel; Containing a Short Sum of All the Divinity Necessary for a Christian Conscience" (1548). In this sermon the bodily, "lower" part of human nature received almost no attention. Perhaps, the only exception to this focus on the "spiritual" essence of human nature was a debate on the role of the body in the expected resurrection of the dead for the Last Judgment; see, for instance, C. W. Bynum and P. Freedman, eds., *Last Things. Death and the Apocalypse in the Middle Ages* (Philadelphia, 2000).

22 It should be noted that the teachings of the Russian Orthodox Church draw a distinction between soul (*dusha*) and spirit (*dukh*), with the former denoting human personality (mental traits, cognition, etc.) and the latter the connection between God and a human being. See Joost van Baak and Sander Brouwer, eds., *Telo, dukh i dusha v russkoi literature i kul'ture = Leib, Geist und Seele in der russischen Literatur und Kultur* (München, 2004).

23 See, for instance, I. Gergard, *Myslennyi vertograd, ili Khristiianskoe uprazhnenie, sluzhashchee ko utesheniiu blagochestivykh khristiian v bozhestvennom nastavlenii: Kotoroe soderzhit v sebe piat'desiat i odno sviashchennykh razmyshlenii, kasaiushchikhsia do ispravleniia vnutrennego i vneshnego cheloveka* (Moscow, 1783); this book was a Russian translation of *Meditationes sacrae*, a popular Latin tract written by Johann Gerhard and first published in 1611. See also *Cherty vetkhogo i novogo cheloveka: Molitvennoe razmyshlenie* [Features of the old and the new man: a prayer-discourse] (Moscow, 1818).

24 For a general overview, see L. N. Belenchuk, *Prosveshchenie Rossii: Vzgliad zapadnikov i slavianofilov* (Moscow, 2014); for the concurrent ideas about "a new kind of people," see A. M. Iarinskaia, "K voprosu o planakh sozdaniia 'novoi porody liudei' v pravlenie Ekateriny II," [Towards an issue of plans to create a "new kind of people" during the rule of Catherine the Great], *Vestnik Tomskogo universiteta. Kul'turologiia i iskusstvovedenie*, 1 (2011): 26–38.

25 For a detailed analysis of these ideas in Russian culture of the period, see R. G. Eimontova, *Idei prosveshcheniia v obnovliaiushcheisia Rossii v 50-60-e gody XIX v.* [Enlightenment ideas in the renewing Russia of the 1850s–1860s] (Moscow, 1998).
26 See, for instance, O. N. Goncharova, *"Novye liydi" epokhi 1860-kh: idei-teksty-sotsiopraktiki* ["New men" of the 1860s: ideas-texts-social practices] (St. Petersburg, 2011); and S. N. Nikol'skii, *Russkoe mirovozzrenie. "Novye liudi" kak ideia i iavlenie: opyt osmysleniia v otechestvennoi filosofii i klassicheskoi literature 40-60-kh godov XIX stoletiia* [Russian worldview. "New men" as an idea and phenomenon: the experience of reflections in the native philosophy and classical literature of the 1840s to the 1860s] (Moscow, 2012).
27 For a detailed analysis of the ideas and ideals underpinning the movement, see E. V. Polikarpova, *Ideologiia narodnichestva v Rossii* [The ideology of the *narodniki* in Russia] (Moscow, 2001).
28 See, for instance, N. Zosimskii, *Chto sdelano?* [What has been done?] (St. Petersburg, 1870); D. L. Mordovtsev, *Novye liudi: Povest' iz zhizni shestidesiatykh godov* [New men: a story from the life of the 1860s] (St. Petersburg, 1886); and Aleksei Pletnev, *Novye liudi* [New men], (St. Petersburg, 1897). For a dated but still useful overview of the literature critical of these ideas, see Charles A. Moser, *Antinihilism in the Russian Novel of the 1860s* (The Hague, 1964).
29 See, for instance, Thomas Tetzner, *Der kollektive Gott: Zur Ideengeschichte des «Neuen Menschen» in Russland* (Göttingen, 2013). The emergence and influence of various "supernatural" currents in Russian culture during this period have been documented and examined, though not in relation to the "new men" debates, in several recent studies by Ilya Vinitsky, *Ghostly Paradoxes: Modern Spiritualism and Russian Culture in the Age of Realism* (Toronto, 2009); Julia Mannherz, *Modern Occultism in Late Imperial Russia* (DeKalb, IL, 2012); Maria Carlson, *No Religion Higher Than Truth: A History of the Theosophical Movement in Russia, 1875–1922* (Princeton, NJ, 2012); and George M. Young, *The Russian Cosmists: The Esoteric Futurism of Nikolai Fedorov and His Followers* (New York, 2012).
30 A far from complete list of "occult" periodicals that circulated in the country includes *Rebus* (Moscow, 1881–1915); *Spiritualist* (Moscow, 1905–12); *Smelye mysli* (Moscow, 1906–11); *Golos vseobshchei liubvi: Spiritualisticheskii zhurnal* (Moscow, 1906–11); *Teosofskaia zhizn'* (Smolensk, 1907–9); *Vestnik okkul'tnykh nauk* (Moscow, 1907); *Zapiski Russkogo spiritualisticheskogo obshchestva* (Moscow, 1908); *Voprosy psikhizma i spiritualisticheskoi filosofii* (Moscow, 1908); *Vestnik teosofii* (St. Petersburg, 1908–18); *Izida* (St. Petersburg, 1909–16); *Zhizn' dukha* (Smolensk, 1910); *Izvestiia Rossiiskogo teosoficheskogo obshchestva* (St. Petersburg, 1914–17); and many others.
31 *Spisok izdanii knigoizdatel'stva* [*"Novyi Chelovek"*] *s ukazaniem obshchego soderzhaniia ikh* (Petrograd, 1915).
32 See Aleksei Poroshin [Suvorin], *Novyi chelovek* (St. Petersburg, 1913); F. Zhiro [Girod], *Opytnyi magnetizm* (Petrograd, 1915); R. M. Bekk [Bucke], *Kosmicheskoe soznanie* (Petrograd, 1915); P. D. Uspenskii, *Iskaniia novoi zhizni: Chto takoe ioga* (Petrograd, 1915); and G. T. Fekhner [Fechner], *Zhizn' posle smerti* (Petrograd, 1915).
33 For an insightful discussion of biotypology's role in the "new man" visions, see Francesco Cassata, "Biotypology and Eugenics in Fascist Italy," in *The "New Man" in Radical Right Ideology and Practice, 1919–45*, eds. Matthew Feldman, Jorge Dagnino, and Paul Stocker (London, 2018), 39–63.
34 See, for example, A. Bogdanov, "Sobiranie cheloveka," [The gathering of man], *Pravda* (Moscow), 4 (1904): 158–75; idem, *Iz psikhologii obshchestva* [From the psychology

of society] (St. Petersburg, 1904); Anatolii Lunacharskii, *Religiia i sotsializm* [Religion and socialism] (Moscow, 1908); and A. Bogdanov et al., *Ocherki filosofii kollektivizma* [Essays on the philosophy of collectivism] (St. Petersburg, 1909). See also Coates's chapter in the present volume.

35 From the variations in the sheer size of the corpus of books in different languages scanned by Google to the availability of different kinds of printed materials (newspapers, magazines, books, and so on) in a particular language from various time periods, the differences in the raw data make any analysis of the contents of Google Books databases tentative at best. Nevertheless, the Ngrams do provide vivid illustrations and serve as good indicators for possible avenues of further research.

36 The first upheaval is also often called the "Great October Revolution," or simply the "October Revolution." The second upheaval has been variously described by its actors, as well as its scholars, as the "great break," the "cultural revolution," "the great retreat," and the "revolution from above."

37 The searches in the Google Books Russian corpus with several other synonymic expressions, such as "coming man" (*griadushchii chelovek*), "future man" (*budushchii chelovek*), and "man of the future" (*chelovek budushchego*), yield no results at all, perhaps because of the paucity of available Russian materials. In what follows I use the phrases "new *man*" and "new *men*" interchangeably and will discuss the differences between the two and their meanings in the later part of this chapter.

38 It should be noted that during this time, psychology was still considered to be and was taught as part of philosophy. Tellingly, the major outlet for psychological publications of the time bore the title *Issues in Philosophy and Psychology* [*Voprosy filosophii i psikhologii*] (Moscow, 1889–1918).

39 See, for instance, polemics between occultists and theologians, scientists and occultists, and theologians and scientists in A. N. Nadezhdin, *Spiritizm pered sudom khristianstva* [Spiritism at the court of Christianity] (St. Petersburg, 1896); M. I. Verzhbolovich, *Spiritizm pered sudom nauki i khristianstva* [Spiritism at the court of science and Christianity] (St. Petersburg, 1903); Arkhimandrit Varlaam, *Teosofiia pered sudom khristianstva* [Theosophy at the court of Christianity] (Poltava, 1912); D. V. Stranden, *Teosofiia i ee kritiki* [Theosophy and its critics] (St. Petersburg, 1913); and V. P. Bykov, *Spiritizm pered sudom nauki, obshchestva i religii* [Spiritism at the court of science, society, and religion] (Moscow, 1914).

40 For instance, the supernatural and the naturalistic approaches not infrequently intersected over such subjects as telepathy and hypnosis, with the same materials appearing in both "occult" and scientific/medical periodicals.

41 See, for instance, satirical plays by P. I. Surov, *Spiriticheskii seans* [Spiritist séance] (Moscow, 1890); B. E. Pisarevskii [Shraiber], *Dekadenty: Novye liudi* [Decadents: New men] (Odessa, 1899); R. Z. Chinarov and V. L. Binshtok, *Telepatiia* [Telepathy] (Moscow, 1912); and F. N. Fal'kovskii, *Chudesnye luchi* [Miracle rays] (Petrograd, 1915); and collections of humorous stories by A. M. Seletrennikov, *Spirity i drugie iumoristicheskie rasskazy* [Spiritists and other humorous stories] (Odessa, 1910–11); and by Ar. Bukhov et al., *Vestnik znaniia "Novogo Satirikona." Okkul'tnye nauki. Grafologiia. Khiromantiia. Entsiklopedicheskii slovar'. Khrestomatiia dlia ochen' malen'kikh devochek* [Herald of knowledge by the "New Satyricon." Occult sciences. Graphology. Chiromancy. An encyclopedic dictionary. A reader for very little girls] (Petrograd, 1917).

42 See, for example, A. E. Zarin, *Spirit: Roman* [Spiritist: A novel] (St. Petersburg, 1902); Skif [S. P. Kubenitskii], *Utopiia ili deistvitel'nost': Novyi mir, novyi chelovek i velikaia*

deistvitel'nost' [Utopia or reality: New world, new man, and the great reality] (Odessa, 1905); N. I. Zhenishek, *Chelovek proshlogo. Chelovek nastoiashchego. Chelovek budushchego* [Man of the past. Man of the present. Man of the future] (Moscow, 1906); A. A. Sokolov, *Tsar' zemli—rab zemli: Novyi chelovek* [King of earth—slave of earth: New man] (Moscow, 1907); I. Gorskii, *Grigorii Tuchkin: Povest' o starykh i novykh liudiakh russkoi derevni* [Grigorii Tuchkin: a novel about the old and the new men of the Russian village] (St. Petersburg, 1907); A. Bogdanov, *Krasnaia zvezda* [Red star] (Moscow, 1908); idem, *Inzhener Menni* [Engineer Menni] (Moscow, 1913); and Anna Simionesko, *Novye liudi* [New men] (Simferopol', 1913). See also a collection of contemporary writings on the "image of the future in socio-economic thought at the end of XIXth and the beginnings of the XXth centuries" in Ia. I. Kuz'minov, ed., *Obraz budushchego v sotsial'no-ekonomicheskoi mysli kontsa XIX-nachala XX veka: Izbrannye proizvedeniia* (Moscow, 1994).

43 See "O predelakh nauchnogo poznaniia," *Nauka i zhizn'*, 4 (1890): 50–1; and "Spiritizm i chetvertoe izmerenie," ibid., 46 (1890): 722–4; B. Dinershtein, "Mysliashchie loshadi," *Zhizn' dlia vsekh*, 3–4 (1913): 479–84; and M. Novorusskii, "Nauka i ne nauka," ibid., 10 (1913): 1414–25.

44 Richard Stites, *Revolutionary Dreams: Utopian Vision and Experimental Life in the Russian Revolution* (Oxford, 1989).

45 For details, see Nikolai Krementsov, "Marxism, Darwinism, and Genetics in the Soviet Union," in *Biology and Ideology: From Descartes to Dawkins*, eds. Denis Alexander and Ron Numbers (Chicago, 2010), 215–46.

46 See James T. Andrews, *Science for the Masses: The Bolshevik State, Public Science, and the Popular Imagination in Soviet Russia. 1917–1934* (College Station, TX, 2003).

47 For details, see Nikolai Krementsov, "Thought Transfer and Mind Control between Science and Fiction: Fedor Il'in's 'The Valley of New Life' (1928)," *Osiris*, 34 (2019): 36–54.

48 For details, see Nikolai Krementsov, "Off with Your Heads: Isolated Organs in Early Soviet Science and Fiction," *Studies in History and Philosophy of Biological and Biomedical Sciences*, 40 (2009): 87–100.

49 For details, see Nikolai Krementsov, "A Cinematic and Physiological Puzzle: Soviet Conjoined Twins Research, Scientific Cinema and Pavlovian Physiology," *Medical Movies on the Web* (2015). https://www.nlm.nih.gov/hmd/collections/films/medicalmoviesontheweb/conjoinedtwinsessay.html

50 For details, see Kirill Rossiianov, "Beyond Species: Il'ya Ivanov and His Experiments on Cross-Breeding Humans with Anthropoid Apes," *Science in Context*, 15, no. 2 (2002): 277–316.

51 For examples of such cultural productions, see novels by Alexander Beliaev, *The Head of Professor Dowell* (1926); *Ruler of the World* (1926); and *The Amphibian Man* (1928); Fedor Il'in, *The Valley of New Life* (1928); Mikhail Gireli, *Eozoon: The Dawn of Life* (1929); and Boris Fortunatov, *The Island of Gorilloids* (1929); and a famous film, *Mechanics of the Brain* (1926), directed by the rising star of Soviet cinematography Vsevolod Pudovkin. Some of these productions are discussed in Krementsov's and Schwartz's chapters in the present volume.

52 See L. Vygotskii, "Sotsialisticheskaia peredelka cheloveka," *VARNITSO*, 9–10 (1930): 36–44. Characteristically, the article was published in the mouthpiece of the campaign to subjugate science and technology to the control of party functionaries and Marxist philosophers. For a dated, but still useful, historical account of this newfound

emphasis on the social as opposed to the biological in the specific area of "the conception of personality," see Bauer, *The New Man in Soviet Psychology* (cit. n. 9).

53 P. P. Postyshev, *Stakhanovtsy—novye liudi epokhi sotsializma* (Moscow, 1935).

54 For detailed analyses of the campaign, see Lewis H. Siegelbaum, *Stakhanovism and the Politics of Productivity in the USSR, 1935–1941* (Cambridge, 1988) and Robert Maier, *Die Stachanov-Bewegung 1935–1938. Der Stachanovismus als tragendes und verschärfendes Moment der Stalinisierung der sowjetischen Gesellschaft* (Stuttgart, 1990). For the campaign's expansion to the peasantry, see Mary Buckley, *Mobilizing Soviet Peasants: Heroines and Heroes of Stalin's Fields* (Lanham, MD, 2006).

55 Compare Figure 0.2 and the Ngrams for the expression "new man" for the period from 1890 to 1940 in English-language materials at https://books.google.com/ngrams/graph?corpus=15&year_end=1940&content=%22+new+man+%22&smoothing=5&year_start=1890&case_insensitive=on&direct_url=t4%3B%2C%22%20new%20man%20%22%3B%2Cc0%3B%2Cs0%3B%3B%22%20new%20man%20%22%3B%2Cc0%3B%3B%22%20New%20Man%20%22%3B%2Cc0; in German-language materials at https://books.google.com/ngrams/graph?content=%22+Neue+Mensch+%22%2B%22+neue+Mensch+%22&year_start=1890&year_end=1940&corpus=20&smoothing=5&case_insensitive=true#; in French-language materials at https://books.google.com/ngrams/graph?content=%22+nouvel+homme+%22%2B%22+homme+nouveau+%22&year_start=1890&year_end=1940&corpus=19&smoothing=5&case_insensitive=true; in Italian-language materials at https://books.google.com/ngrams/graph?content=%22+uomo+nuovo+%22&year_start=1890&year_end=1950&corpus=22&smoothing=5&case_insensitive=true; in Spanish-language materials at https://books.google.com/ngrams/graph?content=%22+hombre+nuevo+%22&year_start=1890&year_end=1940&corpus=21&smoothing=5&case_insensitive=true (all accessed on September 1, 2020).

56 J. D. Bernal, *The World, the Flesh and the Devil: An Enquiry into the Future of the Three Enemies of the Rational Soul* (London, 1929).

57 For details, see Nikolai Krementsov, *Revolutionary Experiments: The Quest for Immortality in Bolshevik Science and Fiction* (New York, 2014).

58 Probably the most comprehensive exposition of this current of thought was Nikolai Danilevskii's 1869 voluminous treatise, *Rossiia i Evropa* [Russia and Europe] (St. Petersburg, 1871). For a recent overview of the debate, see Susanna Rabow-Edling, *Slavophile Thought and the Politics of Cultural Nationalism* (Albany, NY, 2006). In various forms, the debate continues unabated to the present day.

59 See https://books.google.com/ngrams/graph?content=%22+new+man+%22%2C%22+new+men+%22&year_start=1890&year_end=1940&corpus=26&smoothing=5&case_insensitive=true (accessed on September 1, 2020).

60 For the British sources, see https://books.google.com/ngrams/graph?content=%22+new+man+%22%2C%22+new+men+%22&year_start=1890&year_end=1940&corpus=29&smoothing=5&case_insensitive=true; for the American sources, see https://books.google.com/ngrams/graph?content=%22+new+man+%22%2C%22+new+men+%22&year_start=1890&year_end=1940&corpus=28&smoothing=5&case_insensitive=true#.

61 See https://books.google.com/ngrams/graph?corpus=31&smoothing=5&content=%22+neue+Mensch+%22%2C%22+neuen+Menschen+%22&year_end=1940&year_start=1890&direct_url=t1%3B%2C%22%20neue%20Mensch%20%22%3B%2Cc0%3B.t1%3B%2C%22%20neuen%20Menschen%20%22%3B%2Cc0 (accessed on September 1, 2020). For possible clues as to the origins of the similarities between the Russian and

German visions of "new *men*," see Fritzsche and Hellbeck, "The New Man in Stalinist Russia and Nazi Germany" (cit. n. 13).

62 See, for instance, Feldman, Dagnino, and Stocker, eds., *The "New Man" in Radical Right Ideology and Practice* (cit. n. 13).

63 See, for instance, Yvonne Howell, "The Liberal Gene: Sociobiology as Emancipatory Discourse in the Late Soviet Union," *Slavic Review*, 69, no. 2 (2010): 356–76; and Colleen McQuillen and Julia Vaingurt, eds., *The Human Reimagined: Posthumanism in Russia* (Brookline, MA, 2018).

64 For instance, such focus might have provided a fruitful direction to the analyses of the "new men" debates in the recent collection by Feldman, Dagnino, and Stocker, eds., *The "New Man" in Radical Right Ideology and Practice* (cit. n. 13).

Chapter 1

1 The research leading to this chapter was supported by a Cohen-Tucker Dissertation Research Fellowship from ASEEES and a grant from the Institute of Slavic, East European, and Eurasian Studies at the University of California, Berkeley. I would like to thank them for their support. On Saint-Simon, see Henri Gouhier, "Un 'Projet d'Encyclopédie' de Saint-Simon," *Revue Internationale de Philosophie*, 14 (1960): 384–98; Pierre Musso, "Le projet de *Nouvelle Encyclopédie* de Saint-Simon," in *La Construction des savoirs: XVIIIe-XIXe siècles*, ed. Lise Andries (Lyon, 2009), 161–75; Henri de Saint-Simon, "Esquisse d'une *Nouvelle Encyclopédie*," in idem, *Oeuvres*, 47 vols., vol. 15 (Paris, 1865–1878), 89–96. On Chernyshevskii, see "Letter to O.S. Chernyshevskaia, October 5, 1862," in N. G. Chernyshevskii, *Polnoe sobranie sochinenii*, ed. V. Ia. Kirpotin et al., vol. 14 (Moscow, 1949), 455–7. Engels on a few occasions writes of the need to produce an encyclopedic summation of his and Marx's worldview; his *Dialectics of Nature* fits this model. See, e.g., Friedrich Engels, *Dialektik der Natur*, in *Karl Marx, Friedrich Engels Gesamtausgabe (MEGA)*, Part 1, vol. 26 (Berlin, 1985), 390–5. On Plekhanov, see Iu. E. Shmushkis, *Sovetskie entsiklopedii: ocherki istorii, voprosy metodiki* (*Soviet Encyclopedias: Outlines of a History, Questions of Methodology*) (Moscow, 1975), 27–32. On Jaurès, see Jean Jaurès, "La Philosophie de Vaillant," *La Petite République*, January 8, 1901. https://www.retronews.fr/journal/la-petite-republique/08-janvier-1901/667/1686561/1; see also Vincent Chambarlhac, "*L'Encyclopédie socialiste*, une forme singulière pour une cause politique?" *Genèses*, 57 (2004): 4–22, for his relationship to the later *Socialist Encyclopedia*. On Wells, see H. G. Wells, *World Brain* (London, 1938). On Neurath, see Otto Neurath, "Unified Science as Encyclopedic Integration," in *Foundations of the Unity of Science: Toward an* International Encyclopedia of Unified Science, eds. Otto Neurath, Rudolf Carnap, and Charles Morris, vol. 1 (Chicago, 1971), 1–27; also Nancy Cartwright, Jordi Cat, Lola Fleck, and Thomas E. Uebel, *Otto Neurath: Philosophy between Science and Politics* (Cambridge, 2008). Jaurès, in particular, was often cited by Soviet encyclopedists as being an intellectual predecessor to their work, including in the *Great Soviet Encyclopedia* itself. See *Bol'shaia Sovetskaia Entsiklopediia*, ed. O. Iu. Shmidt, 1st ed., vol. 64 (Moscow, 1933), 498–9.

2 Denis Diderot, "Encyclopédie," in *Encyclopédie, ou dictionnaire raisonné des sciences, des arts et des métiers, etc.*, eds. Denis Diderot and Jean le Rond d'Alembert (Chicago,

2017), eds. Robert Morrissey and Glenn Roe. https://artflsrv03.uchicago.edu/philologic4/encyclopedie0521/navigate/5/2355/?byte=6753511. An English translation is also available: Diderot, "Encyclopedia," trans. Philip Stewart, in *The Encyclopedia of Diderot & d'Alembert Collaborative Translation Project* (Ann Arbor, MI, 2002). http://hdl.handle.net/2027/spo.did2222.0000.004.

3 See Daniela Steila, "A Proletarian *Encyclopédie*," in *Word and Image in Russian History: Essays in Honor of Gary Marker*, eds. Maria di Salvo, Daniel H. Kaiser, and Valerie A. Kivelson (Brighton, MA, 2015), 90–117. Steila's article became known to me only after this essay had been completed. See also Daniela Steila, *Nauka i revoliutsiia: retseptsiia empiriokrititsizma v russkoi kul'tura, 1877-1910gg.* Translated by O. Popovaia (Moscow, 2013). See also Georgii Gloveli, "V poiskakh 'planomernoi progressivnosti': ideia 'Novoi Entsiklopedii' u Sen-Simona i Bogdanova," *Vestnik Mezhdunarodnogo Instituta A. Bogdanova*, 13 (2003). https://web.archive.org/web/20161026155753/http://www.bogdinst.ru/vestnik/v13_03.htm.

4 For a major recent study of this activity, see Mark J. P. Wolf, *Building Imaginary Worlds: The Theory and History of Subcreation* (New York, 2012). Perhaps the most famous example of the use of an encyclopedia for worldbuilding comes from fiction; see Jorge Luis Borges, "Tlön, Uqbar, Orbis Tertius," in idem, *Collected Fictions*, trans. Andrew Hurley (New York, 1998), 68–81.

5 Aleksandr Bogdanov, *Filosofiia zhivogo opyta* (*The Philosophy of Living Experience*) (St. Petersburg, 1913). There is an English translation: Bogdanov, *The Philosophy of Living Experience: Popular Outlines*, ed. and trans. David Rowley (Leiden, 2015). Vilonov's manuscript is preserved at Russian State Archive of Social-Political History (RGASPI), f. 455 op. 1 d. 10.

6 Aleksandr Bogdanov, *Tektologiia: Vseobshchaia organizatsionnaia nauka* (Tektology: General organizational science) (Moscow, 1989), 79–83.

7 On these experiments, see Nikolai Krementsov, *A Martian Stranded on Earth: Alexander Bogdanov, Blood Transfusions, and Proletarian Science* (Chicago, 2011).

8 On Bogdanov's early years, see Zenovia A. Sochor, *Revolution and Culture: The Bogdanov-Lenin Controversy* (Ithaca, 1988). David Rowley also includes a substantial discussion of Bogdanov's early years in David G. Rowley, *Millennarian Bolshevism, 1900–1920* (New York, 1987). James White has recently published a major biography of Bogdanov, *Red Hamlet: The Life and Ideas of Alexander Bogdanov* (Leiden, 2019). Maria Chehonadskih has drawn on Bogdanov's concepts of the encyclopedia and worldbuilding as a theoretical tool for understanding early Soviet literature and art in Chehonadskih, "Soviet Epistemologies and the Materialist Ontology of Poor Life: Andrei Platonov, Alexander Bogdanov and Lev Vygotsky," PhD diss., (Kingston University, 2017), and Chehonadskih, "The Comrades of the Past: The Soviet Enlightenment Between Negation and Affirmation," *Crisis & Critique*, 4 (2017): 87–105.

9 See Krementsov, *A Martian Stranded on Earth*, 34–7 (cit. n. 7). These works are also the subject of a recent article by David Rowley, "Alexander Bogdanov's Holistic World Picture: A Materialist Mirror Image of Idealism," *Studies in East European Thought*, 73 (2021): 1–18.

10 Aleksandr Bogdanov, *Osnovnye elementy istoricheskogo vzgliada na prirodu* (Fundamental elements of the historical view on nature) (St. Petersburg, 1899), 1–7.

11 On this concept, see David Bates, "Automaticity, Plasticity, and the Deviant Origins of Artificial Intelligence," in *Plasticity and Pathology: On the Formation of the Neural Subject*, eds. David Bates and Nima Bassiri (New York, 2015), 194–218. James had outlined his concept of plasticity in William James, *Principles of Psychology* (New York, 1890).

12 Aleksandr Bogdanov, *Poznanie s istoricheskoi tochki zreniia* (Cognition from a historical point of view) (St. Petersburg, 1901), 47–58; 128–37.
13 Robert C. Williams, *The Other Bolsheviks: Lenin and His Critics, 1904–1914* (Bloomington, 1986), 32–7; Krementsov, *A Martian Stranded on Earth*, 38–9 (cit. n. 7).
14 Aleksandr Bogdanov, "Sobiranie cheloveka" (The gathering of man), in A. A. Bogdanov, *Voprosy sotsializma: Raboty raznykh let* (Problems of socialism: Works from various years), eds. L. I. Abalkin, G. D. Gloveli, V. K. Parmenov, and N. K. Figurovskaia (Moscow, 1990), 28–45.
15 See Karl Marx and Friedrich Engels, *The German Ideology*. https://www.marxists.org/archive/marx/works/1845/german-ideology/ch01a.htm.
16 Ibid.
17 The connection between Bogdanov's epistemology and his theory of revolution vis-à-vis that of Lenin has been noted by David Rowley, although he does not foreground cognition, or Bogdanov's physiological theories specifically. See David G. Rowley, "Bogdanov and Lenin: Epistemology and Revolution," *Studies in East European Thought*, 48 (1996): 1–19. Bogdanov, "Sobiranie cheloveka" (cit. n. 14).
18 See Chad Wellmon, *Organizing Enlightenment: Information Overload and the Invention of the Modern Research University* (Baltimore, 2015).
19 Ann Blair, *Too Much to Know: Managing Scholarly Information before the Modern Age* (New Haven, 2010); Richard Yeo, *Encyclopaedic Visions: Scientific Dictionaries and Enlightenment Culture* (Cambridge, 2001).
20 The topic of information overload has become a popular one in recent years; in addition to the aforementioned works, see Daniel R. Headrick, *When Information Came of Age: Technologies of Knowledge in the Age of Reason and Revolution, 1700–1850* (Oxford, 2000), especially his chapter on dictionaries and encyclopedias, 142–80.
21 V. I. Lenin, *Materialism and Empirio-Criticism* (1908). https://www.marxists.org/archive/lenin/works/1908/mec/. A recent edition of *Empiriomonizm* is A.A. Bogdanov, *Empiriomonizm* (Moscow, 2003); there is also an English translation in Bogdanov, *Empiriomonism: Essays in Philosophy, Books 1-3*, ed. and trans. David Rowley (Leiden, 2020). See also Rowley's introduction and critical essays in that volume.
22 On the history of this period, see David Joravsky, *Soviet Marxism and Natural Science, 1917–1932* (New York, 1961), 1–44; Sochor, *Revolution and Culture* (cit. n. 8); Tamas Krausz, *Reconstructing Lenin: An Intellectual Biography*. Translated by Balint Bethlenfalvy and Mario Fenyo (New York, 2015), 125–41; Williams, *The Other Bolsheviks*, 125–43 (cit. n. 13).
23 See Tovah Yedlin, *Maxim Gorky: A Political Biography* (Westport, CT, 1999), 83–8.
24 Maxim Gorky, "Letter to A. A. Bogdanov, around March 8 (21), 1908," in Maksim Gor'kii, *Polnoe sobranie sochinenii* (Complete collected works), vol. 6 (Moscow, 2000), 200–1; and Maxim Gorky, "Letter to K. P. Piatnitskii, April 9 (22), 1908," in ibid., vol. 6, 220–1.
25 Maxim Gorky, "Letter to G. A. Aleksinskii, 15 (29) May, 1908," in ibid., vol. 6, 240–1. On Gorky's connections with the publishing industry, see Charles A. Ruud, *Russian Entrepreneur: Publisher Ivan Sytin of Moscow, 1851–1934* (Montreal, 1990).
26 Gorky, "Letter to K. P. Piatnitskii, April 9 (22), 1908" (cit. n. 24).
27 Gorky, "Letter to G. A. Aleksinskii, 15 (29) May, 1908" (cit. n. 25).
28 Aleksinskii expressed great interest in the project, offering to write the volume on the history of the church after Vasilii Desnitskii (aka Stroev) declined. See Aleksinskii's

letter to Gorky, dated May 31, 1908, RGASPI f. 75 op. 1 d. 26. Aleksinskii also discusses the encyclopedia in Grégoire Alexinsky, *La vie amère de Maxime Gorki* (Grenoble, 1950).

29 Maxim Gorky, "Letter to G. A. Aleksinskii, 15 (29) May, 1908" (cit. n. 25).

30 Although I do not have access to Bogdanov's letter to Pokrovskii, I say this on the basis of the fact that Pokrovskii referred to the encyclopedia as such in his correspondence with Gorky on the subject a few weeks later, and Bogdanov was the one who first told Pokrovskii about the proposed encyclopedia. See the notes to "Letter to M. N. Pokrovskii, around 3 (16) March, 1909," in Maksim Gor'kii, *Polnoe sobranie socheninii*, vol. 7 (Moscow, 2001), 98–100.

31 M. N. Pokrovskii, "Letter to A. A. Bogdanov, February 1909," in *M. Gor'kii: Neizdannaia perepiska s Bogdanovym, Leninym, Stalinym, Zinov'evym, Kamenevym, Korolenko* (Gorky: Unpublished correspondence with Bogdanov, Lenin, Stalin, Zinoviev, Kamenev, Korolenko), (Moscow, 1998), 80–1. The letter was forwarded by Bogdanov to Gorky; see Bogdanov, "Letter to Gorky, after March 6 (19), 1909," 46–7.

32 Granat had somewhat of a history of being involved with writers on the radical left in Russia. Lenin, for example, wrote the article on "Karl Marx" for their main publication, the *Encyclopedic Dictionary Granat* (*Entsiklopedicheskii slovar' Granat*), in 1914. See V. I. Lenin, "Karl Marx." https://www.marxists.org/archive/lenin/works/1914/granat/.

33 Gorky, "Letter to A. A. Bogdanov, after March 9 (22), 1909," in Gorkii, *Neizdannaia perepiska*, 47–9 (cit. n. 31).

34 Gorky, "Letter to M. N. Pokrovskii, around 3 (16) March, 1909," (cit. n. 30); see also Aleksinskii's letter of March 10, 1909, RGASPI f. 75 op. 1 d. 25.

35 See the notes to Gorky, ibid.

36 It should be noted that, even if the encyclopedia would serve this purpose, it was still a Bolshevik project, and not a project of the wider Party. Gorky had previously noted that the Mensheviks might try to launch a similar project of their own. See Gorky, "Letter to K.P. Piatnitskii, April 9 (22), 1908" (cit. n. 24). He had also once noted with pride that even the Constitutional Democrats were talking about the project. See "Letter to A. A. Bogdanov, around 5 (18) April, 1909", in *Gor'kii v zerkale epokhi*, eds. L. A. Spiridonova, N. N. Primochkina, and M. A. Semashkina (Moscow, 2010), 52–3.

37 Gorky, "Letter to A. A. Bogdanov, after March 9 (22), 1909" (cit. n. 33).

38 Gorky, "Letter to M.N. Pokrovskii, around 3 (16) March, 1909" (cit. n. 30).

39 It is also worth noting that Aleksinskii was apparently surprised by this suggestion, as Bogdanov seems to have told him that nothing definite had been decided. See Aleksinskii (cit. n. 34).

40 Bogdanov, "Letter to Gorky, after March 6 (19), 1909" (cit. n. 31).

41 On the history of the party school, see Jutta Scherrer, "Les Écoles du Parti de Capri et de Bologne: La formation de l'intelligentsia du parti," *Cahiers du Monde russe et soviétique*, 29 (1978): 259–84, as well as Scherrer, "The Relationship between the Intelligentsia and Workers: The Case of the Party Schools in Capri and Bologna," in *Workers and Intelligentsia in Late Imperial Russia: Realities, Representations, Reflections*, ed. Reginald E. Zelnik (Berkeley, 1999), 172–85; Michael David-Fox, *Revolution of the Mind: Higher Learning among the Bolsheviks, 1918-1929* (Ithaca, 1997), 27–37; Williams, *The Other Bolsheviks*, 146–53 (cit. n. 13).

42 See the plan in Scherrer, "Les Écoles du Parti de Capri et de Bologne," 270 (cit. n. 41). See also the plans held in the Grigorii Aleksinskii papers, MS Russ 73, (11) Houghton Library, Harvard University.

43 Bogdanov, "Letter to Gorky, around 12(25) June 1909, Paris," in *Gor'kii v zerkale epokhi*, 66–7 (cit. n. 36).
44 V. I. Lenin, "Pis'mo Lenina uchenikam Kapriiskoi Shkoly, August 30, 1909" ("Letter to the Students of the Capri School, August 30, 1909"), in Grigorii Aleksinskii Papers, MS Russ 73, (5) Houghton Library, Harvard University.
45 A. A. Bogdanov, *Kul'turnye zadachi nashego vremeni* (The cultural tasks of our time) (Moscow, 1911), 42–5.
46 A. Bogdanov, *Nauka ob obshchestvennom soznanii* (The science of social consciousness) (Moscow, 1914). See also the bibliographical note in John Biggart, Georgii Gloveli, and Avraham Yassour, *Bogdanov and His Work: A Guide to the Published and Unpublished Works of Alexander Bogdanov (Malinovsky) 1873-1928* (Aldershot, 1998), which links this work with the encyclopedia project.
47 As Steila shows, Gorky made a number of efforts to solicit funding for the project from prominent Russians, including the operatic bass Fedor Chaliapin and the conductor Serge Koussevitzky. Ultimately, he was unable to secure the level of funding that he considered necessary for the project. See Steila, "A Proletarian *Encyclopédie*", 98–9 (cit. n. 3). Steila also considers disunity to be an important factor in the failure of the project.
48 Bogdanov et al., "Otchet tovarishcham-bol'shevikam ustranennykh chlenov rasshirennoi redaktsii 'Proletariia'" (Report to the Comrades-Bolsheviks of the removed members of the expanded editorial board of *The Proletarian*), in *Neizvestnyi Bogdanov* (*The Unknown Bogdanov*), 3 vols., eds. G. A. Bordiugov, N. S. Antonova, and N. V. Drozdova, vol. 2 (Moscow, 1995), 175. See also V. M. Shuliatikov, ed., *Soveshchanie rasshirennoi redaktsii "Proletariia"* (*Meeting of the expanded editorial board of* The Proletarian) (Moscow, 1934).
49 Bogdanov, *Kul'turnye zadachi nashego vremeni*, 58–80 (cit. n. 45).
50 Ibid.
51 Ibid.
52 A. Bogdanov, *Inzhener Menni* (Engineer Menni) (St. Petersburg, 1919), 115.
53 P. I. Lebedev-Polianskii, ed., *Protokoly Pervoi vserossiiskoi konferentsii proletarskikh kul'turno-prosvetitel'nykh organizatsii* (Protocols of the first all-Russian conference of proletarian cultural-educational organizations) (Moscow), 31–6.
54 Ibid., 42.
55 Ibid., 17–21.
56 See his speech from November 20, 1920, P. I. Lebedev-Polianskii, *O proletarskoi kul'ture* (On Proletarian Culture) (Rostov-on-Don, 1921).
57 See Lynn Mally, *Culture of the Future: The Proletkult Movement in Revolutionary Russia* (Berkeley, 1990), 1–32.
58 Russian State Archive for Literature and Art (RGALI), f. 1230 op. 1 d. 1537 l. 4.
59 RGALI, f. 1230 op. 1 d. 3, 117, 118, 121, 137, 140, 146, 1215, 1215, 1245, 1278, 1524, 1525, 1536, 1537, 1538, 1540. The encyclopedia was *Klubnaia rabota: prakticheskaia entsiklopediia dlia podgotovki klubnykh rabotnikov* (Club work: a practical encyclopedia for the preparation of club workers) (Moscow, 1926).
60 I have outlined the early history of the First Edition of the *BSE* in "Istoricheskie vzgliady na entsiklopedistiku: istoriia sozdaniia *Bol'shoi Sovetskoi Entsiklopedii*" ("Historical perspectives on encyclopedistics: The history of the creation of the *Great Soviet Encyclopedia*"), in *Sovremennaia rossiiskaia entsiklopedistika: mesto i rol' v obshchestve, perspektivy razvitiia* (Contemporary Russian encyclopedistics: its place and role in society, perspectives on its development), ed. U. G. Saitov (Ufa, 2019), 19–25. On the First Edition, see also Brian Kassof, "A Book of Socialism: Stalinist

Culture and the First Edition of the *Bol'shaia sovetskaia entsiklopediia*," *Kritika*, 6 (2005): 55–95; Laurent Mazliak, "The beginnings of the Soviet encyclopedia: The utopia and misery of mathematics in the political turmoil of the 1920s," *Centaurus*, 60 (2018): 25–51; G. V. Iakusheva, *Otto Iul'evich Shmidt – entsiklopedist: kratkaia illiustrirovannaia entsiklopediia* (*Otto Iul'evich Shmidt – Encyclopedist: A Short Illustrated Encyclopedia*), eds. A. M. Prokhorov and B. S. Sokolov (Moscow, 1991); Iu. E. Shmushkis, *Sovetskie entsiklopedii* (cit. n. 1).

61 See *Vestnik Kommunisticheskoi akademii*, 12 (1925): 363–92.

62 See, for example, the statements of Valerian Kuibyshev in RGASPI f. 79 op. 1 d. 858 ll. 1–3.

63 On these types of institutions, see David-Fox, *Revolution of the Mind* (cit. n. 41).

64 Bogdanov, "Vospominanie o detstve" ("Recollections about Childhood"), in *Neizvestnyi Bogdanov*, vol. 1, 25–6.

Chapter 2

1 Michael David-Fox, *Showcasing the Great Experiment: Cultural Diplomacy and Western Visitors to the Soviet Union, 1921–1941* (Oxford, 2012), 1. The research leading to this chapter was supported by a grant from the Russian Science Foundation: Project No 19-18-00414 'Soviet Culture Today (Forms of Cultural Recycling in Russian Art and Aesthetics of the Everyday Life. 1990s–2010s)'.

2 "Priezd amerikanskikh uchenykh v SSSR" (The Visit of American Scholars to the USSR), *Izvestiia*, July 7, 1928.

3 However, one of his principal works on educational theory, *Experience and Education*, was still to be written.

4 According to the trip organizers, it was "a non-political mission of twenty-five American educators to study methods of public instruction in Soviet Russia." The group included "Miss Katherine Devereux Blake, Emer. Principal, N. Y. City. Dr. J. McKeen Cattell, Editor of four scientific journals. President Lotus D. Coffman, University of Minn. President Donald J. Cowling, Carleton College. Professor John Dewey, Columbia University. Professor Robert H. Gault, Northwestern Univ. Professor Mary L. Hinsdale, Grand Rapids College. Florence Holbook, Principal, Chicago, Ill. President Parke R. Kolbe, Polytechnic Institute, Brooklyn. Dr. J. Kunitz, College of the City of New York. President K. G. Matheson, Drexel Institute, Phil. Professor James K. Norris, Mass. Inst. of Tech. President Geo. D. Olds, Amherst College. K. E. Richter, College of the City of N. Y. President Walter Dill Scott, Northwestern Univ. Miss Emily A. Stein, James Monroe High School, N. Y. City. Professor Lucy Textor, Vassar College. Professor Thomas Woody, University of Penn." (1928.05.16 [06418]: Francis Ralston Welsh to State Dept. Collection: Diplomatic Branch. Document: TD. Notes: Stamped "EASTERN EUROPEAN AFFAIRS | MAY 19, 1928 | DEPARTMENT OF STATE"; "RECEIVED | MAY 21, 1928 | Dept. of State") (Special Collection Research Center, Southern Illinois University Carbondale).

5 "Foreign News: To Moscow," *Time*, XI, no. 23 (June 4, 1928): 18.

6 The informer to the State department listed all cases of Dewey's "sympathy" to "the Soviets" concluding that "Professor John Dewey has been very consistently helping the Communist game, both in what he has done in America and what he has said in the past about the Russian Soviets." About the delegation the report said that it is "one more move in the Communist propaganda game engineered by those who have proved willing tools of the Communists in the past and with various non-

Communists drawn in to hide the Communist machinery working underneath" (1928.05.16); (06418): Francis Ralston Welsh to State Dept. (cit. n. 4).

7 The name of Evelyn, who coauthored with Dewey *Schools of Tomorrow*, was known to Soviet educators. Nadezhda Krupskaia (1869–1939), the wife of Vladimir Lenin and a Deputy Head of Narkompros (1929–39), wrote an introduction to Evelyn Dewey's book *The Dalton Laboratory Plan*, published in Moscow in 1923, and reprinted in 1924, 1925.

8 "Priezd amerikanskikh uchenykh v SSSR" (cit. n. 2). Soviet pedagogical publications were happy to report any reaction of foreign educators to the system of Soviet education. See, for example, "Iz otzyvov amerikanskikh pedagogov o russkoi shkole i programmakh GUSa" (From reviews of Russian schools by American educators), *Na putiakh k novoi shkole*, 9 (1926): 188–91; E. Guro, "Inostrantsy o nashem prosveshchenii," *Na putiakh k novoi shkole*, 12 (1929): 62–8.

9 A. V. Lunacharskii, "Vospitanie novogo cheloveka" (Education of the New Man) (1928), in idem, O *vospitanii i obrazovanii* (Moscow, 1976), 282. About American-Soviet parallels in the pre-Stalin system of education, see, for example, V. V. Iakovleva, *Reformirovanie otechestvennogo obrazovaniia v kontekste filiatsii idei v pervoi treti XX veka* (Reform of National Education in the Context of Filiation of Ideas in the First Third of the twentieth century). PhD Dissertation (Perm, 2004); *Ocherki istorii shkoly i pedagogicheskoi mysli narodov SSSR, Konets XIX—nachalo XX veka* (Essays on History of School and Pedagogical Thought of Peoples of the USSR), eds. E. D. Dneprov et al. (Moscow, 1991). On Dewey's role in developing Soviet theory of education see: A. E. Korobova, *Pedagogicheskie idei J. Dewey i ikh interpretatsiia v otechestvennoi pedagogicheskoi teorii i praktike 20–30-kh gg.* (Pedagogical Ideas of John Dewey and Their Interpretation in Russian Pedagogical Theory and Practice). PhD Dissertation (Saratov, 2000).

10 A. V. Lunacharskii, "O vospitanii cheloveka novogo obshchestva" (On Education of the New Society Man) (1925), *Nauka i zhizn'*, 3 (1976): 55.

11 Cf. A. V. Lunacharskii, "Nashi tekushchie zadachi (Kakaia shkola nuzhna proletarskomu gosudarstvu)" (Our Current Tasks [What Kind of School Does the Proletarian State Need]) (1922), in idem, *O vospitanii i obrazovanii* (Moscow, 1976), 101. The project method is a method of teaching that requires joint work of children on a project with minimum guidance of a teacher. See Russian translation of Ellsworth Collings, *Opyt raboty amerikanskoi shkoly po metodu proektov* (*An Experiment with a Project Curriculum*) (Moscow, 1926).

12 Thus, for example, Victor Shulgin (1894–1965), an educator and a historian, a member of the Narkompros collegium, advanced the project method in Soviet schools. Cf. V. N. Shulgin, "Osnovnye voprosy sotsial'nogo vospitaniia," *Na putiakh k novoi shkole*, 4–5 (1927). On application of the project method in Soviet schools see N. K. Krupskaia, "Voprosy teorii i praktiki metoda proektov" (Problems of Theory and Practice of the Project Method), *Na putiakh k novoi shkole*, 5 (1931): 17–24.

13 Jay Martin, *The Education of John Dewey: A Biography* (New York, 2002), 354.

14 John Dewey, "Impressions of Soviet Russia," in idem, *The Later Works, 1925–1953: 1927–1928*, vol. 3 (Carbondale, IL, 1984), 204.

15 Ibid., 222.

16 Ibid., 213.

17 Ibid., 247. For S. Shatskii's recollections of Dewey's visit, see S. T. Shatskii, "Amerikanskie pedagogi u nas v gostiakh" (Our guests are American educators), in idem, *Pedagogicheskie sochineniia v 4 t.*, vol. 3 (Moscow, 1964), 206–14.

18 In the 1920s and early 1930s, "educational" pilgrimage was one of the kinds of pilgrimage of Western intellectuals to the Soviet Union. Communes, including children's labor communes, served as one of the pilgrimage destinations. In addition to Dewey, the famous pilgrims who visited communes, though not children's labor-communes, were Niels Bohr, Bernard Shaw, and Nancy and Walldorf Astor. Thus, in 1931, Shaw and the Astors visited the Irskaia commune in the Tambov region, where descendants of Russian emigres to the United States, the United Kingdom, and Australia had returned to live.

19 Dewey, "Impressions of Soviet Russia," 212 (cit. n. 14).

20 Felix Dzerzhinsky, "Order of the All-Russian Extraordinary Commission," No. 23, Moscow, January 27, 1921. On children's life in the USSR see: Catriona Kelly, *Children's World: Growing Up in Russia, 1890–1991* (Yale University Press, 2008). For literature on *besprizorniki* see Alan M. Ball, *And Now My Soul Is Hardened: Abandoned Children in Soviet Russia, 1918–1930* (Berkeley, 1994); Anne E. Gorsuch, *Youth in Revolutionary Russia: Enthusiasts, Bohemians, Delinquents* (Indiana-Michigan Series in Russian and East European Studies) (Bloomington, IN, 2000).

21 M. Gorky, "Ot 'vragov obshchestva'—k geroiam truda" (From "enemies of the society" to heroes of labor), (1936) in idem, *Sobranie sochinenii v 30-ti tomakh* (Collected works in thirty volumes), 27 (Moscow, 1953), 509. M. David-Fox claims that Gorky played a "key role" in the history of Bolshevo (David-Fox, *Showcasing the Great Experiment*, 158 cit. n. 1).

22 In the 1930s, when the pathos of creating a "new man" would become an empty form, *Perekovka* would be a common name for newspapers published in Stalin's camps.

23 M. David-Fox notes that, interestingly, the Bolshevo commune was not designed as a "showcase for foreigners" but was brought to light by *The Nation*, which published an article about the commune in 1925. David-Fox, *Showcasing the Great Experiment*, 160 (cit. n. 1).

24 *Kommuna v Nikolo-Ugreshe* (Commune in Ugresha Monastery) (Dzerzhinskii, 2012), 23–39.

25 I. L. Auerbach, *Ot prestupleniia k trudu* (From crime to labor), ed. A. Ya. Vyshinskii (Moscow, 1936), 24.

26 Ibid., 5.

27 "The liquidator of homelessness" is a term coined by Gorky. In his essay "Across the Union of Soviets" the writer applies this term to the teachers who worked in the labor communes, that is, Makarenko, Melekhov, Pogrebinskii, and others. Gorky and Pogrebinskii got acquainted in 1928; it was Pogrebinskii who brought to Gorky in Italy a letter from Stalin, proposing him to return to the USSR.

28 See M. S. Pogrebinskii, *Trudovaia kommuna OGPU* (Labor commune of OGPU). Edited by M. Gorky (Moscow, 1928); M. S. Pogrebinskii, *Fabrika liudei* (Making People), (Moscow, 1929); I. Ionin, *Shkola-koloniia Krasnye Zori* (Leningrad, 1933); A. Makarenko, *Pedagogichesksaia poema* (Road to Life) (Moscow, 1935); *Bolshevtsy. Ocherki po istorii Bolshevskoi im. G. G. Iagody trudkommuny NKVD* (The Bolshevs. Essays on history of a labor commune named after G. G. Iagoda), eds. M. Gorky, K. Gorbunov, and M. Luzgin (Moscow, 1936).

29 Pogrebinskii, *Fabrika liudei*, 8–9 (cit. n. 28).

30 Ibid.

31 Ibid.

32 Makarenko, *Bolshevtsy*, 195 (cit. n. 28). See also: A. Makarenko, "Bolshevtsy" (The Bolshevs), *Literaturnaia gazeta*, August 27, 1936.

33 M. Gorky, "Po Soiuzu Sovetov" (Across the Union of Soviets), in idem, *Sobranie sochinenii v 30-ti tomakh* (Collected works in thirty volumes), 17 (Moscow, 1952), 157–8.
34 In 1924, Ionin together with his wife wrote a script of an educational film, *Golden Honey*, about the beekeeping activity of the communards. The script was later used for the documentary *Krasnye Zori* (Red Dawns) about the life and the work in the commune.
35 On the organization of labor in the commune Krasnye Zori see I. V. Ionin, *Shkola-koloniia (kommuna)* (School colony [commune]), ed. N. A. Kuznetsov (Leningrad, 1924); I. Ionin, *Shkola-koloniia Krasnye Zori* (Leningrad, 1933); I. V. Ionin, *K organizatsii opytno-agronomicheskoi raboty v ShKM* (To organization of experimental agriculture in a school colony) (Leningrad, 1932). Under the penname "I. O. Nin" Ionin published a children's story about the pioneers who at the end of the story were awarded an honorary diploma for their "work in developing animal breeding, in particular for the contribution to protection of feed"; see I. O. Nin, *Pochetnyi diplom* (Honorary Diploma) (Moscow, 1931), 38.
36 "The Forge of New People" was the name of the article in the newspaper *Lenin's Sparks* dedicated to the fifteenth anniversary of the commune Krasnye Zori; see "Kuznitsa novykh liudei," *Leninskie iskry*, November 27, 1934. In the late 1920s and the 1930s, "The Forge of New People" became a cliché in examples of *perekovka*. See, for example, A. Otvodnyi, *V kuznitse novogo cheloveka* (In the Forge of the New Man) (Moscow, 1932).
37 Gorky, "Po Soiuzu Sovetov," 181 (cit. n. 33).
38 M. Gorky, *Mother* (New York, 1906), 63.
39 Gorky, "Po Soiuzu Sovetov," 155 (cit. n. 33).
40 M. Gorky, *Publitsisticheskie stat'i* (Publicistic Essays) (Moscow, 1933), 22–3.
41 Ibid.
42 Gorky, "Po Soiuzu Sovetov," 165 (cit. n. 33).
43 Pogrebinskii, *Fabrika liudei*, 10 (cit. n. 28).
44 Ibid., 32.
45 Makarenko, *Bolshevtsy*, 194 (cit. n. 28).
46 Pogrebinskii, *Fabrika liudei*, 34–5 (cit. n. 28).
47 *Leningradskaia Pravda*, November 23, 1934.
48 Gorky, "Po Soiuzu Sovetov," 177 (cit. n. 33).
49 "Krasnye orliata" (Red Little Eagles) (1925), "Ky-Sy-Me" (Komsomol, Young Communist League) (1925), "P. S. R." (Party of free guys) (1928), "Fugas zalozhen" (Explosive bomb is laid) (1928), "Put' sovetskogo khleba" (The Way of Soviet bread) (1929), and so on.
50 Radii Fish, *Nazim Hikmet* (Moscow, 1968), 95.
51 *Vecherniaia Moskva*, September 6, 1926.
52 Well-known film directors, including A. Medvedkin, A. Room, L. Kuleshov, V. Pudovkin, N. Ekk, G. Vasiliev, and others, were often involved in the creation of such films.
53 R. Yanushkevich, "Velikii nemoi zagovoril. Fragmenty vospominanii" (The silent era has spoken. Fragments of memories), *Kinovedcheskie zapiski*, 98 (2011): 59. http://www.kinozapiski.ru/data/home/articles/attache/52-65.pdf. In the 1920s, the OGPU sought to use the creative activity of filmmakers for propaganda purposes; thus, by order of the OGPU a propagandistic film, *Solovki* (1928, directed by A. Cherkasov), was filmed, as well as a number of documentaries about the White Sea channel.

In 1925, the Society of Friends of Soviet Cinema (later Society of Friends of Soviet Cinematography and Photography) was established; the short-term chairman of the board was Dzerzhinsky.

54 In the 1957 restored and edited version of the film approved by N. Ekk, these lines are absent. The industrial vocabulary of "reforging," "remodeling," and "remelting," which was typical for the first postrevolutionary years, disappears from the narrative about the education of the Soviet man making the period of the 1920s to the early 1930s unique in this respect.

55 Sergeev is modeled on several historic "liquidators of homelessness," including Matvei Pogrebinskii, Fiodor Melekhov, a former colleague of Pogrebinskii and the first director of the Liuberetskaia commune, and Mikhail Tipograf, a member of the commission for the elimination of homelessness. Tipograf helped Batalov to find the right approach to his part, to the "grain" of the role. He several times took Batalov to "operations" and even gave him a *kubanka* hat and a leather overcoat that was a popular attire in the Cheka. See M. Zharov, *Zhizn', teatr, kino* (Life, Theatre, Cinema) (Moscow, 1967), 292.

56 In fact, the lack of control from the Cheka authorities and the non-authoritarian behavior of the Chekist Sergeev aroused criticism of some scholars who saw the film as the "glorification of the Chekist experiment." Cf. Cristina Vatulescu, "Secret Police Shots at Filmmaking: The Gulag and Cinema," in idem, *Police Aesthetics: Literature, Film, and the Secret Police in Soviet Times* (Stanford, 2010), 123–60.

57 A similar episode is described by A. S. Makarenko in his book *Road to Life* (1935): Makarenko trusts a revolver and the commune money to a former criminal Semion Karabanov (Semion Kalabalin). A. S. Makarenko, *Pedagogicheskaia Poema* (*Road to Life*, 1935), vol. 1 (Moscow, 2018), 163. There is rather extensive literature on Makarenko's pedagogical experiments that often foreshadows the educational activity of other labor-communes' organizers. See, for example, J. Bowen, *Soviet Education: Anton Makarenko and the Years of Experiment* (Madison, 1965).

58 Pogrebinskii, *Trudovaia kommuna OGPU* (cit. n. 27), 7–8.

59 Auerbach, *Ot prestupleniia k trudu*, 32 (cit. n. 25).

60 See, for example, Auerbach's story about "reeducation" in a Stalin camp of the poorly working brigade that starts with washing hands before lunch, followed by morning neck washing; see Auerbach, *Ot prestupleniia k trudu*, 48 (cit. n. 25), or the struggle for cleanliness that requires for each communard to have his own toothbrush and toothpowder in Makarenko, *Bolshevtsy*, 215 (cit. n. 28).

61 Reportedly, according to Meyerhold, the success of *The Road to Life* was based on two smiles: Batalov's and Ivan Kyrlia's. See: E. Margolit, "Svoi! V nature!" "Putevka v zhizn" kak obrazets "obshchestvennogo zakaza" ("Ours! In fact!" *The Road to Life* as an example of "social request"), *Séance*, September 13, 2015. https://seance.ru/articles/svoj-v-nature/.

62 Harry Alan Potamkin, "Tendencies in the Soviet Films," *New Masses*, VII (12) (1932): 18.

63 Ibid.

64 Ibid.

65 Yanushkevich, "Velikii nemoi zagovoril. Fragmenty vospominanii," 63 (cit. n. 53).

66 A. Mikhailov, "Putevka v zhizn'" (Road to Life), *Proletarskoe kino*, 5–6 (1931): 25.

67 Ibid., 26, 28.

68 K. R. "Film o besprizornikakh ili besprizornyi film" (Film About Homeless Children or Homeless Film), *Izvestiia*, May 10, 1931.

69 Ibid.
70 Ibid.
71 The First Experimental Station (1919–36), a network of institutions, was, probably, the most radical experimental educational institution in the world.
72 See: N. S. Kirichko, "Shatskii i zarubezhnaia pedagogika," in *S. T. Shatskii (1878–1934)*, ed. M. S. Epstein (Moscow, 1934), 100–8; V. I. Malinin, "Russkie pedagogi o shkole SShA" (Russian Educators about American School), *Sovetskaia pedagogika*, 4 (1987): 116–24.
73 John Dewey, *The Later Works, 1925–1953: 1935, Vol. 10, Art as Experience* (Carbondale, IL, 1989), 50.
74 John Dewey, *The Later Works, 1925–1953: 1938, Vol. 12, Logic: The Theory of Inquiry* (Carbondale, IL, 1986), 72.
75 John Dewey, *The Later Works, 1925–1953: 1939–1941, Vol. 14, Essays, Reviews, and Miscellany* (Carbondale, IL, 1988), 16.
76 Ibid., 17.
77 John Dewey, *The Middle Works, Vol. 8, 1899–1924: Essays and Miscellany in the 1915 Period; German Philosophy and Politics; Schools of Tomorrow* (Carbondale, IL, 1979), 391.
78 John Dewey, *The Middle Works, Vol. 9, 1899–1924: Democracy and Education, 1916* (Carbondale, IL, 1980), 82.
79 John Dewey, "My Pedagogic Creed," *School Journal*, 54 (January 1897): 77–80.
80 Later Krupskaia criticized the uncritical application of the Dalton plan in the Soviet system of education. The Resolution of the Central Committee of the party in 1932 (August 25) condemned the laboratory-brigade method of learning.
81 Evelyn Dewey, *The Dalton Laboratory Plan* (New York, 1922), 1.
82 Dewey, "Impressions of Soviet Russia," 233 (cit. n. 14).
83 John Dewey, "The Public and Its Problems," in idem, *The Later Works, 1925–1953: 1925–1927*, vol. 2 (Carbondale, IL, 1984), 328.
84 Dewey, "Impressions of Soviet Russia," 236 (cit. n. 14).
85 Ibid., 246–7.
86 Ibid., 248. N. S. Iulina believes that Dewey was "cheated in his expectations," not because he was not far-sighted, but because he was too rational. The chances that the Soviet state had were not used because of irrational reasons, voluntarist decisions of the authorities, ideological dogmas, an atmosphere of fear, and so on; that is, because there was just "an exceptional turn in the natural course of events," N. S. Iulina, "Ob ocherke Dzhona D'iui 'Vpechatleniia o Sovetskoi Rossii'" (On John Dewey's essay "Impressions of Soviet Russia"), *Istoriia filosofii*, 5 (2000): 272.
87 Dewey, "Impressions of Soviet Russia," 243 (cit. n. 14).
88 *Survey* 61 (1928): 348–9. For a sampling of English-language commentary on Dewey's relation to Soviet educational experiments, see, for example, William W. Brickman, "John Dewey in Russia," *Educational Theory*, 10 (1960): 83–6, and "Soviet Attitudes toward John Dewey as an Educator," in *John Dewey and the World View*, eds. Douglas E. Lawson and Arthur E. Lean (Carbondale, 1964), 64–149; "Dr. Dewey Praises Russia's School," *New York Times*, December 6, 1928, 3; Elena Rogacheva, "Russian Education in Search of Democracy: The Relevance of John Dewey's Model of the School," *East/West Education*, 15 (1994): 49–61.
89 *Film Daily*, April 15, 1932, 4.
90 In the version shown in Germany, the opening speech was given by Egon Erwin Kisch, a Czech-German journalist and writer, communist, and one of the founders of

the Communist Party of Austria. Kisch, who saw *The Road to Life* in 1931 in Moscow, defended the film from criticism: "Three years ago, *Putievka* would have been a reportage, but now when homelessness has been liquidated, the film is a serious social and political document." Cited in Margolit, "Svoi! V nature!" (cit. n. 61).

91 John Dewey cited in Bowen, *Soviet Education*, 4 (cit. n. 57).

92 Dewey, "Impressions of Soviet Russia," 207 (cit. n. 14).

93 John Dewey, "Making Soviet Citizens," in idem, *The Later Works, 1925–1953: 1925–1927,* vol. 6 (Carbondale, IL, 1985), 293–4.

94 John Dewey, "Statement to the Conference on Curriculum for the College of Liberal Arts," in idem, *The Later Works, 1925–1953: 1925–1927,* vol. 6 (Carbondale, IL, 1985), 423.

95 "O nachal'noi i srednei shkole" (On primary and secondary school), *Kommunisticheskaia partiia Sovetskogo Soiuza v rezoliutsiiakh i resheniiakh s"ezdov, konferentsii i plenumov TsK: 1929–1932* (Moscow, 1983), 356.

96 See Judy Kutulas, *The Long War: The Intellectual People's Front and Anti-Stalinism, 1930–1940* (Durham, NC, 1995), 116–18. For an account of Soviet-era commentary on Dewey's philosophy see John Ryder, *Interpreting America: Russian and Soviet Studies of the History of American Thought* (Nashville, 1999), especially Chapter 4.

97 Makarenko, "Bolshevtsy" (cit. n. 32).

98 David-Fox, *Showcasing the Great Experiment*, 173 (cit. n. 1).

Chapter 3

1 See Mikhail Heller, *Mashina i vintiki. Istoriia formirovaniia sovetskogo cheloveka* (A cog and the wheel. The development of Homo Sovieticus) (London, 1994), 28; Maja Soboleva, "The Concept of the 'New Soviet Man' and Its Short History," *Canadian-American Slavic Studies*, 51 (2017): 64–85; and the "introduction" to the present volume.

2 This metaphor was used by the Head of the People's Enlightenment Department at the Petrograd Executive Committee Z. I. Lilina (Zinov'eva) in 1918.

3 A. V. Lunacharskii and N. A. Skrypnik, *Narodnoe obrazovanie v SSSR v sviazi s rekonstruktsiei narodnogo khoziaistva. Doklady na VII s"ezde Soiuza rabotnikov prosveshcheniia* (People's education in the USSR in relation to the reconstruction of people's economy. Presentations at the Seventh Congress of the Union of Enlightenment Workers), (Moscow, 1929), 131–2. Here Lunacharskii uses the Russian folk saying "*gorbatogo mogila ispravit*" that is roughly equivalent to "a leopard can't change its spots."

4 On the notion of "re-forging" (*perekovka*), see Lyubov Bugaeva's contribution to the present volume.

5 About Eugenii Radin, see Nikolai Krementsov, *With and Without Galton: Vasilii Florinskii and the Fate of Eugenics in Russia* (Cambridge, 2018), 279–80.

6 M. A. Radina-Kornil'eva and E. P. Radin, *Novym detiam novye igry: Podvizhnye igry shkol'nogo i vneshkol'nogo vozrastov ot 7 do 18 let v refleksologicheskom i pedologicheskom osveschenii* (New games for new children: Physical games for in-school and out-of-school age, from seven to eighteen, from the reflexology and pedology perspectives), 4th ed. (Moscow, 1927), 4.

7 Yu. M. Lotman, "Kukly v sisteme kultury" (Dolls in the system of culture), in idem., *Izbrannye stat'i*, vol. 1 (Tallinn, 1992), 380.

8 Catriona Kelly, *Children's World: Growing Up in Russia, 1890–1991* (New Haven, 2007), 714; A. A. Sal'nikova, *Rossiiskoe detstvo v XX veke: Istoriia, teoriia i praktika issledovaniia* (Russian Childhood in the 20th Century: History, Theory and Practice of Research) (Kazan, 2007), 256; and Yu. G. Salova, "Igrovoe prostranstvo sovetskogo rebenka-doshkol'nika v 1920-e gody" (Playing domain of a Soviet preschool-age child in the 1920s), in *Kakoreia. Iz istorii detstva v Rossii i drugikh stranakh. Sbornik statei i materialov*, ed. G. V. Makarevich (Moscow–Tver, 2008), 114–23.

9 M. V. Gavrilova, "Transformatsiia traditsionnyh russkih igr v sovetskoi pedagogike (1920–1930-e gg.)" (Transformation of traditional Russian games in Soviet pedagogy [1920s–1930s]), *Antropologicheskii forum*, 19 (2013): 130–75.

10 Mia Heinimaa, Julia Ivanova, Maria Marchenko, and Tatjana Stserbina, *Sankarilliset lelut: Neuvostoleikkikalun lyhyt historia* (Jyväskylä, 2005), 120.

11 M. Kostiukhina, *Igrushka v detskoi literature* (Toy in children's literature) (St. Petersburg, 2008), 208; and idem, *Zapiski kukly. Modnoe vospitanie v literature dlia devits kontsa XVIII- nachala XX veka* (Doll's notes. Fashion education in the late-eighteenth- early-twentieth-century literature for maidens) (Moscow, 2017), 225.

12 This issue, perceived broadly, has lately been actively discussed at international fora. It can be handled by integrating a meticulous retrieval of written sources, such as children's diaries and correspondence, with the search for traces of toy use or misuse. See Megan Brandow-Faller, ed., *Childhood by Design: Toys and the Material Culture of Childhood, 1700-Present* (New York, 2018); and "Forum: V poiskah detskoi sub'ektivnosti" (Forum: In search of children's subjecthood), *Antropologicheskii Forum*, 42 (2019): 9–106.

13 A similar situation was observed in communist China, where the authorities also tried to create a politically relevant toy for "new children." See Valentina Boretti, "Patriotic Fun: Toys and Mobilization in China from the Republican to the Communist Era," in *War and Childhood in the Era of the Two World Wars,* eds. Mischa Honeck and James Marten (Cambridge, 2019), 17–34.

14 L. Orshanskii, "Istoricheskii ocherk razvitiia igrushek i igrushechnogo proizvodstva na Zapade i v Rossii" (A historical overview of the development of toys and toy-making in the West and in Russia), in *Igrushka. Ee istoriia i znachenie*, ed. N. D. Bartram (Moscow, 1912), 61–2.

15 Juliette Peers, "Doll Culture," in *Girl Culture: An Encyclopedia*, eds. Claudia A. Mitchell and Jacqueline Reid-Walsh, vol. 1 (Westport, CT, 2008), 25–38, on 27.

16 Heinimaa et al., *Sankarilliset lelut*, 21, 52 (cit. n.10).

17 Gavrilova, "Transformatsiia traditsionnyh russkih igr v sovetskoi pedagogike (1920–1930-e gg.)," 130–75 (cit. n. 9).

18 A. V. Lunacharskii, "Vmesto vvedeniia" (In lieu of introduction), in *Igra: Neperiodicheskoe izdanie, posviaschennoe vospitaniiu posredstvom igry* (Petrograd-Moscow, 1918), 1–4, on 2.

19 For a detailed history of pedology in Russia, see Andy Byford, *Science of the Child in Late Imperial and Early Soviet Russia* (Oxford, 2020).

20 See, N. A. Rybnikov, "Pedologicheskie uchrezhdeniia respubliki" (Pedological institutions of the republic), *Pedologiia*, 1 (1928): 181–92.

21 Andy Byford, *Russian Child Science in International and Contemporary Context* (Durham University, 2012). https://www.dur.ac.uk/resources/russianchildscience/Report1Nov12.pdf: 5.

22 "Komissiia po detskim igrushkam Tsentral'nogo pedologicheskogo instituta" (Commission on child toys at the Central Pedological Institute), in *Rebenok i igrushka,* ed. N. A. Rybnikov, 2nd ed. (Moscow, 1924), 3–6, on 4–5.
23 "O postoiannoi vystavke igrushek" (About permanent toy exhibition), in Ibid., 74–7, on 75–6.
24 K. Kornilov, "K psihologii detskoi igry v kukly" (Towards the psychology of child's play with dolls), in ibid., 36–50, on 36.
25 See Loren R. Graham, *Science, Philosophy, and Human Behavior in the Soviet Union* (In Russ.) (Moscow, 1991), at scepsis.net/library/id_852.html (accessed on August 5, 2019).
26 A. A. Faivusiovich, "Ob osobennostiakh detei preddoshkol'nogo vozrasta" (About specific features of children before preschool age), *Pedologiia*, 2 (1928): 24–46.
27 V. N. Osipova, "Shkola V. M. Bekhtereva i pedologiia" (V. M. Bekhterev's school and pedology), *Pedologiia*, 1 (1928): 10–26; on 26.
28 For reflections on semantic coupling of Pavlov's hypotheses and the discourse on the creation of the "new man," see K. A. Bogdanov, "Pravo na son i uslovnye refleksy: kolybel'nye pesni v sovetskoi kul'ture (1930–1950-e gody)" (The right to sleep and conditional reflexes: lullabies in Soviet culture [1930s–1950s]), *Novoe literaturnoe obozrenie* 4 (2007). magazines.gorky.media/nlo/2007/4/pravo-na-son-i-uslovnye-refleksy-kolybelnye-pesni-v-sovetskoj-kulture-1930-1950-e-gody.html (accessed on June 26, 2019).
29 Radina-Kornil'eva and Radin, *Novym detiam novye igry*, 14 (cit. n. 6).
30 A. N. Antonov, "Igra v kukly i ee obschestvennoe znachenie" (Playing with dolls and their social significance), *Pedologicheskii zhurnal*, 3 (1924): 1–27, on 27.
31 Kornilov, "K psikhologii detskoi igry v kukly," 48 (cit. n. 24).
32 On the "young pioneer" movement in Soviet Russia, see Lisa A. Kirschenbaum, *Small Comrades: Revolutionizing Childhood in Soviet Russia, 1917–1932* (New York, 2001).
33 Marie Gasper-Hulvat, "Public Nostalgia and the Infantilization of the Russian Peasant: Early Soviet Reception of Folk Art Toys," in *Childhood by Design: Toys and the Material Culture of Childhood, 1700-Present*, ed. Megan Brandow-Faller (New York, 2018), 273–92.
34 A. Ames'evskii, "Igrushka v politike i revoliutsii" (The toy in politics and revolution), *Kustar'-kooperator*, 3 (1927): 7–8.
35 A. Suvorov, "Vmesto mekkano... banki dlia gutalina" (Instead of meccano... shoe blackener tins), *Pionerskaia pravda* (April 1, 1932): 3.
36 See, for instance, E. V. Ianovskaia, *Skazka, kak factor klassovogo vospitaniia* (Fairy-tale as a factor of class upbringing) (Kharkov, 1923). The second, expanded edition of this book that came out two years later bore an even more polemical title, *Does a proletarian child need the fairy-tale?*
37 N. Sats and S. Rozanov, *Teatr dlia detei* (Theater for children) (Leningrad, 1925), 22, 33, 34; see also N. I. Sats, *Deti prikhodiat v teatr* (Children come to the theater) (Moscow, 1961), 86.
38 Evgenii Shvarts, "*Dnevnikovaia zapis' 17 oktiabria 1952 g.*" (Dairy record of October 17, 1952). https://prozhito.org/notes?date=%221952-01-01%22&diaries=%5B74%5D (accessed on April 7, 2019).
39 Cited in Salova, "Igrovoe prostranstvo sovetskogo rebenka-doshkol'nika v 1920-e gody," 116 (cit. n. 8). *Mossel'prom* was an abbreviation for the Moscow Regional Association of Agricultural Enterprises of the Food Industry.

40 L. N. Mazur, "Istoriia rannesovetskoi sem'i: problemy tipologii" (History of early-Soviet family: typology issues), *Dokument. Arkhiv. Istoriia. Sovremennost'*, 15 (Ekaterinburg, 2015): 115–25.

41 E. M. Bykovskie, *Kartonazhnye igrushki svoimi rukami* (Handmade cardboard toys). Edited by N. Bartram (Moscow–Leningrad, 1927), 76–9.

42 Heinimaa et al., *Sankarilliset lelut*, 22 (cit. n. 10).

43 For reflections on the use of dolls as substitute objects in archaic cultures, see I. A. Morozov, *Fenomen kukly v traditsionnoi i sovremennoi kul'ture. Krosskul'turnoe issledovanie ideologii antropomorfizma* (Phenomenon of the doll in traditional and modern culture. A cross-cultural study of the anthropomorphism ideology) (Moscow, 2011), 86–96.

44 A. B. Zalkind, *Pedologiia v SSSR* (Pedology in the USSR) (Moscow, 1929), 5.

45 N. A. Rybnikov, "Ideologiia sovremennogo shkol'nika" (The ideology of a modern schoolchild), *Pedologiia*, 1 (1928): 150–8.

46 Yu. G. Salova, *"Novyi chelovek": vzgliad na problemu v 1920-e gody* ("The new man": a take on the issue in the 1920s) (Iaroslavl', 1998), 37–8.

47 A. B. Zalkind, "Osnovy piatiletnego plana po nauchno-issledovatel'skoi pedologicheskoi rabote" (Foundations of the five-year plan for pedological research), *Pedologiia*, 3 (1929): 273–314, on 281–2, 284.

48 For a more general relation of the Soviet ethnic policies and the notions of the "new man," see Stanislav Petrashin's chapter in the present volume.

49 L. Vorontsova, "Sovetskaia kukla" (The Soviet doll), *Sovetskoe iskusstvo*, January 8, 1939, 3.

50 *Ob uchebnykh posobiiakh, uchebnom oborudovanii i o sovetskoi igrushke. Postanovleniia Kollegii NKP RSFSR ot 13–14 iiulia 1931 g.* (About learning aids, educational toolkit and the Soviet toy. Resolutions of the Board of the RSFSR People's Commissariat of Enlightenment of July 13–14, 1931) (Moscow–Leningrad, 1931), 11–12.

51 V. N. Shul'gin, *Deti i Oktiabr'skaia revoliutsiia. Ideologiia sovetskogo shkol'nika* (Children and the October Revolution. The ideology of the Soviet schoolchild) (Moscow, 1928), 3.

52 "Ot redaktsii" (Editorial), in *Sovetskaia igrushka: Sbornik*, vol. 1 (Moscow, 1931), 3–5; on 4.

53 E. A. Flerina, "Igrushka kak ona est'" (The toy as it is), in ibid., 8–14. All subsequent quotations are from this source.

54 I. I. Vasilevskii, "Igrushechnyi promysel v sisteme promkooperatsii" (The toy industry in the system of industrial cooperation), in ibid., 34.

55 "Revoliutsiia trebuet novykh igrushek (Iz itogov obsledovaniia igrushechnoi promyshlennosti brigadoi TsK VLKSM)" (The revolution demands new toys [Some findings of the toy industry survey by a Komsomol Central Committee taskforce]), in ibid., 54.

56 A. P. Babushkin, "Eklektika i reaktsionnaia kleveta na sovetskogo rebenka i podrostka. «O psikhologii rebenka i podrostka» A. A. Smirnova" (Eclecticism and reactionary slander against the Soviet child and teenager. "On child and teenage psychology" by A. A. Smirnov), *Pedologiia*, 1–2 (1932): 40.

57 Ibid., 36.

58 Ibid., 41.

59 L. N. Kurlova and F. S. Litvin, *Igra s kukloi* (Doll playing) (Sverdlovsk, 1936), 4.

60 Kornilov, "K psikhologii detskoi igry v kukly," 45 (cit. n. 24).

61 Kurlova and Litvin, *Igra s kukloi*, 3 (cit. n. 59).
62 For details, see Andy Byford, "Zagrobnaia zhizn 'nauki' pedologii: k voprosu o znachenii 'nauchnyh dvizhenii' (i ikh istorii) dlia sovremennoi pedagogiki" (The afterlife of the "science" of pedology: on the significance of scientific movements [and their history] for contemporary pedagogy), *Prepodavatel' XXI vek*, 1 (2013): 43–54, on 47–9.
63 *Preiskurant otpusknykh tsen na igrushki sistemy promkooperatsii, kooperatsii invalidov i razlichnyh obschestvennyh organizatsii Moskovskoi oblasti s 1-go iiulia 1937 goda* (Price list of producer prices for toys in the system of industrial cooperatives, disabled persons cooperatives, and various social organizations of the Moscow Region since July 1, 1937) (Moscow, 1937), 3.
64 The State Archive of the Russian Federation (Gosudarstvennyi arkhiv Rossiiskoi Federatsii—GARF), fond A-312, opis' 1, delo 452; and F. E. Maizler, *Pamiatka prodavtsu igrushek* (Short instructions for toy seller) (Moscow, 1937).
65 Stalin made this declaration at the First All-Union Conference of Stakhanovite Workers on November 17, 1935.
66 Kostiukhina, *Zapiski kukly*, 225 (cit. n. 11).
67 These power practices of controlling and standardizing corporeality are brought to light in classic studies by Michel Foucault, Jean Baudrillard, and Bryan Turner.
68 Tricia Starks, *The Body Soviet: Propaganda, Hygiene, and the Revolutionary State* (Madison, 2008), 313.
69 "Igrushki khoroshego kachestva" (Quality toys), *Sovetskaia igrushka*, 12 (1936): 10–12.
70 Vorontsova, "Sovetskaia kukla" (cit. n. 49).
71 *Ob uchebnykh posobiiakh, uchebnom oborudovanii i o sovetskoi igrushke* (cit. n. 50), 22.
72 Zinbakh, "Razve zaitsy nosiat plat'e?" (Do hares really wear dress?), *Pionerskaia pravda* (April 1, 1933): 3.
73 Suvorov, "Vmesto mekkano... banki dlia gutalina," (cit. n. 35).
74 "Revoliutsiia trebuet novykh igrushek" (cit. n. 55).
75 For details, see Starks, *The Body Soviet* (cit. n. 68).
76 See I. Beletskii, "O kukol'noi dramaturgii" (About puppet dramatic arts), *Detskaia Literatura*, 5 (1938): 41–3.
77 M. Moskovtsev, "Pochetnyi dolg igrushechnikov" (Toy-makers' honor duty), *Igrushka*, 2 (1938): 11.
78 This situation resembled the state of affairs in the doll market in Germany during the First World War or in the United States during the Second World War, when the escalating demand for "militarized" dolls initially had to be satisfied by industrial-scale re-clothing of "peacetime dolls." See Heike Hoffmann, "Schwarzer Peter im Weltkrieg. Die deutsche Spielwarenindustrie 1914–1918," in *Kriegserfahrungen. Studien zur Sozial- und Mentalitätsgeschichte des Ersten Weltkriegs*, eds. Gerhard Hirschfeld et al. (Essen, 1997), 323–35; and Peers, "Doll Culture," 29 (cit. n. 15).
79 E. Flerina, "Nuzhen reshitel'nyi sdvig" (A decisive shift is needed), *Igrushka*, 3 (1938): 6–7.
80 Kurlova and Litvin, *Igra s kukloi*, 37 (cit. n. 59).
81 Ibid., 47.
82 Ibid., 29–30.
83 A. Davydova, "Pogranichniki" (Border guards), *Igrushka*, 2 (1938): 12–13.
84 N. Panova, "Voennye igry oktiabriat" (Military games of the Little Octobrists), *Igrushka*, 11–12 (1939): 20.
85 Davydova, "Pogranichniki," 13 (cit. n. 83).

86 See, Peers, *Doll Culture*, 36 (cit. n. 15).
87 Zalkind, "Osnovy piatiletnego plana po nauchno-issledovatel'skoi pedologicheskoi rabote," 285 (cit. n. 47).

Chapter 4

1 For a detailed analysis of the essay, see Natal'ia Kornienko, "Chevengurskie mechtaniia o 'novom cheloveke' v stat'iakh Platonova 1920-kh gg." (The Chevengur dreams about the "new man" in Platonov's essays of the 1920s), in *"Strana Filosofov" Andreia Platonova: Problemy tvorchestva* ("The Philosophers' Country" of Andrei Platonov), vol. 6 (Moscow, 2005), 483–519. The parallel texts of the original essay, titled "*Pitomnik novogo cheloveka*" (The breeding pen of the new man), and its final, revised version, titled "*Chelovek, kotoryi budet*" (The man that will be), appear on 505–15. All the subsequent quotations from the essay are from this source.
2 Emphasis added. A standard English translation of the word *pitomnik* is nursery, and the title of Platonov's essay is usually translated as "Nursery of the New Man." See, for instance, Nariman Skakov, "Soul Incorporated," *Slavic Review*, 73, no. 4 (2014): 772–800, on 790. However, *nursery* somewhat inadequately represents the meaning of the Russian word, which has a much narrower meaning, denoting *exclusively* a place where one breeds and/or propagates particular species and varieties of animals and plants, such as a dog kennel, a fish hatchery, a cattery, an alligator farm, or a potting shed. Its use at the time was confined almost exclusively to agricultural literature. It is completely devoid of the typical reference to child-rearing and childcare characteristic of the English word "nursery." It also lacks the connotations typical of the word "nursing," though it does resonate strongly with the meanings of the word "nurturing"; indeed its root "*pitanie*" means food or feeding.
3 The literature on the history of interactions between science and religion is enormous. Useful introductions to the subject can be found in Gary B. Ferngren, ed., *Science and Religion: A Historical Introduction* (Baltimore, 2002); Richard G. Olson, *Science and Religion, 1450–1900. From Copernicus to Darwin* (Baltimore, 2004); and Peter Harrison, ed., *The Cambridge Companion to Science and Religion* (New York, 2010).
4 Of course, what exactly constituted the study of life, and hence what word "biology" actually signified, varied considerably in different settings. In English, arguably, the most comprehensive concurrent discussion of the subject could be found in Herbert Spencer, *The Principles of Biology*, 2 vols. (London, 1864–7).
5 Charles Lyell, *Principles of Geology: Being an Attempt to Explain the Former Changes of the Earth's Surface, by Reference to Causes Now in Operation*, 3 vols. (London, 1830–33). Lyell was certainly not alone in advancing the new geology during the first half of the nineteenth century. For a good introduction to the history of geology, see Gabriel Gohau, *A History of Geology* (New Brunswick, 1990).
6 Lyell elaborated this framework of causal uniformity in the past and present geological changes to challenge the view of the Earth geological history as the result of unique catastrophic events. For a detailed analysis of the debate between the proponents of catastrophism and uniformitarianism, see Chapters 10–12 in Gohau, *A History of Geology*, 125–58 (cit. n. 5).
7 Charles Darwin, *On the Origin of Species by Means of Natural Selection, Or the Preservation of Favoured Races in the Struggle for Life* (London, 1859), 488.

8 See, for instance, Charles Lyell, *Geological Evidences of the Antiquity of Man* (London, 1863); Matthias J. Schleiden, *Das Alter des Menschengeschlechts* (Leipzig, 1863); and Carl Vogt, *Vorlesungen über den Menschen, seine Stellung in der Schöpfung und in der Geschichte der Erde* (Giessen, 1863).

9 See T. H. Huxley, *Evidence as to Man's Place in Nature* (London, 1863).

10 See Maximien Rey, *Dégénération de l'espèce humaine et sa régénération* (Paris, 1863); Francis Galton, "Hereditary Talent and Character," *Macmillan's Magazine*, 12 (1865): 157–66; 318–27; V. M. Florinskii, "Usovershenstvovanie i vyrozhdenie chelovecheskogo roda," (The perfection and degeneration of mankind) *Russkoe slovo*, 8 (1865): 1–57; 10: 1–43; 11: 1–25; 12: 27–43; and Eduard Reich, *Ueber die Entartung der Menschen, ihre Ursachen und Verhütung* (Erlangen, 1868).

11 For details, see Nikolai Krementsov, *With and Without Galton: Vasilii Florinskii and the Fate of Eugenics in Russia* (Oxford, 2018).

12 For a useful overview, see Joseph Carroll, *Literary Darwinism: Evolution, Human Nature, and Literature* (New York, 2004).

13 See Roslynn D. Haynes, *H. G. Wells: Discoverer of the Future. The Influence of Science on His Thought* (London, 1980).

14 For details, see the introduction to this volume.

15 See V. V. Bitner, *Otkuda, kto i kuda my?* in idem, *Na rubezhe stoletii: obzor glavneishikh nauchnykh i kul'turnykh priobretenii XIX veka*, vol. 2 (St. Petersburg, 1903).

16 K. S. Merezhkovskii, *Rai zemnoi ili Son v zimniuiu noch'. Skazka-utopiia XXVII veka* (Berlin, 1903). For a detailed analysis of the novel and its contexts, see Ricardo Nicolosi, *Degeneration erzählen: Literatur und Psychiatrie im Russland der 1880er und 1890er Jahre* (Paderborn, 2017).

17 See V. M. Shimkevich, *Budushchee chelovechestva s tochki zreniia naturalista* (St. Petersburg-Moscow, 1906).

18 See a pioneering study of such visions of the life sciences and their practitioners in Philip J. Pauly, *Controlling Life: Jacques Loeb and the Engineering Ideal in Biology* (New York, 1987).

19 M. M. Zavadovskii, *Pol i razvitie ego priznakov* (Sex and the development of its characteristics) (Moscow, 1922), 235.

20 See his groundbreaking analysis in Mark B. Adams, "Last Judgment: The Visionary Biology of J. B. S. Haldane," *Journal of the History of Biology*, 33 (2000): 457–91.

21 I. I. Mechnikov, *Etiudy o prirode cheloveka* (Moscow, 1961), 236. I use here the "academic" Russian edition based on a careful comparison of the Essays' manuscript and published versions prepared by A. E. Gaisinovich.

22 Ibid, 245.

23 I. P. Pavlov, "Nobelevskaia rech'," in idem, *Polnoe sobranie sochinenii*, vol. 2, part 2 (Leningrad, 1951), 347–60, on 360.

24 Literature on the history of eugenics is huge. For a recent voluminous overview, see Alison Bashford and Philippa Levine, eds., *The Oxford Handbook on the History of Eugenics* (New York, 2010). For a detailed analysis of the history of eugenics in Russia, along with the overview of relevant secondary literature, see Krementsov, *With and Without Galton* (cit. n.11).

25 That is how the essence of eugenics was defined at the Second International Eugenics Congress held in 1921 in New York City, see Harry H. Laughlin, *The Second International Exhibition of Eugenics* (Baltimore, 1923), 15.

26 V. Slepkov, *Evgenika. Uluchshenie chelovecheskoi prirody* (Moscow, 1927).

27 For a short, but insightful, overview, see Mark B. Adams, "The Quest for Immortality: Visions and Presentiments in Science and Literature," in *The Fountain of Youth: Cultural, Scientific, and Ethical Perspectives on a Biomedical Goal*, eds. Stephen G. Post and Robert H. Binstock (New York, 2004), 38–71.

28 It is a well-known fact that Aldous was thinking of following in the footsteps of his illustrious grandfather and only problems with his eyesight prevented him from becoming a physician or a biologist. For detailed accounts of his life and works, see Sybille Bedford, *Aldous Huxley: A Biography* (Chicago, 2002) and Nicholas Murray, *Aldous Huxley* (London, 2003).

29 There are literally hundreds of publications, from short articles to massive volumes, that have examined the novel from every possible perspective. See, for example, Peter Edgerly Firchow, *The End of Utopia: A Study of Aldous Huxley's Brave New World* (Lewisburg, PA, 1984); Raychel H. Reiff, *Aldous Huxley: Brave New World* (New York, 2010); John S. Feinberg and Paul D. Feinberg, *Ethics for a Brave New World, Updated and Expanded* (Wheaton, IL, 2010); Jonathan Greenberg and Nathan Waddell, eds., *"Brave New World": Contexts and Legacies* (London, 2016).

30 For more details on "scientific foundations" of *Brave New World*, see I. V. Golovacheva, *Nauka i literatura: Arkheologiia nauchnogo znaniia Oldosa Khaksli* (Science and literature: The archeology of Aldous Huxley's scientific knowledge) (St. Petersburg, 2008); and idem, *Putevoditel' po "Divnomu novomu miru" i vokrug* (A guide to "Brave New World" and its surroundings) (Moscow, 2017).

31 See H. G. Wells, Julian Huxley, and G. P. Wells, *The Science of Life*, 3 vols. (London, 1929). Some subsequent editions came out in two-volume and even single-volume formats.

32 Julian Huxley, *Memories*, vol. 1 (London, 1970), 155–6.

33 Ibid., 160.

34 J. B. S. Haldane, *Daedalus, or Science and the Future: A Paper Read to the Heretics, Cambridge on February 4th, 1923* (London, 1923). The subsequent quotations are from this source. For a detailed analysis of the series, see Max Saunders, *Imagined Futures. Writing, Science, and Modernity in the To-Day and To-Morrow Book Series, 1923-31* (Oxford, 2019).

35 On the essay's profound impact on contemporary thought, see Krishna R. Dronamraju, ed., *Haldane's Daedalus Revisited* (New York, 1995).

36 Bertrand Russell, *Icarus, or the Future of Science* (London, 1924). On the Haldane-Russell exchange and its impact on British scientists and writers, see Adams, "Last Judgment" (cit. n. 20); and Charles T. Rubin, "Daedalus and Icarus Revisited," *The New Atlantis: The Journal of Technology and Society*, 8 (2005): 73–91.

37 J. B. S. Haldane, "The Last Judgment," *Harper's Magazine*, 154 (1926–7): 413–20; and in idem, *Possible Worlds and Other Essays* (London, 1927), 287–312. For a detailed analysis of the essay, see Adams, "Last Judgment," (cit. n. 20). For a different interpretation of the relationship between Huxley's and Haldane's ideas, see Saunders, *Imagined Futures*, 309–13 (cit. n. 34).

38 See Julian Huxley, "The Tissue-Culture King," *Yale Review*, 15 (1926): 487–504; and "The Tissue-Culture King: A Biological Fantasy," *Cornhill Magazine*, 60 (1926): 422–57.

39 Aldous Huxley, "Foreword," in idem, *Brave New World* (London, 1956), 10. (The Vanguard Library edition).

40 Teo Eli (F. N. Il'in), *Dolina novoi zhizni* (Moscow, 1928). All subsequent quotations are from this edition.

41 The penname was actually a Latinized and abbreviated name of the author, Fedor (Theodor) and Il'in (the son of Elie). For more details on the novel and its author, see Nikolai Krementsov, "Thought Transfer and Mind Control between Science and Fiction: Fedor Il'in's 'The Valley of New Life' (1928)," *Osiris*, 34 (2019): 36–54.

42 Undoubtedly, the "prototype" for the Petrvoskii character was Il'ia Ivanov, a pioneer in artificial insemination and its uses for interspecies hybridization. On Ivanov and his research, see Kirill Rossiianov, "Beyond Species: Il'ya Ivanov and His Experiments on Cross-Breeding Humans with Anthropoid Apes," *Science in Context*, 15 (2002): 277–316; and Nikolai Krementsov, "From a 'prominent biologist' to a 'Red Frankenstein': Il'ia Ivanov in Soviet and Post-Soviet Biographies," in *What Is Soviet Now? Identities, Legacies, Memories*, eds. Thomas Lahusen and Peter H. Solomon Jr. (Berlin, 2008), 120–32.

43 Eli, *Dolina novoi zhizni*, 33 (cit. n. 40).

44 Aldous Huxley, *Brave New World* (London, 1956), 187, 189.

45 For details on such transformation of scientific knowledge into a cultural resource, see Nikolai Krementsov, *Revolutionary Experiments: The Quest for Immortality in Bolshevik Science and Fiction* (New York, 2014).

46 The subgenre of popular-science writing has generated lively debates on its origins, purposes, and permutations among historians of science. For illuminating discussions of "popular science" in Western contexts, see, for instance, Stephen Hilgartner, "The Dominant View of Popularization: Conceptual Problems, Political Uses," *Social Studies of Science*, 20 (1990): 519–39; Roger Cooter and Stephen Pumfrey, "Separate Spheres and Public Places: Reflections on the History of Science Popularization and Science in Popular Culture," *History of Science*, 32 (1994): 237–67; and five contributions to the special "Focus" section on "Historicizing 'Popular Science'," *Isis*, 100 (2009): 310–68.

47 For a further elaboration of the notion of science as a cultural resource, see Krementsov, "Thought Transfer and Mind Control" (cit. n. 41).

48 As is the case with popular science, the genre's origins and permutations remain the subject of debates that show no sign of abating; compare, for instance, Edward James and Farah Mendlesohn, eds., *The Cambridge Companion to Science Fiction* (New York, 2003); Mark Bould and Sherryl Vint, *The Routledge Concise History of Science Fiction* (London, 2011); and Adam Roberts, *The History of Science Fiction* (Basingstoke, 2016). See also Matthias Schwartz's chapter in the present volume.

49 For instance, a few such "subspecies" could be found in a voluminous 1928 collection with the characteristic title *Life and Technology of the Future*, see Ark. A-n and E. Kol'man, eds., *Zhizn' i tekhnika budushchego* (Moscow–Leningrad, 1928).

50 See, for instance, the analyses of the uses of existing blood transfusion technologies in Bogdanov's writings in Nikolai Krementsov, *A Martian Stranded on Earth: Alexander Bogdanov, Blood Transfusions, and Proletarian Science* (Chicago, 2011); and of imaginary "mind control" technologies, based on extensive contemporary experimental studies of telepathy, in the writings of several Soviet writers in idem, "Thought Transfer and Mind Control" (cit. n. 41).

51 Indeed, these processes were not confined to the first third of the twentieth century or to the "new man" visions. The same processes could be seen unfolding in historical and contemporary debates over many "hot" bio-psycho-medical subjects, ranging from race and emerging epidemic diseases, like AIDS and Covid-19, to artificial intelligence and genetic engineering.

52 This neglect is particularly pronounced in Russian cultural studies. To give just one example, a very detailed and insightful typology of various personages in Mikhail

Bulgakov's writings does not include Professors Persikov and Preobrazhenskii, the lead protagonists of the writer's famous novellas, "Fateful Eggs" and "Dog's Heart." See E. A. Iablokov, *Khudozhestvennyi mir Mikhaila Bulgakova* (The artistic world of Mikhail Bulgakov) (Moscow, 2001), 260–307.

53 One of the forefathers of biology, leading eighteenth-century French naturalist George Buffon has asserted forcefully more than two centuries ago that "we know nothing except by comparison." Cited from James Smith Barr, ed., *Buffon's Natural History*, vol. X (London, 1807), 30.

54 Kornienko, "Chevengurskie mechtaniia," 509 (cit. n. 1). This formulation appears in the essay's second version.

55 For a detailed analysis of ideas about "international" science and their evolution from the late nineteenth through the mid-twentieth centuries, see Nikolai Krementsov, *International Science between the World Wars: The Case of Genetics* (London, 2005).

56 See D. B. Kholden and Bertran Ressel', *Dedal i Ikar (Budushchee nauki)* (Leningrad-Moscow, 1926).

57 See, for example, David N. Livingstone, *Putting Science in Its Place: Geographies of Scientific Knowledge* (Chicago, 2004); and Kapil Raj, *Relocating Modern Science: Circulation and the Construction of Knowledge in South Asia and Europe, 1650–1900* (Basingstoke, 2007).

58 Detailed analyses of such changes, their sources, mechanisms, and consequences, see in Nikolai Krementsov, *Stalinist Science* (Princeton, NJ, 1997); idem, "Big Revolution, Little Revolution: Science and Politics in Bolshevik Russia," *Social Research*, 73 (2006): 1173–204; idem, *A Martian Stranded on Earth* (cit. n. 50); and Evgeniia Dolgova, *Rozhdenie sovetskoi nauki: uchenye v 1920-1930-e gg.* (The birth of soviet science: Scientists in the 1920s-1930s) (Moscow, 2020).

59 See Nikolai Krementsov, "Marxism, Darwinism, and Genetics in the Soviet Union," in *Biology and Ideology: From Descartes to Dawkins*, eds. Denis Alexander and Ron Numbers (Chicago, 2010), 215–46.

60 On the Bolsheviks' efforts in fulfilling their promises to the peasantry, see Olga Elina's chapter in the present volume.

61 Richard Stites, *Revolutionary Dreams: Utopian Vision and Experimental Life in the Russian Revolution* (Oxford, 1989). For various original pronouncements on the subject by leading Bolshevik figures, see a two-volume collection by William G. Rosenberg, ed., *Bolshevik Visions*, 2 vols. (Ann Arbor, MI, 1990).

62 See, for instance, John C. O'Brien, "The Instauration of the New Man of Marxism: A Critique," *International Journal of Social Economics*, 14 (1987): 22–33; and idem, "Marxism and the Instauration of Man," ibid., 19 (1992): 107–26.

63 See Krementsov, *A Martian Stranded on Earth* (cit. n. 50) and Michael Coates's chapter in the present volume.

64 L. Trotskii, *Literatura i revoliutsiia* (Literature and revolution) (Moscow, 1923), 195–7. There is no doubt that Trotsky's use of the word *sverkhchelovek* was a reference to Friedrich Nietzsche's *Übermensch*. Nietzsche's ideas were highly influential among Russian intellectuals, including Marxists. See Bernice G. Rosental, ed., *Nietzsche in Russia* (Princeton, NJ, 1986).

65 N. Semashko, "O biologicheskom podkhode k postanovke polovogo vospitaniia" (On a biological approach to the organization of sexual upbringing), *Zvezda*, 5 (1924): 150–3, on 150.

66 For an example of these processes, see a detailed analysis of the development of Soviet endocrinology, in Nikolai Krementsov, “Hormones and the Bolsheviks: From Organotherapy to Experimental Endocrinology, 1918–1929,” *Isis*, 99 (2008): 486–518.

67 According to far from complete contemporary data, only from November 1917 to October 1924, the number of popular-science books and pamphlets on biological issues (excluding medicine/public health, education, and agriculture) grew 30-fold and reached 240 separate titles annually. By the end of October 1924, the total number of such publications reached 642, with a median print run of 3,000 copies each. Considering that during the civil war of 1918–21, publishing industry was at a virtual standstill, these numbers indeed are very telling. The number of similar publications in the daily press, popular magazines, and journals is impossible to estimate, but nearly all such periodicals, including the Bolsheviks’ major mouthpieces, *Pravda* and *Izvestiia*, carried such articles on a regular basis. For details, see Krementsov, *Revolutionary Experiments* (cit. n. 45).

68 For a detailed analysis of Russian pedology, see Andy Byford, *Science of the Child in Late Imperial and Early Soviet Russia* (New York, 2020). For an example of how this new discipline contributed to the “new man” visions embedded in children’s dolls, see Olga Ilyukha’s chapter in this volume.

69 For an overview of the history of psychotechnology in Russia, see V. I. Oleshkevich, *Istoriia psikhotekhniki* (Moscow, 2002); for the discipline’s cultural impact, see Margarete Vöhringer, *Avantgarde und Psychotechnik. Wissenschaft, Kunst und Technik der Wahrnehmungsexperimente in der frühen Sowjetunion* (Göttingen, 2007).

70 See Iu. P. Frolov, *Uchenie ob usluvnykh refleksakh, kak osnova pedagogiki* (Moscow, 1928), and I. A. Ariamov, *Refleksologiia i pedagogika* (Moscow, 1930), 6th ed. See also Lyubov Bugaeva’s chapter in the present volume.

71 John Watson, *Behaviorism* (London, 1930), 82.

72 See, for instance, Thomas Tetzner, *Der kollektive Gott: Zur Ideengeschichte des «Neuen Menschen» in Russland* (Göttingen, 2013); and the introduction to the present volume.

73 As another example, one can mention a short story by Ilya Ehrenburg, titled “Uskomchel.” The story’s title is an abbreviation of a phrase, “Improved communist man” (*Usovershenstvovannyi kommunisticheskii chelovek—Us-kom-chel*). It was published in Berlin in 1922, but forbidden for publication in Soviet Russia, according to some evidence, by Joseph Stalin personally. For an analysis of Bulgakov’s novella, see Irina Golovacheva’s chapter in the present volume.

74 Eli, *Dolina novoi zhizni*, 63 (cit. n. 40).

75 Ibid.

76 For a recent overview of this revolution, see Faramerz Dabhoiwala, *The Origins of Sex: A History of the First Sexual Revolution* (Oxford, 2012); for the particularities of the Russian case, see Eric Naiman, *Sex in Public: The Incarnation of Soviet Ideology* (Princeton, NJ, 1997); and Gregory Carleton, *Sexual Revolution in Bolshevik Russia* (Pittsburgh, PA, 2005). For detailed analyses of the influence of Freudian theories in Russian and Soviet cultures, see Alexander Etkind, *Eros of the Impossible. The History of Psychoanalysis in Russia* (Boulder, CO, 1997); and Martin A. Miller, *Freud and the Bolsheviks: Psychoanalysis in Imperial Russia and the Soviet Union* (New Haven and London, 1998). On the particularities of Soviet sexology, see Susan G. Solomon, “Soviet Social Hygienists and Sexology after the Revolution: Dynamics of ‘Capture’ at Home and Abroad,” *Ab Imperio*, 4 (2014): 107–35; and Brian J. Baer, “Translating Sexology in Late-Tsarist and Early Soviet Russia: Politics, Literature, and the Science

of Sex," in *Sexology and Translation: Cultural and Scientific Encounters across the Modern World*, ed. Heike Bauer (Philadelphia, 2015): 115–34.

77 See Susan E. Lederer, *Frankenstein: Penetrating the Secrets of Nature* (New Brunswick, NJ, 2002). It is worth noting that in Russia Shelly's novel was little known and, hence, its protagonists did not become as important icons of the cultural resource described by the phrase "new man," as in the United States or Britain, until the last third of the twentieth century. For detailed analyses of the image of "evil" or "mad" scientist in Western cultures, see Roslynn D. Haynes, *From Faust to Strangelove: Representations of the Scientist in Western Literature* (Baltimore, 1994); idem, *From Madman to Crime Fighter: The Scientist in Western Culture* (Baltimore, 2017); and Christopher Frayling, *Mad, Bad and Dangerous?: The Scientist and the Cinema* (London, 2006). See also Irina Golovacheva's chapter in this volume.

78 For details, see Nikolai Krementsov, "Off with Your Heads: Isolated Organs in Early Soviet Science and Fiction," *Studies in History and Philosophy of Biological and Biomedical Sciences*, 40 (2009): 87–100.

79 See Robert C. Tucker, *Stalin in Power: The Revolution from Above, 1928–1941* (New York, 1990).

80 The full text of the novel would appear in print only in the 1970s, while the majority of Platonov's writings would remain unpublished until the dissolution of the Soviet Union.

81 Indeed, in the 1930s all discussions of eugenics were reduced to its condemnations as a "bourgeois" and "fascist" science, while projects to create a "proletarian" eugenics, so popular during the 1920s, were abandoned. For details, see Krementsov, *With and Without Galton* (cit. n. 11).

82 See Nikolai Krementsov, "Eugenics, Rassenhygiene, and Human Genetics in the late 1930s: The Case of the Seventh International Genetics Congress," in *Doing Medicine Together: Germany and Russia between the Wars*, ed. Susan G. Solomon (Toronto, 2006), 369–404.

83 See "Mysli Marksa i Lenina ob obshchestvennom razdelenii truda i 'novom cheloveke,'" *Revoliutsiia i kul'tura*, 8–10 (1929): 121–4.

84 V. I. Kremianskii, "Perekhod ot vedushchei roli estestvennogo otbora k vedushchei roli truda," *Uspekhi sovremennoi biologii*, 14, no. 2 (1941): 356–71. For details, see Krementsov, *With and Without Galton* (cit. n. 11).

85 See, for instance, A. Lunacharskii, *Vospitanie novogo cheloveka* (The upbringing of the new man) (Leningrad, 1928), or the contributions to a long debate published weekly over the course of six months in the newspaper *Komsomol Truth* under the general headlines "Who is the builder of socialism?" and "What man do we need?" See *Komsomol'skaia pravda*, 1928, June 24 to December 4.

86 On the origins and uses of the phrase "engineers of human souls," see O. Ronen, "'Inzhenery chelovecheskikh dush': K istorii izrecheniia" (Engineers of human souls: Towards a history of the phrase), *Lotmanovskii sbornik*, 2 (1997): 393–400.

87 Partially this process is examined in Krementsov, *With and Without Galton* (cit. n. 11).

Chapter 5

1 H. G. Wells, *Russia in the Shadows* (New York, 1921), 57.

2 H. G. Wells, "It Seems to me That I Am More to the Left Than You, Mr. Stalin," *New Statesman and Nation*, October 27, 1934. https://www.newstatesman.com/politics/20

14/04/h-g-wells-it-seems-me-i-am-more-left-you-mr-stalin (accessed on September 15, 2019); on the aftereffects of the interview, see Matthew Taunton, "Russia and the British Intellectuals. The Significance of 'The Stalin-Wells Talk'," *Russia in Britain, 1880–1940: From Melodrama to Modernism,* eds. Rebecca Beasley and Philip Ross Bullock (Oxford, 2013), 209–24.

3 Halina Stephan, "Aleksei Tolstoi's Aelita and the Inauguration of Soviet Science Fiction," *Canadian American Slavic Studies,* 18 (1984): 63–75.

4 N. A. Rynin, *Mezhplanetnye soobshcheniia,* t. 1, no. 1–3; t. 2, no. 4–6, t. 3, no. 7–9 (Leningrad, 1928–32). Because of their pioneering role the volumes were translated into English in 1970 and 1971 by the Israel Program for Scientific Translations; see N. A. Rynin, *Interplanetary Flight and Communication* (vol. 1, no. 1—vol. 3, no. 9) (Jerusalem, 1970–1).

5 Grigorii Mishkevich, *Doktor zanimatel'nykh nauk. Zhizn' i tvorchestvo Iakova Isidorovicha Perel'mana* (Moscow, 1986), 114–21; Iurii Kovalev, "Uells v Peterburge i Leningrade," *Vtorzhenie v Persei,* eds. E. Brandis and Vl. Dmitrevskii (Leningrad, 1968), 415–34.

6 Boris Liapunov, *V mire fantastiki. Obzor nauchno-fantasticheskoi i fantasticheskoi literatury,* 2nd ed. (Moscow, 1975), 51.

7 Grigorii Mishkevich, "Vstrecha v 'Astorii'," *Ural'skii sledopyt,* 7 (1962): 36–9; idem, "Tri chasa u velikogo fantasta," in *Vtorzhenie v Persei,* eds. Brandis and Dmitrevskii, 345–442.

8 Ibid., 441.

9 Mishkevich, for example, quotes Wells with praise for having read Perelman's *Entertaining Physics* (1913) and Beliaev's novels *Professor Dowell's Head* (story 1924–5, novel 1937) and *The Amphibian Man* (1928) with pleasure, although none of the books were translated into English at the time and Beliaev did not rewrite the short story *Professor Dowell's Head* into a novel until 1937. See ibid.; Mishkevich, "Vstrecha v 'Astorii'," (cit. n. 7).

10 When Wells was there for the first time in January 1914, the city was still called St. Petersburg; on his second visit it was already called Petrograd, before it was renamed Leningrad after Lenin's death in 1924.

11 Wells, *Russia in the Shadows,* 64 (cit. n. 1).

12 Ibid., 54.

13 Ibid., 163.

14 Ibid., 162. Italics in the original.

15 *The Science of Life. A Summary of Contemporary Knowledge about Life and Its Possibilities* was a popular-scientific work Wells wrote together with Julian Huxley and his son George Philip, which was first published in a serialized way from 1929 to 1930.

16 Wells, *Russia in the Shadows,* 57 (cit. n. 1).

17 See, for example, Richard Stites, *Revolutionary Dreams: Utopian Vision and Experimental Life in the Russian Revolution* (New York, 1989); John E. Bowlt and Olga Matich, eds., *Laboratory of Dreams: The Russian Avant-Garde and Cultural Experiment* (Stanford, 1990); Margarete Vöhringer, *Avantgarde und Psychotechnik. Wissenschaft, Kunst und Technik der Wahrnehmungsexperimente in der frühen Sowjetunion* (Göttingen, 2007).

18 Boris Groys and Michael Hagemeister, eds., *Die Neue Menschheit. Biopolitische Utopien in Russland zu Beginn des 20. Jahrhunderts* (Frankfurt am Main, 2005).

19 Igor J. Polianski, "Das Unbehagen der Natur. Sowjetische Populärwissenschaft als semiotische Lektüre," in *Laien, Lektüren, Laboratorien. Kunste und Wissenschaften*

in Russland 1860–1960, eds. Matthias Schwartz, Wladimir Velminski, and Torben Philipp (Frankfurt a. M., 2008), 71–113. For a more differentiated picture of the later period, see Nikolai Krementsov, *Stalinist Science* (Princeton, NJ, 1997), Alexei Kojevnikov, "Games of Stalinist Democracy. Ideological Discussions in Soviet Sciences, 1947–52," in *Stalinism. New Directions*, ed. Sheila Fitzpatrick (London, 2000), 142–75; Daniel Beer, *Renovating Russia. The Human Sciences and the Fate of Liberal Modernity, 1880–1930* (Ithaca, 2008).

20 Nikolai Krementsov, *Revolutionary Experiments: The Quest for Immortality in Bolshevik Science and Fiction* (Oxford, 2014), 8.

21 H. G. Wells, *The Shape of Things to Come: The Ultimate Revolution* (1933) (London, 1935). The novel is written in the form of a history book from the year 2106; ibid., *Things to Come. A Film Treatment* (London, 1935). http://leonscripts.tripod.com/scripts/THINGSTOCOME.htm (accessed on September 15, 2019).

22 Geoffrey O'Brien, "*Things to Come*: Whither Mankind?," *The Criterion Collection*, June 20, 2013. https://www.criterion.com/current/posts/2812-things-to-come-whither-mankind (accessed on September 15, 2019).

23 H. G. Wells, *Anticipations of the Reaction of Mechanical and Scientific Progress upon Human Life and Thought* (London, 1901, 1902). In *Mankind in the Making* (1903) and the novel *A Modern Utopia* (1903), Wells continued these reflections on the future of humanity.

24 H. G. Wells, *The Open Conspiracy. Blue Prints for a World Revolution* (New York, 1928). The book was revised and republished under different titles between 1930 and 1933 several times, before the final version was issued in 1933 under the original title. See also: Richard Nate, "Scientific Utopianism in Francis Bacon and H. G. Wells. From Salomon's House to the Open Conspiracy," *Critical Review of International Social and Political Philosophy*, 3, nos. 2–3 (2000): 172–88.

25 Wells, *Anticipations*, 279–318 (cit. n. 23). Although Wells later distanced himself from this eugenic vision of the New Man, the question of how a new, better humanity could emerge continued to occupy him from then on and also reappears in his film script for *Things to Come*. On Wells's ambivalent views, see Philip Coupland, "H. G. Wells' Liberal Fascism," *Journal of Contemporary History*, 35, no. 4 (2000): 541–58.

26 Wells, *Things to Come* (cit. n. 22).

27 Ibid.

28 Thus, on the surface the Progress Party wins with its moon flight, but the personal names of the two characters send a different signal: Here the technocrat bears the name Cabal, that of the intriguer who destroys all happiness and love between people, as we know him from Friedrich Schiller's 1784 tragedy *Love and Intrigue* (*Kabale und Liebe*). Meanwhile the doubter is Passworthy: The one who is worthy of passing into the future.

29 Nicholas Ruddick, "An Unsuitable Memorial: Stover's Edition of H. G. Wells's Things to Come," *Science Fiction Studies*, 35, no. 1 (2008): 121–6.

30 Erhard Schütz, "Wahn-Europa. Mediale Gas-Luftkrieg-Szenarien der Zwischenkriegszeit," in *Krieg in den Medien*, ed. Heinz-Peter Preußler (Amsterdam, 2005), 127–48.

31 Also Roger Luckhurst, *Science Fiction* (Cambridge, 2005), 13–75.

32 This motif of escape from human catastrophes with the help of space flight was readopted decades later by Arkadii and Boris Strugatsky in their famous short novel *Escape Attempt* (1962).

33 Wells, *Things to Come* (cit. n. 22).

34 See in detail, Matthias Schwartz, *Expeditionen in andere Welten. Sowjetische Abenteuerliteratur und Science Fiction von der Oktoberrevolution bis zum Ende der Stalinzeit* (Köln, 2014), 49–91; James T. Andrews, *Science for the Masses. The Bolshevik State, Public Science, and the Popular Imagination in Soviet Russia. 1917–1934*, (College Station, 2003).
35 Ibid., 69–81.
36 Gerbert Uells (Herbert Wells), *Oblik griadushchego* (An Image of the Future) (Moscow, 1937).
37 Ibid., 57–69; Evgenii Dobrenko, *Formovka sovetskogo chitatelia. Sotsial'nye i ėsteticheskie predposylki retseptsii sovetskoi literatury* (S-Peterburg 1997), 70–1, 126–7.
38 See Zeev Bar-Sella, *Aleksandr Beliaev* (Moscow, 2013); Schwartz, *Expeditionen in andere Welten*, 215–33 (cit. n. 34).
39 See I. Zlobnyi, "Fantasticheskaia literatura," *Revoliutsiia i kul'tura*, 2 (1930): 47–9.
40 I. Svistunov, "Ob uvlekatel'nom i poleznom chtenii. Eshche o nauchno-fantasticheskom zhanre," *Literaturnaia gazeta* (October 17, 1933), 3.
41 A first definition of the term by Evgeny Zamiatin as early as 1922, however, did not have any consequences for the further debate. For the first time, the composite was systematically used as a thematic title by the journal *Vsemirnyi sledopyt*, founded in 1925, which was subtitled "Journal of Adventure, Travel and Scientific Fantasy." From then on, the term was used repeatedly as a characterization of works dealing with scientific fiction or as a series title, but more precise definitions as a genre designation only began to emerge under cultural-political pressure during the first five-year plan (1928–32) from the beginning of 1928. Beliaev started to use the subtitle regularly for his literary works since 1928 and made an early attempt at a definition in a sketch, added to his volume *Battle in the Ether*, which received little attention at the time due to the small circulation of 5,000 copies. Aleksandr Beliaev, "Fantastika i nauka. Ocherk," *Bor'ba v efire. Nauchno-fantasticheskii roman* (Moscow, 1928), 309–21; on the broader context, see Schwartz, *Expeditionen in andere Welten*, 249–54 (cit. n. 34). I thank Nikolai Krementsov for calling my attention to Beliaev's article.
42 Matthias Schwartz, "How 'Nauchnaya fantastika' Was Made: The Debates About the Genre of Science Fiction from NEP to High Stalinism," *Slavic Review*, 2 (2013): 224–46.
43 Abram Palei, "Sovetskaia nauchno-fantasticheskaia literatura," *Revoliutsiia i kul'tura*, 23–4 (1929): 63–8.
44 Ibid., 64–6. As models for such literature he named Alexander Bogdanov's utopian works *Red Star* (1908) and *Engineer Menni* (1913) or Aleksei Tolstoi's *Aelita*. Ibid., 63.
45 [Eds.], "Redaktsiia zhurnala 'Vsemirnnogo sledopyta' ob"iavliaet Vsesoiuznyi literaturnyi konkurs" 1928 g., *Vsemirnyi sledopyt*, 5 (1928): 392–3; (Zhiuri), "O literaturnom konkurse 'Vsemirnogo sledopyta'," *Vsemirnyi sledopyt*, 12 (1928): 956.
46 [Eds.], "Litkonkurs 'Sledopyta' 1928 g.," *Vsemirnyi sledopyt*, 2 (1929): 148–9.
47 See Schwartz, "How 'Nauchnaya fantastika' Was Made," 232–8 (cit. n. 42).
48 Here quoted after Aleksandr Beliaev, "Zvezda KETs" (1935), *V mire fantastiki i prikliuchenii* (Leningrad, 1959), 375–528.
49 On the popularity of Tsiolkovsky and his ideas in the 1930s, see (Anon.), "Konstantin Ėduardovich Tsiolkovsky," *Vorkug sveta*, 10 (1935): 14–16; Iakov Perel'man, *Tsiolkovsky. Zhizn' i tekhnicheskie idei* (Moscow, 1937); James T. Andrews, *Red Cosmos. K. E. Tsiolkovsky, Grandfather of Soviet Rocketry* (College Station, 2009).

50 Beliaev, "Zvezda KETs," 500 (cit. n. 48).
51 Ibid., 503.
52 Ibid., 510.
53 Katerina Clark, "The Changing Image of Science and Technology in Soviet Literature," in *Science and Soviet Social Order*, ed. Loren Graham (Cambridge, 1990), 259–98; Karl Schlögel, *Traum und Terror. Moskau 1937* (Munich, 2008), 386–410.
54 See Matthias Schwartz, "Guests from Outer Space: Occult Aspects of Soviet Science Fiction," in *The New Age of Russia. Occult Esoteric Dimensions*, eds. Brigit Menzel, Michael Hagemeister, and Bernice Glatzer Rosenthal (Munich, 2011), 209–35.
55 Matthias Schwartz, "A New Poetics of Science: On the Establishment of 'Scientific-Fictional Literature' in the Late Stalin Period," *The Russian Review*, 79 (2020): 415–31.
56 Samuil Marshak, "Sodoklad S. Ia. Marshaka o detskoi literature," in *Pervyi vsesoiuznyi s'ezd sovetskikh pisatelei 1934. Stenograficheskii otchet* (Moscow, 1934), 20–38, 31.
57 Ibid., 31.
58 Maxim Gorky, "Preface," M. Il'in, *Men and Mountains. Man's Victory over Nature* (London, 1935), 5–6.
59 See M. Il'in, *New Russia's Primer: The Story of the Five-Year Plan* (Boston, 1931).
60 See Matthias Schwartz, "Factory of the Future. On M. Il'in's 'Scientific-Fictional Literature'," *Russian Literature*, 103–5 (2019): 259–81.
61 M. Il'in and E. Segal, *Kak chelovek stal velikanom* (Moscow, 1940).
62 Aleksandr Ivich, *Prikliucheniia izobretenii* (Leningrad, 1930); extended and corrected editions were published in 1935 and 1939.
63 Ibid., 3–7.
64 Ibid., 8–33.
65 Ibid., 58. However, in the second revised edition of his book, Ivich points out that all of Wells's mistakes were ultimately understandable, since "no imagination" and no science could actually enable anyone to see beyond the horizons of his own time, which is why most "utopias were very interesting, but not very similar to the truth." See Aleksandr Ivich, *Prikliucheniia izobretenii* (Izdanie vtoroe, pererabotannoe) (Leningrad, 1935), 121.
66 That was probably why such very different authors as Viktor Shklovskii and Varlam Shalamov were so fascinated by this new genre. See Varlam Shalamov, "Nauka i khudozhestvennaia literatura," *Front nauki i tekhniki*, 12 (1934): 84–91; Aleksandr Ivich, Viktor Shklovskii, "Uėlls i Zhiul' Vern," *Detskaia literatura*, 5 (1939): 14–18.
67 See Schwartz, *Expeditionen in andere Welten*, 331–40 (cit. n. 34).
68 Russian State Archive for Literature and Art (Rossiiskii gosudarstvennyi arkhiv literatury i isskustva, RGALI), fond 630, opis 1, edinitsa 287 (Fond Gosudarstvennogo Izdatel'stva Detskoi literatury, Stenogramma soveshchaniia po obsuzhdeniiu knigi Il'ina M. i Segal E. "Kak chelovek stal velikanom." 02.06.1940), listy 1–66.
69 Angela Schwarz, *Der Schlüssel zur modernen Welt. Wissenschaftspopularisierung in Grossbritannien und Deutschland im Übergang zur Moderne (ca. 1870–1914)* (Stuttgart, 1999).
70 See Catriona Kelly, "New Boundaries for the Common Good. Science, Philanthropy, and Objectivity in Soviet Russia," in *Constructing Russian Culture in the Age of Revolution. 1880–1940*, eds. Catriona Kelly and David Shepherd (Oxford 1998), 238–55; Elizabeth A. Hachten, "In Service of Science and Society. Scientists and the Public in Late Nineteenth-Century Russia," *Osiris*, 17 (2002): 171–209; Joseph

Bradley, *Voluntary Associations in Tsarist Russia: Science, Patriotism, and Civil Society* (Cambridge, MA, 2009).

71 For all biographical details, see Mishkevich, *Doktor zanimatel'nykh nauk* (cit. n. 5).

72 The two-volume *Entertaining Physics* alone was published in nine repeatedly revised editions until 1929; see Iakov Perel'man, *Zanimatel'naia fizika. Paradoksy, golovolomki, zadachi, opyty, zamyslovatye voprosy i rasskazy iz oblasti fiziki*, 2 vol. (Leningrad, 1929).

73 From 1918 to 1973 alone his books were printed with a total circulation of twelve million copies in Russian; see Mishkevich, *Doktor zanimatel'nykh nauk*, 183 (cit. n. 5).

74 Tellingly, in his history of science popularization in Russia and the Soviet Union, Ivich does not even mention Perel'man. His greatest and most successful opponent is simply removed from history in the Stalinist manner. See Aleksandr Ivich, *Poeziia nauki. O literature nauchno-populiarnoi i nauchno-khudozhestvennoi* (Moskva, 1967).

75 Accordingly, the subtitle of the collective volume *Science at Leisure* (1935) was "Collection of Entertaining Tasks, Riddles, Tricks, Games from the Field of Physics, Mathematics, Geography, Astronomy, Meteorology, Chemistry," cf. Ia. I. Perel'man, S. V. Gliazer, V. I. Priannikov, and V. V. Riumin, *Nauka na dosuge. Sbornik zanimatel'nych zadach, golovolomok, fokusov, igr iz oblasti fiziki, matematiki, geografii, astronomii, meteorolgii, khimii* (Leningrad, 1935); see also Eleonora A. Lazarevich, *Iskusstvo populiarizatsii. Akademiki S. I. Vavilov, V. A. Obruchev, A. E. Fersman—Populiarizatory nauki* (Moscow, 1960), 62–109.

76 Quoted after A. Kruber, "Akademik A. E. Fersman. Tri goda za poliarnym krugom [1923]," *Pechat' i revoliutsiia*, 3 (1924): 222–3, 222. Similarly, Perel'man writes in his Introduction to *Entertaining Physics* (1929): "The author tried as hard as he could to give the presented an outwardly interesting form, to tell excitingly about the object [. . .]. The main goal [. . .] is—to encourage the reader to *think scientifically*, to enable him *to think* physically." Perel'man, *Zanimatel'naia fizika*, 3–4 (cit. n. 72). Emphasis in the original.

77 D. Mikhailov, "Iak. I. Perel'man. Mezhplanetnye puteshestviia," *Pechat' i revoliutsiia*, 3 (1924): 223. Perel'man also writes in this sense in 1929: "The author has used the material [of the scientific-fantastic fiction] particularly extensively, because he considered it most suitable for the aims of the volume: Sections from the generally known novels and stories of Jules Verne, Wells, Mark Twain and others have been consulted." Perel'man, *Zanimatel'naia fizika*, 3 (cit. n. 72).

78 Thus, it obviously also followed the logic of the cabinets of curiosities from the eighteenth century.

79 However, to protect it from being suppressed or banished, sometimes quotations of Lenin and later also Stalin as well as allusions to day-to-day politics were incorporated into the texts. See for instance the Stalin quote in Ia. I. Perel'man and V. I. Prianishnikov, *Vechera zanimatel'noi nauki* (Leningrad, 1936), 3; V. A. Kamskii, ed., *Dom zanimatel'noi nauki* (Leningrad, 1940), 27; V. A. Kamskii, ed., *Dom zanimatel'noi nauki v pomoshch' shkole* (Leningrad, 1941), 3.

80 See Mishkevich, *Doktor zanimatel'nykh nauk*, 143–77 (cit. n. 5).

81 Nowadays one of its wings houses the Akhmatova Museum.

82 Ibid., 143.

83 Lev Uspenskii, "De-Ze-En," *Tekhnika - molodezhi*, 6 (1972): 34–6.

84 Mishkevich, *Doktor zanimatel'nykh nauk*, 175–6 (cit. n. 5).

85 Uspenskii, "De-Ze-En," 34 (cit. n. 83).

86 Whereas in 1936 there were only eleven, in 1938 there were already thirty-seven "travelling evenings" on offer, by 1941 there were almost a hundred events to choose from, during which films, slides, and experiments were shown in connection with lectures and discussions. The eleven subject areas ranged from "science and defence" to "cultural history," from "the life of remarkable people" to "entertaining mathematics." See Otdel massovoi politiko-kul'turno-prosvetitel'noi raboty Lensoveta, *Dom Zanimatel'noi Nauki* (Leningrad, 1936); Dom zanimatel'noi nauki, *Vyezdnye vechera zanimatel'noi nauki* (Leningrad, 1938); ibid., *Vyezdnye vechera Doma zanimatel'noj nauki. Nauchno-popular'nye lektsii i besedy* (Leningrad, 1941). The brochures and booklets, which had a circulation of 30,000–200,000, reached a total circulation of four million copies. See Mishkevich, *Doktor zanimatel'nykh nauk*, 174 (cit. n. 5).

87 Mishkevich, *Doktor zanimatel'nykh nauk*, 173 (cit. n. 5).

88 A. Ioffe, Ia. Frenkel', M. Frank et al., "Propagandist nauki," *Izvestiia* (December 4, 1939): 4.

89 Korr. 'Pravdy', "Iubilei vydaiushchegosia nauchnogo populiarizatora," *Pravda* (December 9, 1939): 4.

90 Mishkevich, *Doktor zanimatel'nykh nauk*, 175 (cit. n. 5).

91 Ia. Perel'man, "Romantik nauki. K 110-letiiu so dnia rozhdeniia Zhiulia Verna," *Izvestiia* (February 5, 1938): 4; Ia. Perel'man, "Chto takoe zanimatel'naia nauka?" (1939), *Tekhnika—molodezhi*, 11 (1972): 18–20.

92 Mishkevich, *Doktor zanimatel'nykh nauk*, 176 (cit. n. 5).

93 Vladimir Vainshtok presented a very similar picture of the erudite scholar in the figure of geographer Jacques Paganel in his 1936 film adaptation of Jules Verne's *Les Enfants du Capitaine Grant* (1868); see Matthias Schwartz, "Die Kinder des Kapitän Grant. Zur Geopoetik des Abenteuers in Vladimir Vajnštoks Verne-Verfilmung von 1936," in *Geopoetiken. Geographische Entwürfe in den mittel- und osteuropäischen Literaturen*, eds. Magdalena Marszałek and Sylvia Sasse (Berlin, 2010), 189–224.

94 The political context is mostly completely ignored: A brochure, for instance, explains the accuracy of bombers or cannons in the same style as the precision of land surveying. See G. N. Mamaev and E. Pavlov, *Zadachi o samolete (Dom zanimatel'noi nauki)* (Leningrad, 1940), 8, 14; Perel'man and Prianishnikov, *Vechera*, 61–7 (cit. n. 79).

95 At the same time, many of these "achievers" (vydvizentsy) and renowned scientists were also affected by terror, although not to the same extent as other population groups. See Sheila Fitzpatrick, "Stalin and the Making of a New Elite," in *The Cultural Front: Power and Culture in Revolutionary Russia* (London 1992), 149–82; Kendall E. Bailes, *Technology and Society Under Lenin and Stalin: Origins of the Soviet Technical Intelligentsia, 1917–1941* (Princeton, NJ, 1978), 159–262.

96 Ivich, *Prikliucheniia izobretenii* (cit. n. 62).

97 Only Alexander Ivich survived the Second World War as a front reporter, but in the postwar period he came into the focus of the anti-Semitic campaign against cosmopolitanism as "Enemy No. 1 of Children's Literature" (Alexander Fadeev). From 1954 onward, however, he was able to publish again as an author of children's books and popular-science writings until his death in 1978.

98 See Ethan Pollock, *Stalin and the Soviet Science Wars* (Princeton, 2007).

99 See Schwartz, "A New Poetics of Science" (cit. n. 55).

Chapter 6

1 On film adaptations of M. Shelley's *Frankenstein*, see James A. W. Heffernan, "Looking at the Monster: Frankenstein and Film," *Critical Inquiry*, 24, no. 1 (1997): 133–58; Michael Grant, "James Whale's *Frankenstein*: The Horror Film and the Symbolic Biology of the Cinematic Monster," in *Frankenstein: Creation and Monstrosity*, ed. Stephen Bann (London, 1994), 113–35; Caroline Joan Picart, "Re-birthing the Monstrous: James Whale's (Mis)reading of Mary Shelley's *Frankenstein*," *Critical Studies in Mass Communication*, 15, no. 4 (1998): 382–404.

2 The phrase "to create a Frankenstein monster" was a popular cliché in the political rhetoric of the 1820s, particularly referring to the French Revolution. See Fred Botting, *Making Monstrous: Frankenstein, Criticism, Theory* (Manchester, 1991).

3 On the details of creation of Monster's image, see Alberto Manguel, *Bride of Frankenstein* (London, 1997); Robert Horton, *Frankenstein* (London and New York, 2014), 13–26; David J. Scal, "The 1931 Film Makes Frankenstein a Cultural Icon," *Readings on Frankenstein*, ed. Don Nardo (San Diegom CA, 2000), 129–37; Stephen Jones, *The Frankenstein Scrapbook: The Complete Movie Guide to the World's Most Famous Monster* (New York, 1995).

4 Cited in Scal, "The 1931 Film," 132. For more details of the preparatory stage of shooting of *Frankenstein*, see Elizabeth Fee and Susan E. Lederer, *Frankenstein: Penetrating the Secrets of Nature: An Exhibition by the National Library of Medicine. National Library of Medicine (U.S.)* (New Brunswick, 2002).

5 *The Hollywood Reporter*'s original review headlined "Frankenstein 100% Shocker—Old Horror Tale Full of Thrills." Cited in *The Hollywood Reporter*. https://www.hollywoodreporter.com/news/frankenstein-thrs-1931-review-749292 (accessed on December 23, 2019).

6 See Harry Hamilton Laughlin, *The Second International Exhibition of Eugenics Held September 22 to October 22, 1921, in Connection with the Second International Congress of Eugenics in the American Museum of Natural History, New York: An Account of the Organization of the Exhibition, the Classification of the Exhibits, the List of Exhibitors, and a Catalog and Description of the Exhibits* (Baltimore, 1923): 28–9, 118.

7 On the work on the Monster's makeup and other visual features, see more in Fee and Lederer, *Frankenstein*, 39; Gregory William Mank, *It's alive! The Classic Cinema Saga of Frankenstein* (San Diego and New York, 1981), 14; Fernando Vidal, "Frankenstein's Brain: 'The Final Touch,'" *SubStance*, 45, no. 2, issue 140 (2016): 88–117.

8 Angela M. Smith, *Hideous Progeny: Disability, Eugenics, and Classic Horror Cinema* (New York, 2011), 66.

9 On the Lombrosian influence on Whale's movie, see Nicole Rafter, Michelle Brown, *Criminology Goes to the Movies: Crime Theory and Popular Culture* (New York, 2011), 28–46.

10 Havelock Ellis, *The Criminal* (New York, 1890), 49–51.

11 Ibid., 61–2.

12 Cited in Smith, *Hideous Progeny*, 66 (cit. n. 8).

13 Ibid.

14 Ellis, *The Criminal*, 71 (cit. n. 10).

15 Cited in Manguel, *Bride of Frankenstein*, 20 (cit. n. 3). Emphasis added.

16 On "criminal brain," see Charles Davenport, "Crime, Heredity and Environment," *Journal of Heredity*, 19, no. 7 (1928): 307–13; Nicole Rafter, Chad Posick, and Michael

Roque, *The Criminal Brain: Understanding Biological Theories of Crime*, 2nd ed. (New York, 2016); Stephen Gould, *The Mismeasure of Man* (New York, 1981).

17 Frankenstein's Monster is not the only degenerative character in the movie. Fritz, the humping hunchback, also demonstrates the classical Lombrosian set of atavistic characteristics. Similar to the Monster, Fritz has "degeneration stigmata" such as unrestrained primitive instincts, cognitive and communicative problems, as well as cruelty.

18 One can frequently come across the statement on the relatedness of Professor Preobrazhensky to the ambitious Victor Frankenstein, the protagonist of Shelley's novel. For example, see Natalia Dame, "Why Is Sharikov dead? The Fate of 'the Soviet Frankenstein' in Bulgakov's 'A Dog's Heart,'" *Canadian Slavonic Papers*, 61, no. 1 (2019): 25–56. However, compared to Frankenstein, Bulgakov's surgeon was hardly going to create a brand new man. Neither was he going to meddle with crossbreeding a man and a dog.

19 These last names directly derived from the words for "divine protection," "resurrection," and "epiphany," resp. Preobrazhensky, in turn, is derived from the word for Transfiguration.

20 On these and other medical doctors who influenced Bulgakov, see Iu. G. Vilenskii, *Doktor Bulgakov* (Dr. Bulgakov) (Kiev, 2005); I. S. Likhtenstein, "Doktor Mikhail Afanas'evich Bulgakov" (Dr. Mikhail Afanas'evich Bulgakov), in *Etiudy o literature. Glazami vracha* (Haifa, 2009), 88–109.

21 S. A. Preobrazhenskii, "Khirurgicheskaiia profilaktika vyrozhdeniia" (The surgical prevention of degeneration), *Sovremennaia psikhiatriia*, 2 (1912): 110–17.

22 For rejuvenation in "The Heart of a Dog," see Nikolai Krementsov, *Revolutionary Experiments: The Quest for Immortality in Bolshevik Science and Fiction* (Oxford, 2014), 127–59.

23 Mikhail Bulgakov, *The Heart of a Dog*, trans. Michael Glenny (London 1989), 109.

24 Ibid.

25 On degeneration topic in Russian cultural, mostly literary, discourse, see Riccardo Nicolosi, *Degeneration erzählen: Literatur und Psychiatrie im Russland der 1880er und 1890er Jahre* (Paderborn, 2012).

26 Bulgakov, *The Heart of a Dog*, 109 (cit. n. 23).

27 For the various "faces of eugenics," see Nikolai Krementsov, *With and Without Galton: Vasilii Florinskii and the Fate of Eugenics in Russia* (Cambridge, 2018), 1–21; Nikolai Krementsov, "The Strength of a Loosely Defined Movement: Eugenics and Medicine in Imperial Russia," *Medical History*, 59, no. 1 (2015): 6–31.

28 See Nikolai Krementsov, "Mezhdunarodnaia evgenika i rossiiskoe meditsinskoe soobschestvo, 1900–1917" (International Eugenics and the Russian Medical Community), *Istoriko-biologicheskie issledovaniia*, 7, no. 1 (2015): 7–40.

29 Bulgakov, *The Heart of a Dog*, 108 (cit. n. 23).

30 Ibid., 37.

31 Ibid., 67.

32 Ibid., 64, 68.

33 Ibid., 68.

34 See P. I. Kovalevskii, *Vyrozhdenie i vozrozhdenie. Prestupnik i bor'ba s prestupnost'iu* (Degeneration and revival. The criminal and the struggle against crime), 2nd ed. (St. Petersburg, 1903); D. A. Dril', "Prestupnyi chelovek" (The Criminal), *Iuridicheskii vestnik*, 11 (1882): 401–22; 12 (1882): 483–550; V. F. Chizh, "K ucheniiu ob organicheskoi prestupnosti" (On the theory of organic crime), *Arkhiv psikhiatrii, nevrologii i psikhopatologii*, 16, no. 1 (1893): 137–76; V. F. Chizh, "Prestupnii

chelovek pered litsom vrachebnoi nauki" (The criminal man as judged by medical science), *Nevrologicheskii vestnik*, 2, no. 1 (1894). Supplement: 1–41; P. I. Liublinskii, "Novaia mera bor'by s vyrozhdeniem i prestupnost'iu" (A new measure of fighting degeneration and crime), *Russkaia mysl'*, 3 (1912): 31–56; S. Ukshe, "Vyrozhdenie, ego rol' v prestupnosti i mery bor'by s nim" (Degeneration, its role in crime and the measures of fighting it), *Vestnik obshchestvennoi gigieny*, 6 (1915): 798–816. On the development of Russian criminal anthropology, see Louise McReynolds, "P. I. Kovalevskii: Ugolovnaia antropologiia i russkii natsionalizm" (Criminal anthropology and Russian nationalism), *Novoe literaturnoe obozrenie*, 144 (2017): 360–82.

35 P. I. Kovalevskii, *Sudebno-psikhiatricheskie analizy: sostavleny dlia medikov i iuristov* (Psychiatric analyses in law-court: Compiled for medical doctors and legal professionals), 2nd ed. (Khar'kov, 1881), 93.

36 V. M. Bekhterev, "Voprosy vyrozhdeniia i bor'ba s nim" (The issues of degeneration and fighting it), *Obozrenie psikhiatrii i nevrologii*, 9 (1908): 518–21.

37 The topic of hereditary alcoholism was extensively covered in a whole number of eugenic works. See, for instance, I. V. Sazhin, *Nasledstvennost' i spirtnye napitki* (Heredity and alcohol) (St. Petersburg, 1908); N. K. Koltsov, "Alkogolism i nasledstvennost'" (Alcohol addiction and heredity), *Priroda*, 4 (1916): 502–5. N. K. Kol'tsov, "K voprosu o nasledovanii posledstvii alkogolizma" (On inheriting the outcomes of alcohol addiction), *Priroda*, 10 (1916): 1189.

38 Bulgakov, *The Heart of a Dog*, 62 (cit. n. 23).

39 Ibid., 91.

40 V. F. Chizh, *Lektsii po sudebnoi psikhologii* (Lectures on psychology for the court of law) (St. Petersburg, 1890); V. F. Chizh, *Uchebnik psikhiatrii* (Textbook on Psychiatry) (Iur'ev, 1902).

41 Bulgakov, *The Heart of a Dog*, 64 (cit. n. 23).

42 For an overview of the early Soviet studies of the criminal, see Kenneth M. Pinnow, "From All Sides: Interdisciplinary Knowledge, Scientific Collaboration, and the Soviet Criminological Laboratories of the 1920s," *Slavic Review*, 76, no. 1 (2017): 122–46.

43 Nikolai Bukharin, *Problemy teorii i praktiki sotsializma* (The problems of theory and practice of socialism) (Moscow, 1989), 168.

44 Leon Trotsky, *Literature and Revolution*. Edited by W. Keach, R. Strunsky (Chicago, 2005), 206. The word "coagulated" does not adequately convey the meaning of the original word "zastyvshii." A more accurate translation is "stagnant," "rigid," or "inveterate" Homo sapiens.

45 N. K. Kol'tsov, "Uluchshenie chelovecheskoi porody. Rech' v godichnom zasedanii Russkogo evgenicheskogo obshchestva 20 oktiabria 1921 goda" (On the Improvement of Human Race: The Speech at the Annual Meeting of the Russian Eugenic Society, October 20, 1921), cited from V. V. Babkov, *Zaria genetiki cheloveka. Russkoe evgenicheskoe dvizhenie i nachalo genetiki cheloveka* (The dawn of human genetics. Russian eugenic movement and the birth of human genetics) (Moscow, 2008), 77–100, cit. 90.

46 A famous psychiatrist E. K. Krasnushkin, who worked at the Serbsky Institute of Forensic Psychiatry, claimed that the criminal was biologically deficient. See E. K. Krasnushkin, "Kriminal'nye psikhopaty sovremennosti i bor'ba s nimi" (Criminal psychopaths of our days, and how to fight them), *Prestupnyi mir Moskvy* (Moscow, 1924), 192–7; E. K. Krasnushkin, "Chto takoe prestupnik?" (What is the criminal?), *Prestupnik i prestupnost'*, 1 (Moscow, 1926): 6–33. However, the psychiatrist did not think that such deficiency was hereditary. On Russian criminology of that time, see

L. O. Ivanov and L. V. Il'ina, *Puti i sud'by otechestvennoi kriminologii* (Ways and fates of national criminology) (Moscow, 1991), especially Chapter III: "Criminological institutions in the RSFSR" and Chapter IV. "Work of Departments Studying Criminal Identities and Crime."

47 On the history of Soviet eugenics, see Mark B. Adams, "The Soviet Nature-Nurture Debate," in *Science and the Soviet Social Order*, ed. Loren Graham (Cambridge, 1990), 94–138; Mark B. Adams, "The Politics of Human Heredity in the USSR, 1920–40," *Genome*, 31 (1989b): 879–84; Loren R. Graham, "Science and Values: The Eugenics Movement in Germany and Russia in the 1920s," *American Historical Review*, 82 (1977): 1133–64; Nikolai Krementsov, "Eugenics in Russia and the Soviet Union," in *The Oxford Handbook of the History of Eugenics*, eds. Alison Bashford and Philippa Levine (Oxford, 2010), 413–29; Nikolai Krementsov, "'From Beastly Philosophy' to Medical Genetics: Eugenics in Russia and the Soviet Union," *Annals of Science*, 68 (2011): 61–92; Nikolai Krementsov, *With and Without Galton: Vasilii Florinskii and the Fate of Eugenics in Russia* (Open Book Publishers, 2018), 308–20.

48 See B. I. Slovtsov, *Uluchshenie rasy. (Evgenika)* (The betterment of race [Eugenics]) (Petrograd, 1923).

49 M. Volotskoi, *Podniatie zhiznennyh sil racy (Novyi put)* (Raising the vitality of race: A new way) (Moscow, 1923).

50 V. V. Bunak, "Antropologocheskoe izuchenie prestupnika, ego sovremennoe polozhenie i zadachi" (The anthropological study of the criminal, his present condition and goals), *Arkhiv kriminologii i sudebnoi meditsiny*, 23 (Khar'kov, 1927): 535–69.

51 On the closeness of psychological degeneration theory with the criminal-anthropological concept of atavism, see Nicolosi, *Degeneration erzählen*, 299–37 (cit. n. 25); Riccardo Nicolosi, "Criminality, Deviance, and Antropological Diversity: Narratives of Inborn Criminality and Atavism in Late Imperial Russia (1880–1900)," in *The Born and the Common Criminal. The Discourse on Criminality and the Practice of Punishment in Late Imperial Russian and Early Soviet Union*, eds. Riccardo Nicolosi and Anne Hartmann (Bielefeld, 2017), 85–117.

52 Bulgakov, *The Heart of a Dog*, 71 (cit. n. 23). Lombrosian fashion seemed to have passed into oblivion in Russia by the 1920s but was occasionally revived in just another effort to disclose the biological origin of crime.

53 Ibid., 95.

54 Ibid., 87.

55 Most likely, Sharikov's intellectual deficiency explains why rather deep, even ironical, reflections of the stray dog are not replaced by a similar interior monologue of Sharikov. Apparently, such a "subhuman" narrative did not seem of any interest to the author. On the "endocrinological" explanation of the shift in Sharikov's speech, see Elena Fratto, "Endoctrine Glands and the Anthropocene: Metabolic Storytelling in Mikhail Bulgakov's 'Heart of a Dog,'" *Russian Literature*, 114–15 (2020): 45–65.

56 Marina Mogilner, "The Empire-Born Criminal: Atavism, Irrational instincts, and the Fate of Russian Imperial Modernity," in *The Born and the Common Criminal. The Discourse on Criminality and the Practice of Punishment in Late Imperial Russian and Early Soviet Union*, eds. Riccardo Nicolosi and Anne Hartmann (Bielefeld, 2017), 31–62.

57 On disputes about the inheritance of acquired characteristics in Soviet Russia, see: Adams, "The Soviet Nature-Nurture Debate" (cit. n. 47); Krementsov, *With and Without Galton*, 308–20 (cit. n. 47).

58 On Lamarckism in "The Heart of a Dog," see Yvonne Howell, "Eugenics, Rejuvenation, and Bulgakov's Journey into the Heart of Dogness," *Slavic Review*, 65, no. 3 (2006): 544–62.
59 See Daniel Todes, *Ivan Pavlov: Exploring the Animal Machine* (New York, 2000), 87–92; Krementsov, *With and Without Galton*, 359–60 (cit. n. 47).
60 Bulgakov, *The Heart of a Dog*, 68 (cit. n. 23).
61 Ibid., 107.
62 Ibid., 74.
63 Ibid., 127. Emphasis added.
64 The only English translation, which retained the subtitle, is Mikhail Bulgakov, *A Dog's Heart: An Appalling Story*. Translated by Andrew Bromfield (London, 2007).
65 Jeffrey Andrew Weinstock, "Introduction: Monsters Are the Most Interesting People," in *The Ashgate Encyclopedia of Literary and Cinematic Monsters*, ed. Jeffrey Andrew Weinstock (Berlington, VT, 2014), 1; Jeffrey J. Cohen, "Monster Culture (Seven Theses)," in *Monster Theory: Reading Culture*, ed. Jeffrey J. Cohen (Minneapolis, 1997), 4.
66 On the danger of the monsters' procreation as represented in contemporary fantasy, see Irina Golovacheva, "Opasnye sviazi: Chelovek i monstr v sovremennoi massovoi culture" (Dangerous liaisons: Man and monster in contemporary mass culture), *Neprikosnovennyi zapas*, 6, no. 86 (2012): 144–62.

Chapter 7

1 A. V. Chayanov (I. Kremnev), "Puteshestvie moego brata Alekseia v stranu krest'ianskoi utopii" (My brother Alexei's journey to the country of peasant utopia), *Ne publikovavshiesia i maloizvestnye raboty A. V. Chayanova* (Moscow, 2003), 245–311; cit. 260, 261, 270. For a detailed analysis and recent interpretation of Chayanov's novel, see I. V. Gerasimov, *Dusha cheloveka v period perekhoda: sluchai Aleksandra Chayanova* (Human soul in transition: The case of Alexander Chayanov) (Kazan', 1997); A. M. Nikulin, "Chayanovskii utopizm: Balansiruia sredi krizisov intensifikatsii optimumov" (Chayanov's utopianism: Balancing among crises of intensification of optimums), *Krest'ianovedenie*, 2, no. 1 (2017): 6–29; D. Raskov, "Socialist Agrarian Utopia in the 1920s: Chayanov," *OEconomia: History, Methodology, Philosophy*, 4, no. 2 (2014): 123–46. English translation: Ivan Kremnev (1920), "The Journey of my Brother Alexei to the Land of Peasant Utopia," *Journal of Peasant Studies*, 4, no. 1 (1976): 63–108.
2 Chayanov proposed the microeconomic theory of the peasant household, which argued for an equilibrium between the consumption needs and labor force of peasant household members (the *consumption-labor-balance principle*). On Chayanov's theory, see K. Bruisch, *Als das Dorf noch Zukunft War: Agrarismus und Expertise Zwischen Zarenreich und Sowjetunion* (Köln, 2014), 60–6, 312–17; D. W. Darrow, "From Commune to Household: Statistics and the Social Construction of Chaianov's Theory of Peasant Economy," *Comparative Studies in Society and History*, 43, no. 4 (2001): 788–818.
3 For experimental studies of the "new man" in Soviet Russia and their interpretation in literature, see, for example, N. Krementsov, *Revolutionary Experiments: The Quest for Immortality in Bolshevik Science and Fiction* (New York, 2014). An extensive historiography on the "new man" is analyzed in "Introduction" to this volume.

4 As the examples of such literature, see L. Attwood, *The New Soviet Man and Woman: Sex-Role Socialization in the USSR* (Basingstoke, 1990); C. Kelly, "The New Soviet Man and Woman," *The Oxford Handbook of Modern Russian History*, ed. S. Dixon (New York, 2015).

5 See T. Shanin, *The Awkward Class. Political Sociology of Peasantry in a Developing Society. Russia 1910–1925* (Oxford, 1972).

6 *Rossiiskii Gosudarstvennyi arkhiv ekonomiki*—RGAE (Russian State Archive of Economy), fond 480, opis' 1, delo 129b, list 19. Hereafter such references will be given as RGAE, f. 480, op. 1, d. 129b, l. 19.

7 RGAE, f. 480, op. 1, d. 3, l. 5. See also N. Gratsianov, "Vystavka i tekhnicheskie uluchchsheniia krestianskikh trudovykh khoziaistv" (The Exhibition and technical improvement of peasant labor households), *Vestnik Glavnogo vystavochnogo komiteta*, 2 (1922–3): 18–19; cit. 19.

8 On education of the new man, see also the contribution to this volume by L. Bugaeva, "The Road to Life": Educating the New Man.

9 On the ideology of Russian agrarianism, and politics of modernity, see, for instance: D. Atkinson, *The End of the Russian Land Commune, 1905–1930* (Stanford, 1983); Bruisch, *Als das Dorf noch Zukunft war* (cit. n. 2); I. V. Gerasimov, *Modernism and Public Reform in late Imperial Russia: Rural Professionals and Self-Organization, 1905–30* (Basingstoke, 2006).

10 V. I. Lenin, "O kooperatsii" (On cooperation), *Polnoe sobranie sochinenii v 55 tt.* vol. 45 (Moscow, 1970), 369–77; cit. 370.

11 For details on the NEP, see A. Ball, "Building a New State and Society: NEP, 1921–1928," in *The Cambridge History of Russia. Volume III: The Twentieth Century*, ed. R. Grigor Suny (Cambridge, 2006), 168–91; S. Fitzpatrick et al., eds., *Russia in the Era of NEP* (Bloomington, 1991).

12 B. P. Danilov, *Sovetskaia dokolkhoznaia derevnia: nasledie, zemlepol'zovanie, khoziaistvo* (Soviet pre-kolkhoz village: Population, land use, farming) (Moscow, 1977), 106–7.

13 In connection with the Stolypin reforms, Stephen Frank reflects on the "islands of enlightenment": The "enlightened peasants" who possessed "the instinct of private property." S. Frank, "Conforming the Domestic Other: Rural Popular Culture and Its Enemies in Fin-de-Siècle Russia," in *Cultures in Flux: Lower-Class Values, Practices, and Resistance in Late-Imperial Russia,* eds. S. Frank and M. Steinberg (Princeton, NJ, 1994), 97–103; cit. 103.

14 On the Stolypin reforms, see D. A. Macey, "Reflections on Peasant Adaptation in Rural Russia at the Beginning of the Twentieth Century: The Stolypin Agrarian Reforms," in *Rural Adaptation in Russia*, ed. S. K. Wegren (London, 2005), 38–64; K. Matsuzato, "Stolypinskaia reforma i russkii agrotekhnicheskii perevorot" (Stolypin reform and the Russian agrotechnical revolution), *Acta Slavica Japonica,* 10 (1992): 33–42.

15 For litterateurs' reflections on the prerevolutionary "new peasantry," see, O. Elina, "Mechty o "Novom krest'ianine" v publitsistike perioda Stolypinskikh reform" (Dreams on "New peasant" in the writings of publicists during the Stolypin reforms), *Krest'ianovedenie*, 2021 (in print). For examples of such writings, see I. A-v, *"Novyi krest'ianin"* ("New peasant") (Odessa, 1915).

16 Y. Kotsonis, *Making Peasants Backward: Agricultural Cooperatives and the Agrarian Question in Russia, 1861–1914* (New York, 1999); Gerasimov, *Modernism and Public reform in late Imperial Russia* (cit. n. 9), 99–122.

17 See, for instance, V. G. Tiukavin and V. I. Skriabin, "Primenenie mashin v sel'skom khoziaistve Rossii v kontse XIX—nachale XX veka" (The use of machinery in Russian agriculture in the late nineteenth and early twentieth centuries), *Agrarnaia evolutsiia v Rossii i SShA v XIX—nachale XX veka* (Moscow, 1991), 271–92.

18 N. P. Mel'nikov, *Chudesa vystavki v Chikago 1893 goda* (Miracles of the 1893 Exhibition in Chicago) (Odessa, 1894), 28–9. The Russian Department of the Columbian Exhibition was headed by Vladimir Kovalevsky as a general commissioner, who later became one of the organizers of VSKhV.

19 For an overview of literature on Russian agricultural exhibitions, see: O. Yu. Elina, "Nauka na agragno-promyshlennykh vystavkakh Rossii: sotsial'nye transformatsii i smena khudozhestvennykh obrazov: pervaia tret' XX veka" (Science at agricultural exhibitions in Russia: Social transformation and change of art images: The first third of the XX century), in *Vikhrevaia dinamika razvitiia nauki i techniki. Rossiia-SSSR. Pervaia polovina XX veka,* ed. Yu. M. Baturin, 2 vols., vol. 1 (Saratov, 2018), 370–413. On world exhibitions, see: A. C. T. Geppert, *Fleeting Cities. Imperial Expositions in Fin-de-Siècle Europe* (Basingstoke, 2010).

20 *Materialy i dokumenty. Vserossiiskaia sel'skokhoziaistvennaia vystavka s inostrannym otdelom* (Materials and documents. All-Russian Agricultural and Handicraft Industrial Exhibition with a foreign department) (Moscow, 1922), 18.

21 GVK had a staff of 700 people and managed nine operating sectors; 108 provincial, district, and republican exhibition committees were organized to work "on the ground"; see RGAE, f. 480, op. 1, d.129b, l.19; f. 478, op. 1, d. 34, l. 5–6.

22 *Materialy i dokumenty,* 1922, 18 (cit. n. 20).

23 RGAE, f. 480, op. 1, d. 129b, l. 62.

24 Vladimir Kovalevsky, a specialist in agricultural statistics and soil cartography, was a senior official of both the Ministry of Finance and the Ministry of Agriculture. He participated in the organization of Russian departments at several world exhibitions (see cit. n. 18). Since 1917 he headed the Agricultural Scientific Committee of Narkomzem. Kovalevsky was the chief editor of the *Great Agricultural Encyclopedia,* published in 1925–8.

25 RGAE, f. 478, op. 1, d. 1081, l. 174–5.

26 RGAE, f. 480, op. 1, d. 3, l. 69.

27 *Vremennaia arkhitektura Parka Gor'kogo* (Temporary Structures in Gorky Park), eds. M. V. Evstratova and S. V. Koluzakov (Moscow, 2019); *Obzor deiatel'nosti Glavnogo vystavochnogo komiteta. Oktiabr'-dekabr' 1922 goda* (Review of the activities of the Main Exhibition Committee, okt.-dec. 1922) (Moscow, 1922), 8–11.

28 RGAE, f. 480, op. 13, d. 34, l. 18; d. 1, l. 80.

29 For a sample of book-length studies, see *Vremennaia arkhitektura* (cit. n. 27); *Vystavochnye ansambli SSSR. 1920–1930-e gody: materialy i dokumenty* (Exhibition ensembles of the USSR. 1920–1930s: Materials and documents), ed. V. P. Tolstoy (Moscow, 2006).

30 VSKhV was first opened on August 15, for the experts' visits; see RGAE, f. 480, op. 13, d. 8, l. 6.

31 RGAE, f. 480, op. 13, d. 8, l. 5–7; op. 1, d. 129b, l. 7–9.

32 RGAE. f. 480. op. 1, d. 28, l. 12.

33 RGAE, f. 480, op. 1, d. 1, l. 63.

34 RGAE, f. 480, op. 13, d. 34, l. 56–7. APO worked under the guidance of the Agitation and Propaganda section of the Central Committee Secretariat of the Bolshevik party.

35 RGAE, f. 480, op. 13, d. 34, l. 56. Emphasis added.
36 *Krest'ianskoe khoziaistvo i vystavka. Posobie dlia mestnykh uchrezhdenii* (Peasant household and the Exhibition. Instruction for local institutions), eds. D. L. Slobodchikov, M. A. Tsvetkov, P. K. Gratsianov, and I. V. Vladykin (Moscow, 1923), 23.
37 RGAE, f. 480, op. 1, d. 129b, l. 48–52.
38 RGAE. F. 480, op. 1. d. 129b. l. 85.
39 RGAE, f. 480, op. 13, d. 5, l. 258–61.
40 RGAE, f. 480, op. 13, d. 5, l. 5.
41 RGAE, f. 480, op. 1, d. 34, l. 37.
42 RGAE, f. 480, op. 13, d. 34, l. 55.
43 It is worth mentioning that many peasant women participated at VSKhV. They took active part in the debates and discussions, wrote articles for the exhibition magazines, and so on. See RGAE, f. 480, op. 13, d. 5, l. 16.
44 RGAE, f. 480, op. 13, d. 34, l. 7.
45 RGAE, f. 480, op. 13, d. 5, l. 258–60.
46 *Sbornik programm otdelov Pervoi Vserossiiskoi sel'skokhoziaistvennoi i kustarno-promyshlennoi vystavki SSSR* (Collection of programs of the Departments of the First Agricultural and Handicraft Industrial Exhibition of the USSR) (Moscow, 1923), 93.
47 *Ukazatel' otdelov Pervoi sel'skokhoziaistvennoi i kustarno-promyshlennoi vystavki* (Index of departments of the First Agricultural and Handicraft Industrial Exhibition) (Moscow, 1923), 33.
48 M. A. Bulgakov, "Zolotistyi gorod" (A Golden City) / M. A. Bulgakov, *Sobranie sochinenii v 8 tt*, vol. 3 (Moscow, 2009); RGAE, f. 480, op. 1, d. 159, l. 8.
49 *Ukazatel' otdelov*, 15–16 (cit. n. 47).
50 *Sbornik programm otdelov*, 39–42 (cit. n. 46).
51 *Gosudarstvennyi muzei arkhitektury im. A. V. Shchuseva* - GMA (A. V. Shchusev State Museum of Architecture). Dep. of photos, f. XI, 2022, 2024.
52 GMA. Dep. of photos, f. XI, 2022, 2023, 2025.
53 *Vremennaia arkhitektura*, 76–85 (cit. n. 27)
54 *Sbornik programm otdelov*, 28 (cit. n. 46).
55 *Vremennaia arkhitektura*, 86–7 (cit. n. 27).
56 *Sbornik programm otdelov*, 21–3 (cit. n. 46).
57 RGAE, f. 480, op. 1, d. 129b, l. 43.
58 RGAE, f. 480, op. 1, d. 3, l. 29.
59 RGAE, f. 480, op. 1, d. 2, l. 8.
60 RGAE, f. 480, op. 1, d. 2, l. 8–8bp.
61 RGAE, f. 480, op. 1, d. 3, l. 22.
62 *Krest'ianskoe khoziaistvo i vystaka*, 7 (cit. n. 36).
63 Ibid., 11–12.
64 RGAE, f. 480, op. 1. d. 70, l. 1.
65 RGAE, f. 480, op. 1. d. 159, l. 159–60; d. 129b, l. 47–8.
66 RGAE, f. 480, op. 13, d. 9, l. 4–4bp.
67 The Commandant secured a place for them in a dormitory, but one of the family members would have to stay at "Old Village" section to care for the cattle. "Separation of families" was seen as undesirable, so their resettlement was therefore not allowed; see RGAE, f. 480, op. 1, d. 159, l. 159.

68 *Vremennaia arkhitektura*, 70–1 (cit. n. 27).
69 *Ukazatel' otdelov*, 6–7 (cit. n. 47).
70 RGAE, f. 480, op. 13, d. 26, l. 121–2.
71 For details, see Geppert, *Fleeting Cities* (cit. n. 19).
72 RGAE. f. 480. op. 1. d. 87. l. 135; op. 13. d. 27. l. 4.
73 RGAE, f. 480, op. 13, d. 8, l. 47–50.
74 Ibid.
75 RGAE, f. 480, op. 13, d. 8, l. 47bp.
76 RGAE, f. 480, op. 13, d. 8, l. 56.
77 M. Rolf, *Soviet Mass Festivals, 1917–1991* (Pittsburgh, 2013), 7.
78 RGAE, f. 480, op. 13, d. 12, l. 7.
79 The highlight for the peasants was the animal awards ceremony, followed by an animal parade at the hippodrome and a carnival in the Neskuchnyi Garden. RGAE, f. 480, op. 13, d. 8, l. 44–5.
80 RGAE, f. 480, op. 13, d. 8, l. 31–2.
81 V. V. Mayakovsky, "Rasskaz pro Klima iz chernozemnykh mest, pro Vserossiiskuiu vystavku i rezinotrest" (A story about Klim from black soil places, about the All-Russian Exhibition and Rezinotrest), in idem, *Polnoe sobranie sochinenii v 13 tt.*, vol. 5 (Moscow, 1955), 315–37.
82 K. N. Altaisky (Korolev), "Na Vserossiiskoi Vystavke" (At the All-Russian Exhibition), *Vyatskaia Pravda*, 36 (1923): 4.
83 M. N. Kovrov, "O Vystavke" (On the Exhibition), *Vyatskaia Pravda*, 38 (1923): 6.
84 RGAE, f. 480, op. 1, d. 129b, l. 85.
85 See on this, H. Hudson, "The Kulakization of the Peasantry: The OGPU and the End of Faith in Peasant Reconciliation, 1924–1927," *Jahrbücher für Geschichte Osteuropas,* 60, no. 1 (2012): 34–57.
86 RGAE, f. 480, op. 1, d. 129b, l. 85a.
87 See, Gerasimov, *Dusha cheloveka v period perekhoda* (cit. n. 1); Darrow, *From Commune to Household* (cit. n. 2).
88 See, O. B. Mozokhin, *Delo "Trudovoi Krest'ianskoi partii"* (Case of the "Labour Peasant Party") (Moscow, 2021).

Chapter 8

1 J. E. Bowlt and O. Matich,"Introduction," in *Laboratory of Dreams: The Russian Avant-Garde and Cultural Experiment*, eds. J. E. Bowlt and O. Matich (Stanford, CA, 1996), 1–2, 11.
2 See for example Mutual Art, "Vasilii Vatagin." https://www.mutualart.com/Artist/Vasily-Vatagin/A289679751E697EB/Artworks (accessed on April 16, 2020).
3 "Darvinovskii muzei" (Darwin Museum), in *Bol'shaia sovetskaia entsiklopedia* (The Great Soviet Encyclopedia), vol. 20, ed. O. Yu Shmidt (Moscow, 1930), 472; A. F. Kots, "O muzee evoliutsionnoi istorii Moskovskikh Vyskikh Kursakh uchenii god 1913–1914" (On the museum of evolutionary history of the Moscow Higher Courses teaching year 1913–1914) (Moscow, May 6, 1914), Archive of the State Darwin Museum Moscow (*Arkhiv gosudarstvennogo darvinovskogo muzeia*—AGDM), fond 12430, opis' 32, ed.khraneniia 165.

4 This was demonstrated in Kots's response to Trofim Lysenko's speech "The situation in biological science," given to the All-union Academy of Agricultural Sciences (VASSKhNIL) Session, July 31, 1948, in *Agrobiology. Essays on the Problems of Plant Breeding and Seed Growing* (Moscow, 1954), 515–53. See A. F. Kots, "Ob itogakh sessii vsesoiuznoi akademii s.kh. nauk po dokladu akad. Lysenko 'O polozhenii v biolog. nauke' v primenenii k eksponanture gosudarstvennogo darvinovskogo muzeia" (On the summary of the session of the All-union Academy of Agricultural Sciences about the address by academician Lysenko "On the Situation in Biological Science" in application to the exhibitions of the State Darwin Museum) (July 31, 1948), AGDM f.10141, o.101, ed.khr.33. See also P. Simpson, "Lysenko, 'Michurinism' and art at the Moscow Darwin Museum 1930s-1950s," in *The Lysenko Controversy as a Global Phenomenon*, vol. 1, *Genetics and Agriculture in the Soviet Union and Beyond*, eds. W. deJong-Lambert and N. Krementsov (Palgrave Macmillan, 2017), 129–76.

5 I choose to call these theorizations "crypto-Lamarckian" because although there were some scientists and thinkers who did explicitly espouse Lamarck, according to Alexander Vucinich, there were many supporters of Darwin who made no clear differentiation between the ideas of Lamarck and Darwin. See A. Vucinich, *Darwin in Russian thought* (Berkeley, Los Angeles, Oxford, 1989), 384.

6 See: M. Foucault, "Truth and Power," in *Power/Knowledge: Selected Interviews and Other Writings 1972–1977 by Michel Foucault*, ed. C. Gordon, trans. C. Gordon, L. Marshall, J. Mephan and K. Soper (New York, 1980), 131–2; Michel Foucault, *Discipline and Punish: the Birth of the Prison*, trans. A. Sheridan (London, 1979), 184; Michel Foucault, *The History of Sexuality*, vol. 1, *The Will to Knowledge*, trans. R. Hurley (London, 1998), 77–80, 106, 116, 120–7, 131, 145, 154–7.

7 "From the history of the museum: chronic[k]le of leading events," *Darwin Museum Report 1996–2000*. http://www.darwin.museum.ru/report/1996-2000-en/e_hist.htm, (accessed on November 16, 2008) (now inaccessible online but I have a print-out).

8 Ibid.

9 P. S. Kogan, "Novaia sistema tvorchestva" ("A new system of creation"), May 3, 1926, in *Assotsiatsiia khudozhnikov revoliutsionnoi Rossii. Sbornik vospominanii, statei, dokumentov AKHRR* (*The Association of Artists of Revolutionary Russia, AKhRR. An Anthology of Memoires, Articles and Documents of AKhRR*), eds. I. M. Gronskii and V. N. Perel'man (Moscow, 1973), 227.

10 B. Taylor, "On AKhRR," in *Art of the Soviets. Painting, Sculpture and Architecture in a One-Party State*, eds. M. Cullerne Bown and B. Taylor (Manchester, 1993), 61.

11 L. Dickerman, "Monumental Propaganda," *October*, 165 (2018): 182.

12 V. A. Vatagin, "Vospominia," in *Vospominaniia. Zapiski Animalista. Stat'i* (*Memoires. Notes of an Animalist. Articles*), compiled by I. V. Vatagin, ed. V. A. Vatagin (Moscow, 1980), 10, 59, 61–2, 161, 192.

13 See "The work of the sculptor V. A. Vatagin, *Andrei Rublev*, 1918–1919, gypsum, toning. From the collection of the State Darwin Museum." https://soviet-art.ru/soviet-sculptor-vasily-alekseevich-vatagin-1883-1969/the-work-of-the-sculptor-v-a-vatagin-andrei-rublev-1918-1919-gypsum-toning-from-the-collection-of-the-state-darwin-museum/ (accessed on July 30, 2019).

14 C. Lodder, "Lenin's Plan for Monumental Propaganda," in *Art of the Soviets*, eds. Cullerne Bown and Taylor, 26.

15 See also P. Simpson, "Beauty and the Beast: Imaging Human Evolution at the Moscow Darwin Museum in the 1920s," in *Picturing Evolution and Extinction:*

Regeneration and Degeneration in Modern Visual Culture, eds. F. Brauer and S. Keshavjee (Newcastle-upon-Tyne, 2015), 159–60. For an Image of Iuon's *New Planet*, see: https://www.wikiart.org/en/konstantin-yuon/new-planet-1921 (accessed on August 4, 2019).

16 A. Dobrokhotov, "GAKhN: An Aesthetics of Ruins or Alexei Losev's Failed Project," *Studies in East European Thought*, 63, no. 1 (2011): 31–42. See also N. Mislev, "Towards an Exact Aesthetics," in *Laboratory of Dreams* (cit. n. 1), 118–32.

17 Ia. A. Tugendkhol'd, "Nasha skul'ptura" ("Our sculpture"), *Novyi mir*, May 05, 1926, 161–7; A. V. Lunacharskii, "Po vystavkam" [About the exhibition], *Izvestiia TsIK i VTsIK SSSR*, cited in Vatagin, *Vospominaniia* (cit. n. 12), 189. For an image of Iuon's painting see: Laura Cumming, "Revolution: Russian Art 1917–1932," review of the eponymous exhibition at the Royal Academy, *The Observer*, London, February 12, 2017. https://www.theguardian.com/artanddesign/2017/feb/12/revolution-russian-art-1917-1932-review (accessed on October 10, 2019).

18 C. R. Darwin, *On the Origin of Species by Means of Natural Selection, or the Preservation of Favoured Races in the Struggle for Life* (London, 1859), 488; C. R. Darwin, *The Descent of Man and Selection in Relation to Sex*, 2 vols, vol. 2 (London: 1871), 389.

19 Darwin, *Origin of Species* (cit. n. 18), 60–79; Darwin, *The Descent of Man,* vol. 1 (cit. n. 18), 61, 136, 154, 174, 180, 185, 257, 320; vol. 2, 389.

20 See the Rodin Museum website for a plaster version made before 1888: https://collections.musee-rodin.fr/es/museum/rodin/toilette-de-venus/S.02898?materiauxUtilises%5B0%5D=Pl%C3%A2tre+enduit&position=4 (accessed on August 03, 2019).

21 Rodin's *Eve* is now held at the Pushkin Museum in Moscow. See: https://pushkinmuseum.art/data/fonds/europe_and_america/sk/sk_254/index.php?lang=en (accessed on August 3, 2019). The Pushkin Museum also holds Maillol's *Pomona* (1910), and three works commissioned by Morozov, *Flora* (1911), *Spring* (1912) and *Summer* (1912), that were available in the Museum of Modern Western Art in the 1920s. See: https://pushkinmuseum.art/data/fonds/europe_and_america/sk/sk_243/index.php?lang=en (accessed on August 03, 2019).

22 Shchukin's art collection was sequestered on October 29 1918, and Morozov's on December 18, 1918. Initially the collections were named the First and Second Museums of Modern Western Art but were merged as a single museum in 1923. http://www.newestmuseum.ru/history/gmnzi/index.php?lang=en (accessed on August 3, 2019).

23 Tugendkhol'd, "Nasha skul'ptura" (cit. n. 17).

24 See, F. Brauer, "Introduction. The Janus Face of Evolution: Degeneration, Devolution and Extinction in the Anthropocene," in *Picturing Evolution and Extinction*, eds. Brauer and Keshavjee, xv–xlii (cit. n. 15).

25 See for example: Tricia Starks, *The Body Soviet: Propaganda, Hygiene and the Revolutionary State* (Madison, 2008); F. Bernstein, "Envisioning Health in Revolutionary Russia: the Politics of Gender in Sexual Enlightenment Posters of the 1920s," *The Russian Review*, 57 (1998): 191–217; J. E. Muller et al., "The Soviet Health System: Aspects of Relevance for Medicine in the United States," *New England Journal of Medicine*, 286 (1972): 700. http://www.nejm.org/doi/full/10.1056/NEJM197203302861305 (accessed on August 04, 2019); Roger I. Glass, "The SANEPID service in the USSR," *Public Health Reports*, 91, no. 2 (1976): 155–8. http://www.ncbi.nlm.nih.gov/pmc/articles/PMC1438525/pdf/pubhealthrep00155-0056.pdf (accessed on August 4, 2019).

26 N. W. Gilham, "Sir Francis Galton and the Birth of Eugenics," *Annual Review of Genetics*, 35 (2000): 83–101.
27 See also N. Krementsov: "The 'beastly philosophy': Eugenics in Imperial Russia," "Science and Ideology: Eugenics in Bolshevik Russia," and "Eugenics in a Revolutionary Society," in *The Oxford Handbook of the History of Eugenics*, eds. A. Bashford and P. Levine (Oxford, 2010), respectively 414–16, 416–21, 421–4. A more detailed overview of Soviet eugenics and its differences from Western eugenics discourse is given in: N. Krementsov, "From 'beastly philosophy' to medical genetics: eugenics in Russia and the Soviet Union," *Annals of Science*, 68, no. 1 (2011): 61–92, and especially, N. Krementsov, *With and without Galton: Vasilii Florinskii and the Fate of Eugenics in Russia* (Cambridge, 2018).
28 In an exhibition about Soviet eugenics at the Darwin Museum entitled *The younger sister of genetics*, December 2010, two volumes of the *Russian Eugenics Journal* held in the museum's collection were displayed: 2 (1923), 4 (1926).
29 Krementsov, "From 'beastly philosophy' to Medical Genetics," 61–92 (cit. n. 27).
30 The following books from Kots's library were displayed in December 2010 in the exhibition *The Younger Sister of Genetics:* Karl Pearson, *Life and Letters of Francis Galton*, 2 vols. (Cambridge, 1914 & 1924); F. Galton, *Natural Inheritance* (London, 1889); F. Galton, *Nasledstvennost' talanta ee zakony i posledstviia* (*Hereditary genius. An inquiry into its laws and consequences*—(a translation of the 1869 edition) (St. Petersburg, 1875); C. Lombroso, *Genialnost' i pomeshatel'stvo* (*Genius and madness*, 1872). Translated by G. Tetiushinova, 1885 (1892); T. I. Iudin, *Evgenika* (Moscow, 1925). Alexander Kots's handwritten personal library catalogue contains scientific books and papers by an array of American, German, and British scientist/eugenicists including the United States—Vernon Kellogg, C. B. Davenport, H. F. Osborn, W. K. Gregory, H. J. Müller; Germany—A. Weisman, E. Haeckel, P. Kammerer; Britain—R. C. Punnett, W. Bateson. It shows a preference for British writings on eugenics, including a 1926 Russian translation of Reginald Ruggles-Gates, *Inheritance and Eugenics* (1923), as well as Julian Huxley and H. G. Wells, *The Science of Life* (1931): AGDM, Rare Books Room, N5. Inventarnaia kniga, C1, no.2160. Nadezhda Kots's library included significant works relating to eugenics by Yerkes including "Eugenic bearing of measurements of intelligence in the United States Army," 1928: Irina Kalacheva, *Arkhivnyi fond Ladygina-Kots, Nadezhdy Nikolaevny (1889–1963), Opis no.1* (AGDM, 2010), 286.
31 See for example: H. F. Osborn to A. F. Kots, 25/03/30, AGDM f.10141, op.492, ed.khr .1293, no.1409; A. F. Kots to W. K. Gregory, American Museum of Natural History (AMNH), no date, AGDM f.12497, op.1080, ed.khr.1239, no.1410; A. F. Kots to H. F. Osborn, AGDM f.12497, op.1081, ed.khr. 1239, no.1411; R. Yerkes to A. F. Kots and N.N Ladygina-Kots, 25/03/30, AGDM f.10141 op.376, ed.khr.1239, no.1409; Yerkes to Kots and Ladygina-Kots 30/01/30, AGDM f.10141, op.502, ed.khr.1304, no.2057. Yerkes visited the Darwin Museum in 1929, on his way to the Soviet monkey and ape station at Sukhumi on the Black Sea coast: correspondence between N. N. Ladygina-Kots and R. Yerkes 1929, AGDM kpf.15111, op. 2396, khr.112, stellazh (shelving unit) 3, polka (shelf) 3.
32 Krementsov, "From 'beastly philosophy' to Medical Genetics" (cit. n. 27), 73.
33 A. Kollontai, "The First Steps Towards the Protection of Motherhood," in *From my Life and Work*, ed. A. Kollontai (Moscow, 1974), 336–40.
34 See, P. Simpson, "Bolshevism and Sexual Revolution: Visualising New Soviet Woman as the Eugenic Ideal," in *Art, Sex, and Eugenics: Corpus Delecti*, eds. F. Brauer and A. Callen (Aldershot, 1988), 209–38.

35 N. A. Semashko, *Nauka o zdorovè* (1922), 53, cited in Joravsky, *The Lysenko Affair* (Chicago, 1970), 259.
36 N. I. Bukharin, *Pravda*, October 11, 1923, cited in A. K. Gastev, “Shatunovshchina kak metodika,” *Krasnaia nov’* (January–February 1924): 237; L. Trotsky, *Literature and Revolution*. Translated by Rose Strunsky (Ann Arbor, 1968), 252–6.
37 A.V. Lunacharskii, “VIII vystavka AKhRR,” *Bor’ba za realizm v izobrazitel’nom iskusstve, 20kh godoov, materialy dokumenty, vospominaniia*, ed. V.N. Perelman (Moscow, 1962) 225–227, cited in B. Taylor, “ON AKhRR”, in *Art of the Soviets. Painting, Sculpture and Architecture in a One-Party State 1917–1992*, ed. B. Taylor and M. Cullerne Bown (Manchester and New York, 1993).
38 Krementsov, “From ‘beastly philosophy’ to Medical Genetics” (cit. n. 27), 90.
39 Vucinich, *Darwin in Russian thought* (cit. n. 5), ix, 151, 156–8, 161–5, 200, 321, 381, 391.
40 F. Engels, *The Dialectics of Nature* (Moscow, 1966); F. Engels, *The Part Played by Labour in the Origin of Man from Apes.* Translated by Clemens Dutt (Moscow, 1934), Marxists.org archive. https://www.marxists.org/archive/marx/works/1876/part-played-labour/ (accessed on October 10, 2019).
41 S. Sobol’, “Bor’ba za sushchestvovanie” (“The struggle for existence”), in *Bolshaiia Sovetskaiia Entsiklopedia* (*The Great Soviet Encyclopedia*), vol. 7 (Moscow, 1927), 204–14.
42 See W. deJong-Lambert and N. Krementsov, eds., *Lysenko as a Global Phenomenon*, 2 vols. (Cham, 2017).
43 N. Krementsov, “Marxism, Darwinism, and Genetics in the Soviet Union,” in *Biology and Ideology: From Descartes to Dawkins*, eds. D. Alexander and R. Numbers (Chicago, 2010), 215–46.
44 Darwin, *Origin of Species* (cit. n. 18)
45 C. R. Darwin, *The Descent of Man and Selection in Relation to Sex* (1879), republished by Penguin Books (London, 2004), 178–84.
46 Sobol, “Bor’ba za sushchestvovanie” (cit. n. 41).
47 Darwin, *Origin of Species*, 60–79 (cit. n. 18).
48 Ibid.
49 David R. Oldroyd, *Darwinian Impacts: An Introduction to the Darwinian Revolution* (Milton Keynes, 1980), 67–8. See also: D. P. Todes, *Darwin without Malthus: the Struggle for Existence in Russian Evolutionary Thought* (New York, 1989); and D. Beer, *Renovating Russia: The Human Sciences and the Fate of Liberal Modernity* (Ithaca and London, 2008), 38, 45.
50 K. Marx, *Capital*, 2 vols. (London, 1972), vol. 1 (1867), 148, 149, 209, 326, 371.
51 Marx, *Capital*, vol. 2, 574 (cit. n. 50).
52 Engels, Letter to Friedrich Albert Lange in Duisberg, 29 March 1865, in S. W. Ryaznonova, ed., *Marx and Engels Selected Correspondence*. Translated by I. Lasker (Moscow, 1975), 161–2. A Comprehensive account of the “struggle for existence problem” is offered in: Todes, *Darwin without Malthus* (cit. n. 49). See also D. Beer, *Renovating Russia* (cit. n. 49), 38, 45.
53 Engels, *The Dialectics of Nature* (cit. n. 40); Engels, *The Part Played by Labour in the Origin of Man from Apes* (cit. n. 40).
54 Sobol, “Bor’ba za sushchestvovanie” (cit. n. 41). See also Engels, *The Part Played by Labour in the Origin of Man from Apes* (cit. n. 40).
55 See P. Simpson, “Imag[in]ing Post Revolutionary Evolution: The Taylorised Proletarian, ‘Conditioning’ and Soviet Darwinism in the 1920s,” in *The Art of Evolution: Darwin, Darwinisms and Visual Culture*, eds. B. Larson and F. Brauer (New Hampshire, 2009), 226–61.

56 See P. Simpson, "A Sort of Vitalist Modernism? Soviet Darwinism as a Means to Regenerate the Wounded in WWII," Ch. 4 in *Modern art and Vitalist Modernism: Organicism and the New Sciences*, ed. F. Brauer (London and New York, forthcoming).
57 L. Attwood, *The New Soviet Man and Woman: Sex Role Socialisation in the USSR* (Bloomington and Indianapolis, 1990), 127, 170–1, 177, 178, 205, 212.
58 See Krementsov, "From 'beastly philosophy' to Medical Genetics" (cit. n. 27), 73–4, for the link between Okhrmat'mlad, Semashko and contemporary Soviet eugenics discourse.
59 See Simpson, "Bolshevism and Sexual Revolution" (cit. n. 34), 209–38.
60 See https://commons.wikimedia.org/wiki/File:Auguste_Rodin_Eternal_Spring_IMG_6895.JPG, photo © Deror avi 07/10/2009. https://commons.wikimedia.org/wiki/User:Deror_avi (accessed on October 10, 2019).
61 Vatagin, *Vospominaniia* (cit. n. 12), 17, 24; Oleg Sopotsinsky, ed., *Art of the Soviet Union: Painting, Sculpture, Graphic Arts*, 1977 (Leningrad, 1978), 402.
62 "Anna Golubkina, *Mound*. Bronze.1904," Sputnik Images. http://sputnikimages.com/hier_rubric/photo/761050.html (accessed on April 14, 20).
63 Engels, *Dialectics of Nature* (cit. n. 40), 54.
64 For images of a dominant male and the size difference between male and female orangutans, see Melissa Hogenboom, "Why Male Orangutans Have Such Weird Faces," *BBC Earth*. http://www.bbc.co.uk/earth/story/20151027-new-insights-into-strange-faced-orangutans (accessed on October 10, 2019). This webpage is linked to: P. R. Marty, M. A. Noordwick, M. Hesterman, E. P. Willems, L. P. Dunkel, M. Cadilek, M. Agil, and T. Weingrill, "Endocrinal Correlates of Male Bimaturism in Wild Orangutans," *American Journal of Primatology*, 77 (2015): 1170–8.
65 Ibid. No specific page numbers given in the online version of the Marty et al. article.
66 A. F. Kots, "Vasilii Alekseevich Vatagin i ego raboty v Darvinovskom musee 1902–1952" ("Vasilii Alekseevich Vatagin and his works in the Darwin Museum 1902–1952") no date, AGDM f.10141, op. 623, ed.khr.215: 11.
67 Ibid., 10.
68 Ibid.
69 Vatagin, *Vospominaniia* (cit. n. 12), 60, 73–4.
70 Kots, "V. A. Vatagin 1902–1952" (cit. n. 66), 11.
71 N. Krementsov, "The Dog's Heart and Monkey Glands: Rejuvenation," in idem, *Revolutionary Experiments: The Quest for Immortality in Bolshevik Science and Fiction* (New York, 2014), 139.
72 Nadezhda Ladygina-Kots, "Preface," in *Infant Chimpanzee and Human Child: A Classic 1935 Comparative Study of Ape Emotions and Intelligence*, trans. B. Vekker, ed. F. de Waal (Oxford and New York, 2002), 6.
73 Ibid., 7.
74 Ibid.
75 It is clear from the archival evidence that Vatagin preferred to work from life—or from photographs. Ladygina-Kots may also have posed for Vatagin for this work, as she did so for his sculpture of *Lamarck and his Lamenting Daughters*: Photograph of Vasilii Vatagin, making *Blind Lamarck and his Daughters*, c1921 (sculpture dimensions 125 × 150 × 310 centimeter), with Nadezhda Ladygina-Kots, and the taxidermist of small animals, Dmitri Fedulov posing for him, *c*. 1921, British Museum of Natural History Archive, MSS MUS 8 vols, L.MSS.
76 Ladygina-Kots, "Preface," 393 (cit. n. 72).
77 Ibid., 397.

78 See P. Simpson, "Imag[in]ing Post-Revolutionary Evolution: The Taylorised Proletarian Body," in *The Art of Evolution: Darwin, Darwinisms and Visual Culture*, eds. B. Larson and F. Brauer (Hanover, 2009), 226–61.
79 Anon, "Nested Hierarchies, the order of nature: Carolus Linnaeus," *Understanding Evolution* (Berkeley, n.d). https://evolution.berkeley.edu/evolibrary/article/0_0_0/history_05 (accessed on April 11, 2020).
80 J. van Wyhe and P. C. Kjaergaard, "Going the Whole Orang: Darwin, Wallace and the Natural History of Orangutans," *Studies in History and Philosophy of Biological and Biomedical Sciences*, 21 (2015): 53–6.
81 Ibid.
82 A. F. Kots, "Zoologiia do Darvina i darvinism c tochki zreniia istoricheskogo metoda" ("Zoology until Darwin and Darwinism from the perspective of historical method"), Physico-Chemical Institute advertisement flyer 1909, AGDM f.199, op.10141, ed.khr.774.
83 A. S. Serebrovskii to A. F. Kots (June 10 1920) AGDM f.10141, op.253, ed.khr.1026.
84 Van Wyhe and Kjaergaard, "Going the Whole Orang: Darwin, Wallace and the Natural History of Orangutans," 56–8 (cit. n. 80).
85 Darwin, *Origin of Species* (cit. n. 18), 488.
86 Darwin, *The Expression of the Emotions in Humans and Animals* (London, 1872), 132–45.
87 Darwin, *The Descent of Man* (cit. n. 18), 18, 34, 38, 69–70, 73, 87, 93, 103–4, 178, 180–1, 206–7, 590, 627, 658.
88 Van Wyhe and Kjaergaard, "Going the Whole Orang: Darwin, Wallace and the Natural History of Orangutans," 56–8 (cit. n. 80).
89 Darwin, *The Expression of the Emotions* (cit. n. 86), 132–45. The only illustrations of apes and monkeys are Cynopithecus Niger (Celebes crested macaque) ibid, Figs. 8. 16 and 17: 35, and a chimpanzee, Fig. 8.18: 139.
90 T. H. Huxley, *Evidence to Man's Place in Nature*, 1863 reproduced with no page numbers on the Project Gutenberg website (www.gutenberg.org). https://www.gutenberg.org/files/2931/2931-h/2931-h.htm#linkimage-0002 (accessed on November 14, 2019).
91 Darwin, *The Descent of Man* (cit. n. 18), 178–84.
92 K. Rossianov, "Beyond Species: Il'ya Ivanov and His Experiments on Cross-Breeding Humans with Anthropoid Apes," *Science in Context*, 15, no. 2 (2002): 287–9.
93 See Robert M. Yerkes Papers, Sterling Memorial Library, New Haven (RMY Papers), Collection 569, Box 29, Folders 549–51, correspondence with A. F. Kohts and N. Kohts, 1924–36; A. E. Kohts, N. N. Ladygina-Kots, and R. Yerkes, correspondence, (undated/varied dates late 1920s to 1942), AGDM fol. 12497, op. 650–1, 653–5, 647–9, ezd. khr.1304; fol. 10141, op. 502–4, ezd. khr.1304; R. Yerkes to A. E. Kots, 30/01/30 AGDM fol. 502, op.10141, ezd.khr.1304.
94 *Science Newsletter*, VII (January 9, 1926): 248, cutting about Ivanov's proposed experiment, in E. Slosson to R. M. Yerkes, 18 /01/1926, RMY Papers, Box 69, Folder 1314.
95 See for example: "Soviets Backs Plan to Test Evolution: Experiments to Be Carried Out at Pasteur Institute in Kindia Africa: Support Here Is Alleged. Lawyer for American Atheistic Society Tells of the Project and Will Go Observe it," *The New York Times* (June 17, 1926): 2; "Russian Admits Ape Experiments: Soviets Paying for Scientific Researches in Africa" (special cable, June 18), *The New York Times* (June 17, 1926), "Radio" section: 17; "Ape-child?" *Time Magazine* 8 (August 16, 1926): 7. See

also: A. Etkind, "Beyond Eugenics: The Forgotten Scandal of Hybridising Humans and Apes," *Studies in History and Philosophy of Biological and Biomedical Sciences*, 39 (2008): 205–10.

96 See R. M. Yerkes to Professor Fursikov, October 10, 1929, RMY Papers, Box 63, Biological Station named after I. P. Pavlov and Suchum, Folder 1195 Experimental Station Suchum, Caucasus, USSR.

97 Rossianov, "Beyond Species," 291–2 (cit. n. 92).

98 Ibid.

99 Ibid., 284.

100 N. Krementsov, "Hormones and the Bolsheviks: From Organotherapy to Experimental Endocrinology," *Isis*, 99 (2008): 508–10.

101 Ibid.

102 Ibid.

103 Rossianov, "Beyond Species," 300 (cit. n. 92).

104 Ibid., 306.

105 Ibid.

106 S. Fitzpatrick, "Cultural Revolution in Russia 1928–32," *Journal of Contemporary History*, 9, no, 1 (1974): 33–52. See also Krementsov, "From 'beastly philosophy' to Medical Genetics," 61–92 (cit. n. 27).

107 Rossianov: "Beyond Species," 307–8 (cit. n. 92).

108 N. Ladygina-Kots to R. Yerkes, 06/01/31, RMY Papers, Box 28, Folder 551, Correspondence Kohts, A. E. and Kohts, N. 1931–6.

109 See "Introduction" to this volume.

Chapter 9

1 The Archive of the Russian Museum of Ethnography (*Arkhiv Rossiiskogo etnograficheskogo muzeia*—ARME), fond 2, opis' 1, delo 609, list 114; hereafter such references will be given as ARME, f. 2, op. 1, d. 609, l. 114.

2 William H. Holmes, "Classification and Arrangement of the Exhibits of an Anthropological Museum," *Science*, 404 (1902): 487–504; Ira Jacknis, "Franz Boas and Exhibits: On the Limitations of the Museum Method of Anthropology," in *Objects and Others: Essays on Museums and Material Culture*, ed. George Stocking (Madison, 1985), 77–83; Nélia Dias, "Looking at Objects: Memory, Knowledge in Nineteenth-Century Ethnographic Displays," in *Travellers' Tales: Narratives of Home and Displacement*, eds. Jon Bird, Barry Curtis, Melinda Mash, Tim Putnam, George Robertson, and Lisa Tickner (London, 1994), 165–71. In fact, the majority of museums strove to combine both of these methods to some extent.

3 Johannes Fabian, *Time and the Other: How Anthropology Makes Its Object* (New York, 1983). It was only in the last third of the twentieth century, set against growing movements for political and cultural decolonization, that Western ethnographic museums began gradually to move away from these exhibition methods and seek out new ways to display their collections, see Anthony A. Shelton, "Museums and Anthropologies," in *A Companion to Museum Studies*, ed. Sharon Macdonald (Malden, MA, 2006), 71–9.

4 I. I. Shangina, "Etnograficheskie muzei Moskvy i Leningrada na rubezhe 20–30-kh gg. XX v" (Ethnographic Museums of Moscow and Leningrad in the Late 1920s—Early 1930s), *Sovetskaia etnografiia*, 2 (1991): 71–81.

5 M. F. Komarova, "Rabotat' po-stakhanovski" (Working like a Stakhanovite), *Sovetskii muzei*, 1 (1936): 8–9.

6 In models of mature Stalinism, "new men" were presented as "spontaneous," full of energy and enthusiasm, but lacking sufficient "consciousness"—which made them dependent on the Party and on Stalin personally, to surround them with "fatherly love"; see Katerina Clark, "Utopian Anthropology as a Context for Stalinist Literature," in *Stalinism: Essays in Historical Interpretation*, ed. Robert C. Tucker (New York, 1977), 188. In their spontaneity, they were closer to "the people" than to the political and cultural elite.

7 At the same time, pantheons of national heroes emerged. Yet these pantheons were oriented not toward the glorious present, but toward the constructed "great past" of a particular nationality. They included poets, scholars, and public officials such as Shota Rustaveli, Nizami Ganjavi, Ali-Shir Nava'i, Ulugh Beg, Alexander Pushkin, Alexander Nevsky, and others; see David Brandenberger, "Stalinskii populizm i nevol'noe sozdanie russkoi natsional'noi identichnosti" (Stalinist Populism and the Involuntary Creation of a Russian National Identity), *Neprikosnovennyi zapas*, 4 (2011): 17–33; S. Rumiantsev, "Sovetskaia natsional'naia politika v Zakavkaz'e: konstruirovanie natsional'nykh granits, istorii i kul'tur" (Soviet Nationalities Policy in the South Caucasus: Constructing National Borders, Histories, and Cultures), *Neprikosnovennyi zapas*, 4 (2011): 47–65.

8 Matthew J. Payne, *Stalin's Railroad: Turksib and the Building of Socialism* (Pittsburgh, 2001), 209–45; Mary Buckley, *Mobilizing Stalin's Peasants: Heroines and Heroes of Stalin's Fields* (Lanham, 2006).

9 Sheila Fitzpatrick, *Stalin's Peasants: Resistance and Survival in the Russian Village after Collectivization* (New York, 1994), 273.

10 S. Dimanshtein, "O stakhanovskom dvizhenii v natsional'nykh respublikakh" (On the Stakhanovite Movement in National Republics), *Revoliutsiia i natsional'nosti*, 2 (1936): 18.

11 Nicholas S. Timasheff, *The Great Retreat* (New York, 1946), 354.

12 Lewis H. Siegelbaum, *Stakhanovism and the Politics of Productivity in the USSR, 1935–1941* (Cambridge, 1988), 148.

13 See "Introduction" to this volume.

14 *Rossiiskii etnograficheskii muzei. 1902–2002. Al'bom* (The Russian Museum of Ethnography, 1902–2002. Photo album) (St. Petersburg, 2001), 11.

15 I. V. Dubov, "U istokov Rossiiskogo etnograficheskogo muzeia (k 150-letiiu so dnia rozhdeniia Dmitriia Aleksandrovicha Klementsa)" (The Beginnings of the Russian Museum of Ethnography [for the 150th anniversary of the birth of Dmitry Alexandrovich Klements]), *Etnograficheskoe obozrenie*, 6 (1998): 118–20.

16 *Rossiiskii etnograficheskii muzei. 1902–2002. Al'bom* (cit. n. 14), 32.

17 Francine Hirsch, *Empire of Nations: Ethnographic Knowledge and the Making of the Soviet Union* (Ithaca, 2005), 197–211.

18 ARME, f. 2, op. 1, d. 420.

19 Y. Slezkine, "The Fall of Soviet Ethnography, 1928–38," *Current Anthropology*, 4 (1991): 481.

20 S. Alymov, "Ethnography, Marxism and Soviet Ideology," in *An Empire of Others*, eds. Roland Cvetkovski and Alexis Hofmeister (Budapest, 2014), 121–44; M. Haber, "The Soviet Ethnographers as a Social Engineer: Socialist Realism and the Study of Rural Life, 1945–1958," *The Soviet and Post-Soviet Review*, 2 (2014): 194–219; S. Abashin, "Ethnographic Views of Socialist Reforms in Soviet Central Asia: Collective Farm

(Kolkhoz) Monographs," in *Exploring the Edge of Empire: Soviet Era Anthropology in the Caucasus and Central Asia*, eds. Florian Mühlfried and Sergey Sokolovskiy (Berlin, 2011), 83–98.

21 From 1948—the State Museum of the Ethnography of the Peoples of the USSR; from 1992 to present, the Russian Museum of Ethnography. For details, see V. M. Grusman and V. A. Dmitriev, "Iz istorii Rossiiskogo etnograficheskogo muzeia: k 80-letiiu obreteniia samostoiatel'nosti" (Glimpses of the History of the Russian Museum of Ethnography: The Eightieth Anniversary of Gaining Independence), *Muzei. Traditsiia. Etnichnost'*, 1 (2014): 6–24.

22 "Na novom etape muzeinogo stroitel'stva" (A New Phase of Museum Construction), *Sovetskii muzei*, 1 (1934): 8–9.

23 T. A. Kriukova and E. N. Studenetskaia, "Gosudarstvennyi muzei etnografii narodov SSSR za piat'desiat let sovetskoi vlasti" (The State Museum of Ethnography of the Peoples of the USSR for 50 Years of Soviet Authority) in *Ocherki istorii muzeinogo dela v SSSR* (Essays on the History of Museum Work in the USSR), ed. A. M. Razgon (Moscow, 1971), 42.

24 ARME, f. 2, op. 1, d. 639.

25 ARME, f. 2, op. 1, d. 599, l. 23.

26 Ibid., 22.

27 ARME, f. 2, op. 1, d. 568, l. 2.

28 Ibid., 4.

29 Supinskii was eventually among the victims of Stalinist repressions.

30 Grusman and Dmitriev, "Iz istorii Rossiiskogo etnograficheskogo muzeia" (cit. n. 21), 19.

31 To read more about him, see E. A. Dolgova, "O biografii odnogo stalinskogo upravlentsa: Efim Abramovich Mil'shtein" (One Biography of a Stalinist Manager: Efim Abramovich Milstein), *Noveishaia istoriia Rossii*, 4 (2018): 912–24.

32 Stanislav Petriashin, "Socialist Realism and Ethnography: The Study and Representation of Soviet Contemporaneity in Ethnographic Museums in the 1930s," *Forum for Anthropology and Culture*, 15 (2019): 163–8.

33 N. P. Grinkova, *Byt Voronezhskoi kolkhoznoi derevni (po materialam ekspeditsii v Voronezhskuiu oblast')* (The Way of Life in a Voronezh Collective Farm Village (based on materials from an expedition to Voronezh Oblast), (Leningrad, 1937), 17.

34 ARME, f. 2, op. 1, d. 630; ARME, f. 2, op. 1, d. 566.

35 *Kratkii putevoditel' po vystavke "Russkoe naselenie chernozemnykh oblastei"* (A Brief Guide to the Exhibition "The Russian Inhabitants of the Black Earth Regions") (Leningrad, 1939).

36 Ibid., 25.

37 Ibid., 26.

38 T. D. Lysenko and I. I. Prezent, "Stakhanovskoe dvizhenie i zadachi sovetskoi agrobiologii" (The Stakhanovite Movement and the Goals of Soviet Agrobiology), *Iarovizatsiia*, 3 (1935): 1–12.

39 ARME, f. 2, op. 1, d. 694, l. 7, 7back.

40 *Kratkii putevoditel' po vystavke* (cit. n. 35), 27.

41 ARME, f. 9, op. 3, d. 5, l. 23.

42 *Kratkii putevoditel' po vystavke "Evenki v proshlom i nastoiashchem"* (A Brief Guide to the Exhibition "The Evenks Then and Now") (Leningrad, 1939).

43 ARME, f. 2, op. 1, d. 609, l. 116.

44 ARME, f. 2, op. 1, d. 497, l. 29.

45 ARME, f. 2, op. 1, d. 689, l. 12.
46 Ibid., 15.
47 Clark, "Utopian Anthropology as a Context for Stalinist Literature," 193 (cit. n. 6).
48 Catriona Kelly and Vadim Volkov, "Directed Desires: *Kul'turnost'* and Consumption," in *Constructing Russian Culture in the Age of Revolution: 1881–1940*, eds. Catriona Kelly and David Shepherd (Oxford, 1998), 297–300.
49 ARME, f. 2, op. 1, d. 496, l. 18.
50 ARME, f. 2, op. 1, d. 497, ll. 27–8.
51 ARME, f. 9, op. 3, d. 5, l. 33.
52 ARME, f. 2, op. 1, d. 689, l. 14.
53 Irina Kotkina, "Soviet Empire and Operatic Realm: Stalinist Search for the Model Soviet Opera," *Revue des études slaves*, 3–4 (2013): 505–18; Boram Shin, "National Form and Socialist Content: Soviet Modernization and Making of Uzbek National Opera Between the 1920s and 1930s," *Interventions*, 3 (2017): 416–33.
54 The particular focus on folk art in this exhibition was also a function of the academic interests of Nadezhda Grinkova (1895–1961), who oversaw the creation of the exhibit. She was a well-known folklorist, dialectologist, and ethnographer, who specialized in national costumes.
55 ARME, f. 2, op. 1, d. 615, ll. 19–20.
56 Yuri Slezkine, "The USSR as a Communal Apartment, or How a Socialist State Promoted Ethnic Particularism," *Slavic Review*, 53 (1994): 417–18.
57 A. V. Lunacharskii, "Sotsialisticheskii Realism" (Socialist Realism) in idem, *Stat'i o teatre i dramaturgii* (Moscow–Leningrad, 1938), 17; A. D. Siniavskiy, "CHto takoe sotsialisticheskii realism" (What Is Socialist Realism), in idem, *Literaturnyi protsess v Rossii* (Literary Process in Russia) (Moscow, 2003), 165.
58 Iu. Murashev, "Pis'mo i ustnaia rech' v diskursakh o iazyke 1930-kh godov: N. Marr" (Writing and the Spoken Word in Discussions on the Language of the 1930s: N. Marr), in *Sotsrealisticheskii kanon* (The Socialist Realism Canon), eds. Hans Günther and Evgeny Dobrenko (St. Petersburg, 2000), 599–601.
59 ARME, f. 2, op. 2, d. 142, l. 21.
60 A. I. Savin, "Pis'ma vo vlast' kak spetsificheskaia forma politicheskoi adaptatsii sovetskogo naseleniia (1930-e gg.)" (Letters to the Government as a Specific Type of Political Adaptation by the Soviet Population [1930s]), *Vestnik Novosibirskogo gosudarstvennogo universiteta. Seriia: Istoriia, filologiia*, 15 (2016): 136–8.
61 There were other methods—for instance, an exhibition at the State Museum of Socialist Reconstruction of Agriculture had a diorama entitled *The Harvest On Large-Scale Socialist Farms.* Included as part of the diorama was a combine harvester, on which the museum employees "placed a person, or a whole brigade of people—and not just random people, but specific people with first and last names—*udarniki*, notable people"; see E. I. Okolovich, "Na novom etape (O rabote Gosudarstvennogo muzeia sotsialisticheskoi rekonstruktsii sel'skogo khoziaistva)" (A New Phase [On the Works of the State Museum of Socialist Reconstruction of Agriculture]), *Sovetskii muzei*, 1 (1935): 21.
62 Kriukova and Studenetskaia, "Gosudarstvennyi muzei etnografii narodov SSSR" (cit. n. 23), 52.
63 ARME, f. 2, op. 1, d. 723, l. 72.
64 Kriukova and Studenetskaia, "Gosudarstvennyi muzei etnografii narodov SSSR" (cit. n. 23), 52.
65 Ibid.

66 ARME, f. 2, op. 1, d. 763, l. 13.
67 Ibid., 13–14.
68 Ibid., 15.
69 Hirsch, *Empire of Nations* (cit. n. 17).
70 ARME, f. 2, op. 1, d. 479, l. 68.
71 *Pervoe vsesoiuznoe soveshchanie rabochikh i rabotnits-stakhanovtsev. 14–17 noiabria 1935. Stenograficheskii otchet* (The First All-Union Conference of Stakhanovites. 14–17 November, 1935. Transcript) (Moscow, 1935), 368–70.
72 Ibid., 363, 371–2.
73 Ibid., 363.
74 Stephen E. Hanson, *Time and Revolution: Marxism and the Design of Soviet Institutions* (Chapel Hill, 1997), 165–71.
75 Evgeny Dobrenko, *Political Economy of Socialist Realism* (New Haven, 2007); Hans Günther, "O krasote, kotoraia ne smogla spasti sotsializm" (On the Beauty Which Could Not Save Socialism), *Novoe literaturnoe obozrenie*, 1 (2010): 13–31.

Conclusion

1 Leon Trotsky often emphasized the fact that the "new man" would inhabit a fundamentally different type society in the communist future, that is, there would be an evolutionary fit between the new creature and its new habitat. "The man of the future, the citizen of communism, will no doubt be a very interesting and attractive creature, but his psychology [. . .] will be profoundly different than ours." L. Trotsky, "Zadachi kommunisticheskogo vospitaniia" (The Tasks of Communist Upbringing), 1923. https://www.marxists.org/history/international/comintern/sections/britain/periodicals/communist_review/1923/7/com_ed.htm (accessed on January 20, 2020).
2 Elon Musk and Jeff Bezos are the most recognizable faces in a surge of activity, mostly privately financed, to step up exploration of Mars. See, for instance. https://techcrunch.com/2019/11/07/elon-musk-says-building-the-first-sustainable-city-on-mars-will-take-1000-starships-and-20-years/ (accessed on January 31, 2020).
3 The Transhumanist Declaration was drafted in 1998 and adopted by the Humanity+ board in 2009. https://humanityplus.org/philosophy/transhumanist-declaration/ (accessed on January 31, 2020).
4 See Anya Bernstein, *The Future of Immortality* (Princeton, NJ, 2019), 20; and Robert Ranisch and Stefan Lorenz Sorgner, eds., *Post-and Transhumanism: An Introduction* (Peter Lang, 2014), 7–8.
5 See Bernstein, *The Future of Immortality* (cit. n. 4), 21; and Steve Fuller, "Evolution," in *Post- and Transhumanism* (cit. n. 4), 201–2.
6 For an excellent overview of posthumanist themes in late Soviet and post-Soviet literature and culture, see Colleen McQuillen and Julia Vaingurt, eds., *The Human Reimagined: Posthumanism in Russia* (Boston, MA, 2019).
7 http://transhumanist-party.org/ (accessed on April 25, 2020).
8 According to Peter Joosten, a Dutch ideologue of the "Superhuman Era," contemporary transhumanism has the following internal directions and thought-leaders: Singularitarians expect the sudden emergence of a superintelligence (Ray Kurzweil); the Hedonistic Imperative sees the goal of transhumanism to eliminate human suffering (David Pearce); democratic versus libertarian transhumanists

differ on the role of government; Survival transhumanism focuses on life extension (Zoltan Istvan); Religious transhumanism sees an alignment between its biotechnical philosophies and the religious ideas of the Mormons and or Buddhism; and Cosmism makes a reappearance in contemporary transhumanist circles as a movement with "an attitude of growth, happiness, and a more limited role for science" (Giulio Priso). https://superhumantalks.com/ (accessed on April 25, 2020).

9 In an interview on the IQ2 series. https://www.youtube.com/watch?v=JJ1yS9JIJKs&t=537s (accessed on May 2, 2020) promoting his 2017 book *Homo Deus*. The book is not an endorsement of transhumanist tactics, but it makes the argument that we have reached a level of scientific-technological control over our environment that thwarts the power of biological evolution to shape the future of the species. From now on, the book argues, we are "like gods," able to shape the future through "intelligent design."

10 Krementsov, Introduction to this volume.

11 Istvan Csiscery-Ronay, *The Seven Beauties of Science Fiction* (Middletown, CT, 2011).

12 See Bernstein, *The Future of Immortality* (cit. n. 4), 165–80; and "How Close Are We to Terraforming Mars?" https://www.youtube.com/watch?v=wkkBR-W4XA8 (#Mars #Terraforming #RedPlanet) (accessed on April 25, 2020).

13 https://www.businessinsider.com/elon-musk-plans-1-million-people-to-mars-by-2050-2020-1 (accessed on April 25, 2020).

14 The influence of spiritual ideals on the origins of Soviet science fiction is discussed Anindita Banerjee, *We Modern People: The Making of Russian Modernity* (Middletown, CT, 2013), and Asif Saddiqi, *The Rocket's Red Glare: Spaceflight and the Soviet Imagination* (Cambridge, 2010).

15 The dates of Gorky's conversation in the Summer Garden with Alexander Blok are hazy, as Gorky does not provide a date in his *Reminiscences*. The plausibility of 1919 is established by A. M. Kryukova, "K istorii lichnykh i tvorcheskikh otnoshenii Gorkogo i Bloka," http://litnasledstvo.ru/site/book/id/69 (accessed on January 11, 2020).

16 At our conference in St. Petersburg in May 2019, Irene Delic, in her presentation of "Genius for All: Brain Research," provided the invaluable citation to this telling interchange.

17 The original reads: "—Лично мне—больше нравится представлять человека аппаратом, который претворяет в себе так называемую «мертвую материю» в п сихическую энергию и когда-то, в неизмеримо отдаленном будущем, превратит весь «мир» в чистую психику." http://gorkiy-lit.ru/gorkiy/vospominaniya/a-a-blok.htm (accessed on January 10, 2020).

18 The original reads: "Глаза Блока почти безумны." "Походка его на первый взгляд кажется твердой, но, присмотревшись, видишь, что он нерешительно качается на ногах." http://gorkiy-lit.ru/gorkiy/vospominaniya/a-a-blok.htm (accessed on January 10, 2020).

19 Nikolai Fedorov's 1892 essay "Karazin: Meteorologist or Meteourge?" juxtaposes his notion of Buddhism ("life is evil, so the aim is self-destruction") to his notion of Christianity, where "life is good, [wherein] lies the motivation for restoring it [by resurrecting our ancestors]", translated in Yvonne Howell, ed., *Red Star Tales: A Century of Russian and Soviet Science Fiction* (Montpelier, VT, 2015), 36. Gorky seems to be using a similar logic in his "Conversation with A. A. Blok," when he objects to the "absolutely incomprehensible and some kind of Buddhist thought" in Blok's views. See http://gorkiy-lit.ru/gorkiy/vospominaniya/a-a-blok.htm (accessed on January 10, 2020).

20 Seminal texts include Fredric Jameson, *The Cultural Logic of Late Capitalism* (Durham, NC, 1991); Slavoj Zizek, in articles and the imposing satirical documentary "A Pervert's Guide to Ideology" (Sophie Fiennes, director, 2012); Bill McKibben, *Deep Economy* (London, 2007); idem, *Falter: Has the Human Game Begun to Play Itself Out?* (Henry Holt & Co, 2019); and many books and articles in between.

21 Klaus Schwab, *The Fourth Industrial Revolution* (Currency, January 3, 2017); online preview publication made available to Davos Forum participants in 2016.

22 Andy Clark makes the case for the ancient origins of humanity's adaptive adoption of cognitive prostheses. See *Natural-Born Cyborgs: Minds, Technology, and the Future of Human Intelligence* (Oxford, 2004).

23 Brad Tabas, "Of Earthlings and Aliens. Space Mining and the Challenge of Post-Planetary Eco-Criticism." Paper draft available on author's site. https://ensta-bretagne.academia.edu/BradTabas (accessed on January 11, 2020)

24 For his translated selected works, see Konstantin Tsiolkovsky, *Dreams of Earth and Sky* (New York, 2004).

25 Donella Meadows, Jurgen Randers, and Dennis Meadows, *Limits to Growth: 30 Years Later* (White River Junction, VT, 2004).

26 See Tabas, "Of Earthlings and Aliens" (cit. n. 23).

27 Howell, *Red Star Tales,* 120 (cit. n. 19).

28 Kazemir Malevich (1879–1935), one of the central figures in Russian avant-garde art of the revolutionary period. Founder of the Suprematist movement (manifesto: *From Cubism to Suprematicism*, 1915). The first infamous *Black Square* composition was exhibited in 1915 in Petrograd. Malevich pushed the boundary of nonrepresentational art to its ultimate extreme in *White on White* (1918). The painting was exhibited in Berlin in 1927 and remained in Germany until 1935. After the artist's death *White on White* was taken to the Museum of Modern Art (MOMA) in New York, where it is now part of the permanent exhibition. https://www.moma.org/collection/works/80385

29 Space mining is a global industry. Sahar Fatima and Vince Morello, "The Space Mining Race Is on, as Countries Pass New Laws and Ramp Up Research Efforts," *CIM* (Canadian Institute of Mining) *Magazine*, 11, no. 4 (2016). https://magazine.cim.org/en/technology/another-giant-leap-for-mankind/ (accessed on April 24, 2020); Luxembourg Space Agency, White Paper on "Major Take-Aways of the Mining Space Summit 2019." https://space-agency.public.lu/dam-assets/publications/2020/MINING-SPACE-SUMMIT-2019-Paper.pdf; Namrata Goswami, "China in Space: Ambitions and Possible Conflict," *Strategic Studies Quarterly*, 12, no. 1 (2018): 74–97. www.jstor.org/stable/26333878 (accessed on April 26, 2020).

30 See Banerjee, *We Modern People* (cit. n. 14); and Anindita Banerjee, ed., *Science Fiction Circuits of the South and East* (Peter Lang, 2018).

31 For more on the "science-fictionality" of Russian culture, see Yvonne Howell, "Arkady and Boris Strugatsky: The Science Fictionality of Russian Culture," in *Lingua Cosmica. Science Fiction from Around the World*, ed. Dale Knickerbocker (Champaign, IL, 2018), 201–20.

32 Translated in Howell, *Red Star Tales*, 161 (cit. n. 19).

33 The novel begins memorably with the problem of a barely functioning car on a nearly impassable northern road, which takes a young computer programmer with barely any change in his pocket to his unexpected destination—a fabulously innovative high-energy physics institute.

34 I. V. Stalin, *Sochineniia*, vol. 13 (Moscow, 1951), 29–42.

35 Mary Finley-Brook, "Extreme Energy Injustice and the Expansion of Capital," in *Organized Violence and the Expansion of Capital*, eds. Dawn Paley and Simon Granovsky-Larsen (Regina, SK, 2019), 23–47.

36 Pavel Luksha, founder of the "Rapid Foresight" method for envisioning development strategies, as quoted in Bernstein, *The Future of Immortality* (cit. n. 4), 198. This comment would have been made sometime in 2015.

37 Ibid.

Further Reading

Muller, Derek, *Der Topos des Neuen Menschen in der russischen und sowjetrussischen Geistesgeschichte*. Bern, 1998.

Pietrow-Ennker, Bianka, *Russlands "neuen Menschen": Die Entwicklung der Frauenbewegung von den Anfängen bis zur Oktoberrevolution*. Frankfurt, 1999.

Lepp, Nicola, Martin Roth, and Klaus Vogel, eds. *Der neue Mensch: Obsessionen des 20. Jahrhunderts. Katalog zur Ausstellung im Deutschen Hygiene-museum Dresden 22. 4.–8. 8. 1999*. Ostfildern-Ruit, 1999.

Haynes, John, *New Soviet Man: Gender and Masculinity in Stalinist Soviet Cinema*. Manchester, 2003.

Wedemeyer-Kolwe, Bernd, *"Der neue Mensch": Körperkultur im Kaiserreich und in der Weimarer Republik*. Würzburg, 2004.

Groys, Boris and Michael Hagemeister, eds. Die neue Menschheit. Biopolitische Utopien in Russland zu Beginn des 20. *Jahrhunderts*. Frankfurt am Main, 2005.

Hellbeck, Jochen, *Revolution on My Mind: Writing a Diary under Stalin*. Cambridge, MA, 2006.

Cheng, Yinghong, *Creating the "New Man": From Enlightenment Ideals to Socialist Realities*. Honolulu, 2009.

Cassata, Francesco, *Building the New Man: Eugenics, Racial Science and Genetics in Twentieth-Century Italy*. Budapest, 2011.

Tetzner, Thomas, *Der kollektive Gott: Zur Ideengeschichte des «Neuen Menschen» in Russland*. Göttingen, 2013.

Thomsen, Mads R., *The New Human in Literature: Posthuman Visions of Changes in Body, Mind and Society after 1900*. London, 2013.

Vaissié, Cécile, *La fabrique de l'Homme nouveau après Staline: les arts et la Culture dans le Projet soviétique*. Rennes, 2016.

Vujosevic, Tijana, *Modernism and the Making of the Soviet New Man*. Manchester, 2017.

McCallum, Claire E., *The Fate of the New Man: Representing & Reconstructing Masculinity in Soviet Visual Culture, 1945–1965*. DeKalb, IL, 2018.

McQuillen, Colleen and Julia Vaingurt, eds., *The Human Reimagined: Posthumanism in Russia*. Brookline, MA, 2018.

Feldman, Matthew, Jorge Dagnino, and Paul Stocker, eds., *The "New Man" in Radical Right Ideology and Practice, 1919–45*. London, 2018.

Voigt, Wolfgang, Dorothea Deschermeier, and Peter Cachola Schmal, eds., *New Human, New Housing: Architecture of the New Frankfurt, 1925–1933*. Berlin, 2019.

Gelderloos, Carl, *Biological Modernism: The New Human in Weimar Culture*. Evanston, IL, 2020.

Contributors

Lyubov Bugaeva is an associate professor at St. Petersburg State University, Russia. She is the author of two books in Russian: *Literature and* Rite De Passage (St. Petersburg, 2010) and *What's Up, Doc? Cinema as Thought* (St. Petersburg, 2021); and of nearly 200 articles (in Russian and English) on film studies, literary theory, Russian literature, and American pragmatism. Her most recent publications include "Black Mountain College as a Form of Life", *Pragmatism Today* 11 (2) (2020): 146–53; and "Fear on the Small Screen", *Russian Journal of Communication* 13 (1) (2021): 29–41.

Michael Coates is a PhD candidate in history at the University of California, Berkeley. He is currently writing a dissertation on the history of the *Great Soviet Encyclopedia* and its role in constructing Soviet knowledge, for which he received a Cohen-Tucker Dissertation Research Fellowship. He has published some of his research as "Istoricheskie vzgliady na entsiklopedistiku: istoriia sozdaniia *Bol'shoi Sovetskoi Entsiklopedii*" ("Historical Perspectives on Encyclopedistics: The History of the Creation of the *Great Soviet Encyclopedia*"), in *Sovremennaia rossiskaia entsiklopedistika: mesto i rol' v obshchestve, perspektivy razvitiia* (*Contemporary Russian Encyclopedistics: Its Place and Role in Society, Perspectives on its Development*), ed. U. G. Saitov (Ufa, 2019), 19–25.

Olga Elina is a chief research fellow at the Institute for the History of Science and Technology, the Russian Academy of Sciences. She published extensively on the history of Russian and Soviet agricultural sciences. Her most recent publications include: "Passion for Plants: Collections and Power Games in Botany in the 18th—beginning of the 19th century Russian Empire," *Centaurus*, 60 (4) 2018: 257–75; "Lysenko Predecessors: The Demchinskys and the Bed Cultivation of Cereal Crops," *The Lysenko Controversy as a Global Phenomenon.* In 2 Vols. / W. DeJong-Lambert and N. Krementsov (eds). Vol. 1. 2017, 37–66; "Science at Agricultural Exhibitions in Russia: Social Transformation and Change of Artistic Images: The First Third of the XX Century," *Vikhrevaia dinamika razvitiia nauki i techniki. Rossiia / SSSR. Pervaia polovina XX veka.* In 2 Vols. / Yu. Baturin (ed.). Vol. 1. (Saratov, 2018), 370–413 (in Russian).

Irina Golovacheva is a professor at St. Petersburg State University. Her major publications include three books in Russian: *A Guide to "Brave New World" and Around* (Moscow, 2017); *Fantastika and the Fantastic* (St.-Petersburg, 2013); *Science and Literature: the Archeology of Aldous Huxley's Knowledge* (St.-Petersburg, 2008). She also published numerous chapters and articles on the fantastic, utopia, British and American fiction and biography, literature, and science in English. The most recent is "In the Maze of Ethical Relativism: Huxley at the Cradle of Bioethics," in *Aldous Huxley* *and Self-Realization*, ed. Dana Sawyer, Julian Piras, Uwe Rasch (Zurich: LIT Verlag, 2019); and "From Poe to James via Dostoevsky: Doppelgangers in American and Russian Short Story," in *Connection and Influence in the Russian and American Short Story*, ed. Jeff Birkenstein and Robert Hauthart. Lexington Books (London: Rowman & Littlefield, 2021)".

Yvonne Howell is a professor of Russian and Global Studies at the University of Richmond. She has published extensively on Russian and Soviet science fiction. Her most recent publications include *Red Star Tales: A Century of Soviet and Russian Science Fiction* (Montpelier, VT: RIS Publications, 2015); "The Science Fictionality of Russian Culture: Literature by Arkady and Boris Strugatsky," in *Lingua Cosmica: Science Fiction from around the World*, ed. Dale Knickerbocker (Urbana-Champagne: University of Illinois Press, 2017); "The Genetics of Morality: Policing Science in Dudintsev's 'White Robes,'" in *Policing Literary Theory*, ed. Michailescu and Takayuki (Leiden, London: Brill 2017); and "Through a Prism, Translated: Culture and Change in Russia," in *Prismatic Translation*, ed. Matthew Reynolds (Oxford: Legenda, 2019).

Olga Ilyukha is the director of and a leading research fellow at the Institute of Linguistics, Literature, and History of the Karelian Research Centre, the Russian Academy of Sciences. Her most recent publications include *Shkola i detstvo v karel'skoi derevne v kontse XIX—nachale XX veka* (School and childhood in the Karelian village in the late nineteenth and early twentieth centuries: The modernization and ethno-cultural tradition] (St.-Petersburg, 2007); *Eremeevy-Riaikhia: chelovek, sem'ia, politika v karel'skom pogranich'ye nachala XX veka. Issledovanie. Dokumenty. Materialy. Еремеевы-Ряйхя: человек, семья, политика в карельском пограничье начала XX века. Исследование. Документы. Материалы / Jeremejev-Räihä: ihminen, perhe ja politiikka Karjalan raja-alueella 1900-luvun alussa. Tutkielma. Asiakirjat. Aineistot* (Eremeevs-Riaikhia: person, family, politics in the Karelian borderland of the beginning of the XX century. Study. Documents. Materials) (Petrozavodsk, 2017) (in Russian and Finnish).

Nikolai Krementsov is a professor at the Institute for the History and Philosophy of Science and Technology, University of Toronto. He published numerous books and articles on the history of biomedical sciences in Russia and the Soviet Union. The latest include *Revolutionary Experiments: The Quest for Immortality in Bolshevik Science and Fiction* (New York, 2014); *With and without Galton: Vasilii Florinskii and the Fate of Eugenics in Russia* (Oxford, 2018); and "Thought Transfer and Mind Control between Science and Fiction: Fedor Il'in's 'The Valley of New Life' (1928)," *Osiris* 34 (2019): 36–54.

Stanislav Petriashin is a research fellow at the Russian Museum of Ethnography, St. Petersburg. His work focuses specifically on the anthropology of time and materiality, and history of anthropology (Soviet ethnography). His recent publications include: "Life-Size Dioramas in the 1930s Soviet Ethnographic Museum: Ideology, Science and Spectacle," *Novoe literaturnoe obozrenie* 1 (2021): 151–64 (in Russian); "Socialist

Realism and Ethnography: The Study and Representation of Soviet Contemporaneity in Ethnographic Museums in the 1930s," *Forum for Anthropology and Culture* 15 (2019): 155–82; "Chemical Industry, the Environment, and Russian Provincial Society: The Case of the Kokshan Chemical Works (1850–1925)," *Ambix* 2 (2018): 143–68, (co-authored with Andrei Vinogradov).

Matthias Schwartz is head of the program area "World Literature" at the Leibniz Center for Literary and Cultural Research (ZfL), Berlin, Germany. His research interests include the cultural history of Russian and Soviet adventure literature, science-fiction and science popularization; Eastern European youth cultures, memory cultures and contemporary literatures in a globalized world. Recent publications include *Shalamov. Readings* (co-edited, 2018), *Cultural Hero: Genealogies—Constellations—Media Practices* (co-edited, 2016), *Expeditions into Other Worlds: Soviet Adventure Literature and Science Fiction from the October Revolution to the End of the Stalin Era* (2014); *Gagarin as an Archive Body and Memory Figure* (co-edited, 2014, all in German); and *Eastern European Youth Cultures in a Global Context* (co-edited, 2016).

Pat Simpson is a reader in Social History of Art, and Research Tutor at the School of Creative Arts, University of Hertfordshire, UK. She has published extensively on the late-nineteenth- to twenty-first-century Russian, Soviet, and post-Soviet cultural discourse. Her latest publications include "A Cold War curiosity? The Soviet collection at the Darwin memorial museum, Down House, Kent," *Journal of the History of Collections* 30 (3) (2017): 487–509; "Lysenko's 'Michurinism' and Art at the Darwin Museum 1935–1964," in *Lysenkoism as a Global Phenomenon: Genetics and Agriculture in the Soviet Union and Beyond*, deJong-Lambert, W. & Krementsov, N. (eds.) (New York: Palgrave Macmillan, 2017), vol. 1, 129–75.

Index

Note: Numbers in **Bold** indicate that the term appears in the caption to an illustration

www.ingramcontent.com/pod-product-compliance
Lightning Source LLC
Chambersburg PA
CBHW060245100726
47907CB00003B/773

* 9 7 8 1 3 5 0 2 3 2 8 4 6 *